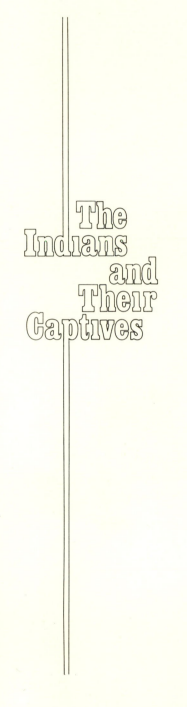

The Indians and Their Captives

The Indians and Their Captives

Edited and Compiled by

James Levernier
and Hennig Cohen

Contributions in American Studies, Number 31

GP GREENWOOD PRESS

WESTPORT, CONNECTICUT • LONDON, ENGLAND

Library of Congress Cataloging in Publication Data
Main entry under title:

The Indians and their captives.

(Contributions in American studies ; no. 31)
Bibliography: p.
Includes index.
1. Indians of North America—Captivities. 2. American literature—19th century. 3. Indians of North America—Captivities—Literary collection.
I. Levernier, James. II. Cohen, Hennig.
E85.I523 970.'004'97 76-57831
ISBN 0-8371-9535-7

Library of Congress Catalog Card Number: 76-57831
ISBN: 0-8371-9535-7
ISSN: 0084-9227

First published in 1977

Greenwood Press, Inc.
51 Riverside Avenue, Westport, Connecticut 06880

Printed in the United States of America

Contents

ILLUSTRATIONS ix
ACKNOWLEDGMENTS xi
INTRODUCTION xiii

PART ONE
THE DISCOVERY OF THE INDIAN

A Spaniard Among Florida Indians 3
From Samuel Gardner Drake, *Indian Captivities . . .* (1839), first published in the *True Relation of the Gentleman of Elvas . . .* (1557)

Captain John Smith Meets the Princess Pocahontas 12
From Captain John Smith, *The Generall Historie of Virginia, New-England, and the Summer Isles . . .* (1624)

PART TWO
TRIALS OF THE SPIRIT

A Letter from a Jesuit in New France 23
From John Dawson Gilmary Shea, *Perils of the Ocean and Wilderness . . .* (1857), first published under the title *Breve Relatione d'Alcune Missioni . . .* (1653)

A Sermon on the Deliverance of a Puritan Woman X 31
From Cotton Mather, *Magnalia Christi Americana . . .* . . . (1702), first published by Mather in *Humiliations Follow'd with Deliverances* . . . (1697)

A Quaker Journal Records God's Protecting Providence 40
From Jonathan Dickinson, *God's Protecting Providence* . . . (1699)

PART THREE
THE LAND IMPERATIVE

A Puritan Minister Describes French Savagery and Treachery X 47
From John Norton, *The Redeemed Captive . . .* (1748)

An Indian Trader Held by the British 50
From *A Narrative of the Capture and Treatment of John Dodge . . .* (1779)

The Captive as Naturalist, Anthropologist, and Plagiarist 55
From the *Memoirs of Charles Dennis Rousoe d'Eres* . . . (1800)

An Almanac Promotes Colonization in the Old Southwest 60
"A True and Faithful Narrative of the Captivity and

1/17/79 Emery Pratt 1750

Travels of Capt. Isaac Stewart . . ." from *Bickerstaff's Genuine Boston Almanack for 1787*

Faked Atrocity Stories 64
An Affecting Narrative of the Captivity and Sufferings of Mary Smith . . . (1818)

"War! War!! War!!! Women and Children Butchered!" 76
From the *Narrative of the Capture and Providential Escape of Misses Frances and Almira Hall* . . . (1832)

A Propaganda Broadside During the Second Seminole War 85
"Captivity and Sufferings of Mrs. Mason, with an Account of the Massacre of Her Youngest Child" (c. 1836)

Attack on a Wagon Train 90
From Fanny Kelly, *Narrative of My Captivity Among the Sioux Indians* . . . (1871)

An Indian Idyll 97
From Edwin James, *A Narrative of the Captivity and Adventures of John Tanner* . . . (1830)

"She Lov'd the Indian Style of Life" 110
From James Seaver, *A Narrative of the Life of Mrs. Mary Jemison* . . . (1824); and Gordon M. Fisk, *Story of the Female Captive* . . . (1844)

A White Savage: "I Kill My First Man" 124
From Jonathan H. Jones, *Indianology* (1899)

PART FOUR

BEHIND THE FRONTIER

An Antiquarian Records an Incident in the Deerfield Massacre 131
From Elihu Hoyt, *A Brief Sketch of the First Settlement of Deerfield* . . . (1833)

Washington Irving on John Colter's Race 135
From Irving, *Astoria, or, Anecdotes of an Enterprise Beyond the Rocky Mountains* (1836)

George Bancroft on the MacCrea Abduction 141
From Bancroft, *History of the United States . . . (1834-1885)*

Francis Parkman on the Conspiracy of Pontiac 143
From Parkman, *The Conspiracy of Pontiac* (1870), first published in 1851

Henry David Thoreau on Hannah Duston's Captivity 156
From Thoreau, *A Week on the Concord and Merrimack Rivers (1849)*

The Legend of Murderer's Creek 160
From *McGuffey's Newly Revised Eclectic Third Reader* (1846)

The Ballad of "The White Captive" 165
"The White Captive" from Helen Flanders, Elizabeth Ballard, et al., *New Green Mountain Songster* (1939); and "Bright Amanda" from Lester A. Hubbard, *Ballads and Songs from Utah* (1961)

Folktales About the Escapes of Tim Murphy 171
From Harold Thompson File, New York State Historical Society; and Emelyn Gardner, "Folk-Lore from Schoharie County, New York," *Journal of American Folklore* (1914)

Daniel Boone and the Indians 174
From John Filson, "The Adventures of Col. Daniel Boon" in *The Discovery, Settlement and Present State of Kentucke* (1784); and Timothy Flint, *Biographical Memoir of Daniel Boone* (1833)

The Christian Hermit 178
From the *Narrative of the Massacre, by the Savages, of the Wife and Children of Thomas Baldwin . . .* (1836)

Sal Fink: "How She Cooked Injuns" 186
"Sal Fink, the Mississippi Screamer" from *Crockett's Almanac* for 1854

MOCCASIN BILL, a Dime Novel 189
From Paul Bibbs, *Moccasin Bill; or, Cunning Serpent the Ojibwah, a Romance of Big Stone Lake* (1873)

A Cowboy Captured by Indians 200
From *The Life and Adventures of Nat Love . . .* (1907)

PART FIVE

BEYOND THE FRONTIER

The Frontiers of Fantasy 209
From *A Surprising Account, of the Captivity and Escape of Philip M'Donald, and Alexander M'Leod, of Virginia . . .* (1786)

The Pocahontas Plays 214
From James Nelson Barker, *The Indian Princess; or, La Belle Sauvage* (1808)

YAMOYDEN, a Narrative Poem 218
From James W. Eastburn and Robert C. Sands, *Yamoyden, a Tale of the Wars of King Philip . . .* (1820)

Nathaniel Hawthorne's "The Duston Family" 224
From *The American Magazine of Useful and Entertaining Knowledge* (May 1836)

The Captivity of the Munro Sisters from James Fenimore Cooper's THE LAST OF THE MOHICANS 231
From Cooper, *The Last of the Mohicans* (1826)

Thomas Cole Paints the Death of Cora **253**
Cole, detail from "A Scene from *The Last of the Mohicans*" (1827)

An Indian's Love Lyric **257**
"The Stolen White Girl" from John Rollin Ridge, *Poems* (1868)

Erastus Dow Palmer Captures a White Captive in Marble **260**
Palmer, "White Captive" (1858); and "Palmer's 'White Captive,'" *Atlantic Monthly* (January 1860)

"The Escape" from Herman Melville's TYPEE **264**
From Melville, *Typee, a Peep at Polynesian Life* (1846)

BIBLIOGRAPHICAL NOTE 275
INDEX 279

Illustrations

Title page decoration from *Indian Anecdotes and Barbarities . . . ,* 1837 frontis

Portrait of Pochantas from the *Generall Historie of Virginia* by Captain John Smith 13

The torture of two "helpless virgins" from the *Affecting History of . . . Frederick Manheim's Family* 70

Frontispiece to the *Narrative of . . . Misses Frances and Almira Hall* 79

"The Attack and Capture of Our Train, July 12, 1864" from Fanny Kelly's *Narrative of My Captivity Among the Sioux Indians* 95

"Mary [Jemison] Being Arrayed in Indian Costume" 116

"Colter Pursued by the Indians" 139

Fold-out from the *Narrative of the Massacre . . . of the Wife and Children of Thomas Baldwin* 183

Thomas Baldwin, "the Christian Hermit" 184

Portrait of Sal Fink from the *Crockett Almanac for 1854* 187

Cover of the dime novel *Moccasin Bill* 190

"The Escape of the Duston Family" 227

Detail from Thomas Cole's "A Scene from *The Last of the Mohicans*" 255

"White Captive," statue by Erastus Dow Palmer 262

Frontispiece to the *Narrative of the Capture . . . of Mrs. Eliza Fraser* 266

Acknowledgments

For the use of their collections, we would like to thank the Library Company of Philadelphia, the American Philosophical Society, the Rosenbach Foundation, and the Van Pelt Library of the University of Pennsylvania. We would especially like to make known our appreciation to the Newberry Library for giving us access to its incomparable holdings of Indian captivity materials, and to John Aubrey, Assistant Curator of Special Collections at the Newberry Library, for his generous assistance. We are indebted to Daniel Littlefield and James Parins of the University of Arkansas at Little Rock for allowing us to consult their unpublished research on John Rollin Ridge. During the preparation of this manuscript we were Visiting Research Fellows of the Newberry Library.

For permission to reproduce materials, we are indebted to the following:

"The White Captive" from Helen Flanders, Elizabeth Ballard, *et al.*, *The New Green Mountain Songster* (Yale University Press, 1939), pp. 256-258. Reprinted by permission of James H. Flanders, executor of the estate of Helen Flanders.

"Bright Amanda" from Lester A. Hubbard, *Ballads and Songs from Utah* (University of Utah Press, 1961), pp. 98-99. Reprinted by permission of the University of Utah Press.

Folktales about Tim Murphy from the Harold Thompson File, courtesy of the New York State Historical Society, and from Emelyn E. Gardner, "Folk-Lore from Schoharie County, New York," *Journal of American Folklore* 27 (1914), p. 305, reprinted by permission of the American Folklore Society.

Erastus Dow Palmer's "White Captive," photographed and printed courtesy of the Metropolitan Museum of Art, gift of Hamilton Fish, 1894.

Illustration of Sal Fink, reprinted courtesy of the American Antiquarian Society.

Cover of *Moccasin Bill*, photographed and reprinted courtesy of the Swen Parson Library of Northern Illinois University at De Kalb.

Illustration from Fanny Kelly's *Narrative of My Captivity Among the Sioux Indians*, reprinted courtesy of the Everett D. Graff Collection, the Newberry Library, Chicago.

Illustrations from *Indian Anecdotes and Barbarities* and from the John Smith, Manheim, Hall, Mason, Jemison, Baldwin, Hawthorne, and Fraser narratives, reproduced courtesy of the Edward E. Ayer Collection, the Newberry Library, Chicago.

All other illustrations were supplied courtesy of the Van Pelt Library of the University of Pennsylvania.

Introduction

When Rip Van Winkle failed to return from a hunting trip into the Catskills, it was assumed that he had been "carried away by the Indians." The assumption was fairly safe. During the French and Indian Wars, which ended about the time Rip disappeared, possibly as many as two thousand captives were carried to Canada by the Indians as war prisoners. Countless others were adopted into Indian tribes and lost forever to white society. The Indian captivity was a massive historic reality. It helped to shape the national character, it provided substance for the artistic imagination, it defined basic issues in the white culture, and it was made to serve a variety of purposes, not all of which were noble.

This collection and the commentary which accompanies it are designed to illustrate the scope and significance of the captivity narratives as they changed, through time, in the details of their subject matter, style, literary form, attitudes toward Indian culture, and the purposes to which they were applied. The narratives are divided into five phases, corresponding to the major historical and cultural preoccupations of the captivity tradition. These phases have been labeled: 1) THE DISCOVERY OF THE INDIAN, as revealed in narratives about the captivities of a conquistador, the Spaniard, Juan Ortiz,* and an adventurer, or, more accurately, "planter," Captain John Smith;* 2) TRIALS OF THE SPIRIT, undergone in the captivities of Jesuits, Puritans, and Quakers, who interpreted Indian captivity primarily within a religious framework; 3) THE LAND IMPERATIVE, which dominated narratives written during the French and Indian Wars, the American Revolution, and the later Indian wars on the American frontier, and which transformed captivity narratives into propaganda for the removal, assimilation, or destruction of any obstacle of the moment—French, British, or Indian—to westward imperial expansion; 4) BEHIND THE FRONTIER, narratives collected and retold in the settled regions through elite, folk, and popular media during the nineteenth century in which the captivity experience, retrospectively considered, enhanced the historic heritage and the socializing process; and 5) BEYOND THE FRONTIER, movement into the realm of the artistic imagination where

*Items included in our collection are marked with an asterisk the first time they are referred to in the Introduction whether the reference is in full or in part.

the captivity theme became a structure and metaphor for complex, pretentious art forms.

These phases show a steady chronological progression, but Captain John Smith, who belongs to the first phase, was not lacking in literary imagination or skill in the manipulation of language, and the pseudonymous authors of *A Surprising Account, of the Captivity and Escape of Philip M'Donald, and Alexander M'Leod . . .* (1786),* while they command attention for the imaginative leap into art they attempted, are imitative and subliterary. Prevailing opinions likewise tended to move with the times and the westering frontier, with dissent following behind. For instance, from the first in every region, there are narratives which depict the Indian lifestyle affirmatively and, on occasion, idyllically. Certain narratives reveal odd dimensions of the captivity tradition. Sal Fink,* daughter of the Mississippi keelboatman, Mike Fink, presents a boisterously comic spectacle unexpected in a genre dominated by horrors, pathos, and pragmatic application, and, while her story inhabits the ill-defined terrain between folklore and popular culture, its imaginative artistry almost qualifies it for a place in the section BEYOND THE FRONTIER.

If one defines the captivity narrative as a work which was based on fact or one intended to be accepted as fact, the canon (according to a checklist presently being compiled at the Newberry Library) consists of approximately two thousand items, different editions of the same item included, about the experiences of more than five hundred captives, beginning in the early sixteenth century and continuing through the 1870s. If fictive works such as historical romances and poems significantly incorporating the captivity theme are included, the number becomes even more extensive. Recently, a scholar, Louise K. Barnett, compiled a list of eighteenth- and nineteenth-century frontier romances, at least twenty-four of which have captivity incidents, and Arthur Hobson Quinn's survey of American plays before the Civil War includes twelve which can be identified as including Indian captivity. In addition, there is a substantial number of nineteenth-century paintings and statues depicting captivity episodes. The captivity materials (tales and songs) from folklore are considerable and from the popular culture (for instance, the dime novel), enormous. In short, the corpus is large and complex, and while it yields to categorization, categories overlap and result in loss of nuance.

Much of the material in this collection is obscure to the extent that it has not been reprinted in the present century. Better known items, such as selections from Cooper's *The Last of the Mohicans* (1826)* and Melville's *Typee* (1846),* assume new significance when read within the context of the other narratives in the captivity canon. Certain more familiar narratives have been excluded in favor of others less familiar but equally significant. For example, an account of the captivity of another Puritan woman, Hannah

Swarton,* usurps the place which might otherwise have been given to Mary Rowlandson's *The Sovereignty and Goodness of God . . .* (1682).

The earliest captivity narratives, those written during the period designated THE DISCOVERY OF THE INDIAN, were a by-product of sixteenth- and seventeenth-century exploration and colonization of the New World. They were intended to supply information about the newly discovered Americas. Even for some time after colonization, Europeans knew little about Indians, and what they did know was often based less on direct observation (which was, and remains, distorted by preconceptions) than on the abstract formulations of philosophers, theologians, and historians. They agreed only on the proposition that if Indians were indeed human beings—and not every one was sure of this—then they must somehow be descended from Adam, possibly through Cain or the illegitimate children of Noah, but more probably through the Lost Tribes of Israel. No one knew for certain whether the Indians were the "wild men" of medieval folklore, given over to unspeakable depravities; gentle innocents like the "cannibals" of Montaigne's *Essays* (I. xxxi [1580]) who lived in harmony with natural law; or, perhaps, subhuman degenerates like Caliban in Shakespeare's *The Tempest* (1611), whose mother was a witch and father a devil. Initial contacts between Europeans and Indians were cautious, tentative, and filled with misunderstanding on both sides. The conflicting reports about Indians which reached Europe from the New World compounded the confusion. They ranged from Sir Francis Drake's (c. 1543-1596) descriptions of a "people of a tractable, free and loving nature, without guile or treachery" to the monstrous "Anthropophagi, or devourers of human flesh" described by Martin Frobisher (c. 1543-1594), another British seafarer and explorer. The sketches of Jacques Le Moyne, the French artist who visited Florida in 1564 in the expedition led by René Laudonnière, almost innocently capture this double vision of the Indian. Le Moyne painted savage Indians indulging in man-eating and other revolting practices, but also Indians with the noble configuration of demigods besporting themselves in Arcadia. Theodor de Bry's engravings after Le Moyne's drawings which illustrated his narrative in the *Great and Small Voyages* (Frankfurt, 1590) became known throughout Europe. Le Moyne's double vision was to persist, usually as image and counterimage, but sometimes in uneasy combination. It came to be a feature of the captivity narratives which, on the face of it, could be expected to portray the Indian as abhorrent, not ambivalently or favorably.

Stereotypes of the Indian emerged when colonization of the New World succeeded exploration and it became necessary to have fixed views so that the Indians could be dealt with. These stereotypes varied with the aims of the colonizing nations and were based on preconceptions about how they hoped Indians would behave. The earliest captivity stories reflect these preconceptions and in turn were used as evidence to confirm and hence to perpetuate them. Spain, for example, wanted to exploit the riches of the New World. Indians were considered part of the spoils. It took the papal bull of Paul III, *Sublimus Deus* (1537), to settle the matter that they were "truly men . . . capable of understanding the Catholic faith," and not "dumb brutes created for our service." Narratives of captive Spanish conquistadors like Núñez Cabeza de Vaca's *Relation . . .* (1542) and the story of Juan Ortiz in the *True Relation of the Gentleman of Elvas . . .* (1557) encouraged further despoilment by describing Indians as inhuman and untrustworthy. France, on the other hand, wanted to trade with the Indians. Its colonists cultivated Indian friendship, married into their tribes, and, Samuel de Champlain explains, brought missionaries "to teach the [Indian] people the knowledge of God, and inform them" about French culture, "so that together with the French language, they may also acquire a French heart and spirit." To captive Jesuits in New France, the Indians were souls to be saved from Satan's power and won over for the greater glory of God and France.

English attitudes toward the Indian tended to vary in terms of the origins of the various colonies, though even within individual colonies these attitudes shifted with time and contained contrary elements. For instance, the Virginia colonists hoped for profitable commerce with the Indians. Initially, and from this viewpoint, they saw the land in Arcadian terms—"Earth's only Paradise," as it was called by the poet Michael Drayton in his ode "To the Virginian Voyage" (1606)—and they envisioned Indians as children of a beneficent nature. The British explorer, Arthur Barlowe, "found the people [of Virginia] most gentle, loving, and faithful, void of all guile and treason and such as lived after the Golden Age." This view was shared by the Hakluyts and other British promoters of commerce between the homeland and the New World, and it is confirmed in the captivity episode in Captain John Smith's *Generall Historie of Virginia, New-England, and the Summer Isles . . .* (1624). The initial success of Jamestown depended in large measure on a friendly relationship with the Indians and on continued support from Britain in the form of supplies and additional colonists. Sir Walter Raleigh's Roanoke expedition (1585) had failed because the threat of the Spanish Armada prevented supply ships from reaching it in time to save the colonists from their unknown misfortune—if the legend of Virginia Dare is to be believed, their captivity by the Croatans. Like the adventurers who financed the Virginia expedition, Smith understood that if the Virginia enterprise was to succeed, it was important not to "offend the naturals" or to present an essentially unfavorable image of them to the British public. In Pennsylvania, William Penn hoped that rather than "devour and destroy one another," Quakers and Indians would "live together as neighbours and friends." He considered Indians "under a dark Night in Things relating to *Religion*," and, like John Woolman and other Quaker leaders after him, believed that through "universal righteousness" they might be brought to value a "spirit of love and peace." Jonathan Dickinson's journal* about his captivity among the

Indians of Florida supported the view that Indians were "savage men" in need of enlightenment and that "God's Protecting Providence" would succor all his creatures, Indians and Quakers alike.

In general, the Pilgrims and Puritans who colonized New England regarded the Indian with grave suspicion. Despite the dissent of the Reverend John Eliot (1604-1690), the kindly "apostle to the Indians," the opinion prevailed that the Indians were, in the words of the Puritan poet, Benjamin Tompson (1642-1714), "monsters shapt and fac'd like men." Many Puritans, the Mathers among them, thought that Indians were in league with Satan, if not devils themselves. This view of the Indian extends back to the time of the explorer John Cabot (c. 1450-1499), when they were thought to resemble "bruite beasts," and it was shared by William Bradford, John Winthrop, and even, at times, the gentle Separatist, Roger Williams, and is confirmed in the Puritan captivities. It was a religious view foreshadowing the secular doctrine of Manifest Destiny, which held as a corollary that Indians were degenerates incapable of progress and therefore without right to the lands they inhabited. This attitude toward primitive cultures resembles that of the ancient Greeks toward the barbarians, and the British toward the native Irish whose lands they colonized in the sixteenth century. Together, then, these diverse views penetrated the captivity narrative during its initial phase, when the Indian was being discovered. Behind their diversity and the stereotypes which derived from it lay an unsaid assumption: in America, European culture would be tested and the Indian would be the means. In its most intense form, the Indian captivity, the test would involve forced submission to an alien culture. The traumatic potential was greater even than migration across the ocean. In fact, it was its logical extension.

For Puritans, Catholic priests, and Quakers who had come to the New World primarily for religious reasons, Indian captivities were also TRIALS OF THE SPIRIT. Puritans saw history as a cosmic struggle betwen God and Satan. To help assure God's victory, they founded a government based on a covenant with God to obey his laws to the letter. Following biblical precedent, they modeled their government after the theocracy of the ancient Israelites and thought of themselves as a New Chosen People. Massachusetts was a New Israel won from the Canaan wilderness of New England. It followed that the Indians were Canaanites who would be conquered by the Puritan Israelites. The Puritans extended this thinking to the point that Indians became not just Canaanites, but "devils incarnate," in Cotton Mather's words. To be taken captive, then, meant to fall into Satan's power. Indian captivity was an ordeal which had religious implications for both the captive and the Puritan community.

Above all, Indian captivity was a spiritual affliction that God, for some inscrutable reason, had chosen to visit upon his servants. "I cannot express to man the afflictions that lay upon my Spirit," wrote Mary Rowlandson about her captivity during King Philip's War: "The portion of some is to have their affliction by drops, now one drop and then another; but the dregs of the Cup, the Wine of astonishment, like a sweeping rain that leaveth no food, did the Lord prepare to be my portion." Her feeling was shared by Jonathan Dickinson, a Quaker for whom captivity was an "afflicting tryal," and, in a modified form, by captive Jesuit priests like Father Francis Joseph Bressani,* who saw in the ordeal of Indian captivity an opportunity for purgatorial suffering leading to sanctification: "What consoled me much was, to see that God granted me the grace of suffering some little pain in this world, instead of the incomparably far greater torments, which I should have had to suffer for my sins in the next world," Father Bressani wrote. The Puritan recognized Indian captivity as punishment for sin. Hannah Swarton was convinced that she had invited and deserved her chastisement. She recalled that she and her husband "had left the Publick Worship and Ordinances of God . . . to remove to the North Part of *Casco Bay,* where there was no Church or *Minister* of the Gospel, . . . thereby exposing our Children, to be bred Ignorantly like *Indians.*" In this context, Indian captivity became the symbolic equivalent of a journey into hell, an identification which Mary Rowlandson evokes in her description of an Indian feast she observed on the first night of her captivity: "Oh the roaring, and singing and danceing, and yelling of those black creatures in the night, which made the place a lively resemblance of hell." Puritans ordinarily thought of the Indians as "copper-colored," a description Cotton Mather frequently applied to them. They called Satan "the black man."

Surviving Indian captivity was deemed a sign of God's favor, perhaps an indication of election. There is a suggestion of this typological thinking in the title John Williams chose for his narrative: *The Redeemed Captive Returning to Zion . . .* (1707). Perhaps his ordeal and redemption in this world prefigured what was in store for him in the world to come. Captives carefully recorded any "special providences" which befell them during their captivities. An extra portion of food, a moment of unexpected relaxation, anything out of the ordinary which benefited the captive was read as a sign of divine favor. Sometimes God's providence worked in mysterious ways. Among the "remarkable passages of providence" which Mary Rowlandson took "special notice of in [her] afflicted time" was "the wonderfull providence of God in preserving the heathen for farther affliction to our poor Countrey." About her own captivity she exalts: "O the wonderfull power of God that I have seen, and the experience that I have had: I have been in the midst of those roaring Lyons, and Salvage Bears, that feared neither God, nor Man, nor the Devil, by night and day, alone and in company: sleeping all sorts together, and yet not one of them ever offered me the least abuse of unchastity to me, in word or action." So preemptive was her religious indoctrination and so profound was her ignorance of Indian folkways that it never occurred to her that, in fact, she was in little danger of "abuse." Her view of Indian captivity as a manifestation of God's providence was shared by Catholic and Protestant alike. It is displayed in the title of Jonathan Dickinson's *God's Protecting Providence Man's Surest Help and Defence in Times of the Greatest Difficulty and Most Imminent Danger* (1699) and appears repeatedly in the testimony of captive Jesuits. Among the "signal favors" which God provided Father Bressani during his captivity were faith, humility, obedience, sacrifice, and the opportunity to convert the Indians through preaching and good will.

Puritan, Catholic, and Quaker learned lessons from their captivities which they took care to teach others. Puritan captivities take on the dimension of spiritual autobiography, a mode with didactic potential. By recording the events of a captivity in the sequence that God permitted them to happen, the captive could extract lessons and patterns from the experience which might be evident only in retrospect. But in addition, the Puritan community was, as John Winthrop put it, "knitt together . . . as members of the same body." Salvation could only be attained if, in the words of Thomas Hooker, the individual did "willingly binde and ingage himself to each member of that society to promote the good of the whole." The obligation of the captive extended to both the individual and the Christian community. Religious leaders in their turn saw didactic benefits to be derived from a reading of captivity narratives and took an active interest in their publication and, in some instances, their composition. The Dickinson journal was published by the Society of Friends. Its preface features an analysis of the spiritual lessons it contains. The avowed purpose of *The Jesuit Relations*, issued annually between 1632 and 1673, was to teach by way of example. Puritan ministers incorporated captivity exempla into their sermons and ecclesiastical histories. Cotton Mather included accounts of the captivities of Hannah Duston and Hannah Swarton, written by himself, in his sermon, *Humiliations Follow'd with Deliverances*, preached in Boston on March 6, 1697, in preparation for a public fast. In this context, they were a warning to the faithful that God could, if he so desired, use the Indians to scourge New England for its wickedness and spiritual decline. Mather then reprinted the Duston narrative in *Decennium Luctuosum . . .* (1699), where it is used as an example of spiritual fortitude during the difficult time of King William's War. Both the Duston and Swarton narratives appear yet again in the *Magnalia Christi Americana . . .* (1702) as examples of "memorable providences" and "wonderful deliverances." Mather was more prolific and ingenious than most clerics, and he may have overexploited his material. But it is obvious that the Indian captivity narrative had its practical applications for the pious.

THE LAND IMPERATIVE, the demand for more and more territory, changed the character of the Indian captivity narrative. From the eighteenth century onward, it became increasingly secular, serving primarily as an instrument to control or counter any force that stood in the way of territorial expansion along the frontier. Specifically and in chronological succession, this meant first the French and then the British and always the Indian. The process began during the imperialistic struggles between France and England which culminated in the Seven Years' War (1756-1763). Although often their stated purpose is to provide a lesson in the mysterious workings of divine providence, narratives written during the French and Indian Wars are at bottom intended to elicit hatred toward the French, whom they accused of inciting Indian depredations. Accordingly, *An Account of the Captivity of Elizabeth Hanson . . .* (1760) had an ostensible purpose, that "the merciful kindness and goodness of God might thereby be manifested; and the reader stirred up with more care and fear to righteousness and humility," but throughout Mrs. Hanson points to atrocities committed by the French through the Indians. After a rather evocative description of the technique of scalping, Mrs. Hanson adds: "And it has been currently reported, that the French, in their wars with the English, have given the Indians a pecuniary reward for every scalp they brought to them."

Similar anti-French propaganda can be found in the *Memoirs of Odd Adventures, Strange Deliverances, &c. in the Captivity of John Gyles, Esq. . . .* (1736), John Norton's *The Redeemed Captive . . .* (1748),* *A Narrative of the Sufferings and Surprizing Deliverances of William and Elizabeth Fleming . . .* (1756), *A Faithful Narrative of the Many Dangers and Sufferings as Well as Wonderful Deliverances of Robert Eastburn . . .* (1758), *A Plain Narrative of the Uncommon Sufferings and Remarkable Deliverance of Thomas Brown . . .* (1760), among other narratives. Presumably written "to glorify God, for his Goodness and Faithfulness to the Meanest of his Servants, and to encourage others to trust in him," the Eastburn narrative is replete with examples of the "prodigious Iniquity" of the French, who use the Indians to accomplish "their ambitious and unjust Designs" against the English. William and Elizabeth Fleming claim that the French gave the Indians "a certain Sum per Scalp and for Prisoners, if they were young, and fit for Business," but that "the old People and Children" were to be "kill'd and scalped, as well as such as were refractory and not willing to go with them." In this way, they charge, the French encouraged the Indians to kill the helpless and infirm rather than to take them captive. Peter Williamson's *French and Indian Cruelty . . .* (1757) is blatantly aggressive; the 1758 edition contains a map "of the most convenient roads for the British forces to invade Canada in three divisions, and make themselves masters of it the next campaign."

Since American Protestants feared the spread of Roman Catholicism even more than they feared a French political conquest, much of this anti-French sentiment is directed against the church. "Having heard much of the Papists torturing the Protestants," John Gyles is reduced to tears of terror when he

discovers that the Indians have sold him to the French. *A Jou*
Captivity of Jean Lowry . . . (1760) terminates in a spirited debat
Mrs. Lowry and her Catholic captors on the relative merits of C
and Catholicism, which, she reports without surprising the reader, sl
The subtitle of the Fleming narrative, an inflammatory pamphlet ai
military recruits, parades its anti-French bias and accuses Catholic priests of instigating the atrocities committed by the Indians: *A Narrative Necessary to be Read by All Who are Going in the Expedition, as Well as Every British Subject. Wherein It Fully Appears That the Barbarities of the Indians Is Owing to the French and Chiefly Their Priests.* When her Indian captors told Elizabeth Fleming about the many "old People and Children they kill'd and scalped," she "asked them if they did not think it was a Sin to shed so much innocent Blood." The Indians promptly responded "*That the* French *were much better off than the* English, *for they had a great many old Men among them that could forgive all their Sins, and these Men had often assured the* Indians *it was no Sin to destroy Hereticks, and all the* English *were such.*"

The British supplanted the French as an object of hatred in Indian captivity narratives written at the time of the Revolutionary War. *A Narrative of the Capture of Certain Americans at Westmorland . . .* (c. 1780) begins by explaining that the British are responsible for the Indian atrocities it will describe: "The savages who occasioned the following scenes, were sent from the British garrison at Niagara, some time in the fore part of March A.D. 1780, through a deep snow, on a wretched skulking Indian expedition, against a few scattered people which they hoped to find about the Susquehannah; especially those who were making sugar in the woods at that time of the year." Among the Indian brutalities it details are scalpings, murders, tortures, and forced marches through deep snows. Because the Indians receive a bounty for scalps but not for captives, they use their prisoners as bearers until the war party reaches Niagara. Then they murder them for their scalps. Similar accusations are made in *A Narrative of the Capture and Treatment of John Dodge . . .* (1779),* one of the more vehemently anti-British accounts. According to Dodge, the Indians are "no ways interested in the unhappy dispute between Great-Britain and America" until the British arouse them by offering twenty dollars for each American scalp and by telling them that the Americans intend "to murder them all and take their lands." Dodge is incensed at the inhumanity of the British officials at Detroit who ordered Indian war parties "not to spare man, woman, or child" because "the children would make soldiers, and the women would keep up the flock."

After the Revolutionary War, when Indians became the main obstacle to frontier expansion, the captivity narratives became almost exclusively a device for anti-Indian propaganda. A few narratives presented a sympathetic picture of Indian life, but most of them were shaped by publishers exploiting a mass market that thrived on sensationalism, in a natural alliance with land speculators who wanted to implement a policy of Indian extermination in the interest of real estate development. Accounts like *An Affecting Narrative of the Captivity and Sufferings of Mrs. Mary Smith . . .* (1818),* *A Narrative of the Sufferings of Massy Harbison . . .* (1825), the *Narrative of the Captivity and Providential Escape of Mrs. Jane Lewis . . .* (1833), R. B. Stratton's *Captivity of the Oatman Girls . . .* (1857), and Fanny Kelly's *Narrative of My Captivity Among the Sioux Indians . . .* (1871),* among dozens of others, were designed to horrify audiences into hating what the novelist Hugh Henry Brackenridge (1748-1816), an editor of captivity narratives, referred to as "the animals, vulgarly called Indians." Pulp thrillers, shilling shockers, and penny dreadfuls, they constitute the stereotypical Indian captivity narrative. In them, the Indian is painted as so irredeemably brutish that he deserves to be deprived of his lands. Their setting follows the frontier: first the western borders of Pennsylvania and New York, then the Ohio River Valley, and eventually the Far West, where the Apache, Comanche, and Sioux opposed white settlement with extreme hostility. In the end, the setting is in the South Seas, where sailors and shipwrecked travelers are held captive by Polynesians described in language originally applied to American Indians.

The major Indian wars were another factor which stimulated the publication of anti-Indian narratives. *The Remarkable Adventures of Jackson Johonnot . . .* (1791) tells about its author's captivity among the Kickapoo Indians in 1791 while serving as a soldier in the expedition led by Generals Josiah Harmar and Arthur St. Clair to subdue the Indians in the Ohio Territory. *A Narrative of the Life and Sufferings of Mrs. Jane Johns . . .* (1837) takes place in East Florida during the Second Seminole War. The setting of the Mary Smith narrative is the Mississippi River Valley west of Natchez shortly after the Tecumseh uprising. The *Narrative of the Capture and Providential Escape of Misses Frances and Almira Hall . . .* (1832)* is about a captivity in Illinois during Black Hawk's War. Nelson Lee's *Three Years Among the Comanches . . .* (1859) and Sarah Larimer's *The Capture and Escape . . .* (1870) concern captivities which occur in the West during the period of warfare with the Plains Indians.

To achieve their ends, the anti-Indian captivity narratives feature accounts of harrowing cruelties. No excesses, no matter how outrageous, are spared the reader. The torture scenes in the Mary Smith narrative exemplify these overflows of sensationalism. Equally lurid are the Indian atrocities described in the Hall and Kelly narratives: a baby roasted in an oven before its mother's eyes, a man left bound and naked to starve in the desert, and other incidents "too shocking for publication." Such narratives are characterized by exaggeration, outright fiction, and plagiarism. Mrs. Jane Johns is shot, scalped, and set on fire. She uses the blood from her wounds to extinguish the flames and lives to tell the story.

For obvious reasons, captivity narratives depicting Indian life favorably are rare. Many captives chose to remain among the Indians when offered the opportunity to return, but few of them wrote narratives. Tribalized, they discarded their white identity and with it the white man's language and the desire to communicate with whites. Indifference, usually, but also the fear that the government might force their return caused them to avoid white culture. Many treaties stipulated the return of captives without regard for personal preferences. Of the some two hundred captives recovered through a treaty negotiated by Col. Henry Bouquet with the Delawares and Shawnees during the Rebellion of Pontiac in 1764, few left the Indians willingly. In fact, so many captives tried to return to their adoptive tribes that it was necessary to bind and guard them. "Unless they are closely watch'd," reported Lt. Gov. Francis Fauquier of Virginia, "they will certainly return to the Barbarians," and, when given the opportunity, many of them did just that. The accounts of tribalized captives extend from the idyllic descriptions of Indian life in *A Narrative of the Captivity and Adventures of John Tanner . . .* (1830)* to Jonathan H. Jones's *Indianology* (1899),* the story of Herman Lehmann, an Indianized captive more savage than his Apache captors. Between these extremes is *A Narrative of the Life of Mrs. Mary Jemison . . .* (1824),* the testimony of a captive who describes Indian life with little prejudice, Indian or white. Relatively speaking, then, captivity narratives sympathetic toward the Indian did not get written, published, or read. White Americans did not want to read favorable accounts of a culture they were destroying.

Propaganda narratives, however, were widely read, whether anti-French, anti-British, or anti-Indian. Their effectiveness as propaganda depended on mass circulation, and to guarantee a market they were published inexpensively, usually as pamphlets of from twenty to a hundred pages printed on cheap paper, but also as broadsides or as filler material in almanacs hawked by booksellers and roving peddlers. The broadside narrative, "Captivity and Sufferings of Mrs. Mason . . ." (c. 1836),* was published at the height of the Second Seminole War for the purpose of turning public opinion against the Seminoles, who had many sympathizers, especially in the Northeast. Copies of these narratives are rare today because they were intended for immediate consumption and were literally read to pieces. Many narratives were collected into anthologies, the nature of which is obvious from such titles as Archibald Loudon's *A Selection of Some of the Most Interesting Narratives of Outrages Committed by the Indians in Their Wars with the White People . . .* (1808-1811) and the anonymously edited *Indian Anecdotes and Barbarities: Being a Description of Their Customs and Deeds of Cruelty, with an Account of the Captivity, Sufferings and Heroic Conduct of Many Who Have Fallen into Their Hands, or Who Have Defended Themselves from Savage Vengeance; All Illustrating the General Traits of Indian Character . . .* (1837). The Cherokee Removal, ordered by Andrew Jackson, and the Seminole War were in progress (if that is the word) at the time.

By the 1830s, BEHIND THE FRONTIER, in the East, the Indian was a matter of history, though on the western frontier he was another matter. Crazy Horse and Sitting Bull, Red Cloud and Chief Joseph are all figures of the 1870s. Geronimo surrendered in 1866. The massacre of the Sioux at Wounded Knee took place on December 18, 1890. As late as 1911, a small band of Shoshones rose against the whites near Humbolt, Nevada. The difference between eastern and western attitudes is apparent in the public response to the Sauk chief, Black Hawk, after his surrender in 1832. In the East he became a celebrity. He was received by President Jackson and presented with a medal by former President John Quincy Adams. When he traveled through Michigan and Illinois, however, where the memory of the war he led was still fresh, he was jeered, and a military escort had to be called out for his protection. In the East there had emerged a sentimental and antiquarian interest in the past and a concern for primitive culture inherited from the Enlightenment *philosophes* and reinforced by their Romantic successors, such as Chateaubriand. The Indian came to be imaged less as a savage enemy of civilization than a pathetic anachronism, cast aside as civilization marched forward. He was abandoned to the historian, the teller of folktales, the ballad singer, and the hack.

Captivity narratives can be found with predictable frequency in eastern state and town histories. The function of these local histories was to reclaim the past, or perhaps to devise a past which could inspire the present. The Indian captivity of the Deerfield pastor, John Williams, originally written at the insistence of Cotton Mather to affirm God's providence, was rewritten in another, more secular age by a local historian, Elihu Hoyt,* to foster patriotism. The Hannah Duston captivity went through a number of more complex permutations. Cotton Mather used it first, to demonstrate a part of the heaven-ordained historical design. For the Transcendentalist Henry David Thoreau,* the history of Hannah Duston, like the river on which both he and she journeyed, flowed mystically betwen past and present, the remote and close by. It was a symbolic event which suggested that man must accept his whole history as part of his humanity but that he need not be crushed beneath its weight.

Accounts of Indian captivity appear in such military histories as Henry White's *Indian Battles . . .* (1859), Joseph Pritts's *Incidents of Border Life . . .* (1859), and Samuel Gardner Drake's *A Particular History of the Five Year French and Indian War in New England . . .* (1870), where they hold up for emulation the sturdy example of pioneers during the times of early border warfare. For the same reason, they were included in periodicals which featured historical materials such as *The American Pioneer* (1842-1843), *The Olden Time* (1846-1847), and *The American Whig Review* (1850-1852).

Indian histories were another medium for the historical preservation of captivity narratives. In many cases, narratives emphasize affirmative aspects of Indian culture. Parts of the Tanner narrative, for instance, are reprinted in *A Collection of Indian Anecdotes . . .* (1837). Anna C. Miller reshaped Mary Jemison's captivity for inclusion in *The Iroquois; or, the Bright Side of Indian Character . . .* (1855), where it shows Indian life in a favorable light. In an attempt to be objective, some historians simply reprinted verbatim as many captivity narratives as they could readily collect. They believed posterity would distinguish fact from fiction. Dozens of captivity stories appear in the histories of Samuel Gardner Drake, Henry Rowe Schoolcraft, and James Wimer. Collected and edited with care, their works remain an important repository of information about Indians and Indian-white relations, in contrast to the propaganda anthologies whose concern was engendering anti-Indian sentiment.

Indian captivity narratives also are interwoven into the works of more sophisticated historians. The captivity episodes in George Bancroft's *History of the United States . . .* (1834-1885)* convey his negative assumptions regarding the place of the Indian in American history. He uses captivity episodes in his accounts of Indian wars to document the arrested development of the Indian, whose barbaric conduct put him beyond the pale. For example, in explaining Puritan behavior toward the Indian at the time of King Philip's War, Bancroft refers to Mary Rowlandson's captivity to show that "There was no security but to seek out the hiding-places of the natives" and to destroy them "by surprise." Though his scholarship is massive and his literary achievement considerable, Bancroft comes to the same conclusion as the hacks: because Indians are unwilling or unable to accept the benefits of civilization, their extermination is an inevitable necessity.

The stated aim of Francis Parkman's first historical work, *The Conspiracy of Pontiac* (1851)* is to portray "the American forest and the American Indian." This theme brought together Parkman's romantic fascination with nature in its wild state, his admiration for the heroic, his patrician demand for mastery, and his belief in American, democratic progress. At the same time, it dramatized a conflict both personal and cultural: the attraction of the forest primeval was retrogressive and anarchic, yet in his superior moralistic way, Parkman, along with most Americans, subscribed to the cult of progress. No wonder Cooper's *Leatherstocking Tales* were at the top of his favorite reading, or that the plight of the white captives was a subject that touched him. He makes it climactic in *Pontiac* when he recounts the tragedy of the captives who do not want to return to white civilization. Parkman could identify positively with the Indian values that caused the captive to cling to a tribal life—such affirmative values as independence, self-reliance, and freedom—for they are also professed by white American culture. But unable to concede them to the Indianized white, he qualifies them with adjectives. Modified, they become "reckless independence," "haughty self-reliance," "irresponsible freedom," and the Indianized white is branded, "a wanderer and an Ishmaelite." Such was his subliminal response when he encountered the reality of the Indianized white. In fictional guise, however, the white Indian was harmless, even admirable. He could write of *Leatherstocking:* "There is something admirably felicitous in the conception of this hybrid offspring of civilization and barbarism, in whom uprightness, innate philosophy and the truest moral perceptions are joined with the wandering instincts and hatred of restraint which stamp the Indian or the Bedouin."

Written or rewritten for children, narratives of captivity served to entertain the young and to teach reading, writing, history, and moral behavior, not necessarily in that order, and to perpetuate conventional attitudes, among them the conviction of white superiority. *The Stolen Boy* (1830) by Barbara Hofland recounts the adventures of a boy held captive by the Comanches. Mrs. Hofland intrudes to sermonize: "Here let my young reader pause . . . . Let him devoutly and humbly thank his Almighty Father that he was born of Christian parents, in a Christian land; let him rejoice in that his heart is tender, . . . lest he should in any degree become hard-hearted, cruel, and revengeful like the Indian of whom we speak." *The Deerfield Captive; an Indian Story; Being a Narrative of Facts for the Instruction of the Young* (1831) is based on John Williams's *The Redeemed Captive.* Its anonymous author points out in a preface "what trials our ancestors were compelled to endure in laying out these fair settlements which it is our lot to inherit." He expresses the hope that "the sufferings of the first civilized inhabitants of New England" will impress "the tender mind . . . with the deepest gratitude to GOD for the privileges and the blessings which by their labors and privations, have been secured to their children." He excuses the cruelty of the Indians on the grounds that "they were exceedingly ignorant" although he thinks nothing of describing their "unfeeling and wicked" behavior. The captivity tales in *McGuffey's Readers** are forthrightly didactic. They supply history and morality embedded in a pedagogical apparatus.

Folktales and ballads, other modes of history, flourished behind the frontier. Folktales about Indian captivity originated in the East during the late eighteenth and early nineteenth centuries. Many of them center on an incident in which a captive, despite the physical superiority of his captors, outwits them and escapes. In some instances, folk heroes evolved whose fame in large measure rested on ingenious escapes from Indian captivity. Tim Murphy* is a case in point. As time passed, certain escape techniques developed into folk formulas which became attached to various figures of note and contributed to their elevation to legendary status. One of the classic American trickster tales concerns a captive who escapes from the Indians by persuading them to place their hands in a crack in a log from which he removes a wedge and entraps them. It has been told about Tim Murphy, Tom Quick, Davy Crockett, Jim Bridger, and Daniel Boone, among other frontier heroes.

The evolution of the Daniel Boone legend is an illustrative case of how a notable personality may be transformed into legend with some assistance from folklore but far more from the elaborations of rather imaginative popular historians. Boone was still alive and in his prime, and not a figure about whom folktales were being told, when John Filson wrote "The Adventures of Col. Daniel Boon" (1784).* Filson included relatively mild Indian captivity materials which were expanded by subsequent writers like Timothy Flint, who, in his *Biographical Memoir of Daniel Boone* (1883),* describes escapes involving superhuman feats. At this point, on the one hand, folkloristic captivity incidents began to gravitate toward him and, on the other, he became a commodity for the mass media, especially the enormously successful dime novels of the 1860s and 1870s which featured frontier adventures among the Indians.

In their final phase, Indian captivity narratives move BEYOND THE FRONTIER of historical reality into frontiers of the artistic imagination where they provide structures for complex, sophisticated works. The beginning of this phase can be identified in obscure eighteenth-century fantasies such as the M'Donald and M'Leod narrative, in which two soldiers explore the Pacific Northwest and find a utopia, or Abraham Panther's *An Account of a Beautiful Young Lady . . .* (1787), the story of a girl who murders her Indian captor and lives in a cave until she is discovered by the narrator nine years later. Its maturity occurred during the nineteenth century in response to the efforts of writers like Cooper and Simms, who struggled to fashion a distinctively American literary tradition. They saw one practical possibility: infusing established forms with American materials. Dramatic, exotic, and uniquely American, the Indian captivity narrative afforded an artistic opportunity of considerable promise. It could easily be adapted to traditional literary forms, and it had the further advantage of including highly charged features of the American scene: the wilderness and the Indian. Playwrights, for instance, recognized the promise of Indian captivity as drama and spectacle. James Nelson Barker's *The Indian Princess; or, La Belle Sauvage* (1808),* on the rescue of John Smith by Pocahontas, was so favorably received that it provoked imitators and eventually a burlesque. Captivity stories also inspired verse. The narrative poem, *Yamoyden, a Tale of the Wars of King Philip . . .* (1820)* was the attempt of two aspiring young authors, James W. Eastburn and Robert C. Sands, to write poetry about American history. Its novelty lay in its blend of history and the romance, a form popularized by Scott, and its American substance, Indian-white relations at the time of the Puritans, captivities, of course, included. Cooper was shortly to follow this successful course.

But it was in the novel that Indian captivity most significantly influenced the development of American literature. Among the better known American novelists to use the patterns of the Indian captivity are Charles Brockden Brown, James Fenimore Cooper, William Gilmore Simms, Robert Montgomery Bird, Edgar Allan Poe, and Herman Melville. The first to experiment with a captivity novel was Ann Eliza Bleecker, whose *The History of*

Maria Kittle (1797) is basically a captivity narrative molded to fit the modes of the "novel of sensibility," the most popular literary form in late eighteenth-century America. The conventions of the novel of sensibility include a heroine in the power of an unrelenting villain and a series of emotionally draining episodes in which she faces grave danger until rescued and fortuitously reunited with her lover or spouse. In *The History of Maria Kittle,* a frontier heroine whose virtue stems from her contact with the pristine American wilderness is taken captive by Indians whose "unfeeling hearts" allow them to commit atrocities and in general make them ideal villains. The journey through the wilderness furnishes occasion for a series of mishaps in which Mrs. Kittle displays her virtue and resourcefulness, and the Indians their lack of sentiment. Finally, and coincidentally, she is reunited with her husband, but only after telling her story to a group of compassionate Canadian women who offer her "sympathy and tea."

What Mrs. Bleecker did for the sentimental novel Charles Brockden Brown did for the gothic novel, and it was with *Edgar Huntly; or, Memoirs of a Sleepwalker* (1799) that Indian captivity entered the American literary mainstream. In a prefatory note Brown states his purpose. He will write a novel "growing out of the condition of our country" which will engage "the sympathy of the reader" because "incidents of Indian hostility and the perils of the Western wilderness are far more suitable" for gothic fiction than the "Puerile superstitions and exploded manners . . . usually employed for this end." In this novel about somnambulism, murder, Indian warfare, and obsession, the wilderness associated with Indian captivity is a metaphor for the intricacies of the human mind, and the savagery often associated with the Indian is seen as a human condition lurking in the subconscious of the most civilized.

It is with the *Leatherstocking Tales* of James Fenimore Cooper that the Indian captivity narrative has made the most obvious impression on American, and indeed international, literary culture. Leatherstocking is a frontier hero in the tradition of Daniel Boone. Parkman recognized their affinity when he wrote in an essay on Cooper for the *North American Review* (1852) that the "quiet, unostentatious courage of Cooper's hero had its counterpart in the character of Daniel Boone; and the latter had the same unaffected love of nature which forms so pleasing a feature in the mind of Leatherstocking." With all due respect to their natural habitat, they also owe an allegiance to civilization. The Boone of historical legend and the Leatherstocking of frontier romance live in a divided world. Leatherstocking spends his life as brother to noble Indians like Chingachgook and Uncas, almost allegorical types of natural goodness, when he is not himself escaping from savage Indians, types of evil in nature, or helping various civilized types, like Cora and Alice Munro of *The Last of the Mohicans,* escape. Through the captivity narrative, Cooper leads the reader into Leatherstocking's world, permitting him to follow its emotional and ethical ramifications within a whirling pattern of pursuit, capture, escape, and pursuit.

Essentially alone, insistently white by blood but clearly Indian in outlook, Leatherstocking dies childless. His death is a typical Cooper stage piece which reveals the extent of his divided allegiances. The scene is the outskirts of a Pawnee village, Leatherstocking having declined to live in the village itself. At his side are his surrogate children—the Indian chief Hard-Heart from the nearby village, the aristocratic Captain Duncan Middleton, come from civilization a thousand miles away, and Paul Hover, a frontiersman who will help to build a civilization in the backwoods. Leatherstocking pronounces his benediction and then addresses himself directly, in the terminology of the Indian, to "the Great Spirit" who will at last redeem him from his captivity in this imperfect and divided world.

Cooper experienced life on the western frontier at second hand. Washington Irving, after his long years abroad, explored the western prairies almost as if he were a foreign tourist. Francis Parkman's frontier journey along the Oregon Trail, whatever it might have meant as psychic therapy or the field work of a fledgling historian, and whatever its rigors, was an artificial and temporary arrangement. Herman Melville was the only major writer to experience the frontier, in his case the frontiers of both the land and sea, immediately and out of natural necessity. And he was the only one to be held captive, an experience he was to draw on more or less extensively in his fiction. His first novel, *Typee* (1846), is identifiably close to his adventures as a sailor in the Pacific who deserted his ship, was taken captive by island tribesmen, and was rescued by a landing party. America was pushing beyond the land itself, and it did not stretch the imagination to identify Polynesians with Indians or the Pacific Ocean with the western wilderness. Cooper was to do the same in his South Sea island novel, *The Crater* (1848), which followed Melville's by two years. In *Mardi* (1849), an American sailor rescues a white captive maiden of mysterious origin from a Polynesian priest, killing the priest and provoking the vengeful pursuit of his three sons, armed with bows and arrows, in their canoe. In a later novel, *Pierre* (1852), he compares the isolation of his young hero in the city wilderness of New York to the plight of "a frontier man" who has been "carried far and deep into the wilderness, and there held captive, with no slightest probability of eventual deliverance." In "Benito Cereno" (1855), his tale of a slave insurrection aboard ship in the Pacific, the Spanish captain, in a complex charade, is held by African blacks, whose traits appear alternately noble and savage.

As a sailor on a whaleship, the narrator of *Typee* is subject to the restraints and demands of civilization until he escapes to the freedom of his white captivity among the Polynesians. Leatherstocking flees civilization for the freedom of the frontier, but he eventually recognizes the demands of civilization and also realizes that, in responding to them, he is an instrument in the destruction of the wilderness environment that has nurtured him. The narrator of *The Conspiracy of Pontiac* reveals the attractiveness of "forest life" unwittingly in the language he uses to describe the Indianized white men and, at the same time, the secure bonds that tie him to civilization. Washington Irving's "Rip Van Winkle" is an amiable statement of an identical tension. We know that Rip is not carried off by the Indians, at least not exactly. But he is carried away by values the Indian symbolized.

Rip, Leatherstocking, and the narrators of *Typee* and *Pontiac* are projections of ourselves in the culture. The historical experience of Indian captivity supplied a metaphor for embodying the tension between civilization and the wilderness. The metaphor embraced ambivalences. Captivity in the wilderness was horror, and yet many captives saw civilization as a worse captivity. Civilization represented the fulfillment of man's highest aspirations, and yet its attractions meant nothing to untold numbers who chose the freedom of the wilderness. When the terms of the opposing values of civilization and wilderness are specified—in American society principally technology and nature, social obligation and individualism, man's limitation and his possibility—they lay bare the depth of the captivity metaphor. The Melvilles, Coopers, Parkmans, Irvings, and Erastus Dow Palmers, and the unknown ballad singers in their simplicity and the dime novelists with their stereotypes are the voice of our culture, lamenting and exulting in our captivity.

PART ONE

The Discovery of the Indian

A Spaniard Among Florida Indians

What is known about Juan Ortiz is to be found in this narrative. The conquistador Panfilo de Narváez, who had a grant from Charles V to take up lands in Florida, had met with misfortune. His wife sent out a relief party from Cuba, of which Juan Ortiz was the commander. He was captured and enslaved in 1529 by aborigines in the vicinity of Tampa Bay and was rescued in 1539 by Hernando De Soto, to whom he rendered vital service as a translator. He died some three years later. His story is told in the anonymous *True Relation of the Gentleman of Elvas . . .* (Evora, 1557), written in Portuguese by a member of the De Soto expedition. An English translation is included in Richard Hakluyt's *Virginia Richly Valued . . .* (London, 1609), a work designed to promote British colonization in America.

Ortiz's narrative is above all a lively adventure story which includes his escape from death by torture through the intercession of a chieftain's daughter (cf. Pocahontas), his grisly task guarding an Indian charnel house against the depredations of wolves, and his dramatic rescue by De Soto's soldiers, who at first mistake him for an Indian. The narrative also contains observations on Indian religion, superstitions, and customs, important because Ortiz was one of the first Europeans to live among native Americans. When compared with captivity narratives by early French missionaries and British settlers, his story provides an insight into differences in national attitudes toward the Indians. The French Jesuits in Canada were inclined to view the Indians as potential converts to Catholicism. The New England Puritans saw them as creatures of the devil, avoided them, and looked forward to their extermination as evidence of God's goodness. The Spanish, on the other hand, were

---

SOURCE: From *Indian Captivities . . .* (Boston, 1839) by Samuel Gardner Drake, who condenses the information about Ortiz found in Hakluyt's translation into a unified narrative. The introductory information and the passages of graveyard moralizing are likewise Drake's contribution.

less personal and more secular. Like the land the Indians inhabited, they were there to be exploited, to be used up.

Another sixteenth-century narrative containing a captivity episode is the *Relation . . .* (Zamora, 1542) of Núñez Cabeza de Vaca, a survivor of the Narváez expedition who brought back tales of the Seven Cities of Cibola. Hans Standen's *Warhaftige Historia . . .* (Marburg, 1557) is a German sailor's description of captivity among the Tupi Indians of Brazil, and Job Hortop's *The Travailes of an Englishman . . .* (London, 1591) contains an account of an English sailor captured in 1567 by Mexican Indians.

In the year 1528 Pamphilo de Narvaez, with a commission, constituting him governor of Florida, or "all the lands lying from the river of Palms to the cape of Florida," sailed for that country with 400 foot and 20 horse, in five ships. With this expedition went a Spaniard, named John Ortiz, a native of Seville, whose connections were among the nobility of Castile. Although we have no account of what part Ortiz acted in Narvaez's expedition, or how he escaped its disastrous issue, yet it may not be deemed out of place to notice briefly here that issue.

This Narvaez had acquired some notoriety by the manner in which he had executed a commission against Cortez. He had been ordered by the governor of Cuba to seize the destroyer of Mexico, but was himself overthrown and deserted by his men. On falling into the hands of Cortez, his arrogance did not forsake him, and he addressed him thus: "Esteem it good fortune that you have taken me prisoner." "Nay," replied Cortez, "it is the least of the things I have done in Mexico." To return to the expedition of which we have promised to speak.

Narvaez landed in Florida not very far from, or perhaps at the bay of Apalachee, in the month of April, and marched into the country with his men. They knew no other direction but that pointed out by the Indians, whom they compelled to act as guides. Their first disappointment was on their arrival at the village of Apalachee, where, instead of a splendid town, filled with immense treasure, as they had anticipated, they found only about 40 Indian wigwams. When they visited one Indian town its inhabitants would get rid of them by telling them of another, where their wants would be gratified. Such was the manner in which Narvaez and his companions rambled over 800 miles of country, in about six months' time, at a vast expense of men and necessaries which they carried with them; for the Indians annoyed them at every pass, not only cutting off many of the men, but seizing on their baggage upon every occasion which offered. Being now arrived upon the coast, in a wretched condition, they constructed some miserable barks corresponding with their means, in which none but men in such extremities would embark. In these they coasted toward New Spain. When they came near the mouths of the Mississippi they were cast away in a storm, and all but 15 of their number perished. Out of these 15, 4 only lived to reach Mexico, and these after 8 years wholly spent in wanderings from place to place, enduring incredible hardships and miseries.

The next year after the end of Narvaez's expedition, the intelligence of his disaster having reached his wife, whom he left in Cuba, she fitted out a small company, consisting of 20 or 30 men, who sailed in a brigantine to search after him, hoping some fortuitous circumstance might have prolonged his existence upon the coast, and that he might be found. Of this number was John Ortiz, the subject of this narrative.

On their arrival there, they sought an opportunity to have an interview with the first Indians they should meet. Opportunity immediately offered, and as soon as Indians were discovered, the Spaniards advanced towards them in their boats, while the Indians came down to the shore. These wily people practised a stratagem upon this occasion, which to this day seems a mysterious one, and we have no means of explaining it.

Three or four Indians came near the shore, and setting a stick in the ground, placed in a cleft in its top a letter, and withdrawing a little distance, made signs to the Spaniards to come and take it. All the company, except John Ortiz and one more, refused to go out for the letter, rightly judging it to be used only to ensnare them; but Ortiz, presuming it was from Narvaez, and containing some account of himself, would not be persuaded from venturing on shore to bring it, although all the rest but the one who accompanied him strenuously argued against it.

Now there was an Indian village very near this place, and no sooner had Ortiz and his companion advanced to the place where the letter was displayed, than a multitude came running from it, and surrounding them, seized eagerly upon them. The number of the Indians was so great, that the Spaniards in the vessels did not dare to attempt to rescue them, and saw them carried forcibly away. In this first onset the man who accompanied Ortiz was killed, he having made resistance when he was seized.

Not far from the place where they were made prisoners, was another Indian town, or village, consisting of about 8 or 10 houses or wigwams. These houses were made of wood, and covered with palm-leaves. At one end of this village there was a building, which the captive called a temple, but of what dimensions it was he makes no mention. Over the door of entrance into this temple there was placed the figure of a bird, carved out in wood, and it was especially surprising that this bird had gilded eyes. No attempt is made by Ortiz even to conjecture how or by whom the art of gilding was practised, in this wild and distant region, nor does he mention meeting with any other specimen of that art during his captivity. At the opposite extremity of this village stood the house of the chief, or cazique, as he was often called, upon an eminence, raised, as it was supposed, for a fortification. These things remained the same ten years afterwards, and are mentioned by the historian of Fernando De Soto's Invasion of Florida. The name of the chief of this village was Ucita, before whom was presented the captive, Ortiz, who was condemned to suffer immediate death.

The manner of his death was by torture, which was to be effected in this wise. The executioners set four stakes in the ground, and to these they fastened four poles; the captive was then taken, and with his arms and legs extended, was by them bound to these poles, at such a distance from the ground, that a fire, made directly under him, would be a long time in consuming him. Never did a poor victim look with greater certainty to death for relief, than did John Ortiz at this time. The fire had already begun to rage, when a most remarkable circumstance happened to save his life—a daughter of the stern Ucita arose and plead for him. Among other things she said these to her father: "My kind father, why kill this poor stranger? he can do you nor any of us any injury, seeing he is but one and alone. It is better that you should keep him confined; for even in that condition he may sometime be of great service to you." The chief was silent for a short time, but finally ordered him to be released from his place of torture. They had no sooner taken the thongs from his wrists and ankles, than they proceeded to wash and dress his wounds, and to do things to make him comfortable.

As soon as his wounds were healed, Ortiz was stationed at the entrance of the temple, before mentioned, to guard it against such as were not allowed to enter there; but especially to guard its being profaned by wild beasts; for as it was a place of sacrifices, wolves were its constant visitors. He had not long been in this office, when an event occurred, which threw him into great consternation. Human victims were brought in as sacrifices and deposited here; and not long after Ortiz had been placed as sentinel, the body of a young Indian was brought and laid upon a kind of sarcophagus, which, from the multitudes that had from time to time been offered there, was surrounded with blood and bones! a most rueful sight, as ever any eye beheld!—here an arm fresh torn from its place, reeking with blood, another exhibiting but bone and sinews from the mangling jaws of wild beasts! Such was the place he was ordered to guard, through day and night—doomed to sit himself down among this horrible assemblage of the dead. When left alone he reflected that his escape from fire was not so fortunate for him as he had hoped; for now, his naturally superstitious mind was haunted by the presence of innumerable ghosts, who stalked in every place, and which he had from his youth been taught to believe were capable of doing him all manner of injuries, even to the depriving of life.

There was no reflection in those remote ages of the real situation of all the living, in respect to the great valley of death in which all beings are born and nursed, and which no length of years is sufficient to carry them through. Let us for a moment cast our eyes around us. Where are we? Not in the same temple with Ortiz, but in one equally vast. We can see nothing but death in every place. The very ground we walk upon is composed of the decayed limbs of our own species, with those of a hundred others. A succession of animals have been rising and falling for many thousand years in all parts of the world. They have died all around us—in our very places. We do not distinctly behold the hands, the feet, or the bones of them, because they have crumbled to dust beneath our feet. And cannot the ghosts of these as well arise as of those slain yesterday? The affirmative cannot be denied.

As we have said, Ortiz found himself snatched from one dreadful death, only, as he imagined, to be thrust into the jaws of another, yet more terrible. Experience, however, soon proved to him, that the dead, at least those with whom he was forced to dwell, either could or would not send forth their spirits in any other shape than such phantoms as his own mind created, in dreams and reveries. We can accustom ourselves to almost anything, and it was not long before our captive contemplated the dead bodies with which he was surrounded, with about the same indifference as he did the walls of the temple that encompassed them.

How long after Ortiz had been placed to guard the temple of sacrifices the following fearful midnight adventure happened, we have no means of stating with certainty, nor is it very material; it is, however, according to his own account, as follows: A young Indian had been killed and his body placed in this temple. Late one night, Ortiz found it closely invested by wolves, which, in spite of all his efforts, entered the place, and carried away the body of the Indian. The fright and the darkness were so heavy upon Ortiz that he knew not that the body was missing until morning. It appears, however, that he recovered himself, seized a heavy cudgel, which he had prepared at hand, and commenced a general attack upon the beasts in the temple, and not only drove them out, but pursued them a good way from the place. In the pursuit he came up with one which he gave a mortal blow, although he did not know it at the time. Having returned from the hazardous adventure to the temple, he impatiently awaited the return of daylight. When the day dawned, great was his distress at the discovery of the loss of the body of the dead Indian, which was especially aggravated, because it was the son of a great chief.

When the news of this affair came to the ears of Ucita, he at once resolved to have Ortiz put to death; but before executing his purpose he sent out several Indians to pursue after the wolves, to recover, if possible, the sacrifice. Contrary to all expectation, the body was found, and not far from it the body of a huge wolf also. When Ucita learned these facts, he countermanded the order for his execution.

Three long years was Ortiz doomed to watch this wretched temple of the dead. At the end of this time he was relieved only by the overthrow of the power of Ucita. This was effected by a war between the two rival chiefs, Ucita and Mocoso.

The country over which Mocoso reigned was only two days' journey from that of Ucita, and separated from it by a large river or estuary [St. Johns River]. Mocoso came upon the village of Ucita in the night with an army, and attacked his castle, and took it, and also the rest of his town. Ucita and his people fled from it with all speed, and the warriors of Mocoso burnt it to the ground. Ucita had another village upon the coast, not far from the former, to which he and his people fled, and were not pursued by their enemies. Soon after he had established himself in his new residence, he resolved upon making a sacrifice of Ortiz. Here again he was wonderfully preserved, by the same kind friend that had delivered him at the beginning of his captivity. The daughter of the chief, knowing her intreaties would avail nothing with her father, determined to aid him to make an escape; accordingly, she had prepared the way for his reception with her father's enemy, Mocoso. She found means to pilot him secretly out of her father's village, and accompanied him a league or so on his way, and then left him with directions how to proceed to the residence of Mocoso. Having travelled all night as fast as he could, Ortiz found himself next morning upon the borders of the river which bounded the territories of the two rival chiefs. He was now thrown into great trouble, for he could not proceed farther without discovery, two of Mocoso's men being then fishing in the river; and, although he came as a friend, yet he had no way to make that known to them, not understanding their language, nor having means wherewith to discover his character by a sign. At length he observed their arms, which they had left at considerable distance from the place where they then were. Therefore, as his only chance of succeeding in his enterprise, he crept slyly up and seized their arms to prevent their injuring him. When they saw this they fled with all speed towards their town. Ortiz followed them for some distance, trying by language as well as by signs to make them understand that he only wished protection with them, but all in vain, and he gave up the pursuit and waited quietly the result. It was not long before a large party came running armed towards him, and when they approached, he was obliged to cover himself behind trees to avoid their arrows. Nevertheless his chance of being killed seemed certain, and that very speedily; but it providentially happened, that there was an Indian among them who now surrounded him, who understood the language in which he spoke, and thus he was again rescued from another perilous situation.

Having now surrendered himself into the hands of the Indians, four of their number were dispatched to carry the tidings to Mocoso, and to learn his pleasure in regard to the disposition to be made of him; but instead of sending any word of direction, Mocoso went himself out to meet Ortiz. When he came to him, he expressed great joy at seeing him, and made every profession that he would treat him well. Ortiz, however, had seen enough of Indians to warn him against a too implicit confidence in his pretensions; and what added in no small degree to his doubts about his future destiny, was this very extraordinary circumstance. Immediately after the preliminary congratulations were over, the chief made him take an oath, "after the manner of Christians," that he would not run away from him to seek out another master; to which he very readily assented. At the same time Mocoso, on his part, promised Ortiz that he would not only treat him with due kindness, but, that if ever an opportunity offered by which he could return to his own people, he would do all in his power to assist him in it; and, to keep his word inviolate, he swore to what he had promised, "after the manner of the Indians." Nevertheless, our captive looked upon all this in no other light than as a piece of cunning, resorted to by the chief, to make him only a contented slave; but we shall see by the sequel, that this Indian chief dealt not in European guile, and that he was actuated only by benevolence of heart.

Three years more soon passed over the head of Ortiz, and he experienced nothing but kindness and liberty. He spent his time in wandering over the delightful savannahs of Florida, and through the mazes of the palmetto, and beneath the refreshing shades of the wide-spreading magnolia—pursuing the deer in the twilight of morning, and the scaly fry in the silver lakes in the cool of the evening. In all this time we hear of nothing remarkable that happened to Ortiz, or to the chief or his people. When war or famine does not disturb the quiet of Indians they enjoy themselves to the full extent of their natures—perfectly at leisure, and ready to devote days together to the entertainment of themselves, and any travellers or friends that may sojourn with them.

About the close of the first three years of Ortiz's sojourning with the tribe of Indians under Mocoso, there came startling intelligence into their village, and alarm and anxiety sat impatiently upon the brow of all the inhabitants. This was occasioned by the arrival of a runner, who gave information that as some of Mocoso's men were in their canoes a great way out at sea fishing, they had discovered ships of the white men approaching their coast. Mocoso, after communing with himself a short time, went to Ortiz with the information, which, when he had imparted it to him, caused peculiar sensations in his breast, and a brief struggle with conflicting feelings; for one cannot forget his country and kindred, nor can he forget his savior and protector. In short, Mocoso urged him to go to the coast and see if he could make a discovery of the ships. This proceeding on the part of the chief silenced the fears of Ortiz, and he set out upon the discovery; but when he had spent several days of watchfulness and eager expectation, without seeing or gaining any other intelligence of ships, he was ready to accuse the chief of practising deception upon him, to try his fidelity; he was soon satisfied, however, that his suspicions were without foundation, although no other information was ever gained of ships at that time.

At length, when six years more had elapsed, news of a less doubtful character was brought to the village of Mocoso. It was, that some white people had actually landed upon their coast, and had possessed themselves of the village of Ucita, and driven out him and his men. Mocoso immediately imparted this information to Ortiz, who, presuming it was an idle tale, as upon the former occasion, affected to care nothing for it, and told his chief that no worldly thing would induce him to leave his present master; but Mocoso persisted, and among arguments advanced this, that he had done his duty, and that if Ortiz would not go out and seek his white brethren, and they should leave the country, and him behind, he could not blame him, and withal seriously confirming the news. In the end he concluded to go out once more, and after thanking his chief for his great kindness, set off, with twelve of his best men whom Mocoso had appointed for his guides, to find the white people.

When they had proceeded a considerable part of the way, they came into a plain, and suddenly in sight of a party of 120 men, who proved to be some of those of whom they had heard. When they discovered Ortiz and his men, they pressed towards them in warlike array, and although they made every signal of friendship in their power, yet these white men rushed upon them, barbarously wounding two of them, and the others saved themselves only by flight. Ortiz himself came near being killed. A horseman rushed upon him, knocked him down, and was prevented from dealing a deadly blow only by a timely ejaculation in Spanish which he made. It was in these words: "I am a Christian—do not kill me, nor these poor men who have given me my life."

It was not until this moment that the soldiers discovered their mistake, of friends for enemies, for Ortiz was, in all appearance, an Indian; and now, with the aid of Ortiz, his attending Indians were collected, and they were all carried to the camp of the white men, each riding behind a soldier upon his horse.

Ortiz now found himself among an army of Spaniards, commanded by one Fernando De Soto, who had come into that country with a great armament of 600 men in 7 ships, in search of riches; an expedition undertaken with great ostentation, raised by the expectation of what it was to afford, but it ended, as all such undertakings should, in disgrace and mortification.

Soto considered the acquisition of Ortiz of very great importance, for although he could not direct him to any mountains of gold or silver, yet he was acquainted with the language of the Indians, and he kept him with him during his memorable expedition, to act in the capacity of interpreter.

It was in the spring of 1543, that the ferocious and savage Soto fell a prey to his misguided ambition. Ortiz had died a few months before, and with him fell the already disappointed hopes of his leader. They had taken up winter quarters at a place called Autiamque, upon the Washita, or perhaps Red River, and it was here that difficulties began to thicken upon them. When in the spring they would march from thence, Soto was grieved, because he had lost so good an interpreter, and readily felt that difficulties were clustering around in a much more formidable array. Hitherto, when they were at a loss for a knowledge of the country, all they had to do was to lie in wait and seize upon some Indian, and Ortiz always could understand enough of the language to relieve them from all perplexity about their course; but now they had no other interpreter but a young Indian of Cutifachiqui, who understood a little Spanish; "yet it required sometimes a whole day for him to explain what Ortiz would have done in four words." At other times he was so entirely misunderstood, that after they had followed his direction through a tedious march of a whole day, they would find themselves obliged to return again to the same place."

Such was the value of Ortiz in the expedition of Soto, as that miserable man conceived; but had not Soto fallen in with him, how different would have been the fate of a multitude of men, Spaniards and Indians. Upon the whole, it is hard to say which was the predominant trait in the character of Soto and his followers, avarice or cruelty.

At one time, because their guides had led them out of the way, Moscoso, the successor of Soto, caused them to be hanged upon a tree and there left. Another, in the early part of the expedition, was saved from the fangs of dogs, at the interference of Ortiz, because he was the only Indian through whom Ortiz could get information. It is as difficult to decide which was the more superstitious, the Indians or the self-styled "Christian Spaniards;" for when Soto died a chief came and offered two young Indians to be killed, that they might accompany and serve the white man to the world of spirits. An Indian guide being violently seized with some malady, fell senseless to the ground. To raise him, and drive away the devil which they supposed was in him, they read a passage over his body from the Bible, and he immediately recovered.

Captain John Smith Meets the Princess Pocahontas

John Smith's rescue by Pocahontas is undoubtedly the most famous episode in the genre of Indian captivities. It has been the subject of novels, short stories, plays (see Barker, pp. 214-217), poems, paintings, and even sculpture and has been thoroughly absorbed into American popular lore. The story was first told in Smith's *Generall Historie of Virginia, New-England, and the Summer Isles* (1624). It epitomizes a crucial shift in the attitudes of Virginia colonists toward the Indian.

Whether the incident actually occurred will probably never be known. Although it supposedly took place in December 1607, Smith makes no mention of it in his *True Relation* of the following year. The first published mention of the captivity appears in a 1622 revision of Smith's *New Englands Trials,* originally published in 1620. Here Smith simply states that "God made *Pocahontas,* the King's daughter the meanes to deliver me." Smith said that in 1616 he sent Queen Anne "a little Booke" relating how "after some six weeks fatting amongst those Salvage Courtiers, at the minute of my execution, she [Pocahontas] hazarded the beating out of her own braines to save mine," but the little book is known only from his abstract in the *Generall Historie,* which also contains the extended account of the now famous captivity.

It is indeed strange that Smith waited so long before he publicized this romantic tale and stranger still that it survives only in versions post-dating the death of Pocahontas in 1617. Perhaps Smith was chagrined that he owed his life to the whim of a girl of thirteen. Possibly he considered the incident too trivial to mention in the *True Relation,* in which he had so much else of importance to say. Even in the *Generall Historie* the incident takes up only a few paragraphs. In any event, the publication of the tale corresponds with the arrival in 1616 of Pocahontas in England at a time when Smith was in disfavor and wanted to return to

---

SOURCE: Captain John Smith, *The Generall Historie of Virginia, New-England, and the Summer Isles* . . . (London, 1624).

Portrait of Pocahontas from the *Generall Historie.* The original caption reads: "Matoaks al[ia]s Rebecka daughter to the mighty Prince Powhatan Emperour of Attanoughkomouck al[ia]s virginia converted and baptized in the Christian faith, and wife to the wor[thy] Mr. Joh[n] Rolff." From a contemporary engraving by Simon van de Passe. *Courtesy of the Edward E. Ayer Collection, the Newberry Library.*

Virginia but was without the means to do so. Pocahontas was entertained at court, and the attention she received was perhaps what Smith needed to attract support. If he told the story to the Queen in 1616, then it is probably based on fact since Pocahontas, who spoke English well, could have discredited it. If not, then Smith waited until her death before he linked himself with the "renowned princess" whose fame he could then more safely exploit. In either case, there is little doubt that Smith told the story to his advantage.

Perhaps the most noteworthy feature of the Smith captivity narrative, besides its obvious dramatic appeal, is its reflection of changing attitudes toward the Indian, which becomes more obvious when it is placed in the context of the *Generall Historie*. Early Virginia adventurers respected the rights of the Indians. The Virginia Company had explicitly warned the colonists not to "offend the naturals." Virginia was commonly referred to as a new Eden, and the Indians were seen as children of nature. Only when it became evident that converting Indian lands into tobacco plantations was more promising than commerce or gold mining did the stereotype of the Indian as demonic savage begin to emerge. This stereotype Smith himself indirectly encouraged when he described the "Conjurations" of the shamans in diabolical terms and the race as a whole, following the massacre of Virginia settlers in 1622, as "cruel beasts" and "a perfidious and inhumane people." The massacre provided an excuse, long desired in some quarters, for the eventual subjugation of the Virginia Indians.

. . . And now the winter approaching, the rivers became so covered with swans, geese, duckes, and cranes, that we daily feasted with good bread, Virginia pease, pumpions, and putchamins, fish, fowle, and diverse sorts of wild beasts as far as we could eate them: so that none of our Tuftaffaty humorists [irresponsible wags] desired to goe for *England*. But our *Comædies* never endured long without a *Tragedie;* some idle exceptions being muttered against Captaine *Smith*, for not discovering the head of *Chickahamania* river [James River, perhaps the elusive Northwest Passage], and taxed by the Councell, to be too slow in so worthy an attempt. The next voyage hee proceeded so farre that with much labour by cutting of trees in sunder he made his passage, but when his Barge could passe no farther, he left her in a broad bay out of danger of shot, commanding none should goe a shore till his returne: himselfe with two English and two Salvages went up higher in a Canowe, but hee was not long absent, but his men went a shore, whose want of government, gave both occasion and opportunity to the Salvages to surprise one *George Cassen*, whom they slew, and much failed not to have cut of[f] the boat and all the rest. *Smith* little dreaming of that accident, being got to the marshes at the rivers head, twentie myles in the desert, had his* two men slaine (as is supposed) sleeping by the Canowe, whilst him-

***Jehu Robinson* and *Thomas Emry* slain.

selfe by fowling sought them victuall, who finding he was beset with 200 Salvages, two of them hee slew, still defending himselfe with the ayd of a Salvage his guid, whom he bound to his arme with his garters, and used him as a buckler, yet he was shot in his thigh a little, and had many arrowes that stucke in his cloathes but no great hurt, till at last they tooke him prisoner. When this newes came to *James* towne, much was their sorrow for his losse, fewe expecting what ensued. Sixe or seven weekes those Barbarians kept him prisoner, many strange triumphes and conjurations they made of him, yet hee so demeaned himselfe amongst them, as he not onely diverted them from surprising the Fort, but procured his owne libertie, and got himselfe and his company such estimation amongst them, that those Salvages admired him more then their owne *Quiyouckosucks* [priests]. The manner how they used and delivered him, is as followeth.

The Salvages having drawne from *George Cassen* whether Captaine *Smith* was gone, prosecuting that opportunity they followed him with 300 bowmen, conducted by the King of *Pamaunkee,* who in divisions searching the turnings of the river, found *Robinson* and *Emry* by the fire side, those they shot full of arrowes and slew. Then finding the Captaine, as is said, that used the Salvage that was his guide as his shield (three of them being slaine and divers other so gauld [galled]) all the rest would not come neere him. Thinking thus to have returned to his boat, regarding them, as he marched, more then his way, slipped up to the middle in an oasie [oozy] creeke & his Salvage with him, yet durst they not come to him till being neere dead with cold, he threw away his armes. Then according to their composition they drew him forth and led him to the fire, where his men were slaine. Diligently they chafed his benummed limbs. He demanding for their Captaine, they shewed him *Opechankanough* [Powhatan's brother], King of *Pamaunkee,* to whom he gave a round Ivory double compass Dyall. Much they marvailed at the playing of the Fly and Needle, which they could see so plainely, and yet not touch it, because of the glasse that covered them. But when he demonstrated by that Globe-like Jewell, the roundnesse of the earth, and skies, the spheare of the Sunne, Moone, and Starres, and how the Sunne did chase the night round about the world continually; the greatnesse of the Land and Sea, the diversitie of Nations, varietie of complexions, and how we were to them *Antipodes,* and many other such like matters, they all stood as amazed with admiration. Notwithstanding, within an houre after they tyed him to a tree, and as many as could stand about him prepared to shoot him, but the King holding up the Compass in his hand, they all laid downe their Bowes and Arrowes, and in a triumphant manner led him to *Orapaks,* where he was after their manner kindly feasted, and well used.

Their order in conducting him was thus; Drawing themselves all in fyle, the King in the middest had all their Peeces and Swords borne before him. Captaine *Smith* was led after him by three great Salvages, holding him fast by each arme: and on each side six went in fyle with their Arrowes nocked.

But arriving at the Towne (which was but onely thirtie or fortie hunting houses made of Mats, which they remove as they please, as we our tents) all the women and children staring to behold him, the souldiers first all in fyle performed the forme of a *Bissom* [broom-like spread] so well as could be; and on each flanke, officers as Serjeants to see them keepe their order. A good time they continued this exercise, and then cast themselves in a ring, dauncing in such severall Postures, and singing and yelling out such hellish notes and screeches; being strangely painted, every one his quiver of Arrowes, and at his backe a club; on his arme a Fox or an Otters skinne, or some such matter for his vambrace [shield]; their heads and shoulders painted red, with Oyle and *Pocones* [red dye plant] mingled together, which Scarlet-like colour made an exceeding handsome shew; his Bow in his hand, and the skinne of a Bird with her wings abroad dryed, tyed on his head, a peece of copper, a white shell, a long feather, with a small rattle growing at the tayles of their snaks tyed to it, or some such like toy. All this while *Smith* and the King stood in the middest guarded, as before is said, and after three dances they all departed. *Smith* they conducted to a long house, where thirtie or fortie tall fellowes did guard him, and ere long more bread and venison was brought him then would have served twentie men, I thinke his stomacke at that time was not very good; what he left they put in baskets and tyed over his head. About midnight they set the meate againe before him, all this time not one of them would eate a bit with him, till the next morning they brought him as much more, and then did they eate all the old, & reserved the new as they had done the other, which made him thinke they would fat him to eat him. Yet in this desperate estate to defend him from the cold, one *Maocassater* brought him his gowne, in requitall of some beads and toyes *Smith* had given him at his first arrivall in *Virginia.*

Two dayes after a man would have slaine him (but that the guard prevented it) for the death of his sonne, to whom they conducted him to recover the poore man then breathing his last. *Smith* told them that at *James* towne he had a water would doe it, if they would let him fetch it, but they would not permit that; but made all the preparations they could to assault *James* towne, craving his advice, and for recompence he should have life, libertie, land, and women. In part of a Table booke he writ his minde to them at the Fort, what was intended, how they should follow that direction to affright the messengers, and without fayle send him such things as he writ for. And an Inventory with them. The difficultie and danger, he told the Salvages, of the Mines, great-gunnes, and other Engins exceedingly affrighted them, yet according to his request they went to *James* towne, in as bitter weather as could be of frost and snow, and within three dayes returned with an answer.

But when they came to *James* towne, seeing men sally out as he had told them they would, they fled; yet in the night they came againe to the same place where he had told them they should receive an answer, and such things as he had promised them, which they found accordingly, and with which they returned with no small expedition, to the wonder of them all that heard it, that he could either divine, or the paper could speake: then they led him to the *Youthtanunds*, the *Mattapanients*, the *Payankatanks*, the *Nantaughtacunds*, and *Onawmanients* upon the rivers of *Raphanock*, and *Patawomek*, over all those rivers, and backe againe by divers other severall Nations, to the Kings habitation at *Pamaunkee*, where they entertained him with most strange and fearefull Conjurations;

As if neare led to hell,
Amongst the Devils to dwell.

Not long after, early in a morning a great fire was made in a long house, and a mat spread on the one side, as on the other; on the one they caused him to sit, and all the guard went out of the house, and presently came skipping in a great grim fellow, all painted over with coale, mingled with oyle; and many Snakes and Wesels skins stuffed with mosse, and all their tayles tyed together, so as they met on the crowne of his head in a tassell; and round about the tassell was as a Coronet of feathers, the skins hanging round about his head, backe, and shoulders, and in a manner covered his face; with a hellish voyce and a rattle in his hand. With most strange gestures and passions he began his invocation, and environed the fire with a circle of meale; which done, three more such like devils came rushing in with the like antique tricks, painted halfe blacke, halfe red: but all their eyes were painted white, and some red stroakes like Mutchato's [another Indian], along their cheekes: round about him those fiends daunced a pretty while, and then came in three more as ugly as the rest; with red eyes, and white stroakes over their blacke faces, at last they all sat downe right against him; three of them on the one hand of the chiefe Priest, and three on the other. Then all with their rattles began a song, which ended, the chiefe Priest layd downe five wheat cornes: then strayning his armes and hands with such violence that he sweat, and his veynes swelled, he began a short Oration: at the conclusion they all gave a short groane; and then layd down three graines more. After that, began their song againe, and then another Oration, ever laying downe so many cornes as before, till they had twice incirculed the fire; that done, they tooke a bunch of little stickes prepared for that purpose, continuing still their devotion, and at the end of every song and Oration, they layd downe a sticke betwixt the divisions of Corne. Till night, neither he nor they did either eate or drinke, and then they feasted merrily, with the best provisions they could make. Three dayes they used this Ceremony; the meaning whereof they told him, was to know if he intended them well or no. The circle of meale signified their Country, the circles of corne the bounds of the Sea, and the sticks his Country. They imagined the world to be flat and round, like a trencher, and they in the middest. After this they brought him a bagge of gunpowder, which they carefully preserved till the next spring, to plant as they did their corne; because they would be acquainted with the nature of that seede. *Opitchapam* the Kings brother invited him to his house, where, with as many platters of bread, foule, and wild beasts, as did environ him, he bid him wellcome; but not any of them would eate a bit with him, but put up all the remainder in Baskets. At his returne to *Opechancanoughs*, all the Kings women, and their children, flocked about him for their parts, as a due by Custome, to be merry with such fragments.

But his waking mind in hydeous dreames did oft see wondrous shapes,
Of bodies strange, and huge in growth, and of stupendious makes.

At last they brought him to *[W]eronocomoco*, where was *Powhatan* their Emperor. Here more then two hundred of those grim Courtiers stood wondering at him, as he had beene a monster; till *Powhatan* and his trayne had put themselves in their greatest braveries. Before a fire upon a seat like a bedsted, he sat covered with a great robe, made of *Rarowcun* [raccoon] skinnes, and all the tayles hanging by. On either hand did sit a young wench of 16 or 18 yeares, and along on each side the house, two rowes of men, and behind them as many women, with all their heads and shoulders painted red; many of their heads bedecked with the white downe of Birds; but every one with something: and a great chayne of white beads about their necks. At his entrance before the King, all the people gave a great shout. The Queene of *Appamatuck* was appointed to bring him water to wash his hands, and another brought him a bunch of feathers, in stead of a Towell to dry them: having feasted him after their best barbarous manner they could, a long consultation was held, but the conclusion was, two great stones were brought before *Powhatan:* then as many as could layd hands on him, dragged him to them, and thereon laid his head, and being ready with their clubs, to beate out his braines, *Pocahontas* the Kings dearest daughter, when no intreaty could prevaile, got his head in her armes, and laid her owne upon his to save him from death: whereat the Emperour was contented he should live to make him hatchets, and her bells, beads, and copper; for they thought him aswell of all occupations as themselves. For the King himselfe will make his owne robes, shooes, bowes, arrowes, pots; plant, hunt, or doe any thing so well as the rest.

They say he bore a pleasant shew,
But sure his heart was sad.
For who can pleasant be, and rest,
That lives in feare and dread:
And having life suspected, doth
It still suspected lead.

Two dayes after, *Powhatan* having disguised himselfe in the most fearefullest manner he could, caused Capt. *Smith* to be brought forth to a great house in the woods, and there upon a mat by the fire to be left alone. Not long after from behinde a mat that divided the house, was made the most dolefullest noyse he ever heard; then *Powhatan* more like a devill then a man with some two hundred more as blacke as himselfe, came unto him and told him now they were friends, and presently he should goe to *James* towne, to send him two great gunnes, and a gryndstone, for which he would give him the Country of *Capahowosick,* and for ever esteeme him as his sonne *Nantaquoud.* So to *James* towne with 12 guides *Powhatan* sent him. That night they quarterd in the woods, he still expecting (as he had done all this long time of his imprisonment) every houre to be put to one death or other: for all their feasting. But almightie God (by his divine providence) had mollified the hearts of those sterne *Barbarians* with compassion. The next morning betimes they came to the Fort, where *Smith* having used the Salvages with what kindnesse he could, he shewed *Rawhunt, Powhatans* trusty servant two demi-Culverings [small bore cannon] and a millstone to carry *Powhatan*: they found them somewhat too heavie; but when they did see him discharge them, being loaded with stones, among the boughs of a great tree loaded with Isickles, the yce and branches came so tumbling downe, that the poore Salvages ran away half dead with feare. But at last we regained some conference with them, and gave them such toyes; and sent to *Powhatan,* his women, and children such presents, as gave them in generall full content. Now in *James* Towne they were all in combustion, the strongest preparing once more to run away with the Pinnace; which with hazzard of his life, with Sakre falcon [very small cannon] and musket shot, *Smith* forced now the third time to stay or sinke. Some no better then they should be, had plotted with the President, the next day to have put him to death by the Leviticall law, for the lives of *Robinson* and *Emry,* pretending the fault was his that had led them to their ends: but he quickly tooke such order with such Lawyers, that he layd them by the heeles till he sent some of them prisoners for *England.* Now ever once in foure or five dayes, *Pocahontas* with her attendants, brought him so much provision, that saved many of their lives, that els for all this had starved with hunger.

Thus from numbe death our good God sent reliefe,
The sweete asswager of all other griefe.

His relation of the plenty he had seene, especially at *Werawocomoco,* and of the state and bountie of *Powhatan,* (which till that time was unknowne) so revived their dead spirits (especially the love of *Pocahontas*) as all mens feare was abandoned. Thus you may see what difficulties still crossed any good indevour: and the good successe of the businesse being thus oft brought to the very period of destruction; yet you see by what strange means God hath still delivered it. . . .

PART TWO

Trials of the Spirit

A Letter from a Jesuit in New France

The Jesuit Relations were reports sent to the head Provincial of the order, beginning in 1611 and annually between 1632 and 1673, about the Roman Catholic missions in New France. After careful editing in Europe, they were circulated among a public which eagerly awaited their appearance. Often these reports contained the accounts of priests held captive by Indian tribes especially incensed by the Jesuits' missionary efforts. Many were written in the first person.

This letter was written by Father Francis Joseph Bressani, a native of Rome, while a prisoner of the Iroquois Indians near Sorel, Canada, in 1644. The Iroquois had been implacable enemies of the French and their allies, the Hurons, ever since 1609 when Samuel de Champlain made the mistake of exploring their lands in the company of a Huron war party and frightening them with his firearms. They particularly hated the black-robed Jesuits, whose spiritual power they feared.

After four months of hideous privations and torture, Father Bressani was ransomed by the Dutch and taken to their American colony, New Amsterdam. He reports in a letter from New Amsterdam that his release was easily effected and the ransom low "on account of the little value the Indians attached to me, from my unhandiness at every thing, as well as from their conviction that my sores would never heal." His main regret regarding his captivity by the Iroquois was that he had failed to "impart to them a knowledge of the true God." He returned to his mission among the Hurons until its decline as a result of Iroquois depredations. In 1650 he was sent to Italy. He died there in 1672.

SOURCE: John Dawson Gilmary Shea, *Perils of the Ocean and Wilderness . . .* (Boston, 1857). The narrative was originally written in Italian and published under the title *Breve Relatione d'Alcune Missioni . . .* (Macerata, 1653).

The captivity narratives in *The Jesuit Relations* are important to ethnologists, anthropologists, and historians because they contain the first competent observations of Indian culture before it came under white influence. Like Father Bressani, who was a teacher of literature and philosophy and was reputed to be an eloquent preacher, the Jesuits were distinguished for their learning. They sought out the Indians and valued the captivity experience, which they saw as a means of obtaining forgiveness for sin and advancing God's work. In contrast, the Puritans avoided the Indians and considered captivity a divine punishment (see Swarton, pp. 31-39).

Father Bressani's suffering and piety are not to be gainsaid, but his melodramatic beginning (the "poor cripple" staining the paper he writes on with his own blood) is hardly an instance of Christian humility. The appeal is unquestionable, but perhaps there is a touch of self-satisfaction and pride in his suffering. Or was he accepting the appearance of pride as part of the price exacted to propagate the gospel?

Most reverend Father in Jesus Christ.

PAX CHRISTI—I know not whether your Paternity will recognize the hand-writing of a poor cripple once quite well in body, and well known to you. His letter is badly written and soiled enough, because among other miseries the writer has but one whole finger on his right hand, and can scarcely prevent the paper's being stained by the blood which flows from his yet uncicatrized wounds. His ink is diluted gunpowder, and his table the bare ground. He writes to you from the land of the Iroquois, where he is now a prisoner, and would briefly relate the conduct of Divine Providence in his regard these later days.

I set out from Three Rivers by order of my superiors, the 27th of April last, (1644,) in company with six Christian Indians, and a young Frenchman, who in three canoes were going up to the Huron country.

On the evening of the first day, the Huron who steered our canoe upset us in Lake St. Pierre, by firing at an eagle. I did not know how to swim, but two Hurons caught me and drew me to the shore where we spent the night with our clothes all wet. The Hurons took this accident for an ill-omen, and advised me to return to Three Rivers, which was only eight or ten miles off; "certainly, they cried, this voyage will not prove fortunate." As I feared that there might be some superstitious thought in this resolution, I preferred to push on to another French fort, thirty miles higher up, where we might recruit a little. They obeyed me, and we started quite early the next morning, but the snow and the bad weather greatly retarded our speed, and compelled us to stop at mid-day.

On the third day, when twenty-two or twenty-four miles from Three Rivers, and seven or eight from Fort Richelieu, we fell into an ambuscade of twenty-seven Iroquois, who killed one of our Indians, and took the rest and myself prisoners.

We might have fled or even killed some Iroquois, but, when I saw my companions taken, I thought it better not to forsake them; I looked upon the disposition of our Indians as a mark of the will of God; choosing, as they did, to surrender rather than seek safety by flight.

After binding us, they uttered horrid cries, "sicut exultant victores capta præda," "as conquerors rejoice after taking a prey," (Isaias ix. 3), and made a thanksgiving to the Sun for having delivered into their hands, a Blackgown, as they call the Jesuits. They entered our canoes and seized all their contents, consisting of provisions for the missionaries residing among the Hurons, who were in extreme want, inasmuch as they had for several years received no aid from Europe. They next commanded us to sing, then led us to a little river hard by, where they divided the booty, and scalped the Huron whom they had killed. The scalp was to be carried in triumph on the top of a pole. They cut off the feet, hands, and most fleshy parts of the body to eat, as well as the heart.

The fifth day they made us cross the lake to pass the night in a retired but very damp spot. We there began to take our sleep tied on the ground in the open air, as we continued to do during the rest of our voyage.

My consolation was to think that we were doing the will of God, since I had undertaken this voyage only through obedience. I was full of confidence in the intercession of the Blessed Virgin, and the help of so many souls who prayed for me.

The following day we embarked on a river, and after some miles they ordered me to throw overboard my papers which they had left me till then. They superstitiously imagined that they had made our canoe burst open. They were surprised to see me grieved at this loss, who had never shown any regret for all else. We were two days in ascending this river to the falls which compelled us to land and march six days in the woods.

The next day which was a Friday, (May 6,) we met some Iroquois going out to fight. They added some blows to the terrible threats they made; but the account which they gave to our keepers, of the death of one of their party killed by a Frenchman, was a ground for their commencing to treat us with much greater cruelty.

At the moment of our capture the Iroquois were dying of hunger; so that in two or three days they consumed all our provisions, and we had no food, during the rest of the way, but from hunting, fishing, or some wild roots which they found. Their want was so great that they picked up on the shore a dead beaver already putrefying. They gave it to me in the evening to wash in the river, but, its stench leading me to believe that they did not want it, I threw it into the water. This blunder of mine I expiated by a vigorous penance.

I will not here relate all I had to suffer in that voyage. It is enough to say that we had to carry our loads in the woods by unbeaten roads, where there is nothing but stones, thorns, holes, water and snow, which had not yet entirely disappeared. We were bare-footed, and were left fasting sometimes till three or four o'clock in the afternoon, and often during the whole day, exposed to the rain, and drenched with the waters of the torrents and rivers which we had at times to cross.

When evening was come, I was ordered to go for wood, to bring water, and cook when they had any provisions. When I did not succeed, or misunderstood the orders which I received, blows were not spared; still less when we met other savages going to fish or hunt.

It was not easy for me to rest at night, because they tied me to a tree, leaving me exposed to the keen night air, still cold enough at that period.

We at last arrived at the Lake of the Iroquois, (Lake Champlain.) We had to make other canoes, in which I too was to do my part. After five or six days' sailing, we landed, and marched for three more.

The fourth day, which was the fifteenth of May, we arrived about 20 o'clock, (3 1-4 P. M.,) and before having as yet taken any food, at a river on the banks of which some four hundred savages were gathered, fishing. Hearing of our approach, they came out to meet us, and, when about two hundred paces from their cabins, they stripped off all my clothes, and made me march ahead. The young men formed a line to the right and left, each armed with a club, except the first one, who held a knife in his hand.

When I began my march, this one stopped my passage, and, seizing my left hand, cleft it open with his knife between the little finger and the next, with such force and violence that I thought he would lay open my whole hand. The others then began to load me with blows till I reached the stage which they had erected for our torture. We had to mount on these rough pieces of bark, raised about nine palms high, so as to give the crowd an opportunity to see and insult us. I was all drenched in blood, that streamed from every part of my body, and the wind to which we were exposed was cold enough to congeal it immediately on my skin.

What consoled me much was, to see that God granted me the grace of suffering some little pain in this world, instead of the incomparably far greater torments, which I should have had to suffer for my sins in the next world.

The warriors came next, and were received by the savages with great ceremony, and regaled with the best of all that their fishing supplied.

They bade us sing. Judge whether we could, fasting, worn down by marching, broken by their blows, and shivering from head to foot with cold.

Shortly after, a Huron slave brought me a little Indian corn, and a captain who saw me all trembling with cold, at last, at my entreaty, gave me back the half of an old summer cassock all in tatters, which served only to cover, but not to warm me.

We had to sing till the departure of the braves, and were then left at the mercy of the youth, who made us come down from the scaffold where we had been about two hours, to make us dance in their fashion, and because

I did not succeed, nor was indeed able, these young people beat me, pricked me, plucked out my hair, my beard, etc.

They kept us five or six days in this place for their pastime, leaving us entirely at the discretion or indiscretion of every one. We were obliged to obey even the children, and that in things unreasonable, and often contradictory. "Sing," cries one; "Hold your tongue," says another; if I obeyed the first, the latter tormented me. "Stretch out your hand; I want to burn it." Another burnt it because I did not extend it to him. They commanded me to take fire between the fingers to put in their pipes, full of tobacco, and then let it fall on the ground purposely four or five times, one after another, to make me burn myself, picking it up each time.

These scenes usually took place at night; for, towards evening, the captains cried in a fearful voice around the cabins, "Gather ye young men, come and caress our prisoners."

On this, they flocked together, and assembled in some large cabin. There the remnant of dress which had been given me was torn off, leaving me naked; then some goaded me with pointed sticks; some burnt me with firebrands, or red-hot stones, while others used burning ashes, or hot coals. They made me walk around the fire on hot ashes, under which they had stuck sharp sticks in the ground. Some plucked out my hair, others my beard.

Every night, after making me sing, and tormenting me as above, they spent about a quarter of an hour in burning one of my nails or a finger. Of the ten that I had, I have now but one left whole, and even of that, they have torn out the nail with their teeth. One evening, they took off a nail; the next day the first joint; the day after, the second. By the sixth time, they burned almost six. To the hands merely they applied fire and iron more than eighteen times, and, during this torment, I was obliged to sing. They ceased torturing me only at one or two o'clock at night. They then usually left me tied to the ground in some spot exposed to the rain, with no bed or blanket, but a small skin which did not cover half my body, and often even without any covering; for they had already torn up the piece of a cassock which had been given me. Yet out of compassion they left me enough to cover what decency, even among them, requires to be concealed. They kept the rest.

For a whole month, we had to undergo these cruelties, and greater still, but we remained only eight days in the first place. I never would have believed that man had so hard a life.

One night, that they were as usual torturing me, a Huron, taken prisoner with me, seeing one of his companions escape torments by siding against me, suddenly cried out, in the middle of the assembled throng, that I was a person of rank, and a captain among the French. This they heard with great attention; then, raising a loud shout in sign of joy, they treated me still worse. The next morning, I was condemned to be burnt alive, and to be eaten.

They then began to guard me more narrowly. The men and children never left me alone, even for natural necessity, but came tormenting me to force me to return to the cabin with all speed, fearing that I might take flight.

We left there the 26th of May; and, four days after, reached the first towns of this nation. In this march on foot, what with rain and other hardships, I suffered more than I had yet done. The savage then my keeper was more cruel than the first.

I was beaten, weak, ill-fed, half-naked, and slept in the open air, tied to a tree or post, shivering all night from cold, and the pain caused by my bonds.

In difficult places, my weakness called for help, but it was refused, and, even when I fell, renewing my pain, they showered blows on me again to force me to march; for they believed that I did it purposely to lag behind, and so escape.

One day, among others, I fell into a stream and was like to have drowned. I got out, I know not how, and in this plight had to march nearly six miles more till evening, with a very heavy burthen on my shoulders. They laughed at myself and my awkwardness in falling into the water, yet this did not hinder their burning another of my nails that night.

We at last reached the first village of this nation, and here our reception resembled the first, but was still more cruel. Besides blows from their fists and clubs, which I received in the most sensitive parts of my body—they a second time slit open my left hand, between the middle and fore fingers, and the bastinade was such, that I fell half dead on the ground. I thought I had lost my right eye forever. As I did not rise, because I was unable to do so, they continued to beat me, especially on the breast and head. I should surely have expired beneath their blows, had not a captain literally dragged me out by main strength, up to a stage, made like the former one, of bark. There, they soon after, cut off the middle and mangled the fore finger of my left hand. But at the same moment the rain, attended with thunder and lightning, fell in such torrents, that the savages retired, leaving us exposed naked to the storm, till an Indian, I know not whom, took pity on us, and in the evening took us into his cabin.

We were at this point, tormented with more cruelty and audacity than ever, and without leaving us a moment's rest. They forced me to eat all kinds of filth, and burnt one of my fingers and the still remaining nails. They dislocated my toes, and ran a fire-brand through one of my feet. I know not what they did not attempt another time, but I pretended to faint, so as to seem not to see an indecent action.

After glutting their cruelty here, they sent us into another village, nine or ten miles further. Here they added to the torments of which I have spoken, that of hanging me up by the feet, either in cords or with chains, given them by the Dutch. By night I lay stretched on the ground, naked and bound, according to their custom, to several stakes, by the feet, hands, and neck.

The torments which I had to suffer in this state, for six or seven nights, were in such places, and of such a description, that it is not lawful to describe them, nor could they be read without blushing. I never closed my eyes those nights, which, though the shortest in the year, seemed to me most long. My God! what will Purgatory then be? This consideration greatly alleviated my pains.

After such a treatment, I became so infectious and horrible, that all drew off from me as from carrion, approaching me only to torment. Scarce could I find one charitable enough to put some food in my mouth, for I could use neither of my hands, which were enormously swollen, and a mass of corruption. Thus I had to suffer famine too. I was reduced to eat raw Indian corn, not without danger of my health. Necessity made me even find some relish in chewing chalk, although it was impossible to swallow it.

I was covered with vermin, unable to deliver or shield myself from them. Worms were breeding in my wounds, and one day, more than four fell from one of my fingers.

"I have said to rottenness, Thou are my father; to worms, you are my mother and my sister."—Job xvii. 14. "I became a burthen to myself," so that, had I consulted but my own feelings, I should have "esteemed that to die was gain."

An abscess had formed in my right leg, in consequence of the blows I had received there, and my frequent falls. It gave me no rest, especially after I was no longer anything but skin and bone, with no bed but the bare ground. The savages had, though unsuccessfully, several times endeavored to open it with sharp stones, causing me most intense pain. The apostate Huron, who had been taken with me, had now to act as my surgeon. The day, which, according to my ideas, was the eve of my death, he opened it with four gashes of a knife. The blood and matter gushed out so abundantly, and emitted such a stench, that it drove all the savages from the cabin.

I desired and expected death, though not without experiencing some horror for the torture by fire. Yet I prepared to the best of my power, commending myself to the heart of the Mother of mercy, who is truly, the "Lovely, admirable, powerful, clement Mother, the comfortress of the afflicted." She was, after God, the only refuge of a poor sinner, abandoned by all creatures, in a foreign land, in this place of horror and vast solitude, without speech to give utterance to his thoughts, without a friend to console him, without sacraments to fortify him, without any human remedy to alleviate his woes.

The Huron and Algonquin prisoners, (these latter are called our Indians,) instead of consoling me, were the first to make me suffer in order to please the Iroquois. I did not see our good William Couture until after my deliverance. The child captured with me had been carried off from the moment that they perceived me making him say his prayers, which displeased them. They tormented him also, and, though he was but twelve or thirteen years old, they tore off five of his nails with their teeth. On reaching their country, they had tied his wrists with small cords, drawn as tight as they could so as to give him exquisite pain. They did all this before my eyes to augment my suffering. O! how differently we then value many things which are usually so esteemed! God grant that I may remember and profit by it.

My days then were thus filled up with sufferings, and my nights were spent without repose; this caused me even to count, in the month, five days more than there were, but, looking at the moon one night, I corrected my error.

I was ignorant why the savages so long deferred my death. They told me that it was to fatten me before they ate me; though they took no means to do so.

My fate was at last decided. On the nineteenth of June, which I deemed the last of my life, I begged a captain to put me to death, if possible, otherwise than by fire; but another chief exhorted him to stand firm in the resolution already taken. The first then told me that I was to die neither by fire nor by any other torture. I could not believe it, nor do I know whether he spoke in earnest, yet true it was. Such was the will of God, and of the Virgin Mother, to whom I acknowledge myself indebted for my life, and, what I esteem more highly, for a great fortitude amid my woes. May it please the Divine Majesty that this redound to his greater glory and my good.

The savages themselves were extremely surprised at this result, so contrary was it to their intentions, as they avowed to me, and as the Dutch have written. I was therefore given, with all the usual ceremonies, to an old woman to replace her grandfather, formerly killed by the Hurons, but instead of having me burnt as all desired, and had already resolved, she redeemed me from their hands at the expense of some beads, which the French call porcelaine [wampum].

I live here in the midst of the shadows of death. They can be heard speaking of nothing but murder and assassination. They have recently murdered one of their own countrymen in his own cabin, as useless and unworthy to live.

I have always something to suffer; my wounds are still open; and many of the savages look upon me with no kindly eye. True then it is that we cannot live without crosses; yet this is like sugar in comparison with the past.

The Dutch gave me hopes of my ransom, and that of the boy taken prisoner with me. God's will be done in time and eternity! My hope will be still more confirmed, if you grant me a share in your holy sacrifices and prayers, and those of our Fathers and Brothers, especially of those who knew me in other days.

Territory of the Iroquois, July 15, 1644.

A Sermon on the Deliverance of a Puritan Woman

On May 16, 1690, during King William's War, an Indian war party led by a French officer plundered the Puritan outposts on Casco Bay in Maine. Among the captives was Hannah Swarton, formerly of Beverly, Massachusetts. After an arduous journey through the wilderness, she was turned over to the French at Quebec. In November 1695 negotiations were completed between New England and Canada for the ransom of captives, and Mrs. Swarton was taken by ship to Boston. Her husband had died defending their home, and her eldest son was killed shortly afterwards. She had three other children who had been taken captive with her. Of these only the youngest returned to New England. She never knew the fate of the others.

This account of Mrs. Swarton's captivity appeared in *Humiliations Follow'd with Deliverances . . .* (1697), a sermon preached by Cotton Mather, who later reprinted it in his *Magnalia Christi Americana . . .* (1702). Its wealth of scriptural allusion is typical of his style and suggests that he, rather than Mrs. Swarton, wrote it. Mather collected "illustrious, wonderful providences" and "remarkable salvations," to use the language of his chapter headings in the *Magnalia.* In his diary for November 15, 1696, Mather wrote that there was no better means to "promote the general Repentance" and to "give Testimony to the Justice and Goodness of our Lord Jesus Christ" than to make public the "terrible and barbarous Things undergone by some of our English Captives in the Hands of the Eastern Indians." Mather shared his interest in Indian captivity with his father, Increase, who included a captivity in his *Essay for the Recording of Illustrious Providences . . .* (1684), with an introductory observation on its salutary spiritual benefits.

SOURCE: Cotton Mather, *Magnalia Christi Americana: or, the Ecclesiastical History of New-England . . .* (London, 1702).

The Swarton narrative reveals the Puritan view of Indians and Indian captivity. Indians were creatures of the devil—"loup-garous," or "hell-hounds," as Mather elsewhere calls them. Captivity was a punishment for sin. Specifically, God punished Hannah Swarton and her family because they had *"left the Publick Worship and Ordinances of God, to go to live in a remote Place, without the* Publick Ministry; *depriving our selves and our* Children *of so great a benefit for our* Souls; *and all this for* Worldly Advantages." It was also a lesson to others about God's providence. If he so desired, God might protect man in times of adversity, so that, as Hannah Swarton states, "the works of God might be made manifest."

The structure of the narrative bears this out. It consists of three sections: a trial at the hands of the Indians, which is essentially physical; a trial of faith at the hands of the French, which, although they treated her kindly, she recognized as a "Captivity among the Papists"; and an inner trial, resulting from the combined experience, during which she was tested by her personal sense of sin and doubt. In each case she sustained herself by turning to suitable passages in the Bible. Such a structure is characteristic of Puritan spiritual autobiography.

The Swarton narrative also provides insight into Puritan attitudes toward French culture at the time of King William's War. Although French soldiers were among the Indians who killed her husband and took her captive, Mrs. Swarton does not rebuke them but expresses gratitude for their kindness. She does, however, fear their "false religion." The French exerted pressure to convert their captives to Roman Catholicism. They apparently succeeded in the instance of the daughter from whom Mrs. Swarton was separated, for church records reveal the conversion and marriage of an "Englishwoman" named "Marie Swarton' in Montreal in 1710.

A NARRATIVE *of* Hannah Swarton, *containing* Wonderful Passages, *relating to her Captivity and her Deliverance.*

I was taken by the *Indians* when *Casco* Fort was taken (*May* 1690). My Husband being slain, and four Children taken with me. The Eldest of my Sons they kill'd, about two Months after I was taken, and the rest scatter'd from me. I was now left a Widow, and as bereav'd of my Children; though, I had them alive, yet it was very seldom that I could see 'em, and I had not Liberty to discourse with 'em without danger either of my own Life, or theirs; for our condoling each others Condition, and shewing Natural Affection, was so displeasing to our *Indian Rulers,* unto whose share we fell, that they would threaten to kill us, if we cry'd each to other, or discoursed much together. So that my Condition was like what the Lord threatened the

Jews in *Ezek.* 24.22,23. We durst not *Mourn or Weep* in the Sight of our Enemies, lest we lost our own Lives. For the first times, while the Enemy feasted on our English Provisions, I might have had some with them; but then I was so fill'd with Sorrow and Tears, that I had little Stomach to eat; and when my Stomach was come, our English Food was spent, the *Indians* wanted themselves, and we more: so that then I was pin'd with Want. We had no Corn or Bread; but sometimes *Groundnuts, Acorns, Purslain, Hog-weed,* Weeds, Roots, and some-times *Dogs Flesh,* but not sufficient to satisfie Hunger with these; having but little at a time. We had no Success at hunting; save that one Bear was killed, which I had part of; and a very small part of a Turtle I had another time, and once an *Indian* gave me a piece of a *Moose's* Liver, which was a sweet Morsel to me; and *Fish* if we could catch it. Thus I continued with them, hurry'd up and down the Wilderness, from *May* 20, till the middle of *February*; carrying continually a great Burden in our Travels; and I must go their Pace, or else be killed presently; and yet was pinch'd with Cold for want of Cloathing, being put by them into an *Indian* Dress, with a sleight Blanket, no Stockins, and but one pair of *Indian* Shooes, and of their Leather Stockins for the Winter: My Feet were pricked with sharp Stones and prickly Bushes sometimes, and other times pinch'd with Snow, Cold, and Ice, that I travell'd upon, ready to be frozen, and faint for want of Food; so that many times I thought I could go no further, but must lie down, and if they would kill me, let 'em kill me. Yet then the Lord did so renew my Strength, that I went on still further as my Master would have me, and held out with them. Though many English were taken, and I was brought to some of 'em at times, while we were about *Casco Bay* and *Kennebeck River,* yet at *Norridgawock* we were separated, and no *English* were in our Company, but one *John York* and my self, who were both almost starv'd for Want; and yet told, that if we could not hold up to travel with them, they would kill us. And accordingly *John York* growing weak by his Wants, they killed him, and threatned me with the like. One time my *Indian* Mistress and I, were left alone, while the rest went to look for *Eels;* and they left us no Food from *Sabbath-day* Morning till the next *Saturday;* save that we had a *Bladder* (of Moose I think) which was well fill'd with Maggots, and we boild it, and drank the Broth; but the Bladder was so tough we could not eat it. On the *Saturday* I was sent by my Mistress to that part of the Island most likely to see some *Canoo,* and there to make Fire and Smoke, to invite some *Indians* if I could spie any, to come to relieve us; and I espy'd a *Canoo,* and by Signs invited 'em to come to shore. It prov'd to be some *Squaws;* who understanding our Wants, one of 'em gave me a roasted Eel; which I eat, and it seem'd unto me the most savory Food I ever tasted before. Sometimes we liv'd on *Wortle berries,* sometimes on a kind of *Wild Cherry,* which grew on Bushes, which I was sent to gather once in so bitter a cold Season, that I was not able to bring my Fingers together to hold them fast; Yet under all these Hardships the Lord kept me from any Sickness, or such Weakness as to disenable me from Travelling when they put us upon it.

My *Indian* Mistress was one that had been bred by the *English* at *Black-Point,* and now married to a *Canada Indian,* and turned Papist; and she would say, *That had the* English *been as careful to instruct her in our Religion as the* French *were, to instruct her in theirs, she might have been of our Religion:* and she would say, *That God delivered us into their Hands to punish us for our Sins;* And this I knew was true as to my self. And as I desired to consider of all my Sins, for which the Lord did punish me, so this lay very heavy upon my Spirit many a time, that I had left the Publick Worship and Ordinances of God, where I formerly lived (*viz. at Beverley,*) to remove to the North Part of *Casco Bay,* where there was no Church or *Minister* of the Gospel; and this we did for large Accommodations in the World, thereby exposing our Children, to be bred Ignorantly like *Indians,* and ourselves to forget what we had been formerly instructed in; and so we turned our Backs upon God's Ordinances to get this World's Goods. But now, God hath stript me of these things also; so that I must justifie the Lord in all that has befallen me, and acknowledge that he hath punish'd me less than my Iniquities deserved. I was now bereav'd of Husband, Children, Friends, Neighbours, House, Estate, Bread, Cloaths, or Lodging suitable; and my very Life did hang daily in doubt, being continually in danger of being kill'd by the *Indians,* or pined to Death with Famine, or tired to Death with hard Travelling, or pinch'd with Cold till I died, in the Winter Season. I was so amazed with many Troubles, and hurry'd in my Spirit from one Exercise to another, how to preserve my self in Danger, and supply my self in the Want that was present; that I had not time or Leisure so composedly to consider of the great Concernments of my Soul, as I should have done; neither had I any *Bible* or *Good Book* to look into, or Christian Friend to be my Counsellour in these Distresses: But I may say, *The Words of God,* which I had formerly heard or read, many of them came oft into my Mind, and kept me from *perishing in my Afflictions.* As when they threatned to kill me many times, I often thought of the Words of our Saviour to *Pilate,* Joh. 19.11. *Thou couldest have no Power at all against me, except it were given thee from above.* I knew they had no *Power* to kill me but what the Lord gave them; and I had many times Hope, that the Lord would not suffer them to slay me, but deliver me out of their Hands; and in his time I hoped, return me to my Countrey again. When they told me that my *Eldest Son* was kill'd by the *Indians,* I thought in that of *Jer.* 33.8. *I will cleanse them from all their Iniquities whereby they have sinned against me, and I will pardon all their Iniquities.* I hoped, tho' the Enemy had barbarously killed his Body, yet that the Lord had pardoned his Sins, and that his *Soul* was safe. When I thought upon my many Troubles, I thought of *Job's* Complaint, Chap. 14.16,17. *Thou numbrest my Steps, and watchest over my Sin; my Transgression is sealed up in a Bag; and thou sowest up mine Iniquity.* This was for my Humiliation, and put me upon Prayer to God, for his *Pardoning Mercy* in Christ; and I thought upon *David's* Complaint, *Psalm* 13.1,2. and used it in my Prayers to the Lord; *How long wilt thou forget me, O Lord, for ever! How long wilt thou hide thy Face from me? How long shall I take Counsel in my Soul, having Sorrow in my Heart! How long shall my Enemy be exalted over me*? I sometimes bemoaned my self, as *Job.* Chap. 19.9, 10. *He hath stripped me of my Glory, and hath taken my Crown from my Head; he hath destroyed me on every side, and I am gone, and my hope hath he removed like a Tree.* Yet sometimes encourag'd from *Job* 22.27. *Thou shalt make thy Prayer to him, and he shall hear thee, and thou shalt pay thy Vows.* I made my Vows to the Lord that I would give up my self to him, if he would accept me in Jesus Christ, and pardon my Sins; and I desired and endeavour'd to pay my Vows unto the Lord. I pray'd to him, *Remember not against me the Sins of my Youth;* and I besought him, *Judge me, O God, and plead my cause against an Ungodly Nation; deliver me from the deceitful and unjust Man. Why go I mourning because of the Oppression of the Enemy?* And by many other Scriptures that were brought to my Remembrance, was I instructed, directed and comforted.

I travell'd over steep and hideous Mountains one while, and another while over *Swamps* and Thickets of fallen Trees lying one, two, three Foot from the Ground, which I have stepp'd on from one to another, nigh a thousand in a Day, carrying a great Burden on my Back. Yet I dreaded going to *Canada,* for fear lest I should be overcome by them to yield to their Religion; which I had vowed unto God, *That I would not do.* But the Extremity of my Sufferings were such, that at length I was willing to go to preserve my Life. And after many weary Journies thro' Frost and Snow, we came to *Canada* about the middle of *February* 1690 and travelling over the River my master pitch'd his *Wigwam* in sight of some *French* Houses Westward of us, and then sent me to those Houses to beg Victuals for them; which I did, and found the *French* very kind to me, giving me Beef, and Pork, and Bread, which I had been without near Nine Months before; so that I found a great Change as to Diet. But the Snow being Knee-deep, and my Legs and Hams very sore, I found it very tedious to travel; and my Sores bled; so that as I travell'd, I might be track'd by my Blood that I left behind me on the Snow. I asked leave to stay all Night with the *French* when I went to beg again, which my Master consented unto, and sent me Eastward, to Houses, which were toward *Quebeck* (though then I knew it not:) So, having begg'd Provisions at a *French* House, and it being near Night, after I was refresh'd my self, and had Food to carry to the *Indians,* I signified as well as I could, to make the *French* Woman understand, that I desir'd to stay by her Fire that Night. Whereupon she laid a good Bed on the Floor, and good Coverings for me, and there I lodg'd comfortably; and the next Morning, when I had breakfasted with the Family, and the Men-kind were gone abroad, as I was about to go to my *Indian* Master, the *French* Woman stept out, and left me alone in her House; and I then staid her Return, to give her Thanks for her Kindness; and while I waited, came in two Men, and one of 'em spake to me in *English, I am glad to see you, Countrey Woman*! This was exceedingly reviving to hear the Voice of an *Englishman*, and upon Inquiry I found that he was taken at the *North-West Passage*; and the other was a *French Ordinary Keeper.* After some Discourse, he ask'd me to go with him to *Quebeck*, which he told me, was about four Miles off: I answer'd, my *Indian* Master might kill me for it, when I went back. Then, after some Discourse in *French* with his Fellow-Traveller, he said, This *French* Man engag'd, that if I would go with them, he would keep me from returning to the *Indians*, and I should be ransom'd: And my *French* Hostess being now return'd in-a-doors, perswaded me to go with 'em to *Quebeck*; which I did, and was convey'd unto the House of the *Lord-Intendant, Monsieur le Tonant*, who was Chief Judge, and the Second to the Governour; and I was kindly entertain'd by the Lady; and had *French* Cloaths given me, with good Diet and Lodging, and was carry'd thence unto the Hospital, where I was Physick'd and Blooded, and very courteously provided for. And some time after my *Indian Master* and *Mistress* coming for me, the *Lady Intendant* paid a Ransom for me, and I became her Servant. And I must speak it to the Honour of the *French*, they were exceeding kind to me at first; even as kind as I could expect to find the *English:* so that I wanted nothing for my bodily Comfort which they could help me unto.

Here was a great and comfortable Change as to my *Outward Man*, in my Freedom from my former Hardships, and Hard-hearted Oppressours. But here began a greater Snare and Trouble to my Soul, and Danger to my *Inward Man.* For the Lady my Mistress, the Nuns, the Priests, the Friers, and the rest, set upon me with all the Strength of *Argument* they could from Scripture, as they interpreted it, to perswade me to turn *Papist*; which they press'd with very much Zeal, Love, Intreaties and Promises, if I would turn to 'em; and with many Threatnings, and sometimes hard Usages, because I did not turn to their Religion. Yea, sometimes the Papists, because I would not turn to them, threatned to send me to *France*, and there I should be burn'd, because I would not turn to them. Then was I comforted from that in 2 *Cor.* 1.8,9,10. *We were prest out of measure above Strength, insomuch that we despair'd even of Life; but we had the sentence of Death in our selves, that we should not trust in our selves, but in God, who raises the Dead, who deliver'd us from so great a Death, and doth deliver; in whom we trust that he will yet deliver us.* I knew God was able to deliver me, as he did *Paul*, and as he did the Three Children out of the Fiery Furnace; And I believ'd he would either deliver me from them, or fit me for what he call'd me to suffer, for his Sake and Name. For their praying to *Angels*, they brought the History of the Angel that was sent to the Virgin *Mary*, in the first of *Luke*. I answer'd them from *Rev.* 19.10. and 22.9. They brought *Exod.* 17-11. of *Israel's* prevailing while *Moses* held up his Hands. I told them, we must come to God only by Christ, *Joh.* 6.37,44. For *Purgatory*, they brought *Mat.* 5.25. I told them, to agree with God while here on Earth was, to *Agree with our Adversary in the way;* and if we did not, we should be cast into Hell, and should not come out until we *paid the utmost Farthing*, which could never be paid. But it's bootless for me a poor Woman, to acquaint the World, with what Arguments I used, if I could now remember them; and many of them are slipt out of my Memory.

I shall proceed to relate what Trials I met with in these things. I was put upon it, either to stand to the Religion I was brought up in, and believ'd in my Conscience to be true; or to turn to another, which I believ'd was not right. And I was kept from turning, by that Scripture, *Mat.* 10.32,33. *Whosoever shall confess me before Men, him will I confess before my Father which is in Heaven; and whosoever denies me before Men, him also will I deny before my Father which is in Heaven.* I thought, that if I should deny the Truth and own their Religion, I should deny Christ. Yet, upon their Perswasions, I went to see and be present at their Worship sometimes; but never to receive their Sacrament. And once when I was at their Worship, that Scripture 2 *Cor.* 6.14. to the End, came into my Mind: *What Communion hath Light with Darkness! what Concord hath Christ with Belial! what part hath he that believeth with an Infidel! and what Agreement hath the Temple of God with Idols? Wherefore, come out from among them, and be ye separate, and touch not the unclean thing, and I will receive you, and I will be a Father unto you, and ye shall be my Sons and Daughters, saith the Lord Almighty.* This Scripture was so strong upon my Spirit, that I thought I was out of my way to be present at the Idolatrous Worship, and I resolv'd never to come unto it again. But when the time drew nigh, that I was to go again, I was so restless that Night, that I could not sleep; thinking what I should say to 'em when they urg'd me to go again, and what I should do. And so it was in the Morning, that a *French* Woman of my Acquaintance, told me, if I would not be of their Religion, I did but mock at it, to go to their Worship, and bid me, that if I would not be of their Religion, I should go no more. I answer'd her, *That I would not be of their Religion, and I would go no more to their Worship:* And accordingly I never went more, and they did not force me to it.

I have had many Conflicts in my own Spirit, fearing that I was not truly converted unto God in Christ, and that I had no saving Interest in Christ. I could not be of a False Religion, to please Men; for it was against my Conscience; And I was not fit to suffer for the True Religion and for Christ: For I then fear'd I had no Interest in him. I was neither fit to live, nor fit to die; and brought once to the very Pit of Despair about what would become of my Soul. In this time I had gotten an *English Bible,* and other good Books by the help of my Fellow Captives. I looked over the Scripture, and setled on the Prayer of *Jonah,* and those Words, *I said I am cast out of thy sight, yet will I look again towards thy* Holy Temple. I resolv'd I would do as *Jonah* did: And in the Meditation upon this Scripture the Lord was pleased by his Spirit to come into my Soul, and to fill me with ravishing Comfort that I cannot express it. Then came to mind the History of the Transfiguring of Christ, and *Peter's* Saying, *Matth.* 17.4. *Lord, it is good for us to be here*! I thought it was good for me to be here; and I was so full of Comfort and Joy, I even wish'd I could be so always, and never sleep; or else die in that Rapture of Joy, and never live to sin any more against the Lord. Now I thought God was my God, and my Sins were pardoned in Christ; and now I could suffer for Christ, yea, die for Christ, or do any thing for him. My Sins had been a Burden to me: I desired to see all my Sins, and to repent of them all with all my Heart, and of that Sin which had been especially a Burden to me, namely, *That I Left the Publick Worship and Ordinances of God, to go to live in a remote Place, without the* Public Ministry; *depriving our selves and our* Children *of so great a Benefit for our* Souls; *and all this for* Worldly Advantages. I found an Heart to repent of them all; and to lay hold of the Blood of Christ, to cleanse me from them all.

I found much comfort, while I was among the *French,* by the Opportunities I had sometimes to read the Scriptures and other good Books, and pray to the Lord in secret; and the Conference that some of us Captives had together about things of God and Prayer together sometimes; especially with one that was in the same House with me, *Margaret Stilson.* Then was the Word of God precious to us, and they *that feared the Lord, spake one to another of it,* as we had Opportunity. And Col. *Tyng* and Mr. *Alden,* as they were permitted, did speak to us to confirm and strengthen us in the ways of the Lord. At length the *French* debarr'd our coming together for Religious Conference, or other Duties: And Word was sent us by Mr. *Alden, That this was one kind of Persecution that we must suffer for Christ.*

These are some of the Scriptures which have been my Support and Comfort in the Affliction of my Captivity among the Papists. That in *Ezek.* 16.6-8. I apply'd unto my self, and I desired to *Enter into Covenant with God,* and to be His; and I prayed to the Lord, and hoped the Lord would return me to my Countrey again, That I might *Enter into Covenant* with Him, among his People, and enjoy Communion with Him in his Churches and publick Ordinances. Which Prayers the Lord hath now heard, and graciously answer'd; praised be his Name! The Lord enable me to live suitably to his Mercy, and to those publick and precious Privileges which I now enjoy. So, that in *Ezek.* 11.16,17. was a great Comfort unto me in my Captivity; *Although I have cast them far off among the Heathen, yet will I be a little Sanctuary to them:—I will gather you from the People,—where you have been scattered.*

I found that God was a Little Sanctuary to me there, and hoped, that the Lord would bring me unto the Countrey from whence I had been scattered. And the Lord hath heard the Prayer of the Destitute, and not despis'd my Prayer, but granted me the Desire of my Soul, in bringing me to his House, and my Relations again. I often thought on the History of the Man born blind; of whom Christ, when his Disciples asked, *Whether this Man had sinned, or his Parents?* answered, *Neither this Man nor his Parents; but this was, that the Works of God might be made manifest in him.* So, tho' I had deserved all this, yet I knew not but one Reason of God's bringing all these Afflictions and Miseries upon me, and then enabling me to bear them, was, *That the Works of God might be made manifest.* And in my great Distress I was revived by that in *Psal.* 118.17,18. *I shall not die but live, and declare the Works of the Lord: The Lord hath chastened me sore, but he hath not given me over to Death.* I had very often a secret Perswasion , That I should *Live to declare the Works of the Lord.* And 2 *Chron.* 6,36,37,38,39. was a precious Scripture to me in the Day of Evil. We have read over, and prayed over this Scripture together, and talk'd together of this Scripture, *Margaret* and I; how the Lord had promis'd, Though they were scattered for their Sins, yet there should be a Return, if they did bethink themselves, and turn, and pray. So we did bethink our selves in the Land where we were carried Captive, did turn, did pray, and endeavour to *Return to God with all our Hearts.* And, as they were to *pray towards the Temple,* I took it that I should pray towards Christ; and accordingly did so, and hoped the Lord would hear, and he hath heard from Heaven his Dwelling-place, my Prayer and Supplication, and maintained my Cause, and not rejected me, but returned me. And Oh! how affectionate was my reading of the 84th Psalm in this Condition.

The means of my Deliverance, were by reason of Letters that had passed between the Governments of *New-England* and of *Canada.* Mr. *Cary* was sent with a Vessel, to fetch Captives from *Quebeck*; and when he came, I among others, with my youngest Son, had our Liberty to come away:And by God's Blessing upon us, we arrived in Safety, at *Boston* in *November* 1695, our desired Haven. And I desire to praise the *Lord for his Goodness, and for his wonderful Works to me.* Yet still I have left behind Two Children; a Daughter of *Twenty* Years old, at *Mont Royal,* whom I had not seen in Two Years before I came away; and a son of *Nineteen* Years old, whom I never saw since we parted, the next Morning after we were taken. I earnestly request the Prayers of my Christian Friends that the Lord will deliver them.

What shall I render to the Lord for all his Benefits?

A Quaker Journal Records God's Protecting Providence

In September 1696 a barkentine bound for Philadelphia from Jamaica foundered off the coast of Florida twenty miles north of what is now West Palm Beach. The survivors were taken prisoner by the Jobese Indians, known for their ferocity. Among the captives were a prosperous Quaker merchant, Jonathan Dickinson (also spelled Dickenson), his wife and six-month-old son, and a famous Quaker missionary, Robert Barrow. The prisoners were stripped of their clothing and possessions but eventually managed to make their way to St. Augustine. With the assistance of the Spanish governor, they arrived safely in Philadelphia on April 1, 1697.

God's Protecting Providence . . . (1699), the journal Dickinson kept about his shipwreck and captivity, reveals Quaker attitudes toward Indians and Indian captivity. Dickinson describes how God preserved his "faithful servants" by miraculously afflicting their Indian captors with a state of paralysis at the moment the Indians were preparing to execute them. Quakers shared the Puritan belief that through Indian captivity God manifested his power over human destiny, but not their belief that captivity was a punishment for sin. They also saw the Indian differently. Quakers treated Indians with humanity. They conceived of them as "savage men" in need of enlightenment rather than as fiends from Hell. Hence, Quaker settlements never experienced anything comparable to the systematic Indian uprisings which nearly destroyed Puritan New England.

The journal contains one of the few firsthand accounts of the Florida natives during the seventeenth century. Particularly valuable is the

---

SOURCE: Jonathan Dickinson, *God's Protecting Providence Man's Surest Help and Defence in the Times of the Greatest Difficulty and Most Imminent Danger . . .* (Philadelphia, 1699).

information it provides about Indian attitudes toward the Europeans who colonized the area. From their stronghold at St. Augustine, the Spanish maintained cordial relationships with the Indians, enlisting their aid to ward off British encroachments into Florida. Dickinson and his fellow captives obscure their British identity, for to to have revealed it would have placed them in greater jeopardy. The kindness of the Spanish governor was in accord with a treaty between Spain and England which stipulated that colonial ports aid survivors of maritime disasters, regardless of their nationality.

God's Protecting Providence is one of the most popular Indian captivities. But Dickinson did not intend it to be the colonial best seller it became. In fact, he did not even intend it for publication. He kept a journal of his experiences for reasons of personal edification. The Society of Friends published it in the hope that others might learn the spiritual lessons his life had taught him. Nonetheless, its appeal as an adventure story should not be underestimated.

[Sept.] 22: 3[rd day of week]. This day the storm began at N.E.

[Sept.] 23: 4[th day of week]. About One a Clock in the morning we felt our Vessel strike some few stroaks, and then she Floated again for five or Six minuits before she ran fast a ground, where she beat violently at first: the wind was violent, and it was very dark, that our Mariners could see no land; the Seas broke over us that we were in a quarter of an hour Floating in the Cabin; we endeavoured to get a Candle lighted, which in a little time was accomplished: By this time we felt the Vessell not to strike so often, but severall of her timbers were broken, and some plank started; the seas continued breaking over us and no Land to be seen; We concluded to keep in the Vessel as long as she would hold together. About the Third hour this morning we supposed we saw the Land at some considerable distance and at this time we found the water began to run out of the Vessel; And at Daylight we perceived we were upon the shoar on a beach lying in the breach of the sea, which at times, as the surgis of the Sea reversed, was dry. In taking a view of our Vessell, we found that the violence of the weather had forced many sorts of Sea-Birds on board of our Vessel, some of which were by force of the wind blown into and under our Hen-Cubbs [chicken coops] and many remained alive. Our Hogs and Sheep were washed away and swam on shoar, except one of the Hoggs which remained in the Vessel. We rejoyced at this our preservation from the raging Seas; but at the same Instant feared the sad Consequences that follow'd: yet having hopes still we gott our sick and Lame on shoar, also our Provisions, with sparrs and Sails to make a Tent. I went with one Negroe to view the Land and seek the most convenient place for that purpose; But the Wilderness Countrey looked very dismall, having no Trees, but only Sand hills covered with shrubby Palmetto [small palms], the stalks of which were prickly, that there was no walking amongst them; I espyed a place almost a Furlong within that Beach being a Bottom; to this place I with my Negro soon cutt a Passage, the storm and Rain continuing: Thither I got my Wife and Sick Child being six months and twelve days old, also *Robert Barrow* an aged man, who had been sick about five or six months, Our *Master* who some days past broke his legg, and my kinsman *Benjamin Allen,* who had been very ill with a violent Fever most part of the Voyage: these with others we gott to the place under the shelter of some few Bushes which broke some of the wind but kept none of the Rain from them; I got a Fire made: the most of our people were getting Provisions a shoar; our Chests, Trunks and the rest of our Clothing were all very wett and cold.

About the Eight or Ninth hour came two *Indian-Men* (being naked except a small piece of platted work of straws which just hid their private parts and fastened behind with a Horse-Tail in likeness made of a sort of Silk-grass) from the Southward running fiercely and foaming at the mouth, having no weapons except their knives: and forthwith not making any stop; violently seized the two first of our Men they met with who were carrying Corn from the Vessel to the Top of the Bank where I stood to receive it and put it into a Cask: they used no violence for the men resisted not, but taking them under the Arm brought them towards me. Their Countenance was very Furious and bloody. They had their Hair tyed in a Role behind in which stuck two bones shaped one like a broad Arrow; the other a spear head. The rest of our men followed from the Vessel; asking me what they should do, whether they should get their Guns to kill these two; but I perswaded them otherwise, desiring them to be quiet, shewing their inability to defend us from what would follow; but to put our trust in the Lord who was able to defend to the uttermost. I walkt towards the place where our Sick and Lame were; the two *Indian* men following me, I told them the *Indians* were come and coming upon us. And whilst these two (letting the men loose) stood with a Wild Furious Countenance, looking upon us I bethought my self to give them some Tobacco and Pipes which they greedily snatcht from me, and making a Snuffing noise like a Wild-Beast, turned their Backs upon us and run away.

We Communed together and considered our condition, being amongst a Barbarous people, such as were generally accounted *Man-Eaters,* believing those two were gone to Alarum their People. We satt our selves down expecting Cruelty and hard death except it should please the Almighty God to work Wonderfully for our Deliverance. In this deep Concernment some of us were not left without hopes; Blessed be the Name of the Lord in Whom We trusted.

As We were under a deep Exercise and concernment, a motion arose from one of us that if we should put our selves under the Denomination of *Spaniards* (it being known that that Nation had some Influence on them) and one of us named *Solomon Creson,* speaking the *Spanish* Language well, it was hop't this might be a means for our delivery: To which the most of the Company assented.

Within two or three hours after the departure of the two *Indians,* some of our people being near the *Beach* or *Strand* returned and said, the *Indians* were coming in a very great number all running and shouting: About this time the Storm was much abated, the Rain ceased, and the Sun appeared which had been hid from us many days. The *Indians* went all to the Vessel taking forth what ever they could lay hold on, except Rum, Sugar, Molassoes, Beef and Pork.

But their *Casseekey* [cacique] (for so they call their King) with about thirty more came down to us in a Furious manner, having a dismall Aspect and foaming at the mouth: Their Weapons were large Spanish Knives, except their *Casseekey's,* who had a Bagganett [bayonet] that belong'd to the Master of our Vessel: They rushed in upon us and cryed, *Nickaleez, Nickaleez* [Englishmen]; We understood them not at first: they repeating it over unto us often; At last they cryed, *Epainia* or *Spaniard*: by which we understood them, that at first they meant *English;* but they were answered to the latter in *Spanish* yea, to wich they replyed, No *Spainia* No, but all cryed out, *Nickaleez, Nickaleez.* We sitting on our Chests, Boxes and Trunks, and some on the ground, the *Indians* surrounded us. We stirred nor moved not; but satt all or most of us very calm and still, some of us in a good frame of spirit, being freely given up to the Will of God.

Whilst we were thus sitting, as a People almost unconcerned; these bloody minded Creatures placed themselves each behind one, kicking and throwing away the Bushes that were nigh or under their feet; the *Casseekey* had placed himself behind me, standing on the Chest which I satt upon, they all having their Arms extended with their knives in their hands, ready to execute their bloody design, some taking hold of us by the heads with their Knees sett against our shoulders. In this Posture they seem'd to wait for the *Casseekey* to begin. They were high in words which we understood not. But on a sudden it pleased the Lord to Work Wonderfully for our preservation, and instantly all these savage men were struck dumb, and like men amazed the space of a Quarter of an Hour, in which time their countenances Fell, and they looked like another People. They quitted their places they had taken behind us and came in amongst us requiring to have all our Chests, Trunks & Boxes unlockt; which being done, they divided all that was in them. Our Mony the *Casseekey* took unto himself, privately hiding in the Bushes. Then they went to pulling of our Clothes, leaving each of us only a pair of breeches, or an old Coat, except my Wife & Child, *Robert Barrow* & our *Master,* from Whom they took but little this day.

Having thus done, they asked us again, *Nickaleez, Nickaleez*? But We answered by saying *Pensilvania.* . . .

PART THREE

The Land Imperative

A Puritan Minister Describes French Savagery and Treachery

During the eighteenth century, the imperialistic rivalry between Britain and France for the territories of the New World and the American military campaigns that were the extension of their continental wars resulted in almost continuous frontier warfare, with both sides employing Indian warriors. As loyal subjects of the king, Americans turned vehemently against the French during these conflicts, which they designated as King William's War (1689-1697), Queen Anne's War (1702-1713), King George's War (1739-1748), and the Seven Years' War (1756-1763). These border wars with the French and their Indian allies produced a series of captivity narratives, many of which were reprinted during recurrent periods of conflict.

In *The Redeemed Captive . . .* (1748), the Reverend Mr. John Norton describes a Frenchman turned savage who mutilates and then devours the body of an English soldier. He also details the treachery of a French general who promises to protect the British if they surrender but who later turns them over to his unpredictable Indian cohorts. Norton was a Yale graduate serving as the chaplain at Fort Massachusetts, near the present site of Williamstown, at the time of its capture on August 20, 1746, by French and Indians. He was taken to Canada where he lived in a Quebec prison until his ransom a year later. He died in 1778 at the age of 62. His narrative has little of the self-scrutiny and moralizing of the earlier Puritan captivity accounts; it can be seen as a step in the process of secularization already under way but given impetus by the spirit of nationalism which accompanied the French and Indian and, later, the Revolutionary wars.

SOURCE: John Norton, *The Redeemed Captive . . .* (Boston, 1748).

. . . About twelve o'Clock the Enemy desir'd to Parley: We agreed to it, and when we came to General *De Voudriale* [Pierre François Rigaud de Vaudreuile (1704-c.1770)], he promised us good Quarter if we would surrender; otherwise he should endeavour to take us by Force: The Serjeant told him, he should have an Answer within two Hours. We came into the Fort, and examined the State of it: The Whole of our Ammunition we did not judge to be above three or four Pounds of Powder, and not more Lead: And after Prayer unto God for Wisdom & Direction, we considered our Case, whether there was any Probability of our being able to withstand the Enemy or not; for we supposed that they would not leave us till they had made a vigorous Attempt upon us; and if they did, we knew our Ammunition would be spent in a few Minutes Time, and then we should be obliged to lay at their Mercy: Had we all been in Health, or had there been only those eight of us that were in Health, I believe every Man would willingly have stood it out to the last; for my Part I should; but we feared, that if we were taken by Violence, the Sick, the Wounded, and the Women, would most, if not all of them die by the Hands of the Salvages, therefore our Officer concluded to Surrender on the best Terms he could get: Which were,

I. *That we should be all Prisoners to the French, the General promising that the Salvages should have nothing to do with any of us.*
II. *That the Children should all live with their Parents during the Time of their Captivity.*
III. *That we should all have the Priviledge of being exchanged the first Opportunity that presented.*

Besides these Particulars, the General promised that all the Prisoners should have all Christian Care and Charity exercised towards them; that those who were weak and unable to travel, should be carried in their Journey, that we should all be allowed to keep our Cloathing; and that we might leave a few Lines to inform our Friends what was become of us.

About three of the Clock we admitted the General and a Number of his Officers into the Fort: Upon which he set up his Standard: The Gate was not opened to the rest; the Gentlemen spake comfortably to our People; and on our Petition that the dead Corpse might not be abused, but buried; they said, that it should be buried: But the Indians seeing that they were shut out, soon fell to pulling out the Underpining of the Fort, and crept into it; opened the Gates; so that the Parade was quickly full: they shouted as soon as they saw the Blood of the dead Corpse under the Watch-Box, but the French kept them down for some Time, & did not suffer them to meddle with it: After some Time the Indians seemed to be in a Russle; and presently rushed up into the Watch-Box, bro't down the dead Corpse, carried it out of the Fort, scalpt it, and cut off the Head and Arms: A young Frenchman took one of the Arms and flay'd it, roasted the Flesh, and offer'd some of it to *Daniel Smeed*, one of the Prisoners, to eat; but he refused it. The Frenchman dressed the Skin of the Arms (as we afterwards heard) and made a Tobacco Pouch of it. After they had plundered the Fort, they set it on Fire, and led us out to *their* Camp.

We had been at the Camp but a little Time, when Mons. *Doty*, the General's Interpreter, called me aside, and desired me to speak to our Soldiers & perswade them to go with the Indians; for he said, the Indians were desirous that some of them should go with them; and said, that Serj. *Hawks*, myself, and the Families should go with the French Officers. I answer'd him, that it was contrary to our Agreement, and the General's Promise; and would be to throw away the Lives of some of our Men, who were sick and wounded. He said, no, but the Indians would be kind to them; and tho' they were all Prisoners to the French, yet he hoped some of them would be willing to go with the Indians. We spoke to Serj. *Hawks*, and urged it upon him. We proposed it to some of our Men who were in Health, whether they were willing to go or not, but they were utterly unwilling. I returned to *Doty*, and told him that we should by no Means consent that any of our Men should go with the Indians, we took the General to be a Man of Honour; and we hop'd to find him so; we knew that it was the Manner of the Indians to abuse their Prisoners; and sometimes to kill those that failed in travelling, and carrying Packs, which we knew that some of our Men could not do; and we thought it but little better for the General to deliver them to the Indians, than it would be to abuse them himself; and had I tho't that the General would have delivered any of our Men to the Salvages, I should have strenuously opposed the Surrender of the Fort, for I had rather have died in Fight, than to see any of our Men killed, while we had no Opportunity to resist. He said, that the General would see, that they should not be abused; and he did not like it that I was so jealous and afraid: I told him, I was not the Officer, but as he spake to me, so I had freely spoken my Mind, and discharged my Duty in it; and he had no Reason to be offended, and I hoped the General would not insist on this Thing, but would make good his Promise to all the Prisoners. He went to the General, and after a little Time, the Officers came and took away *John Perry* & his Wife, and all the Soldiers, but Serj. *Hawks, John Smeed* and *Moses Scot* and their Families, and distributed them among the Indians. . . .

An Indian Trader Held by the British

With the outbreak of the Revolution, captivity narratives became vehicles for anti-British propaganda as previously they had served a like purpose against the French during the French and Indian Wars (see Norton, pp. 47-49). *A Narrative of the Capture and Treatment of John Dodge . . .* (1779) not only reports his own difficulties as a prisoner of the British but also tells how the British governor of Detroit, Henry Hamilton, gave Indians a bounty for American scalps, ordering both Indians and British soldiers alike "not to spare man, woman or child," and relates the pathetic story of the American captive whom Dodge saved from torture by the Indians only to see him die from mistreatment in a British military prison.

John Dodge was an Indian trader at Sandusky, Ohio. Because Dodge tried to preserve Indian neutrality, Governor Hamilton ordered a militia of Indians and soldiers to seize him and his property. His narrative about the injustices he witnessed did much to stimulate American patriotism and promote the American cause in Britain where it was published in John Almon's periodical, *The Remembrancer . . .* (1779). Dodge's narrative was so popular that it immediately had several American printings. It brought him to the attention of General Washington, and it was instrumental in the eventual conviction of Hamilton and his subordinates for war crimes. After the war, Dodge was appointed Indian agent for Kaskaskia (now Illinois). He is believed to have died somewhere in Missouri about 1800.

Narratives like Dodge's were written and reprinted whenever hostility erupted between the United States and England. Anti-British propaganda, for example, is especially pronounced in many of the narratives

SOURCE: *A Narrative of the Capture and Treatment of John Dodge, by the English at Detroit. Written by Himself* (Philadelphia, 1779).

published during the 1790s when the British refused to relinquish forts in the Northwest and encouraged the establishment there of an independent Indian state. *The Journal of William Scudder . . .* (1794) and *A True Narrative of the Sufferings of Mary Kinnan . . .* (1795) are examples of narratives written at this time which express antipathy toward the British for behavior similar to that described by Dodge. *Narratives of a Late Expedition Against the Indians . . .* (1783) was twice reprinted between 1796 and 1800. This work describes the execution of the popular Revolutionary War hero, Col. William Crawford, burned at the stake in the presence of Simon Girty, a notorious Tory renegade, who laughed at Crawford's pleas for pity.

. . . In the spring of 1777, I heard there was like to be a good trade at Machilimakanac [Mackinac Island at the juncture of Lakes Michigan and Huron], on which I applied to the Governor, and, with a great deal of trouble, got a pass, went, and met with good trade. On my return Gov. Hamilton, by several low arts, attempted to *pick* my cargo, which as it would spoil the sale of the remainder, I could not allow. As he had no pretence for taking them from me by force, it once more provoked him to wrath against me; he greatly retarded my sales by denying me a permit to draw my powder out of the magazine; also ordered myself and two servants to be ready at a moment's warning to march under Capt. Le Mote on a scouting party with Savages: I told him it was against my inclination to take up arms against my own flesh and blood, and much more so to go with Savages to butcher and scalp defenceless women and children, that were not interested in the present dispute: He said it was not any of my business whether they were interested in the dispute or not; and added if you are not ready when called for, I will fix you. Lucky for me he was soon after called down the country, and succeeded by Capt. Mountpresent as commander, who ordered Le Mote to strike my name out of his books; but my servants with their pay, I lost entirely.

The party of Savages under Le Mote went out with orders not to spare man, woman, or child. To this cruel mandate even some of the Savages made an objection, respecting the butchering the women and children, but they were told the children would make soldiers, and the women would keep up the flock.—Those sons of Britain offered no reward for Prisoners, but they gave the Indians twenty dollars a scalp, by which means they induced the Savages to make the poor inhabitants, who they had torn from their peaceable homes, carry their baggage till within a short distance of the fort, where, in cold blood, they murdered them, and delivered their green scalps in a few hours after to those British barbarians, who, on the first yell of the Savages, flew to meet and hug them to their breasts reeking with the blood of innocence, and shewed them every mark of joy and approbation, by firing of cannon, &c.

One of these parties returning with a number of women and children's scalps, and three prisoners, they were met by the Commander of the fort, and after usual demonstrations of joy, delivered their scalps, for which they were paid; the Indians then made the Commandant a present of two of the prisoners, reserving the third as a sacrifice to the manes [spirit] of one of them that had fell in the expedition. Being shocked at the idea of one of my fellow creatures being tortured and burnt alive by those inhuman Savages, I sought out the Indian who had lost his relative, and to whom, according to the Indian custom, this unhappy man belonged; I found him, took him home with me, and by the assistance of some of my friends, and twenty five-pounds worth of goods, I persuaded the inhuman wretch to sell his life to me. As the rest of the gang had taken the prisoner about two leagues distance, and were making merry over him, we were obliged to lay a scheme to deliver him from their hands, which we did in the following manner,—It being midnight and very dark, the Indian, myself, and two servants, crossed the river in a batteaux to where they were carousing around this unhappy victim. The Indian then went to his companions, and under pretence of taking the prisoner out to answer a call of nature, he delivered him to me who lay at some distance, and I carried him to the batteaux. As soon as he found himself in the hands of his deliverer, his transport was too great for his tender frame; three different times he sunk lifeless in my arms, and as often, by the help of water, the only remedy at hand, I prevented his going to the land of spirits in a transport of joy. None but those who have experienced it, can have an idea of the thoughts that must have agitated the breast of a man, who but a few minutes before saw himself surrounded by Savages, whose dismal yell, and frightful figures, heightened by the glare of a large fire in a dismal wood, which must have harrowed up the soul of an uninterested bystander, much more one who knew that very fire was prepared for his execution, and that every moment the executioner was expected to arrive.—The executioner arrives; he advances towards him; he loosens this unhappy victim from the tree to which he was bound, no doubt, as this young man imagined, to be led to the stake; but as it were in an instant, he finds himself in the hands of his deliverer and fellow-countryman. This, as I said before, was too much for him to bear; however I got his almost lifeless corpse to my house, where I kept him hid. The Indian, according to our agreement, in an hour or two after I was gone, returned seemingly much fatigued, and told his fellow Savages, who were impatiently waiting to begin their brutal sacrifice, that the prisoner had escaped, and that he had in vain pursued him.

Some time after this I found an opportunity, and made an agreement with the Captain of a vessel going to Michilimakanac, to take my unhappy inmate with him, but one of my servants being tempted, by a large reward that was offered for retaking the above prisoner, informed De Jeane that he was hid in my house, on which my habitation was soon surrounded by a party of soldiers under the command of said De Jeane, and myself, the young man and four servants were made prisoners, and having demanded my keys, which I delivered, we were hurried to gaol and confined in different rooms. Here this unhappy young fellow, in high expectations of seeing his friends, was once more plunged into the horrors of imprisonment.

I was sent for and carried before the Commandant, where, on being examined who was the person in my house, I frankly told him it was a young man whom I had bought of the Indians when they were going to burn him, and that I meant to send him to Canada to be out of the way of the Savages, but De Jeane, like other men of bad principles, thinking no man could do a good action without sinister views, said that he believed I had purchased him to serve my own ends, and that he would find them out, which the Commandant ordered him to do as soon as possible, and I was ordered to prison.

De Jeane then took my servant, who was his informant, ironed him, put him in the dungeon, and, after keeping him three days on bread and water, the lad almost frightened out of his senses, sent for De Jeane, and told him that the day before I was taken up I had wrote several letters, and, on his bringing a candle to seal them, that I said, if he told any one that I was writing to Pitsburg, that I would blow his brains out. This suiting De Jeane's purpose, he made the lad swear to it, and then set him, with the rest of my servants, at liberty.

I was now once more called before the Commandant, who told me he understood I was going to send an express to his Majesty's enemies, in consequence of which he had taken an inventory of my effects, and meant to send me to Canada. I told him he was misinformed, he then taxed me with what De Jeane had forced from my servant; asked me where I was writing the day before I was taken. I told him to my correspondents in Montreal; and luckily for me a neighbour of mine, having been at my house, was produced, who declared the truth of what I said, and that, I being hurried, had given him the letters to carry on board the vessel: This, with some other false accusations, being cleared up, I was once more released on giving fresh security.

Though myself and servants were, for want of a pretence for detaining us, set at liberty, it was not so with the unfortunate young man whom I had purchased from the Indian; he still remained in prison, daily tormented with the threats of De Jeane, that he would deliver him to the Indians, which so preyed on his spirits, that in a short time it threw him into a fever. I then applied to Captain Montpresent, the Commandant, who gave me permission, and I removed him to sick Quarters, where I hired Jacob Pue, of Virginia, his fellow prisoner, to attend him: I also, when leisure would permit, attended him myself; but De Jeane, who still haunted him, had so great an effect on him, that one day when I visited him, he called me to his bed side and said to me, that De Jeane had just left him, that he told him to make haste and get well, as the Indians were waiting for him.—Pray, Sir, (said the young man to De Jeane) for God's sake try to keep me from the Indians, for if they get me they will burn me. Keep you from them, said De Jeane, you damn'd Rebel you deserve to be burned, and all your damned countrymen with you, for you need not think Dodge can save you; General Hamilton is now come up, and he will fix you all. I tried to comfort him, and told him to be of good courage:— Oh! replied he, I am almost distracted with the idea of being burnt by the Savages; I had much rather die where I am, than be delivered into the hands of those horrid wretches, from whom I so lately by your hands, escaped, the recollection of which, makes me shudder with horror. He could say no more; he sunk under it, and in a few hours after, death, more kind than his cruel tormentors, released him from his troubles. I paid the last tribute to this my unhappy countryman, and had his corpse decently interred, attended by the Missionary and most of the principal Merchants of the town. . . .

The Captive as Naturalist, Anthropologist, and Plagiarist

Indian captives were among the first white people to view the interior of North America and to observe Indian culture firsthand. It is not surprising, then, that they frequently recorded what they saw and that this information is of value to anthropologists, geographers, naturalists, and historians. Usually such information is interspersed throughout their narratives, but sometimes, as in these excerpts from the *Memoirs of Charles Dennis Rousoe d'Eres . . .* (1800), it appears conveniently categorized in an Appendix devoted to a description of Indian life and natural history. However, scientific data in captivity narratives must be read with caution for they are only as reliable as their narrator. Because these writers were often less interested in advancing knowledge than in entertaining or promoting the settlement of the frontier (see Stewart, pp. 60-63), they sometimes enlivened their narratives with curiosities and extravagances.

This narrative is a case in point. Authorities long considered it fictitious because it contained oddities such as a Canadian monkey and because no one had ever heard of the "Scanyawtauragahrooote" Indians by whom Rousoe d'Eres claimed to have been held. He also claimed to have traveled several thousand miles during an eleven-year captivity which began near Quebec and took him south to Mexico and west to the Red River. But Rousoe d'Eres did exist, and he was an Indian captive taken near Quebec in 1775 and carried west though probably not so far southwest as Mexico. After eleven years he turned up in Spencer, Massachusetts, where he married and opened a blacksmith shop. The name of the tribe, "Scanyawtauragahrooote," is a white man's attempt

SOURCE: *Memoirs of Charles Dennis Rousoe d'Eres . . .* (Exeter, N.H., 1800).

to pronounce "Skaniardaradihronon," an Indian term meaning "those who dwell on the other side of the river." If the river is the Niagara, then Rousoe d'Eres was referring to his captors simply as "Canadian" Indians.

No one will ever know for certain exactly where Rousoe d'Eres traveled and what he saw because he probably did not know himself. To verify his experiences and to add authority and interest to his narrative, he evidently consulted a number of popular sources from which he gained a good deal of misinformation, but in almost every instance the reader can easily distinguish fact from fiction.

His principal source was Jonathan Carver's *Travels Through the Interior Parts of North-America . . .* (London, 1778). The route of Rousoe d'Eres's travels may be traced on the map accompanying Carver's *Travels*, even to the extent of following Carver's geographical inaccuracies. Rousoe d'Eres's Appendix follows Carver's method of organization and his wording is sometimes verbatim. This is true of the selections reprinted here with the exception of the description of the turkey-snake, a reptile neglected by Carver. A British officer, Carver was taken captive by the French and Indians at Fort William Henry in 1757. His *Travels*, often reprinted, was a source for Cooper's *The Last of the Mohicans* (see pp. 231-256).

Of Their Religious Tenets, Modes of Worship, &c.

The Scanyawtauragahrooote Indians hold to a plurality of Gods, as the sun, moon, seven stars, north or polar star. They also suppose that evil geniuses, or bad spirits more or less effect their national and private operations. To the sun, however, they give the preference; ever on its rising and setting, paying homage by bowing &c. towards it, in token of submissive dependance on its power.

The moon and stars are considered as subordinate powers, and take their authority from the sun. The moon on its first appearance, whether in the wane or increase, is particularly attended to. When it first appears in its full orbit, nothing can exceed the joy which pervades the whole village—shouting, dancing, and every other mode of exulting is seen and heard among the inhabitants, ejaculatory prayers are intermixed, asking the moon's interest with the sun, praying that he would be propitious to them, in giving them success in hunting, tilling their lands, &c.

The stars are considered as having rule at night in the absence of the moon; the Indians therefore, pray that they would use their influence with the sun as supreme; that he would hasten the return of the moon, continue its lustre and influence longer than at one time heretofore; that the stars would preside over their traps, give success to their endeavours to catch the Beaver, Fox, Wolfe, and all other animals taken by traps during the night season.

They hold that certain evil spirits have power to counteract the good influence of the sun, moon, &c; that they can, and often do reveal secrets to the Powows or praying Indians. Those Powows are always consulted on public enterprises, such as going to war, &c. The inhabitants suppose the Powows hold a secret correspondence with those evil geniuses.

How those praying Indians come by this secret power, I am at a loss to determine, although when among them I made all the enquiry into this matter. The manner of the Powow's religious operations hath already been fully described.

The Indians appear in their religious principles to be rude, and for want of a knowledge of the scriptures of divine revelation, but a small remove above the brutal creation, not having even a faint idea of any power necessary to exist before, and superior to the sun, moon, &c. in order to create them.

In instances of earthquakes, heavy thunder and lightning, they say it is because the sun, moon, or stars are angry, because they have omitted paying their homage to one or all their deities, or have not in the best manner improved their hunting seasons, or have not (through their own neglect) improved any advantage they have at any time gained over their enemies in battle, &c.

If it happens that earthquakes are not so often repeated, as for the most part is the case among them, they say their Gods are in friendship with them, and that they have nothing to fear from their enemies, and cheerfully pass away time, not even entertaining any notion of a state of future rewards or punishment; but that death puts an end to the difficulties attendant on this life; that the hunter shall no more be obliged to travel so far, and suffer so much as he now does in procuring food, &c. for himself and family; that the state on which they enter at the close of this life, is every way better calculated to make them happy; that good hunting lands, crowded with animals of the first quality and in the greatest plenty and perfection, are there enjoyed; that hunting in the new country will not be fatiguing, but delightful and profitable, beyond present conception. . . .

A Particular Description of the Quadrupeds . . . in the Vicinity of Scanyawtauragahrooote Island . . .

The Buffalo is found in the greatest perfection and plenty in this quarter, and of great consequence to the Scanyawtauragahrooote Indians; it is much larger than a common Ox—has short black horns, with a large beard under its chin; his head is so full of hair that it falls over its eyes, which gives a disagreeable appearance. This animal is distinguished from others by a large bunch on its back, beginning at the haunches, increasing gradually to the shoulders and neck. The whole body is covered with long hair of a dun or mouse colour—its head is larger than a Bull's, with a very short neck—the breast is broad—the body decreaseth towards its rump.—The Buffalo's flesh is excellent food—its hide very useful—its hair much used in manufacturing many articles. . . .

The Hedgehog and Porcupine so nearly resemble each other that in describing one the reader may form an idea of the other, although by some considered as two distinct animals. It is about the bulk of a small Dog, but of shorter legs; its body is covered with hair of a dark brown, and armed with quills on almost every part of the body; those on its back are most substantial. Those quills are this animal's defensive and offensive weapons, which at pleasure he discharges at his enemy. Whenever they enter the flesh in any degree, they will sink into it, and are not to be extracted but by incision. The Indians make use of these quills in boring their ears and noses to insert their pendants, and also as ornaments to their stockings, mogasons, hair, &c; their flesh is esteemed by the Indians.

The Moose by some is said to be of the Deer kind, but on a close examination 'tis found to be an animal of a distinct species from the Deer, both in its bulk and particular formation; the Deer being gant and of a slender body, long leged and light on the foot—its horns long, slender, round and branching. The Moose is in body nearly of the bulk of a well fed horse, its legs shorter and more stockey—its horns near the base are nearly round and large, as they expand, more flat and less branching. This animal sheds his horns annually—its hair is of a light grey, with a small mixture of blackish red—the tail very short—its flesh is good food, nourishing and easy of digestion; the upper lip when properly cook'd is much esteemed—its hide is very proper for leather, being thick, strong, soft and pliable. The Moose never appears when in motion, but on a trot. This animal is rarely to be met with on or near the Scanyawtauragahrooote Island, its haunts being much further north—its food through the winter is the buds and moss of trees. . . .

Of Their Birds . . .

The Humming bird is peculiar to America, and is not known in any other part of the globe; 'tis the smallest of the feathered airy inhabitants—its legs are proportionally small to its body, and are not biger than two small needles—its plumage exceeds description—it has a small tuft on its head of a shining black—its breast is red—the belly white—the back, wings and tail a pale green—small specks of a gold cast are scattered over the whole body—an almost imperceptible down softens the colours, and produces the most pleasing shades—with its bill, which is proportionably small to its body, it extracts moisture from flowers, which is its nourishment; over which it hovers like a Bee, without lighting, constantly moving its wings with such velocity, that the motion is imperceptible; this quick motion causeth a humming noise, from whence it receives its name. . . .

Of SERPENTS . . .

Rattle-Snake. This serpent is of all the serpentile species most to be feared; its bite (if not prevented by some early and proper application) proves fatal—at its full growth 'tis about five feet in length, it measures round its body about eight inches, from its centre it gradually decreaseth both towards its head and tail—the neck is small, the head broad and depressed—they are of a brown colour—the eye appears of a bright red and very piercing—the upper part of its body of a brown, mixed with a ruddy yellow, and chequer'd with many regular lines of a deep black, gradually to a gold colour—the belly is of a pale blue, which grows fuller as it approacheth its sides. This snake gives the traveller notice of his danger by shaking the rattles at its tail; the number denotes its age as one is added every year of its life.

The Turkey-Snake is about six feet in length, proportionally large in its body, and of a dusky colour—this snake takes its name from its preying upon the Wild-Turkey principally. The method of its taking the Turkey is in the manner following.

The snake on finding a tree on which the Turkeys are wont to roost at night, ascends it, to its lowest branches entwines its tail round a branch with its head downwards, draws its body into a small compass, not unlike the form of a Wasp's nest. Whenever the Turkey approaches its wonted place of rest, the Snake suspended as above related, with a hissing noise draws a Turkey directly under its enemy, who, as by a charm seizes its deluded prey, entwines its body round the Turkey's neck, robs it of life, then with its tongue licks every part of the bird, which leaves a certain gluey substance that serves to lubricate the body so that the snake swallows the bird with more ease; thus prepared the serpent takes it by the head and gradually sucks in the body with its feathers, &c. . . .

An Almanac Promotes Colonization in the Old Southwest

Narratives like this one about the "captivity and travels" of Captain Isaac Stewart did more than describe the American wilderness. They encouraged its colonization by providing expansive accounts of the wealth awaiting those brave enough to claim western lands from the Indians, whose deeds of cruelty suggested that they were unworthy of the right to possess the lands. This narrative, published in *Bickerstaff's Genuine Boston Almanack for 1787,* was designed to promote immigration into the territories southwest of the Mississippi at a time when American claims to them were endangered. Under the terms of the Peace of 1783, Spain gained control of the Floridas west to the Mississippi River and threatened to create an empire in the Old Southwest by fortifying its outposts at Natchez and Vicksburg (then called Walnut Hills), prohibiting Americans from moving into its territories, and even encouraging its Indian allies to raid American settlements on the Cumberland and Tennessee rivers. If the United States was to have any claim to the Southwest, it was imperative to sustain it by settling the area immediately.

Because they were so widely read, almanacs afforded a convenient means for publicizing the potential of western lands and the cruelty of the Indians who inhabited them. Moses Coit Tyler explains in his *History of American Literature* (1878) that almanacs were "the supreme and only literary necessity" in America until superseded by newspapers after the Civil War. Their annual publication, usually in the autumn, was eagerly

SOURCE: "A True and Faithful Narrative of the Captivity and Travels of Capt. Isaac Stewart . . . ," *Bickerstaff's Genuine Boston Almanack for 1787.*

anticipated. In addition to calendars, lunar tables, and tidal charts, the typical almanac contained advertisements, historical anecdotes, jokes, proverbs, verse, and just about anything that might interest its audience, including Indian captivity narratives. In fact, *Bickerstaff's Boston Almanack* (1768), the first of the series, contains an account entitled, "Adventure of a Young British Officer Among the Abenakee Savages."

The British periodical in which the Stewart narrative allegedly first appeared remains unidentified, but an American variant, published in the *Columbian Magazine* (February 1787) under the initials "J.C. Esquire," hints at the identity of the author. "J.C." claimed to have heard the narrative from a "*Captain* ISAAC STUART" while on board the *Peacock* in March 1782. According to "J.C.," Stuart [*sic*] was an officer in "*the provincial Cavalry of* South-Carolina" and a friend of Lt. Col. John Cruger (1738-1807), also a Tory officer. During the Revolutionary War, "J.C." states, Captain Stuart [*sic*] commanded "a corp of independent marines, in which capacity he acquitted himself with gallantry."

The Welsh-speaking, light-skinned Indian tribe mentioned in this narrative owes its origin to the legend that during the thirteenth century a Welsh prince named Madoc sailed west and was never heard from again. According to popular lore, both American and European, Prince Madoc and his crew intermarried with a western Indian tribe whose descendants resembled Europeans and spoke a language similar to Welsh. Madoc's story, first told in Humphrey Lloyd's *The Historie of Cambria* (London, 1584) and repeated often thereafter, remains unproved.

A true and faithful Narrative of the Captivity and Travels of Capt. ISAAC STEWART, *taken by the Indians near Fort-Pitt, 1764. Together with an accurate description of the fertility of the southern parts of* AMERICA, *of gold found in brooks, rivulets, Etc. Taken from his own mouth, 1782, and lately published in a London Magazine.—A great part of the particulars, related by the above English Gentleman respecting the fertility of the soil, and immense riches of the Country S.W. of the Ohio River, is corraborated by a Gentleman Officer who lately passed thro' Boston on his way to N. Hampshire, having been taken by the Indians and carried to those parts, while engaged in an expedition against them last war, under the direction of the brave and intrepid Major-General* SULLIVAN.*—These particulars will serve in a striking light to shew that the immense importance of the Southern Parts of this vast Continent* AMERICA, *and the rich treasures it abounds with, were very little known either to* Britain *or* America, *until the late contest; as the Savages were ever cautious of releasing European prisoners that fell into their hands.—Heaven grant that these* UNITED STATES, *thro' the medium and good offices of our worthy and august* CONGRESS, *may be led to their true interest, and improve the rich* Boon *the Arbiter of nations has thrown into their hands, by their emancipation from* British Chains, *and gaining sword in hand their* Independence: *And may we not lose by divisions in the* Cabinet *those glorious laurels we have happily achieved in the* Field *by unanimity and valour unequaled even by the Roman Conquerors.*

I was taken prisoner near Fort-Pitt, by the Indians, and carried with many more White Men to Wabash [Indiana], who were executed with horrid barbarity. It was my good fortune to excite the sympathy of what is called the Good Woman of the town, who was permitted to redeem me from the flames, by giving them a horse. After remaining 2 years in bondage amongst the Indians, a Spaniard came to the nation, having been sent from Mexico on discoveries; he made application to the chiefs for redeeming me and one John Davey; they complied and we took our departure in the company with the Spaniard, and travelled to the Westward, crossing the Mississippi, near the River-Rouge, or Red-River, up which we travelled 700 miles, when we came to a nation of Indians remarkable white, and whose hair was of a redish colour, at least mostly so; they lived on the banks of a small river that empties itself into the Red-River, which is called the River-Post. In the morning of the day after our arrival among these Indians, the Welchman said he would tarry, as the language was like the Welch. My curiosity was excited by this information, and I went with my companion to the chief men of the town, who informed him in a language I had no knowledge of, and not like any other Indian language I ever heard, the forefathers of this nation came from a foreign country, landed on the E. side Mississippi; describing particularly the country now called West-Florida, and that on the Spaniards taking possession of Mexico, they fled to their then abode; to prove what they attested, they produced rolls of parchment carefully tied up in otter-skins, on which were large characters written with blue ink, which I did not understand; and the Welchman being unacquainted with letters, even of his own language, I could not know the writing. They were a bold, hardy people, very warlike, and the women beautiful when compared with other Indians.— We left this nation after being kindly treated, and requested to remain amongst them, being only the Spaniard and myself, and we continued our course up the Red-River, until we came to a nation of Indians called Windots [Wyandots], that had never seen a white man before, and were unacquainted with the use of fire-arms. On our way we came to a transparent stream, which we, to our surprise, found to descend into the earth, and, at the foot of a ridge of mountains, disappeared; it was remarkable clear, and near to it we found the bones of 2 animals, of such size that a man might walk under the ribs, and the teeth were remarkable heavy.— The Indians that had never seen a white man, lived near the source of Red-River, and there the Spaniard discovered to his great joy, gold dust in the brooks and rivulets, and being informed by the Indians that a nation lived farther west, who were very rich, whose arrows were pointed with gold, we set out in hope of reaching their country, and we travelled 500 miles, until we crossed a ridge of mountains, from which the streams run due west, at the foot of which the Spaniard gave proofs of joy and satisfaction, having found gold in abundance. I was not acquainted with the nature of the ore, but I lifted up what he called gold-dust from the bottom of the little rivulets issuing from the cavities of the rocks: It had a yellowish cast and was remarkable heavy; but so much was the Spaniard's satisfaction, he relinquished his plan of a journey, convinced he had found a gold country.— On our return we took a different rout, and when we reached Mississippi, we went in a canoe to the mouth of the Missouri, where we found a Spanish post; there I was discharged by the Spaniard, went to the Chickesaws, thence to the Cherokees, and soon reached 96 [Ninety Six, a British fort], in S. Carolina.— I can't give an adequate description of the country S.W. of Mississippi; I was charmed with the land N.E. of that noble river, till I beheld the other country; the luxuriance of the soil, richness of herbage, majesty of the forests, and fertility of the meadows, which are almost covered with rich grass and clover, 3 feet high; the woods full of deer, elk, buffalo; in the autumn grapes and apples are plenty: In short, every other part of America is a desart compared to Louisiana; the air pure, serene; the climate as healthy as any in the world; nature has been very bountiful in furnishing water; in many places acres of ground are covered with salt-rock, where animals go at certain seasons; it is extremely pleasant to observe the marks of their tongues on the salt-rocks.— No country in the world is better calculated for the culture of rice, indigo and tobacco, when it is considered that, on the banks of the Missouri and Red-River settlements, a quantity of these articles might be made sufficient to supply all Europe; and, for 1000 miles from the confluence of each river, ships could be built, and for 3 months of the year the current runs with such rapidity, they could go down the stream 100 miles in 24 hours.

Faked Atrocity Stories

Melodramatic and chauvinistic, this narrative reinforces the stereotype of the Indian as "merciless savage" which land speculators fostered during the nineteenth century when Indians blocked westward expansion. Indian lands could be settled through treaty or seizure. Treaties required negotiations, and Indians often refused to negotiate. Narratives such as this one, which contained detailed firsthand accounts of Indian cruelty toward innocent white frontiersmen, rationalized the seizure of Indian lands. The vivid descriptions they contained of frontier families cruelly uprooted in the dead of night and tortured in the "most shocking" manners imaginable titillated and horrified audiences into hating Indians.

At first these narratives adhered fairly closely to the facts, but as it became apparent that accounts of Indian cruelty increased their effectiveness as anti-Indian propaganda (and also sold more copies), exaggerations and outright fiction came to abound. No historical records exist to verify the truth of Mrs. Smith's narrative, or even to prove that she ever lived. The passage describing the torture of her "helpless virgin" daughters, said to be "an event the most tragical ere recorded in history," is taken almost verbatim from an *Affecting History of the Dreadful Distresses of Frederick Manheim's Family,* published in 1793, frequently reprinted, and believed fictitious. That an elderly Indian chief threatened Mrs. Smith's chastity seems unlikely. Provocative sexual undertones arise from cultural differences twisted for propaganda purposes. It was not the practice of Eastern Indians to violate their captives. Rape appears in only the most outrageously sensational narratives. But Indians did in fact terrorize isolated frontier families around Natchez in 1814. In 1811 the Shawnee prophet, Tecumseh, attempted to establish an Indian confederacy extending from the Great Lakes to the Gulf of Mexico. Moved by his oratory, the Creeks massacred white families throughout Mis-

---

SOURCE: *An Affecting Narrative of the Captivity and Sufferings of Mrs. Mary Smith, . . . Rescued from the Merciless Savages by a Detached Party of the Army of the Brave General Jackson . . .* (Williamsburgh, Mass., 1818).

sissippi and Alabama. More than four hundred white men, women, and children were killed in 1813 at Fort Mims, Alabama, alone. The "brave General Jackson," upon whom the title of the Smith narrative lavishes praise, crushed the rebellion, but only after almost a thousand Indians, women and children included, were killed. Later, Jackson's militia patrolled the area, suppressing uprisings by tribes such as the Kickapoos, who allegedly captured the Smith family.

The Smith narrative stands in marked contrast to those of John Tanner (pp. 97-109) and Mary Jemison (pp. 110-122), who wrote kindly about their Indian captors; yet this discrepancy is not as misleading as it appears. Indians tortured captives to avenge the deaths of Indians killed by whites, but they also took captives to replenish their dwindling numbers. These captives were usually adopted into the tribe and treated with kindness.

The intrepid and brave General Jackson, with the troops under his command, having so completely effected his object the last season, in so far exterminating the Indians of the Creek nations, as to compel the surviving few to sue for peace—it was conceived advisable by the general to station a few regiments in their neighbourhood, to hold them in awe, in case an enemy should attempt to instigate them to a re-commencement of hostilities. In the interim, the commander was apprized of the incursions of wandering hordes of the Kickapoo nation of Indians, who had committed many depredations on the white inhabitants residing near the Floridas. A detachment from a Tennessee regiment, consisting of a lieutenant, sergeant and thirty-two privates, was ordered on an expedition for the protection of the defenceless inhabitants. This little but brave handful of men quit the main body of the army on the 3d of September, and on the 4th crossed the Yazoo, and not meeting with any but friendly Indians in this quarter, they bent their course further west, and on the 24th fell in with a party of the Choctaws. By these Indians they were informed that they had the day before fallen in with a large body of the Kickapoos and runaway Chickasaws, and that they had with them some white prisoners, and a great number of scalps. Lieut. Brown pushed forward with all possible expedition, and on the day following about sunset, fell in with their trail, and by the fires concluded that the enemy had encamped not far ahead. At the dawn of day the Lieut. despatched two of the most active of his men, to make an observation as to the number and situation of the Indians: they returned with the information that they had discovered the enemy encamped in a swamp a few miles therefrom, that their number exceeded one hundred and were armed with bows and arrows—that they perceived three or four whites lying bound in their centre, one of whom appeared to be a female! these observations were made without any discovery on the part of the enemy.

A consultation was now held among the officers and privates, whether it would be prudent to risk an action with a force so much superior to their own, there probably being four to one! But the idea of rescuing from the merciless hand of their enemies their unfortunate countrymen, who probably were designed as victims to feed their savage fires, inspired the Lieutenant and his little band with unconquerable resolution—not one expressed a doubt of their success, but the whole company begged to be led on to the unequal combat! The commander, placing the utmost confidence in his men, who he knew were well skilled in the Indian mode of bush-fighting, did not hesitate to devise a plan of attack that would insure the release of their unfortunate countrymen: he divided his company into four parties—the sergeant with ten men were designed to gain their rear; two parties of six men each were to flank them on the right and left; while the lieutenant with the remainder of the company were to charge them in front—each party were directed to gain their stations unperceived by the enemy, if possible, and having them thus encompassed, the charge of those in front was to be the signal for the other parties to rush on the enemy. The lieutenant and his little band of invincibles were soon within gun shot of the savages, by whom being at this instant discovered, the latter threw themselves into Indian file, and with a yell peculiar to the savage race, rushed upon their assailants, at whom they hurled their tomahawks and discharged their arrows. At this important crisis, Lt. Brown ordered his little company to charge, which being the signal for a general attack, the detached parties rushed upon the enemy with such impetuosity, in the mean time shouting and discharging their pieces with so good effect, that the latter were soon thrown into disorder and became panic struck; they made no further resistance, but throwing aside their packs, blankets, and even their weapons, attempted each to save himself by flight; but this unexpected opportunity of revenge did not pass unimproved by the lieutenant's brave lads—not having sufficient time to reload their muskets, they assailed the enemy with their own weapons, destroying numbers with the tomahawks, &c. which they had so recently possessed! In less than half an hour the conquering assailants completed their work. At the conclusion of the fight, the unfortunate captives were sought for, whom they found four in number (one a female) bound hand and foot with green withes! Thus did this inferior number of the brave and hardy sons of the western world, attack an enemy in the heart of their own country, and of four times their number, of whom fifty-two were slain, twelve made prisoners, and many wounded, and four unfortunate captives liberated—and all this effected without the loss of a single man on their part, and but four slightly wounded.

The poor female appears to have been peculiarly unfortunate—by these ferocious cannibals, she has been deprived of her husband and three lovely children, and that too in a manner almost too shocking to relate. Her story is such as cannot fail to touch the heart of all not callous to the feelings of humanity.

The name of the late husband of this unfortunate woman was Richard Smith, who with his family (consisting of himself, wife, three children and negro lad) resided at the extreme part of a small township 135 miles west of the Natchez, and at the distance of 12 miles from any other white family—that they remained unmolested until the night of the first of August last, when Mr. Smith was alarmed by the barking of his dog; he rose from his bed and looked from his chamber window, but saw no person, and all appeared to be quiet. He again returned to his bed, but not many minutes after he was once more disturbed by a loud and repeated knocking at the door. The whole family now became greatly alarmed and repaired to the chamber of Mr. Smith, who now hailed from the window, and demanded who was there, but received no other answer, than if he did not immediately open his doors, he should be murdered! He was soon convinced that a party of Indians surrounded his house, and suspecting that their designs were hostile, he armed himself, and ordered the remainder of the family to prepare to defend themselves in the best manner they could. Accordingly Mr. S. with his wife and negro equipped themselves with a loaded musket each, and the two oldest girls with each a hatchet. Being thus prepared, Mr. Smith hailed once more from the window, and with the most horrible threats he was ordered to open his doors, which he peremptorily refused. In a few moments the doors were forced and the hellish tribe rushed in, and were saluted with the three muskets, which caused them to retreat, and gave the brave defenders time to reload; immediately after they again returned and attacked the negro, whom they soon dispatched with their tomahawks. Mr. S. and his wife again discharged their pieces, and then with their daughters retreated to the inner chamber, the door of which they bolted. Here the unfortunate family did not remain long secure, for before they had time to reload, they succeeded in forcing the doors, and with uplifted tomahawks and a hideous yell, rushed into the room! All further resistance now was vain. Mr. S. receiving a severe blow upon the head from an Indian with his tomahawk, fell senseless to the floor! Mrs. S. observing herself and children surrounded by those savage monsters, frightfully painted, and who with their tomahawks and scalping knives menaced them with instant death, begged for mercy: but alas, her intreaties were in vain. They were dragged almost naked out of the house, and bound severally with cords.

By order of one of the savages, who appeared to be chief, about twenty of their gang took charge of the unhappy prisoners, and by whom they were to be conducted to their settlement, about 100 miles distant, without delay; while the remainder were left to pillage and fire the house. They commenced their journey about two in the morning, and travelled through an uncultivated wilderness at the rate of nearly six miles an hour. If either of the prisoners through fatigue slackened their pace, they were most inhumanly beat and threatened with instant death.

After tedious travel of nearly 30 miles, the savages halted in a swamp; here for the first time, from the time of their departure, the prisoners were permitted to sit down.—The Indians kindled a fire, on which they broiled some bear's flesh, but of which they allowed the unfortunate captives but a small portion. After refreshing themselves and extinguishing their fire, they recommenced their journey and travelled until sunset, when the Indians again halted, and began to prepare some covering for the night. The unfortunate children complained much of their feet being swollen: contrary to their expectations, however, they had a tolerable night's rest, and on the succeeding day, though nearly naked and half starved, travelled with much more ease than on the preceding one. The savages occasionally allowing them a little half roasted bear's flesh, sufficient only to keep them alive, they this day travelled according to the reckoning of the Indians nearly 40 miles, and were about sunset joined by the remaining savages who were left behind. They were loaded with the spoils of Mr. Smith's property, among which, unfortunately for the captives, was a small keg of whiskey, of which drinking until they were intoxicated, they diverted themselves in torturing their unhappy prisoners in every way that savage brutality could devise. Mr. S. having lost so large a quantity of blood in consequence of the severe wound that he had received at his house, and now receiving additional bruises and lacerations, became so weak, that on the morning ensuing he was found unable to support himself on his legs. The savages imputing his inability to wilfulness, renewed their acts of barbarity to effect a compulsion; they severally beat him with clubs, cut and gashed his flesh with their knives, and scorched his naked body with brands of fire! Finding, however, that their hellish proceedings had no other effect than to render the poor unhappy sufferer less enabled to travel, they formed the horrid conclusion of putting him to a painful death, and in order to execute the infernal purpose, they stripped and prostrated the wretched victim on his naked back, they then cut holes through his wrists and ankles, between the bones and tendons, in such a manner as to draw green withes through the apertures! then extending his arms and legs to a degree exquisitely painful, they, with the ligiatures abovementioned, lashed him fast to four small trees, about six feet from the ground, which bloody exploit finished, those horrid hell hounds left for a few moments the writhing sacrifice, with an intent to make merry and enjoy, in idea, the excruciating tortures of the sufferer!

In about half an hour they returned, and commenced an Indian dance and pow wow, around the distressed victim; this they continued to do about an hour, when becoming weary of such severe exercise, a strip of bark was placed within a few inches of Mr. Smith's head, as a mark, and at which his cruel tormentors now in succession hurled their tomahawks! At length, either by accident or design, one of those deadly weapons struck the head of their expiring victim and fortunately put an immediate end to his existence! To this horrid spectacle Mrs. Smith and her unfortunate children were compelled to stand witnesses, unable to render their wretched husband and parent any assistance.

The merciless cannibals having sufficiently feasted themselves with a view of the mangled body of the deceased, of which having deprived its scalp, they again resumed their journey toward their settlement, in view of which they encamped that night. At daylight next morning, they gave their prisoners new clothes, painted their faces with various colours, and put into their hands white staffs, tasselled round with the tails of deer; this being done, the savages commenced a dismal yell! in a few moments after, they were joined by a great number of Indians and squaws from the village, to which the unhappy prisoners were now conveyed. They were led in great triumph to the cabin of their principal chief, where they were given to understand their fate was to be determined.

The chiefs of the tribe, after a consultation of an hour or two, conceived it most advisable to put the prisoners to death, as the captors it appeared had disagreed about whose property they should be as they had jointly seized them; and to terminate the dispute, agreeably to the abominable usage of the savages, it was determined by the chiefs of the party, that the prisoners, who gave rise to the contention, should be destroyed; and that their captors should be the principal agents in the execrable business! by them it was resolved that the unhappy girls should immediately suffer, while the death of the mother should be deferred until some future day.

No sooner was the determination of the chiefs made known, than the whole village set up the death cry, and began to make preparations for an event the most tragical ere recorded in history. Two saplings were pruned clear of branches up to the very top around them; while this was doing, two or three of the Indians employed themselves in splitting pitch pine billets into small splinters about five inches in length, and as small as one's little finger, sharpening one end, and dipping the other in melted turpentine.

At length with countenances distorted with infernal fury, and with hideous yells, two or three of the savages leaped into the midst of their circle, and dragged those ill-fated females, the oldest in her 19th, and the youngest in the 11th year of their age, shrieking from the embraces of their helpless mother! these furies assisted by their comrades, stripped the forlorn girls, already convulsed with apprehensions, and tied each to a sapling, with their hands as high extended above their heads as possible: and then, horrid to relate, pitched them from their knees to their shoulders, with upwards of six hundred of the sharpened splinters above described, which, at every puncture, were attended with screams of distress that echoed and re-echoed through the wilderness! and then, to complete the infernal tragedy, the splinters, all

The horrific torture of two "helpless virgins" in the *Affecting Narrative . . . of Mrs. Mary Smith* was plagiarized from a fictitious anti-Indian propaganda collection, the *Affecting History of . . . Frederick Manheim's Family,* in which the above appears as the frontispiece. According to Edwin Wolf II, it is the earliest American illustration of Indian torture. Its ultimate original is John White's sketch of an Indian dance engraved by Theodor de Bry to illustrate his edition of Thomas Hariot's *A Brief and True Report of the New-Found Land of Virginia* (Frankfurt, 1590). *Courtesy of the Edward E. Ayer Collection, the Newberry Library.*

standing erect on the bleeding victims, were every one set on fire, which must have exhibited a scene of monstrous misery, beyond the power of speech to describe, or even the imagination to conceive. It was not until near three hours had elapsed from the commencement of their torments, and that they had lost almost every resemblance of the human form, that these helpless virgins sunk down in the arms of their deliverer, Death.

What could have been the sensations of the poor distressed mother, at witnessing the horrid sacrifice of her tender offspring, I shall not attempt to say: they were unquestionably such as would be impossible for me, or any other person to describe with correctness! let it suffice to say, that she in a fit of distraction, during the tragic scene, broke in twain the withes with which she was bound, and plunged headlong into the flames that were then devouring her dear children!!

She was insensibly drawn from the fire and conveyed to an Indian hut, where she remained in a state of delirium for two or three days; when she had a little recovered she was given to understand, by an Indian who spoke a little broken English, that the hut which she occupied belonged to one of their chiefs, who with four other Indians, were shot in the late attack upon her husband's house. The wretched captive now expected every moment to receive a summons to prepare herself for a fate as horrible as that of her friends! she remained however unmolested for nearly a week; when two aged squaws came to the hut, and made signs to her to follow them, which she did, to the distance of nearly a mile, to a cleared spot of land, where were collected two or three hundred Indians, squaws and children. Mrs. Smith was now addressed by one who appeared to be a chief, and informed of the number of his tribe that had been slain, whose friends, said he, cry for vengeance, and that she was then to suffer torments! The most hideous yells echoed through the woods, a large fire was kindled, and over it they placed a kind of gallows, on which the captive was made to understand she was to be hung. Two large and fierce looking Indians bound her, and with savage ferocity, she was stripped and dragged towards the fire. A ring was formed by the children, a second by the women, and a third by the men round the wretched victim; they then commenced the death song; running back and forth round the flames. After continuing this for near an hour, one of the savages approached the prisoner, and when about to commit her to the devouring element, their attention was suddenly attracted by the harangue of an Indian, apparently a chief, at the conclusion of which the prisoner was unbound, and by the two old squaws was conveyed back to the hut where she had been recently confined. Here she had not remained long, before the old Indian, by whose means her life had been preserved, entered, attended by an interpreter, and by whom she was informed that through the intercession of the old chief her life had been spared, his power was absolute, and he had concluded to adopt her to supply the place of his squaw, who with his two children had been killed by the whites, in one of their former expeditions. The prisoner was now informed that it was left to her choice, whether she would accede to the proposals of the old chief, or would rather resign herself up a victim to savage barbarity.

Here I cannot better describe the feelings of Mrs. Smith, on this trying occasion, than to make use of her own words; they are these—"I now prayed for death, I heartily wished to be delivered from such merciless cannibals! but just escaped from torture, I was reduced to the necessity of becoming a prostitute in order to prevent the most cruel death; but I had but little time to reflect, and that must be employed faithfully: to resign myself as a victim to the barbarity of the savages was a dreadful thought, and to gratify the wishes of one of those vile monsters, was as I conceived, although shocking in the extreme, not quite so bad as to endure their savage torture: of the two impending evils, I was therefore induced to choose the least. I gave the old sachem to understand that I would cheerfully comply, and was conducted immediately to his wigwam. Here I affected great regard for his person, but as I feigned great indisposition, begged of him to suffer me to remain in the situation I then was, until I should in some measure recover my health and spirits, to which, contrary to my expectations, he acceded.

I began now to contemplate seriously upon my disagreeable situation, when the tho't arose in my mind, that by killing this Indian, I might possibly effect my escape: the hut wherein I dwelt was entirely deserted by all other Indians than its owner, therefore my chance was good. I accordingly provided myself with an old scalping knife, which I found in the hut, and which I secreted beneath a quantity of moss which served me for a bed: the night succeeding, the old Indian having prostrated himself on a mattrass near by me, soon fell asleep. I thought this to be the time to effect what I had premeditated. Accordingly I took my knife, and creeping with as little noise as possible to where the savage lay, plunged it into his bosom! He attempted to rise, but at that instant snatching his tomahawk from his belt, [I] gave him a severe blow upon his head which I repeated until I was sure he was dead.

I now hastily collected all the victuals that the hut contained, and left the lonesome place. Nothing was to be heard but the wild beasts, which very much daunted me. I however ventured to proceed, and steered a north-easterly direction. Every shake of a leaf startled me, thinking my enemies were in pursuit. I travelled on through brooks, briars and woods, as fast as my feeble legs would carry me till morning, when I conceived it more prudent to climb some tree and conceal myself in its top than to travel.—While I was thus pondering, I heard a dreadful yelling at a distance, which appeared to be in the same course that I had been travelling. I was so frightened that I knew not what measure to take; at least I resolved to climb a tree near by, which I effected with considerable difficulty. I had not been long in this situation, before I descried twenty or thirty frightful looking Indians, who passed within a few rods of the tree which I had ascended—I recognised some of my old tormentors among them. I kept upon the tree during the day, and at night descended and continued my journey. I had not proceeded far, however, before my ears were again assailed by the dreadful howlings of the wild beasts, which continued till morning: several beasts approached me near enough to distinguish their horrid forms; and some wild-cats appeared also in sight, which, perhaps magnified by my fears, appeared of a most enormous size, nay, there was one of them that advanced nearer to me than any of the rest, but upon my setting up a loud cry, he retreated, after having sent forth a horrid yell, which was echoed back by all the other beasts of the forest.

To avoid these nocturnal enemies, I now resolved to travel only by day. After the fear and fatigue of the night, I could not think of setting forward before I had taken some repose, which I stood in great need of; and, at last, ventured to stretch myself down beneath the branches of a large oak; but the agitations of my mind prevented me from any perfect enjoyment of that blessing, and I slumbered rather than slept, till noon.

I then took a slight repast, which consumed the remainder of my provisions, and began my journey easterly, in hopes of reaching some christian settlement, or falling in with some friendly Indians, who would conduct me thereto. The meeting with the hostile savages was the worst I had apprehended, but now I began to think that a sudden death would be preferable to the state I was then in; passing from one misfortune to another, and exposed to the perishing with hunger, or supplying the wild beasts of the forest with meals to assuage theirs.

My weakness did not suffer me to go far this day, my journey being only about three hours slow pace. I took care to halt before my strength was quite exhausted; the terrors of the night preceding warned me to prepare a safe retreat for the night, from the voracious animals of the wilderness. Fear was the first principle of my actions, which must have been very powerful in me, when it was superior to the pressing calls of hunger. Having selected a tree of easy ascent, on which I had concluded to pass the night, I began to look about for food of any kind; but there was neither roots or vegetables fit for eating, to be found.

As soon as the night fell, I retired with a heavy heart, to what I conceived a safe retreat for the night. The wild beasts did not cause me any alarm until about midnight, when I might well imagine, from the horrid noise, that all the wild beasts throughout the desarts of this new world, had been gathered together, to terrify me with their howlings!

The welcome morn at length arrived, and, by driving the beasts back to their dens, relieved my alarms, which had for the night suspended the cruel sensations of hunger; but as soon as my fears began to abate, these began to operate to a severe degree. Thus was I apparently fated to sustain, alternately, the most bitter ills of life, hunger and fear!

I descended from the tree and prepared to pursue my uncertain journey, in hopes of being able to meet some sort of aliment in my way, to recruit my sinking spirits. I made trials of every species of plant, root or vegetable, I could pick up, but with little success—there was no nourishment in them. My hunger increased every moment, but the hope of being able to assuage it sustained me every step, and enabled me to travel on till afternoon, when I arrived at a piece of rising ground, where I expected to have a view of some fruitful spot, or hospitable village; but all was dreary as before—nothing was to be discovered but a thick and gloomy forest as far as the eye could reach! I was now almost resolved to give up the idea of pursuing any further my fruitless route, in which I could not possibly foresee any end to my wants and miseries, except what I might have received upon the spot where I then was, from death alone.

However, as the day began to draw to a close, I had yet sufficient strength left me to seek my usual place of safety for the night, during which I had little repose, as the continual howlings of the wolves and other beasts prevented it. The morning ensuing I once more set forward, but with as little prospect of meeting with any succour as on the days preceding; a thick wood that I met with in my course, I found it almost impractible to pass through, on account of the strong reeds and briars it was choked up with, which tore my feet and hands in a shocking manner; but fortunately for me, kind Providence seemed willing to reward me, at length, for the pains that I had taken to penetrate a forest so gloomy and uninviting. In the course of my travel this day, when hunger had driven me almost to the last extremity, I had the good fortune to discover a wild turkey's nest, containing thirteen eggs! With what transport of joy did I view this welcomed prize! which to me at that moment was far more acceptable than what would have been their bulk in gold! Such indeed was my hunger at the moment, that I had devoured nearly one half of them, before I gave myself time to reflect that in my then weak bodily state, having been for so great a length of time without food, I ought to have eaten sparingly. Having secured the remainder of the eggs, and feeling much recruited by the unexpected repast, I again set forward with the fond expectation of reaching some settlement, before I should be again compelled to endure the pains of hunger.

But, alas! how true is it, that when we, poor unhappy mortals, conceive ourselves almost within the reach of the object of our pursuit, are unexpectedly precipitated into a state of inconceivable sorrow and disappointment!—such indeed proved the result of my endeavours to reach some hospitable mansion, where I should not only be secure from the further annoyance of the savages, and wild beasts of the forest, but should probably obtain something to satisfy the cravings of nature. Toward the close of the day, I had descended a valley to seek a shelter for the night, when I was aroused by the sound of some shrill voices, which seemed to proceed from a distance—as I conceived myself now not far from some christian settlement, I concluded they were voices of some friendly persons whom kind Providence had selected to extricate me from the difficulties which attend me; whether they be friends or fores (thought I) I will meet them—for I began to conceive it impossible for them to render my situation worse than it was. To prevent being passed unnoticed, I hallooed as loud as the weak state of my lungs would permit me—I soon discovered that I had not only been heard by these people, by their answering, but I soon perceived by the rustling of the leaves that they were approaching the very spot where I stood! the bushes which surrounded me were so extremely thick as to conceal them from my view, until within a few yards of me, when to my inexpressible horror, I perceived them to be savages, and of the very nation from which I had so recently escaped! Thus were all my expectations of a speedy relief in a moment blasted.

They made me their prisoner, and as their number exceeded one hundred and had with them a number of human scalps, and three young men prisoners, I had no doubt but that they were on their return from an expedition against some of the white settlements. They bound me in the manner they had the other unfortunate captives, and weak and emaciated as I was, forced me to keep their pace for three days, when I was fortunately rescued from their merciless hands, by lieutenant Brown, and his brave little company of soldiers."

"War! War!! War!!! Women and Children Butchered!"

While narratives like that of Mary Smith (pp. 64-75) implied that Indians, generally, deserved whatever harsh treatment they received, the narrative of "the Capture and Providential Escape of Misses Frances and Almira Hall, Two Respectable Young Women . . ." (1832) was explicit in what it hoped to achieve. The tortures, scalpings, murders, and barbarities "too shocking to be presented to the public," conventions of the genre, were designed to recruit militia for service in the so-called Black Hawk War (1831-1832). Settlers on the Illinois frontier were incited "to revenge the cruelties perpetrated on the infant, the mother and the defenceless" by enlisting and thereby helping to bring about the immediate extermination of hostile Indians. The narrative also called for the capture and execution of Black Hawk, who himself is said to have ordered the execution of all white captives.

Although exaggerated, garbled, and distorted for purposes of propaganda, the narrative, unlike that of Mary Smith, was based on fact. On May 20, 1832, at the height of the Black Hawk War, Sylvia and Rachel Hall were captured by Sauk and Fox Indians near their family farm in La Salle County, Illinois. Except for themselves, the entire family was murdered. They were eventually ransomed through the intercession of Winnebago Indians. An account of their captivity, given in their own words, can be found in Elmer Baldwin's *History of La Salle County, Illinois* (1877), pp. 98-104.

Angered by a treaty ratified at St. Louis in 1804 in which his tribe ceded its rights to lands east of the Mississippi River, Black Hawk, a subordinate Sauk chief, tried to organize an Indian confederacy of the type envisioned by Pontiac and Tecumseh. He did so in the hope that it

---

SOURCE: *Narrative of the Capture and Providential Escape of Misses Frances and Almira Hall, Two Respectable Young Women (Sisters) of the Ages of 16 and 18—Who Were Taken Prisoners by the Savages, at a Frontier Settlement, Near Indian Creek, in May Last, When Fifteen of the Inhabitants Fell Victims to the Bloody Tomahawk and Scalping Knife; Among Whom Were the Parents of the Unfortunate Females . . .* (New York, 1832).

might block white expansion and nullify the treaty his tribe had signed. Only a few tribes, mainly Sauk and Fox, rallied to his call, and while it was one of the bloodiest Indian wars, it consisted mainly of sporadic raids on frontier farms and villages. (Abraham Lincoln served in the Black Hawk War as a captain of Illinois volunteers.) Frances and Almira Hall, as they are called in this narrative, were captured during one of these forays.

On August 2, 1832, Black Hawk surrendered and was imprisoned briefly. Thereafter, he remained a loyal supporter of the United States. He died in 1838.

The present year (1832) will be long remembered as a year of much human distress, and a peculiarly unfortunate one for the American nation—for while many of her most populous cities have been visited by that dreadful disease, the CHOLERA, and to which thousands have fallen victims, the merciless SAVAGES have been as industriously and fatally engaged in the work of human butchery on the frontiers.

In the month of May last, a considerable body of Indians (principally of the tribes of the Sacs and Foxes) having, as they professed, become dissatisfied with the encroachments of the whites, invaded and made a furious and unexpected attack upon the defenceless inhabitants of the frontier towns of Illinois. The first and most fatal was upon a small settlement on Indian Creek, running into Fox river, where were settled about twenty families, who, not being apprized of their approach, became an easy prey to their savage enemies—indeed so sudden and unexpected was the attack, that they were unalarmed until the savages with their tomahawks in hand, had entered their houses, and began the perpetration of the most inhuman barbarities! No language can express the cruelties that were committed; in less than half an hour more than one half of the inhabitants were inhumanly butchered—they horribly mutilated both young and old, male and female, without distinction of age or sex! among the few whose lives were spared, and of whom they made prisoners, were two highly respectable young women (sisters) of the ages of 16 and 18.

As soon as the melancholy tidings of the horrid massacre were made known to the white inhabitants of the neighboring settlements, a company of volunteers of about 270 in number, were hastily collected and sent in pursuit of the Savages, whom they overtook near Sycamore Creek, and resolutely attacked, but were unfortunately repulsed by a force far superior to their own, and were compelled to retreat with the loss of 50 of their number—many of the Indians were killed, but as they carried off their dead, the exact number could not be ascertained; one only was found on the ground the succeeding day; he had received a mortal wound, and in the agonies of death, had tomahawked one of the whites and cut his head half off, dying in the very act; his last convulsive struggle being an embrace of his enemy even in death! The bodies of the slain whites were cut and mangled in the most cruel manner that savage barbarity could devise; their hearts taken out and their heads cut off!

Immediately on the receipt of the melancholy news of the defeat of the volunteers, Governor Reynolds issued his Proclamation, and a very formidable force (comprised of about 1400 men) were speedily raised, and under command of the Governor and Gen. Atkinson, marched forthwith in pursuit of the murderous foe, but were unable to overtake them, as it appears by the reports of the captives, who have since been ransomed, that after their engagement with the volunteers (the better to evade the pursuit of the whites) they separated into small parties, and fled in different directions. The two unfortunate females, whom they retained as prisoners, and whose unfortunate parents were among those who were inhumanly butchered at Indian Creek, were providentially (by the aid of the Winebagoes) rescued from the hands of the savage monsters, after having been ten days in their power; in which time they were compelled to travel many miles, either on horseback or on foot, through almost impenetrable forests, and subjected to great privations and hardships, and in the expectation at every step of having their heads severed from their bodies, by the bloody tomahawk. . . .

The report of the unfortunate young women (Misses Frances and Almira Hall) communicated to their friends and relatives, on their return from captivity, although treated with less severity, cannot fail to be read with much interest—they state, that after being compelled to witness, not only the savage butchery of their beloved parents, but to hear the heart-piercing screeches and dying groans of their expiring friends and neighbors, and the hideous yells of the furious assaulting savages, they were seized and mounted upon horses, to which they were secured by ropes, when the savages with an exulting shout, took up their line of march in Indian file, bending their course west; the horses on which the females were mounted, being each led by one of their number, while two more walked on each side with their blood-stained scalping knives and tomahawks, to support and to guard them—they thus travelled for many hours, with as much speed as possible, through a dark and almost impenetrable wood; when reaching a still more dark and gloomy swamp, they came to a halt. A division of the plunder which they had brought from the ill-fated settlement, and with which their stolen horses (nine in number) were loaded, here took place, each savage stowing away in his pack his proportionable share as he received it; but on nothing did they seem to set so great a value, or view with so much satisfaction, as the bleeding scalps which they had, ere life had become extinct, torn from the mangled heads of the expiring victims! the feelings of the unhappy prisoners at this moment, can be better judged than described, when

"Two Young Ladies Taken Prisoner by the Savages, May, 1832," frontispiece to the *Narrative of . . . Misses Frances and Almira Hall. Courtesy of the Edward E. Ayer Collection, the Newberry Library.*

they could not be insensible that among these scalps, these shocking proofs of savage Cannibalism, were those of their beloved parents! but, their moans and bitter lamentations had no effect in moving or diverting for a moment, the savages from the business in which they had engaged, until it was completed; when, with as little delay as possible, and without giving themselves time to partake of any refreshment, (as the prisoners could perceive) they again set forward, and travelled with precipitancy until sunset, when they again halted, and prepared a temporary lodging for the night—the poor unfortunate females, whose feelings as may be supposed, could be no other than such as bordered on distraction, and who had not ceased for a moment to weep most bitterly during the whole day, could not but believe that they were here destined to become the victims of savage outrage and abuse; and that their sufferings would soon terminate, as they would not (as they imagined) be permitted to live to see the light of another day! such were their impressions, and such their dreadful forebodings—human imagination can hardly picture to itself a more deplorable situation; but, in their conjectures, they happily found themselves mistaken, as on the approach of night, instead of being made the subjects of brutal outrage, as they had fearfully apprehended, a place separate from that occupied by the main body of the savages, was allotted them; where blankets were spread for them to lodge upon, guarded only by two aged squaws, who slept on each side of them. With minds agitated with the most fearful apprehensions, as regarded their personal safety, and as solemnly impressed with the recollection of the awful scene which they had witnessed the morning previous, in the tragical death of their parents, they spent, as might be expected, a sleepless night; although the savages exhibited no disposition to harm or disturb them—early the morning ensuing, food was offered them, but in consequence of the disturbed state of their minds and almost constant weeping, they had become too weak and indisposed to partake of it, although nearly twenty hours had passed without their having received any sustenance.

The second day they passed much as the first, the Indians travelling with the same speed as on the former one; but nearly at its close, the two unfortunate females had become, through great fatigue and long fasting, too weak to support themselves longer on their horses, and were consequently dismounted and compelled to travel many miles on foot; and not until it was perceived by the savages that they were about to sink under the weight of their miseries, did they consent to come to a halt, and prepare quarters for a second night's lodging—a fire was kindled and some venison broth made, of which the unhappy prisoners were compelled by hunger to partake, and were then permitted to retire and spend the night as they had the preceding one, (as regarded any insult being offered them;) and being unable longer to resist the calls of nature, they the morning ensuing felt much relieved by the undisturbed repose which they had been permitted to enjoy.

During the long travel, or rather flight of the Indians the two preceding days, although they had in two or three instances met with small squads of armed savages, bound as was supposed to commit further depredations on the defenceless inhabitants of the frontier settlements, yet they had not until this the third day of their captivity, met with or beheld the face of any white inhabitant; when, at about noon, a Kentuckian hunter unfortunately fell into their hands; he was immediately seized and pinioned; and after nearly half an hour's consultation among those who appeared to be chiefs, devising, as the prisoner concluded, the best plan to dispose of him, they again put forward, and a few hours before sunset, arrived at one of their Indian settlements, where, in consequence of their enfeebled and emaciated state, it was concluded that the two female captives should remain until recruited; and it was here that it was first communicated to them why their lives had been spared, and why they had been protected from insult, to wit: for the reason that they were to become the adopted wives of the two young chiefs by whom they were first seized! If there was any thing calculated to add more horror to their feelings, it was this, which was indeed calculated to produce a greater shock than the intelligence that they were doomed to become the victims of the most savage torture! Yet however great their afflictions, it was evident that they were supported and protected by that Supreme Being, who has power alone to soften the savage heart—"to break the chains of bondage, and bid the captive go free,"—for, although now completely in the power of the savages, and by every one acknowledged the rightful property of two of their young and distinguished chiefs, yet for the seven days that they passed with them, they received none other but kind and civil treatment—the two young chiefs, by whom it was intended that they should be espoused, manifesting that regard for, and protecting them with as much interest, and apparent good feeling, as if they had been actually their lawfully wedded companions!

On the morning of the 10th day from that of their capture, about fifty of the Winebagoes, (of a neighboring tribe so called) who had been dispatched by the friends of the two young women, in quest of them, with means to ransom them if found alive, arrived—although the prisoners could not but feel overjoyed at this sudden and unexpected prospect of a deliverance, and to hail the tawny messengers as beings commissioned by Heaven, to rescue them from their perilous situation, yet they could not but discover, that on the minds of the two whose companions it was intended they should be, it had quite a different effect; and more particularly with one, who for some time manifested an unwillingness to receive any thing that could be named, in exchange for his highly prized captive! the ransom was however finally effected by adding ten horses more to the number already offered. On parting with her, he insisted upon exercising the right of cutting from her head a lock of her hair, not as a relic which he was desirous to retain in remembrance of one, for whom he felt any uncommon degree of friendship and affection, but to be retained and interwoven into his belt, as an invaluable trophy of his warlike exploits! such indeed is the Indian character—such their love of fame! The price paid in consideration of the ransom of the two female captives, was forty horses, together with a specified quantity of wampum and trinkets—the bargain closed, the prisoners were taken under the protection of the Winebagoes, and conveyed in safety to Galena (Illinois) and although they appear not insensible of the gratitude they owe to God, for their wonderful preservation and final deliverance from the hands of a merciless enemy, yet it is to be expected that they will long remember in sorrow, that fatal day, and the melancholly event, which not only deprived them of their liberty, but of their beloved parents, forever. . . .

Since the commencement of hostilities by the disaffected Indians, in May last, their depredations and shocking barbarities exercised upon the defenceless inhabitants of the frontiers, are some of them of a nature too shocking to be presented to the public—it is sufficient to observe, that the scalping knife and tomahawk, were in some cases the mildest instruments of death! One, of many remarkable instances of whole families having been inhumanly murdered, by the merciless barbarians (of which we have been credibly informed) is that of the truly unfortunate family of Capt. Joseph Naper, near Fort Chicago, comprized of himself, wife, wife's sister, and four children!—when the alarm became general, Naper with many others fled with his family to the fort; but after remaining there a short time, being a bold and daring man, and doubting the hostile views of the savages, he imprudently returned with his family to his log cabin; but, a fatal remove it proved to him, for two days after, every member of his family with himself, were found murdered, and their bodies mangled in the most brutal manner—however shocking the spectacle, the scene of human slaughter afforded a proof that the ill-fated Naper, although single handed, had bravely defended himself and friends—nine of the Indians were found dead near his house, who unquestionably fell before his intrepid arm!

Indian Depredations.

The continual fears and apprehensions of the defenceless inhabitants of the west, since the savage warfare commenced, have been great in the extreme; while some have been driven from their homes, in the most destitute condition, others have retired to and fortified themselves in block-houses, with the determination to defend themselves therein so long as a single man remained alive—in two or three instances these have been attacked, and nobly defended, and in which defence the women took a distinguished part.

A very considerable body of the troops of the United States, (united with more than two thousand of the militia of Kentucky, Illinois, &c.) under command of the brave Gen. Atkinson, have done and are still continuing to do all in their power to check the savage foe, in his murderous career, and prevent the further effusion of innocent blood, but their crafty and distinguished chief, Black Hawk, by cunningly dividing his men into small bodies, with advice to scout in different directions and to act independently of each other, has thereby avoided a general engagement with the whites—with some of these detached parties of the enemy, the troops have had several severe engagements, and in most instances much to the disadvantage of the savages.

Since the commencement of hostilities by the Sacs and Foxes, and in the many depredations committed upon the defenceless inhabitants of the frontier settlements, the lives of but few, who have been so unfortunate as to fall into their hands, have been spared. Their tomahawks have, literally, been made drunk with innocent blood! the virgin's shriek, the mother's wail, and infant's trembling cry, has proved music in their ears! Mothers while entreating for the lives of their poor children, have themselves fallen victims to the bloody tomahawk! no language can express the cruelties which have been committed—and the distressing scene is not unfrequently presented, of whole families lying murdered and scalped, presenting a spectacle too horrid for description. These shocking barbarities have called up the spirit of more than two thousand of the brave and patriotic citizens of Kentucky and Illinois, who have volunteered their services, and have marched against the Savages, determined to revenge the cruelties perpetrated on the infant, the mother and the defenceless. As soon as the horrid massacre of the inhabitants of the white settlement was made known at St. Louis, (Kentucky) the following appeal was published in the form of a hand bill, and generally and expeditiously circulated throughout the state.

"WAR! WAR!! WAR!!!

WOMEN AND CHILDREN BUTCHERED!

Two young ladies taken by the Savages.

Authentic information has been received from the Illinois frontiers, informing of the murder of fifteen defenceless inhabitants of the frontier, most inhumanly butchered, and the women in a most shocking manner mangled and exposed. Two highly respectable young women of 16 and 18 years of age, are in the hands of the Indians, and if not already murdered, are perhaps reserved for a more cruel and savage fate. Whole families are driven from their homes, actually starving, and without a day's provision before them.

Shall we, fellow citizens, quietly look upon these transactions? Can we look upon them without feelings of revenge—without knowing that our assistance is necessary? How soon may it be before our frontiers are in the same way invaded, and our own brothers and sisters scalped? Shall we allow these brutes to dull their tomahawks on the bones of our friends, in order that they may only re-sharpen them for our relations? Allow these murderers further success, and they will be joined by bands from every quarter, and their "border warfare" will be terrible. Rise, fellow citizens of this city and county—let us no longer delay—talk no more, but act. To arms—unloose the spirit of revenge—each one raise a horse, gun, and a few days rations, and put himself under the guidance of some respectable members of the community, (one of experience, and well acquainted with the Indian character, and their mode of warfare) resolved to revenge or die in defence of his relatives and friends. Let us convince our brethren of our neighbor State, that we are willing and able to assist them—and in assisting them to protect ourselves. Let us, as has been already suggested, meet at 5 o'clock this afternoon—form ourselves on the spot, in companies of fifty men each—and the *St. Louis Corps* will march to the seat of war." . . .

A Propaganda Broadside During the Second Seminole War

The "Captivity and Sufferings of Mrs. Mason" was circulated during the Second Seminole War (1835-1841) to inflame public opinon by drawing attention to Indian atrocities. Under the terms of the Treaty of Payne's Landing (1832), the chiefs of the Florida Seminoles were tricked into agreeing to relocate their tribe west of the Mississippi River in return for $15,400, to be divided among the tribe, and a blanket and shirt for each Indian. Many of the Seminoles refused to comply with the treaty, and in 1835 a war began which eventually cost fifteen thousand American lives and more than twenty million dollars. The length of the war, the military success of the Seminoles, and the treachery of American army officers embarrassed the American government, which was under attack by a substantial portion of the public who sympathized with the Indians. Propaganda like this broadside helped justify the war and unify public opinion. Both Mrs. Mason and the events described are probably fictitious.

Broadsides proved an effective means of propaganda because they could be distributed rapidly and widely. The term derives from the way they were produced. Anything printed on one side of a sheet of paper, large or small, is considered a broadside. They were sold by peddlers who carried them in bundles from town to town. Often, they were posted in public places. Their subject matter ranged from official proclamations to songs and ballads, playbills, advertisements for cure-alls, and sensational news items such as murders, shipwrecks, natural catastrophes, and Indian massacres and captivities.

SOURCE: "Captivity and Sufferings of Mrs. Mason, with an Account of the Massacre of Her Youngest Child" (c. 1836).

The format of the Mason broadside reveals a great deal about the medium. Printed on cheap paper and intended for an immediate purpose, the broadside survives only by chance. The illustrations drew immediate attention to the subject matter. The central detail of the main illustration, an Indian with upraised tomahawk, appears on at least two other broadsides about Indian captivity: "Narrative of the Tragical Death of Mrs. Darius Barber. . ." (c. 1816) and "War! War!! War!!! Women and Children Butchered. . ." (c. 1832), a broadside which has not survived in the original but is known from a copy reproduced in an 1833 edition of the *Narrative of the Capture . . . of Misses Frances and Almira Hall,* where it accentuates explicit propaganda (see pp. 76-84). Printers often used the same illustration to enhance entirely different broadsides. The poem further capitalizes on the reader's sensibilities by duplicating in verse the information already presented in other forms.

At the Great Council of the principal Chiefs and Warriors of the different Indian tribes bordering on the Southern frontiers and Florida, assembled in the spring of 1836, the solemn vows then entered into have been kept. The Indians then agreed that so long as the Sun should continue to rise or the grass to grow, they would never leave the land of their farthers. And so inveterate and deadly was their hatred towards the white people that many of them pledged themselves neither to eat or sleep until they had taken the scalp of a pale face.

Under these feelings commenced the *Florida Indian War*. The distress and cruelty which has been inflicted and the hardships endured are beyond description, and although an incessant war has been waged to an enormous expense and the lives of many a brave soldier, the Indians still remain unsubdued, and almost every mail brings the news of some horrid massacre. The following account given by Mrs. Mason of her captivity and suffering, are from her own pen.

(*This is taken from a Letter never befor published.*)

Captivity and Sufferings

Of Mrs. MASON, with an account of the Massacre of her youngest Child.

ST. AUGUSTINE July 3d.

MY DEAR AUNT—The surprise you must feel on receiving a line from one, who you doubtless believed ere this had gone to a happier world, I can but faintly conceive, but it cannot exceed my own when I review the hair-breadth escapes which I have passed since we were separated, that I am still spared, and have once more regained my liberty.

The hope of saving the life of my little Ellen was an exposure, which none but a mother would attempt. O! how fervently have I prayed that I might share her fate. On my return to the dwelling which was already in flames, I found my child still a sleep, unconcious of her exposed situation. I immediately caught her in my arms and flew for safety. But O! what were my feelings when I saw that we should be taken. An Indian who lay in ambush but a short distance from the house suddenly rose, and with his uplifted tomahawk approached us. His first blow was inflicted on my dear child—we both fell, she a mangled corpse, while I fainted. On coming to myself again I saw the very Indian lying cold and dead within a few paces—he was shot by some unknown hand. I now began to think of fleeing and make my escape, and immediately left in hopes of reaching Capt. Clark's plantation. But I had gone but a short distance when I fell in with a number of Squaws who immediately fell upon me in the most desperate manner, beating me and depriving me of my clothing. The great severity and exposure which I now had to endure must have soon terminated in death, but the second day after I made my escape from them, although in a most destitute situation. Thus exposed, I wandered for five days, when on the morning of the sixth day I reached the dwelling of Mr. Martin, where every thing was done for my comfort. Here I stayed but three days as they were fearful of an attack from the Indians, and his dwelling as I afterwards learned was burned and the whole family, consisting of a wife and 5 children inhumanly murdered. To attemp a full account of the various scenes through which I have passed I do not feel myself competent, neither have I space on this sheet. Trusting I shall see you in a few days I close. Yours, M. M.

When midnight calm is on the world,
  A wild strange whoop will rise,
As if the heavens and earth was crushed,
  And rending were the skies.
Thy blood will curdle at the sound,
  Of those death denoting cries.

A thousand dark and dusky forms,
  By stealthy steps, and slow,
Are creeping near that doomed place
  And soon wild shrieks of woe—
And battle shouts, will soon be heard,
  And fierce and chopping blow.

Hark! a thousand yells are ringing,
  Louder than the trump of heaven,
The war-hoop peals right wildly out,
  By thousand voices given—
The red man nears the villager,
  From his burning household driven.

The prayer of woman availeth not,
  They plead to hearts of stone,
The babe is wrenched from its mothers breast,
  She hears its dying groan—
These savage hearts are all unmoved,
  By mothers wail, or beauty's tone.

The eastern sky was light and red—
  The sun rides proud on high,
Its beams fall on a ruined home,
  Where dead and mangled lie—
And smoking embers tell the tale,
  Of ruthless savage butchery.

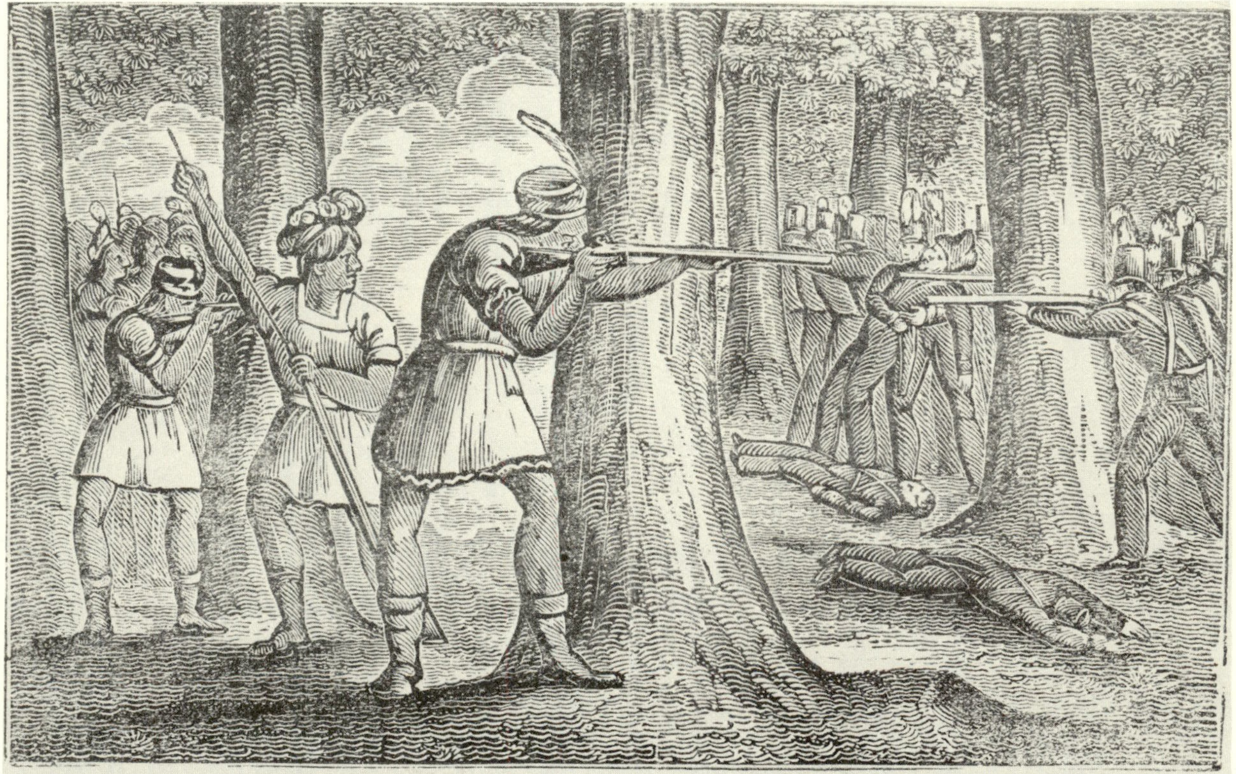

A Battle with the Indians.

Courtesy of the Edward E. Ayer Collection, the Newberry Library.

Attack on a Wagon Train

Fanny Kelly's *Narrative of My Captivity Among the Sioux . . .* (1871) shows what the Indian captivity became during its latter stages when its setting moved west with the receding frontier. Narratives like this were read as exciting adventure stories, factual counterparts of the dime novels (see pp. 189-199) with which they vied for a market. Western tribes sometimes treated their captives with such brutality that a narrative unadorned by exaggeration was sensational enough to meet the demands of both entertainment and anti-Indian propaganda. These narratives were also intended to counter the sentimentalized image of the Indian made popular by novels such as Helen Hunt Jackson's *Ramona* (1884), to the great exasperation of land speculators and settlers following the westward course of empire.

Mrs. Kelly and her daughter, Mary, were taken captive by Oglala Sioux on July 12, 1864, some seventy-five miles northwest of Fort Laramie, Wyoming, during an attack on their wagon train bound from Kansas to Idaho. The Oglala Sioux were among the fiercest of the Sioux tribes and are best known for their defeat of General Custer at Little Big Horn in 1876. This passage from Mrs. Kelly's narrative describes the attack, a situation made familiar by numberless Hollywood and television westerns. Another account of the same raid appears in *The Capture and Escape . . .* (1870) by Sarah Larimer, taken captive at the same time as Mrs. Kelly. "The great emigrant road" described by Mrs. Kelly is the Oregon Trail, which began at Independence, Missouri, and ended at Astoria on the Columbia River and which gave Francis Parkman the title for his classic narrative of overland adventure. Although her daughter was killed while trying to escape, Mrs. Kelly survived Indian captivity. Five months to the day after her capture, she was ransomed by soldiers at Fort Sully in the Dakota Territory and was later reunited with her husband. Congress voted her an appropriation of five thousand dollars for information she had supplied about the Indians.

SOURCE: Fanny Kelly, *Narrative of My Captivity Among the Sioux Indians . . .* (Hartford, Conn., 1871).

In contrast to fictional narratives (see Smith, pp. 64-75) which capitalized on the pathos of a helpless woman held by merciless savages, accounts by actual captives testify to the courage and common sense of women like Fanny Kelly.

CHAPTER II

THE ATTACK AND THE CAPTURE

A TRAIN of wagons were coursing their westward way, with visions of the future bright as our own. Sometimes a single team might be seen traveling alone.

Our party were among the many small squads emigrating to the land of promise.

The day on which our doomed family were scattered and killed was the 12th of July, a warm and oppressive day. The burning sun poured forth its hottest rays upon the great Black Hills and the vast plains of Montana, and the great emigrant road was strewed with men, women, and children, and flocks of cattle, representing towns of adventurers.

We looked anxiously forward to the approach of evening, with a sense of relief, after the excessive heat of the day.

Our journey had been pleasant, but toilsome, for we had been long weeks on the road.

Slowly our wagons wound through the timber that skirted the Little Box Elder [tributary of the North Platte], and, crossing the stream, we ascended the opposite bank.

We had no thought of danger or timid misgivings on the subject of savages, for our fears had been all dispersed by constantly received assurances of their friendliness.

At the outposts and ranches, we heard nothing but ridicule of their pretensions to warfare, and at Fort Laramie, where information that should have been reliable was given us, we had renewed assurances of the safety of the road and friendliness of the Indians.

At Horseshoe Creek, which we had just left, and where there was a telegraph station, our inquiries had elicited similar assurances as to the quiet and peaceful state of the country through which we must pass.

Being thus persuaded that fears were groundless, we entertained none, and, as I have mentioned before, our small company preferred to travel alone on account of the greater progress made in that way.

The beauty of the sunset and the scenery around us filled our hearts with joy, and Mr. Wakefield's voice was heard in song for the last time, as he sang, "Ho! for Idaho." Little Mary's low, sweet voice, too, joined in the chorus. She was so happy in her childish glee on that day, as she always was. She was the star and joy of our whole party.

We wended our way peacefully and cheerfully on, without a thought of the danger that was lying like a tiger in ambush in our path.

Without a sound of preparation or a word of warning, the bluffs before us were covered with a party of about two hundred and fifty Indians, painted and equipped for war, who uttered the wild war-whoop and fired a signal volley of guns and revolvers into the air.

This terrible and unexpected apparition came upon us with such startling swiftness that we had not time to think before the main body halted and sent out a part of their force, which circled us round at regular intervals, but some distance from our wagons. Recovering from the shock, our men instantly resolved on defense, and corralled the wagons. My husband was looked upon as leader, as he was principal owner of the train. Without regard to the insignificance of our numbers, Mr. Kelly was ready to stand his ground; but, with all the power I could command, I entreated him to forbear and only attempt conciliation. "If you fire one shot," I said, "I feel sure you will seal our fate, as they seem to outnumber us ten to one, and will at once massacre all of us."

Love for the trembling little girl at my side, my husband, and friends, made me strong to protest against any thing that would lessen our chance for escape with our lives. Poor little Mary! from the first she had entertained an ungovernable dread of the Indians, a repugnance that could not be overcome, although in our intercourse with friendly savages, I had endeavored to show how unfounded it was, and persuade her that they were civil and harmless, but all in vain. Mr. Kelly bought her beads and many little presents from them which she much admired, but she would always add, "They look so cross at me and they have knives and tomahawks, and I fear they will kill me." Could it be that her tender young mind had some presentiment or warning of her horrid fate?

My husband advanced to meet the chief and demand his intentions.

The savage leader immediately came toward him, riding forward and uttering the words, "How! how!" which are understood to mean a friendly salutation.

His name was Ottawa, and he was a war chief of the Ogalalla band of the Sioux nation. He struck himself on his breast, saying, "Good Indian, me," and pointing to those around him, he continued, "Heap good Indian, hunt buffalo and deer." He assured us of his utmost friendship for the white people; then he shook hands, and his band followed his example, crowding around our wagons, shaking us all by the hand over and over again, until our arms ached, and grinning and nodding with every demonstration of good will.

Our only policy seemed to be temporizing, in hope of assistance approaching; and, to gain time, we allowed them unopposed to do whatever they fancied. First, they said they would like to change one of their horses for the one Mr. Kelly was riding, a favorite race horse. Very much against his will, he acceded to their request, and gave up to them the noble animal to which he was fondly attached.

My husband came to me with words of cheer and hope, but oh! what a marked look of despair was upon his face, such as I had never seen before.

The Indians asked for flour, and we gave them what they wanted of provisions. The flour they emptied upon the ground, saving only the sack. They talked to us partly by signs and partly in broken English, with which some of them were quite familiar, and as we were anxious to suit ourselves to their whims and preserve a friendly intercourse as long as possible, we allowed them to take whatever they desired, and offered them many presents besides. It was, as I have said before, extremely warm weather, but they remarked that the cold made it necessary for them to look for clothing, and begged for some from our stock, which was granted without the slightest offered objection on our part. I, in a careless-like manner, said they must give me some moccasins for some articles of clothing that I had just handed them, and very pleasantly a young Indian gave me a nice pair, richly embroidered with different colored beads.

Our anxiety to conciliate them increased every moment, for the hope of help arriving from some quarter grew stronger as they dallied, and, alas! it was our only one.

They grew bolder and more insolent in their advances. One of them laid hold of my husband's gun, but, being repulsed, desisted.

The chief at last intimated that he desired us to proceed on our way, promising that we should not be molested. We obeyed, without trusting them, and soon the train was again in motion, the Indians insisting on driving our herd, and growing ominously familiar. Soon my husband called a halt. He saw that we were approaching a rocky glen, in whose gloomy depths he anticipated a murderous attack, and from which escape would be utterly impossible. Our enemies urged us still forward, but we resolutely refused to stir, when they requested that we should prepare supper, which they said they would share with us, and then go to the hills to sleep. The men of our party concluded it best to give them a feast. Mr. Kelly gave orders to our two colored servants to prepare at once to make a feast for the Indians.

Andy said, "I think, if I knows any thing about it, they's had their supper;" as they had been eating sugar crackers from our wagons for an hour or more.

The two colored men had been slaves among the Cherokees, and knew the Indian character by experience. Their fear and horror of them was unbounded, and their terror seemed pitiable to us, as they had worked for us a long time, and were most faithful, trustworthy servants.

Each man was busy preparing the supper; Mr. Larimer and Frank were making the fire; Mr. Wakefield was getting provisions out of the wagon;

Mr. Taylor was attending to his team; Mr. Kelly and Andy were out some distance gathering wood; Mr. Sharp was distributing sugar among the Indians; supper, that they asked for, was in rapid progress of preparation, when suddenly our terrible enemies threw off their masks and displayed their truly demoniac natures. There was a simultaneous discharge of arms, and when the cloud of smoke cleared away, I could see the retreating form of Mr. Larimer and the slow motion of poor Mr. Wakefield, for he was mortally wounded.

Mr. Kelly and Andy made a miraculous escape with their lives. Mr. Sharp was killed within a few feet of me. Mr. Taylor—I never can forget his face as I saw him shot through the forehead with a rifle ball. He looked at me as he fell backward to the ground a corpse. I was the last object that met his dying gaze. Our poor faithful Frank fell at my feet pierced by many arrows. I recall the scene with a sickening horror. I could not see my husband anywhere, and did not know his fate, but feared and trembled. With a glance at my surroundings, my senses seemed gone for a time, but I could only live and endure.

I had but little time for thought, for the Indians quickly sprang into our wagons, tearing off covers, breaking, crushing, and smashing all hinderances to plunder, breaking open locks, trunks, and boxes, and distributing or destroying our goods with great rapidity, using their tomahawks to pry open boxes, which they split up in savage recklessness.

Oh, what horrible sights met my view! Pen is powerless to portray the scenes occurring around me. They filled the air with the fearful war-whoops and hideous shouts. I endeavored to keep my fears quiet as possible, knowing that an indiscreet act on my part might result in jeopardizing our lives, though I felt certain that we two helpless women would share death by their hands; but with as much of an air of indifference as I could command, I kept still, hoping to prolong our lives, even if but a few moments. I was not allowed this quiet but a moment, when two of the most savage-looking of the party rushed up into my wagon, with tomahawks drawn in their right hands, and with their left seized me by both hands and pulled me violently to the ground, injuring my limbs very severely, almost breaking them, from the effects of which I afterward suffered a great deal. I turned to my little Mary, who, with outstretched hands, was standing in the wagon, took her in my arms and helped her to the ground. I then turned to the chief, put my hand upon his arm, and implored his protection for my fellow-prisoner and our children. At first he gave me no hope, but seemed utterly indifferent to my prayers. Partly in words and partly by signs, he ordered me to remain quiet, placing his hand upon his revolver, that hung in a belt at his side, as an argument to enforce obedience.

A short distance in the rear of our train a wagon was in sight. The chief immediately dispatched a detachment of his band to capture or to cut it off

"The Attack and Capture of Our Train, July 12, 1864." From Fanny Kelly's *Narrative of My Captivity Among the Sioux Indians*. *Courtesy of the Everett D. Graff Collection, the Newberry Library.*

from us, and I saw them ride furiously off in pursuit of the small party, which consisted only of one family and a man who rode in advance of the single wagon. The horseman was almost instantly surrounded and killed by a volley of arrows. The husband of the family quickly turned his team around and started them at full speed, gave the whip and lines to his wife, who held close in her arms her youngest child. He then went to the back end of his wagon and threw out boxes, trunks, every thing that he possessed. His wife meantime gave all her mind and strength to urging the horses forward on their flight from death. The Indians had by this time come very near, so that they riddled the wagon-cover with bullets and arrows, one passing through the sleeve of the child's dress in its mother's arms, but doing it no personal injury.

The terrified man kept the Indians at bay with his revolver, and finally they left him and rode furiously back to the scene of the murder of our train.

An Indian Idyll

John Tanner provides a far different view of Indians and their life from that described in narratives like those of Mary Smith (pp. 64-75), Frances and Almira Hall (pp. 76-84), and Mrs. Mason (pp. 85-89). In 1789, at the age of nine, Tanner was kidnapped by a band of Shawnee Indians, who sold him to the Ojibwas, by whom he was adopted. His narrative contains idyllic descriptions of hunting in the Minnesota and Canadian wilderness. He speaks warmly of his Indian "mother" who favored him above her own children, describes the justice and humanity Indians showed toward one another, condemns the unjust treatment Indians received from white traders and land speculators, and laments the destruction of Indian culture.

Like Tanner, many captives preferred life among the Indians to white society. Cadwallader Colden was puzzled and distressed by captives at the close of King William's War who refused to leave the Indian families that had adopted them. He wrote in his *History of the Five Indian Nations of Canada . . .* (1747): "No Arguments, no Intreaties, nor Tears of their Friends and Relations, could persuade many of them to leave their new *Indian* Friends and Acquaintance[s]; several of them that were by the Caressings of their Relations persuaded to come Home, in a little Time grew tired of our Manner of living, and run away again to the *Indians,* and ended their Days with them." Crèvecoeur's spokesman flatly states in his *Letters from an American Farmer . . .* (1782) that "thousands of Europeans are Indians," and at the end of the book he is himself residing with a western tribe. Narratives like Tanner's are rare because Indianized captives were usually illiterate and seldom cared to communicate with white audiences. Tanner himself required the help of an editor. Furthermore, Americans sometimes responded uneasily to affirmative accounts of the culture they were destroying.

SOURCE: *A Narrative of the Captivity and Adventures of John Tanner, U.S. (Interpreter at the Sault de Ste. Marie,) During Thirty Years Residence Among the Indians in the Interior of North America. Prepared for the Press by Edwin James, M.D. . . .* (New York, 1830).

Tanner paid a high price for the transculturation he enjoyed. As the Indian culture he admired was obliterated by the rapid expansion of white civilization, Tanner, who had lived as an Indian for more than thirty years, was forced to resume his white identity. For several years he worked as an interpreter for the United States government, but he was so thoroughly tribalized that other whites refused to accept him. Although translated into French and German, Tanner's narrative was not reprinted in America during his lifetime, and his subsequent career is tantalizing and obscure. In the early 1840s he married a white woman from Detroit who ran away in consequence of his alleged brutality. Thereafter, he lived alone, misanthropic and savage, feared by everyone, and perhaps a little mad. In 1846 Tanner reportedly burned his cabin at Sault Ste. Marie, murdered James Schoolcraft (brother of the Indian ethnologist Henry Rowe Schoolcraft), and fled, never to be heard from again.

. . . After a few days, we started to go up the Red River, and in two days came to the mouth of the Assinneboin, where we found great numbers of Ojibbeways and Ottawwaws encamped. As soon as we arrived, the chiefs met, to take our case into consideration, and to agree on some method of providing for us. "These, our relations," said one of the chiefs, "have come to us from a distant country. These two little boys are not able to provide for them, and we must not suffer them to be in want among us." Then one man after another offered to hunt for us; and they agreed, also, since we had started to come for the purpose of hunting beaver, and as our hunters had died on the way, that each should give us some part of what they should kill. We then all started together to go up the Assinneboin river, and the first night we camped among the buffaloe. In the morning, I was allowed to go out with some Indians who went to hunt buffaloes. We killed one of four bulls which we found. We continued to ascend the Assinneboin about ten days, killing many bears as we travelled along. The Assinneboin is broad, shallow, and crooked, and the water, like that of the Red River, is turbid; but the bottom is sandy, while that of Red River is commonly muddy. The place to which we went on the Assinneboin is seventy miles distant by land from the mouth; but the distance by water is greater. The banks of the river, on both sides, are covered with poplar and white oak, and some other trees, which grow to considerable size. The prairies, however, are not far distant, and sometimes come into the immediate bank of the river. We stopped at a place called Prairie Portage, where the Indians directed the trader who was with them, to build his house, and remain during the winter. We left all our canoes, and went up into the country to hunt for beaver, among the small streams. The Indians gave Wa-me-gon-a-biew and myself a little creek, where were plenty of beaver, and on which they said none but ourselves should hunt. My mother gave me three traps, and instructed me how to set them by the aid of a string tied around the spring, as I was not yet able to set them with my hands, as the Indians did. I set my three traps, and on the following morning found beavers in two of them. Being unable to take them out myself, I carried home the beavers and traps, one at a time, on my back, and had the old woman to assist me. She was, as usual, highly gratified and delighted at my success. She had always been kind to me, often taking my side, when the Indians would attempt to ridicule or annoy me. We remained in this place about three months, in which time we were as well provided for as any of the band; for if our own game was not sufficient, we were sure to be supplied by some of our friends, as long as any thing could be killed. The people that remained to spend the winter with us, were two lodges, our own making three; but we were at length joined by four lodges of Crees. These people are the relations of the Ojibbeways and Ottawwaws, but their language is somewhat different, so as not to be readily understood. Their country borders upon that of the Assinneboins, or Stone Roasters; and though they are not relations, nor natural allies, they are sometimes at peace, and are more or less intermixed with each other.

After we had remained about three months in this place, game began to be scarce, and we all suffered from hunger. The chief man of our band was called As-sin-ne-boi-nainse, (the little Assinneboin,) and he now proposed to us all to move, as the country where we were was exhausted. The day on which we were to commence our removal was fixed upon, but before it arrived our necessities became extreme. The evening before the day on which we intended to move, my mother talked much of all our misfortunes and losses, as well as of the urgent distress under which we were then labouring. At the usual hour I went to sleep, as did all the younger part of the family; but I was wakened again by the loud praying and singing of the old woman, who continued her devotions through great part of the night. Very early, on the following morning, she called us all to get up, and put on our moccasins, and be ready to move. She then called Wa-me-gon-a-biew to her, and said to him, in rather a low voice, "My son, last night I sung and prayed to the Great Spirit, and when I slept, there came to me one like a man, and said to me, 'Net-no-kwa, to-morrow you shall eat a bear. There is, at a distance from the path you are to travel to-morrow, and in such a direction, [which she described to him,] a small round meadow, with something like a path leading from it; in that path there is a bear.' Now, my son, I wish you to go to that place, without mentioning to any one what I have said, and you will certainly find the bear, as I have described to you." But the young man, who was not particularly dutiful, or apt to regard what his mother said, going out of the lodge, spoke sneeringly to the other Indians of the dream. "The old woman," said he, "tells me we are to eat a bear to-day; but I do not know who is to kill it." The old woman, hearing him, called him in, and reproved him; but she could not prevail upon him to go to hunt. The Indians, accordingly, all moved off towards the place where they were to encamp that night. The men went first by themselves, each carrying some article of baggage; and when they arrived where the camp was to be placed, they threw down their loads and went to hunt. Some of the boys, and I among them, who accompanied the men, remained with this baggage, until the women should come up. I had my gun with me, and I continued to think of the conversation I had heard between my mother and Wa-me-gon-a-biew, respecting her dream. At length, I resolved to go in search of the place she had spoken of, and without mentioning to any one my design, I loaded my gun as for a bear, and set off on our back track. I soon met a woman belonging to one of the brothers of Taw-ga-we-ninne, and of course my aunt. This woman had shown little friendship for us, considering us as a burthen upon her husband, who sometimes gave something for our support; she had also often ridiculed me. She asked me immediately what I was doing on the path, and whether I expected to kill Indians, that I came there with my gun. I made her no answer; and thinking I must be not far from the place where my mother had told Wa-me-gon-a-biew to leave the path, I turned off, continuing carefully to regard all the directions she had given. At length, I found what appeared at some former time to have been a pond. It was a small, round, open place in the woods, now grown up with grass and some small bushes. This I thought must be the meadow my mother had spoken of; and examining it around, I came to an open place in the bushes, where, it is probable, a small brook ran from the meadow; but the snow was now so deep that I could see nothing of it. My mother had mentioned, that when she saw the bear in her dream, she had, at the same time, seen a smoke rising from the ground. I was confident this was the place she had indicated, and I watched long, expecting to see the smoke; but wearied at length with waiting, I walked a few paces into the open place, resembling a path, when I unexpectedly fell up to my middle into the snow. I extricated myself without difficulty, and walked on; but remembering that I had heard the Indians speak of killing bears in their holes, it occurred to me that it might be a bear's hole into which I had fallen, and looking down into it, I saw the head of a bear lying close to the bottom of the hole. I placed the muzzle of my gun nearly between his eyes, and discharged it. As soon as the smoke cleared away, I took a piece of a stick and thrust it into the eyes and into the wound in the head of the bear, and being satisfied that he was dead, I endeavoured to lift him out of the hole; but being unable to do this, I returned home, following the track I had made in coming out. As I came near the camp, where the squaws had, by this time, set up the lodges, I met the same woman I had seen in going out, and she immediately began again to ridicule me. "Have you killed a bear, that you come back so soon, and walk so fast?" I thought to myself, "how does she know that I have killed a bear?" But I passed by her without saying any thing, and went into my mother's lodge. After a few minutes, the old woman, said, "My son, look in that kettle, and you will find a mouthful of beaver meat, which a man gave me since you left us in the morning. You must leave half of it for Wa-me-gon-a-biew, who has not yet returned from hunting, and has eaten nothing to-day." I accordingly ate the beaver meat, and when I had finished it, observing an opportunity when she stood by herself, I stepped up to her and whispered in her ear, "My mother, I have killed a bear." "What do you say, my son?" said she. "I have killed a bear." "Are you sure you have killed him?" "Yes." "Is he quite dead?" "Yes." She watched my face for a moment, and then caught me in her arms, hugging and kissing me with great earnestness, and for a long time. I then told her what my aunt had said to me, both going and returning, and this being told to her husband when he returned, he not only reproved her for it, but gave her a severe flogging. The bear was sent for, and, as being the first I had killed, was cooked all together, and the hunters of the whole band invited to feast with us, according to the custom of the Indians. The same day, one of the Crees killed a bear and a moose, and gave a large share of the meat to my mother. For some time we had plenty of game in our new residence. Here Wa-me-gon-a-biew killed his first buffaloe, on which occasion my mother gave another feast to all the band. Soon afterwards, the Crees left us to go to their own country. . . .

In the Assinneboin river, at one or two days above the Prairie Portage, is a place called Ke-new-kau-neshe way-boant, (where they throw down the gray eagle,) at which the Indians frequently stop. Here we saw, as we were passing, some little stakes in the ground, with pieces of birch bark attached to them, and on two of these the figure of a bear, and on the others, those of other animals. Net-no-kwa immediately recognized the totems of Pe-shau-ba, Waus-so, and their companions. These had been left, to inform us that Pe-shau-ba had been at this place, and as directions to enable us to find them. We therefore left the traders, and taking the course indicated by the marks which Pe-shau-ba had caused to be made, we found him and his party at the distance of two days from the river. They had returned from the abortive war expedition, to the trading house on Mouse River, finished the canoes which they had left incomplete, and descended along to Kenewkauneshe-wayboant, where, knowing there were good hunting grounds, they had determined on remaining. We found at their camp plenty of game; they had killed, also, a great number of beavers. About this place elks were numberous, and it was now the rutting season. I remember one day, Pe-shau-ba sent me with the two young women, to bring some meat from an elk he had killed at some distance. The women, finding that the elk was large and fat, determined on remaining to dry the meat before they carried it home. I took a load of meat, and started for home by myself. I had my gun with me, and perceiving there were plenty of elk, I loaded it, and concealing myself in a small thicket of bushes, began to imitate the call of the female elk; presently a large buck came bounding so directly towards the spot where I was, and with such violence, that becoming alarmed for my own safety, I dropped my load and fled; he seeing me, turned and ran in an opposite direction. Remembering that the Indians would ridicule me for such conduct, I determined to make another attempt, and not suffer any apprehension for my own safety to be the cause of another failure. So hiding myself again, in a somewhat more carefully chosen place, I repeated my call from time to time, till at length another buck came up, and him I killed. In this manner, a great part of the day had been consumed, and I now perceived it was time to hasten home with my load.

The old woman becoming uneasy at my long absence, sent Wa-me-gon-a-biew to look for me. He discovered me as I was coming out of a piece of woods into a large prairie. He had on a black capot, which, when he saw me, he turned over his head in such a manner as to make himself resemble a bear. At first I took it to be a common black bear, and sought a chance to shoot him; but it so happened that he was in such a situation as enabled him to see me, and I knew he would certainly have turned and fled from me had it been a black bear. As he continued to advance directly towards me, I concluded it must be a grizly bear, so I turned and began to run from him; the more swiftly I ran, the more closely he seemed to follow. Though much frightened, I remembered Pe-shau-ba's advice, never to fire upon one of these animals unless trees were near into which I could escape; also, in case of being pursued by one, never to fire until he came very close to me. Three times I turned, and raised my piece to fire, but thinking him still too far off, turned and run again. Fear must have blinded my eyes, or I should have seen that it was not a bear. At length, getting between him and the lodge, I ran with such speed as to outstrip him, when I heard a voice behind me, which I knew to be that of Wa-me-gon-a-biew. I looked in vain for the bear, and he soon convinced me that I owed all my terror to the disguise which he had effected, with the aid only of an old black coat. This affair being related to the old people when we came home, they reproved Wa-me-gon-a-biew; his mother telling him, that if I had shot him in that disguise, I should have done right, and according to the custom of the Indians she could have found no fault with me for so doing. We continued here hunting beaver, and killing great numbers, until the ice became too thick; we then went to the prairies in pursuit of buffaloes. When the snow began to have a crust upon it, the men said they must leave me with the women, as they were about to go to Clear Water Lake to make canoes, and to hunt beaver on their way down. But previous to their going, they said they would kill something for us to live on while they were gone. Waus-so, who was a great hunter, went out by himself, and killed one buffaloe; but in the night the weather became very cold and stormy, and the buffaloe came in to take shelter in the woods where we had our camp. Early in the morning, Net-no-kwa called us up, saying, there was a large herd close by the lodge. Pe-shau-ba and Waus-so, with Wa-me-gon-a-biew, Sa-ning-wub, and Sag-git-to crept out, and took stations so as nearly to surround the herd. Me they would not suffer to go out, and they laughed at me when they saw me putting my gun in readiness; but old Net-no-kwa, who was ever ready to befriend me, after they were gone, led me to a stand not far from the lodge, near which, her sagacity taught her, the herd would probably run. The Indians fired, but all failed to kill; the herd came past my stand, and I had the good fortune to kill a large cow, which was my first, much to the satisfaction of my mother. Shortly afterwards, having killed a considerable number of buffaloes, the Indians left us; myself, the old woman, one of the young women, and three children, six in all, with no one to provide for them but myself, and I was then very young. We dried considerable of the meat the Indians had killed, and this lasted us for some time; but I soon found that I was able to kill buffaloes, and for a long time we had no want of food. In one instance, an old cow which I had wounded, though she had no calf, ran at me, and I was barely able to escape from her by climbing into a tree. She was enraged, not so much by the wound I had given her, as by the dogs; and it is, I believe, very rare that a cow runs at a man, unless she has been worried by dogs. We made sugar this spring, ten miles above Mouse River Fort. About this time I was much endangered by the breaking of the ice. The weather had become mild, and the beavers began to come up through the holes on to the ice, and sometimes to go on shore. It was my practice to watch these holes, and shoot them as soon as they came up: once, having killed one, I ran hastily up on the ice to get him, and broke in; my snow shoes became entangled with some brush on the bottom, and had nearly dragged me under, but by great exertion I at length escaped. Buffaloes were so numerous about this place, that I often killed them with a bow and arrow, though I hunted them on foot, and with no other aid than that of dogs well trained and accustomed to hunt.

When the leaves began to appear upon the trees, Pe-shau-ba and the men returned in birch canoes, bringing many beaver skins and other valuable peltries. Old Net-no-kwa was now anxious to return to Lake Huron, as was Pe-shau-ba; but Waus-so and Sa-ning-wub would not return, and Pe-shau-ba was unwilling to part with them. Sag-git-to had for some time been very sick, having a large ulcer or abscess near his navel. After having drank for some days, he had a violent pain in his belly, which at length swelled and broke. Pe-shau-ba said to the old woman, "it is not good that Sag-git-to should die here, at a distance from all his friends; and since we see he cannot live much longer, I think it best for you to take him and the little children, and return to Lake Huron. You may be able to reach the rapids, (Saut de St. Marie,) before Sag-git-to-dies." Conformably to this advice, our family was divided. Pe-shau-ba, Waus-so, and Sa-ning-wub remained; Net-no-kwa, and the two other women, with Sag-git-to, Wa-me-gon-a-biew, and myself, with a little girl the old woman had bought, and three little children, started to return to Lake Huron. The little girl was brought from the country of the Bahwetego-weninnewug, the Fall Indians, by a war party of Ojibbeways, from whom Net-no-kwa had bought her. The Fall Indians live near the Rocky Mountains, and wander much with the Black Feet; their language being unlike that of both the Sioux and the Ojibbeways. These last, and the Crees, are more friendly with the Black Feet than they are with the Fall Indians. The little Bahwetig girl that Net-no-kwa had bought, was now ten years of age, but having been some time among the Ojibbeways, had learned their language.

When we came to Rainy Lake, we had ten packs of beaver of forty skins each. Net-no-kwa sold some other peltries for rum, and was drunk for a day or two. We here met some of the trader's canoes, on their way to Red River; and Wa-me-gon-a-biew, who was now eighteen years old, being unwilling to return to Lake Huron, determined to go back to the north with the trader's people. The old woman said much to dissuade him, but he jumped into one of the canoes, as they were about to start off, and although, at the request of the old woman, they endeavoured to drive him out, he would not leave the canoe. Net-no-kwa was much distressed, but could not make up her mind to lose her only son; she determined on returning with him.

The packs of beaver she would not leave with the traders, not having sufficient confidence in their honesty. We therefore took them to a remote place in the woods, where we made a sunjegwun, or deposite, in the usual manner. We then returned to the Lake of the Woods. From this lake the Indians have a road, to go to Red River, which the white men never follow; this is by the way of the Muskeek, or swamp carrying place. We went up a river which the Indians call Muskeego-ne-gum-me-we-see-bee, or Swamp River, for several days; we then dragged our canoes across a swamp for one day. This swamp is only of moss and some small bushes on the top of the water, so that it quakes to a great distance as people walk over it. Then we put our canoes into a small stream, which they called Begwionusk, from the begwionusk, or cow parsley, which grows upon it: this we descended into a small Sahkiegun, called by the same name. This pond has no more than two or three feet of water, and great part of it is not one foot deep; but at this time its surface was covered with ducks, geese, swans, and other birds. Here we remained a long time, and made four packs of beaver skins. When the leaves began to fall, Sag-git-to died. We were now quite alone, no Indians or white men being within four or five days' journey from us. Here we had packs to deposite, as we were about to leave the country; and the ground being too swampy to admit of burying them in the usual manner, we made a sunjegwun of logs, so tight that a mouse could not enter it; in which we left all our packs and other property, which we could not carry. If any of the Indians of this distant region, had found it in our absence, they would not have broken it up; and we did not fear that the traders would penetrate to so poor and solitary a place. Indians who live remote from the whites, have not learned to value their peltries so highly, that they will be guilty of stealing them from each other; and at the time of which I speak, and in the country where I was, I have often known a hunter leave his traps for many days, in the woods, without visiting them, or feeling any anxiety about their safety. It would often happen, that one man having finished his hunt, and left his traps behind him, another would say to him, "I am going to hunt in such a direction, where are your traps?" When he has used them, another, and sometimes four or five, take them in succession; but in the end, they are sure to return to the right owner.

When the snow had fallen, and the weather began to be cold, so that we could no longer kill beaver, we began to suffer from hunger. Wa-me-gon-a-biew was now our principal dependance, and he exerted himself greatly to supply our wants. In one of his remote excursions in pursuit of game, he met with a lodge of Ojibbeways, who, though they had plenty of meat, and knew that he and his friends were in distress, gave him nothing except what he wanted to eat at night. He remained with them all night, and in the morning started for home. On his way he killed a young Moose, which was extremely poor. When this small supply was exhausted, we were compelled to go and encamp with the inhospitable people whom Wa-me-gon-a-biew had seen. We found them well supplied with meat, but whatever we procured from them, was in exchange for our ornaments of silver, or other articles of value. I mentioned the niggardliness and inhospitality of these people, because I had not before met with such an instance among the Indians. They are commonly ready to divide what provisions they have, with any who come to them in need. We had been about three days with these Indians, when they killed two Moose. They called Wa-me-gon-a-biew and me to go after meat, but only gave us the poorest part of one leg. We bought some fat meat from them, giving them our silver ornaments. The patience of old Net-no-kwa was at length exhausted, and she forbade us all to purchase any thing more from them. During all the time we remained with these people, we were suffering almost the extremity of hunger. One morning Net-no-kwa rose very early, and tying on her blanket, took her hatchet and went out. She did not return that night; but the next day, towards evening, as we were all lying down inside the lodge, she came in, and shaking Wa-me-gon-a-biew by the shoulder, said to him, "get up, my son, you are a great runner, and now let us see with what speed you will go and bring the meat which the Great Spirit gave me last night. Nearly all night I prayed and sung, and when I fell asleep near morning, the Spirit came to me, and gave me a bear to feed my hungry children. You will find him in that little copse of bushes in the prairie. Go immediately, the bear will not run from you, even should he see you coming up."

"No, my mother," said Wa-me-gon-a-biew, "it is now near evening: the sun will soon set, and it will not be easy to find the track in the snow. In the morning Shaw-shaw-wa-ne-ba-se shall take a blanket, and a small kettle, and in the course of the day I may overtake the bear and kill him, and my little brother will come up with my blanket, and we can spend the night where I shall kill him."

The old woman did not yield to the opinion of the hunter. Altercation and loud words followed; for Wa-me-gon-a-biew had little reverence for his mother, and as scarce any other Indian would have done, he ridiculed her pretensions to an intercourse with the Great Spirit, and particularly, for having said that the bear would not run if he saw hunters coming. The old woman was offended; and after reproaching her son, she went out of the lodge, and told the other Indians her dream, and directed them to the place where she said the bear would certainly be found. They agreed with Wa-me-gon-a-biew, that it was too late to go that night; but as they had confidence in the prayers of the old woman, they lost no time in following her direction at the earliest appearance of light in the morning. They found the bear at the place she had indicated, and killed it without difficulty. He was large and fat, but Wa-me-gon-a-biew, who accompanied them, received only a small piece for the portion of our family. The old woman was angry, and not without just cause; for although she pretended that the bear had been given her by the Great Spirit, and the place where he lay pointed out to her in a dream, the truth was, she had tracked him into the little thicket, and then circled it, to see that he had not gone out. Artifices of this kind, to make her people believe she had intercourse with the Great Spirit, were, I think, repeatedly assayed by her. . . .

Late in the spring, when we were nearly ready to leave Ke-nu-kau-ne-she-way-bo-ant, an old man, called O-zhusk-koo-koon, (the muskrat's liver,) a chief of the Me-tai, came to my lodge, bringing a young woman, his grand-daughter, together with the girl's parents. This was a handsome young girl, not more than fifteen years old; but Net-no-kwa did not think favourably of her. She said to me, "My son, these people will not cease to trouble you, if you remain here; and as the girl is by no means fit to become your wife, I advise you to take your gun and go away. Make a hunting camp at some distance, and do not return till they have time to see that you are decidedly disinclined to the match." I did so, and O-zhusk-koo-koon apparently relinquished the hope of marrying me to his grand-daughter.

Soon after I returned, I was standing by our lodge one evening, when I saw a good looking young woman walking about and smoking. She noticed me from time to time, and at last came up and asked me to smoke with her. I answered, that I never smoked. "You do not wish to touch my pipe; for that reason you will not smoke with me." I took her pipe and smoked a little, though I had not been in the habit of smoking before. She remained some time, and talked with me, and I began to be pleased with her. After this we saw each other often, and I became gradually attached to her.

I mention this because it was to this woman that I was afterwards married, and because the commencement of our acquaintance was not after the usual manner of the Indians. Among them, it most commonly happens, even when a young man marries a woman of his own band, he has previously had no personal acquaintance with her. They have seen each other in the village; he has perhaps looked at her in passing, but it is probable they have never spoken together. The match is agreed on by the old people, and when their intention is made known to the young couple, they commonly find, in themselves, no objection to the arrangement, as they know, should it prove disagreeable mutually, or to either party, it can at any time be broken off.

My conversations with Mis-kwa-bun-o-kwa, (the red sky of the morning,) for such was the name of the woman who offered me her pipe, was soon noised about the village. Hearing it, and inferring, probably, that like other young men of my age, I was thinking of taking a wife, old O-zhusk-koo-koon came one day to our lodge, leading by the hand another of his numerous grand-daughters. "This," said he, to Net-no-kwa, "is the handsomest and the best of all my descendants; I come to offer her to your son." So saying, he left her in the lodge and went away. This young woman was one Net-no-kwa had always treated with unusual kindness, and she was considered one of the most desirable in the band. The old woman was now somewhat embarrassed; but at length she found an opportunity to say to me, "My son, this girl which O-zhusk-koo-koon offers you, is handsome, and she is good; but you must not marry her, for she has that about her which will, in less than a year, bring her to her grave. It is necessary that you should have a woman who is strong and free of any disease. Let us, therefore, make this young woman a handsome present, for she deserves well at our hands, and send her back to her father." She accordingly gave her goods to a considerable amount, and she went home. Less than a year afterwards, according to the old woman's prediction, she died.

In the mean time, Mis-kwa-bun-o-kwa and myself were becoming more and more intimate. It is probable Net-no-kwa did not disapprove of the course I was now about to take, as, though I said nothing to her on the subject, she could not have been ignorant of what I was doing. That she was not I found, when after spending, for the first time, a considerable part of the night with my mistress, I crept into the lodge at a late hour, and went to sleep. A smart rapping on my naked feet waked me at the first appearance of dawn, on the following morning. "Up," said the old woman, who stood by me, with a stick in her hand, "up, young man, you who are about to take for yourself a wife, up, and start after game. It will raise you more in the estimation of the woman you would marry, to see you bring home a load of meat early in the morning, than to see you dressed ever so gaily, standing about the village after the hunters are all gone out." I could make her no answer, but, putting on my moccasins, took my gun and went out. Returning before noon, with as heavy a load of fat moose meat as I could carry, I threw it down before Net-no-kwa, and with a harsh tone of voice said to her, "here, old woman, is what you called for in the morning." She was much pleased, and commended me for my exertion. I now became satisfied that she was not displeased on account of my affair with Mis-kwa-bun-o-kwa, and it gave me no small pleasure to think that my conduct met her approbation. There are many of the Indians who throw away and neglect their old people; but though Net-no-kwa was now decrepid and infirm, I felt the strongest regard for her, and continued to do so while she lived.

I now redoubled my diligence in hunting, and commonly came home with meat in the early part of the day, at least before night. I then dressed myself as handsomely as I could, and walked about the village, sometimes blowing the Pe-be-gwun, or flute. For some time Mis-kwa-bun-o-kwa pretended she was not willing to marry me, and it was not, perhaps, until she perceived some abatement of ardour on my part, that she laid this affected coyness entirely aside. For my own part, I found that my anxiety to take a wife home to my lodge, was rapidly becoming less and less. I made several efforts to break off the intercourse, and visit her no more; but a lingering inclination was too strong for me. When she perceived my growing indifference, she sometimes reproached me, and sometimes sought to move me by tears and entreaties; but I said nothing to the old woman about bringing her home, and became daily more and more unwilling to acknowledge her publicly as my wife.

About this time, I had occasion to go to the trading-house on Red River, and I started in company with a half breed, belonging to that establishment, who was mounted on a fleet horse. The distance we had to travel has since been called, by the English settlers, seventy miles. We rode and went on foot by turns, and the one who was on foot kept hold of the horse's tail, and ran. We passed over the whole distance in one day. In returning, I was by myself, and without a horse, and I made an effort, intending, if possible, to accomplish the same journey in one day; but darkness, and excessive fatigue, compelled me to stop when I was within about ten miles of home.

When I arrived at our lodge, on the following day, I saw Mis-kwa-bun-o-kwa sitting in my place. As I stopped at the door of the lodge, and hesitated to enter, she hung down her head; but Net-no-kwa greeted me in a tone somewhat harsher than was common for her to use to me. "Will you turn back from the door of the lodge, and put this young woman to shame, who is in all respects better than you are. This affair has been of your seeking, and not of mine or hers. You have followed her about the village heretofore; now you would turn from her, and make her appear like one who has attempted to thrust herself in your way." I was, in part, conscious of the justness of Net-no-kwa's reproaches, and in part prompted by inclination; I went in and sat down by the side of Mis-kwa-bun-o-kwa, and thus we became man and wife. Old Net-no-kwa had, while I was absent at Red River, without my knowledge or consent, made her bargain with the parents of the young woman, and brought her home, rightly supposing that it would be no difficult matter to reconcile me to the measure. In most of the marriages which happen between young persons, the parties most interested have less to do than in this case. The amount of presents which the parents of a woman expect to receive in exchange for her, diminishes in proportion to the number of husbands she may have had. . . .

"She Lov'd the Indian Style of Life"

As best she could remember, Mary Jemison was only twelve when in 1743 a Shawnee war party raided her family's farm near Gettysburg, Pennsylvania, killed her parents, and took her prisoner. Shortly thereafter she was adopted by a kindly Seneca family and was taken to their homeland in the Genesee River Valley of western New York. The Senecas were members of the original Iroquois Confederacy, which also included the Onondaga, Oneida, Cayuga, and Mohawk tribes. Mary Jemison accepted Indian culture, twice married Indian chiefs, and attained a position of leadership within her tribe. She died in 1833, age ninety, much respected by both Indians and whites.

In 1824 a narrative of Mary Jemison's remarkable life was published by James E. Seaver, who claimed to have transcribed the story much as she had told it to him. If for no other reason, this narrative should be read for the humane view it gives of life among the Indians during the late eighteenth and early nineteenth centuries. But Mary Jemison's narrative is also a valuable historical and cultural document, enhanced by her respect for truth. Although she considered herself an Indian in all things but birth, she never forgot that she was also white. Her narrative reflects the tensions of an intelligent, sensitive individual affected by opposing cultures but holding the view that cruelty and kindness are characteristics of human nature rather than peculiarities of race. Her narrative combines compassion, objectivity, and the ability to endure. Compared with those of other Indianized captives, her descriptions of Indian life are less idyllic than John Tanner's (pp. 97-109) and less brutal than Herman Lehmann's (pp. 124-128).

Mrs. Jemison's captivity spanned both the Seven Years' War and the American Revolution, making it historically one of the most signifi-

---

SOURCE: James Seaver, *A Narrative of the Life of Mrs. Mary Jemison . . .* (Canandaigua, N.Y., 1824).

cant in the genre. On more than one occasion she used her wigwam to entertain Joseph Brant, the Mohawk who commanded the Indian allies of the British, and John Butler, the Tory officer blamed for the Wyoming Massacre (1778). She witnessed the execution of William Boyd, a lieutenant in the patrol headed by Gen. John Sullivan which had been sent by General Washington to crush Indian uprisings in the Northwest. Her second husband, Hiokatoo, was present at Braddock's Defeat (1755), was second in command at the Cherry Valley Massacre (1778), and in 1782 took part in the notorious torture of Colonel William Crawford at Sandusky. In the end, Mrs. Jemison lived to see the people of her adopted Seneca nation humiliated and debased by those of her own race.

The following passages from Mary Jemison's narrative record the process of her Indianization, her compassion for human suffering, and her lament that Indians and whites were unable to coexist peaceably. It is impossible to ascertain just where Jemison's words leave off and Seaver's "improvements" begin. Although he claimed "strict fidelity" to the facts, Seaver admitted that "as books of this kind are sought and read with avidity, especially by children, . . . the line of distinction betweeen virtue and vice has been rendered distinctly visible." With an eye toward sales, Seaver undoubtedly enlivened the narrative, but since Mary Jemison was still living at the time of its publication, it seems reasonable to assume that his changes did not distort her story to the point of outright falsification. Seaver's *Narrative* had 24 editions and 32 issues before 1900.

. . . It is a custom of the Indians, when one of their number is slain or taken prisoner in battle, to give to the nearest relative to the dead or absent, a prisoner, if they have chanced to take one, and if not, to give him the scalp of an enemy. On the return of the Indians from conquest, which is always announced by peculiar shoutings, demonstrations of joy, and the exhibition of some trophy of victory, the mourners come forward and make their claims. If they receive a prisoner, it is at their option either to satiate their vengeance by taking his life in the most cruel manner they can conceive of; or, to receive and adopt him into the family, in the place of him whom they have lost. All the prisoners that are taken in battle and carried to the encampment or town by the Indians, are given to the bereaved families, till their number is made good. And unless the mourners have but just received the news of their bereavement, and are under the operation of a paroxysm of grief, anger and revenge; or, unless the prisoner is very old, sickly, or homely, they generally save him, and treat him kindly. But if their mental wound is fresh, their loss so great that they deem it irreparable, or if their prisoner or prisoners do not meet their approbation, no torture, let it be ever so cruel, seems sufficient to make them satisfaction. It is family, and not national, sacrifices amongst the Indians, that has given them an indelible stamp as barbarians, and identified their character with the idea which is generally formed of unfeeling ferocity, and the most abandoned cruelty.

It was my happy lot to be accepted for adoption; and at the time of the ceremony I was received by the two squaws, to supply the place of their brother in the family; and I was ever considered and treated by them as a real sister, the same as though I had been born of their mother.

During my adoption, I sat motionless, nearly terrified to death at the appearance and actions of the company, expecting every moment to feel their vengeance, and suffer death on the spot. I was, however, happily disappointed, when at the close of the ceremony the company retired, and my sisters went about employing every means for my consolation and comfort.

Being now settled and provided with a home, I was employed in nursing the children, and doing light work about the house. Occasionally I was sent out with the Indian hunters, when they went but a short distance, to help them carry their game. My situation was easy; I had no particular hardships to endure. But still, the recollection of my parents, my brothers and sisters, my home, and my own captivity, destroyed my happiness, and made me constantly solitary, lonesome and gloomy.

My sisters would not allow me to speak English in their hearing; but remembering the charge that my dear mother gave me at the time I left her, whenever I chanced to be alone I made a business of repeating my prayer, catechism, or something I had learned in order that I might not forget my own language. By practising in that way I retained it till I came to Genesee flats, where I soon became acquainted with English people with whom I have been almost daily in the habit of conversing.

My sisters were diligent in teaching me their language; and to their great satisfaction I soon learned so that I could understand it readily, and speak it fluently. I was very fortunate in falling into their hands; for they were kind good natured women; peaceable and mild in their dispositions; temperate and decent in their habits, and very tender and gentle towards me. I have great reason to respect them, though they have been dead a great number of years.

The town where they lived was pleasantly situated on the Ohio, at the mouth of the Shenanjee: the land produced good corn; the woods furnished a plenty of game, and the waters abounded with fish. Another river emptied itself into the Ohio, directly opposite the mouth of the Shenanjee. We spent the summer at that place, where we planted, hoed, and harvested a large crop of corn, of an excellent quality.

About the time of corn harvest, Fort Pitt was taken from the French by the English.

The corn being harvested, the Indians took it on horses and in canoes, and proceeded down the Ohio, occasionally stopping to hunt a few days, till we arrived at the mouth of Sciota river; where they established their winter quarters, and continued hunting till the ensuing spring, in the adjacent wilderness. While at that place I went with the other children to assist the hunters to bring in their game. The forests on the Sciota were well stocked with elk, deer, and other large animals; and the marshes contained large numbers of beaver, muskrat, &c. which made excellent hunting for the Indians; who depended, for their meat, upon their success in taking elk and deer; and for ammunition and clothing, upon the beaver, muskrat, and other furs that they could take in addition to their peltry.

The season for hunting being passed, we all returned in the spring to the mouth of the river Shenanjee, to the houses and fields we had left in the fall before. There we again planted our corn, squashes, and beans, on the fields that we occupied the preceding summer.

About planting time, our Indians all went up to Fort Pitt, to make peace with the British, and took me with them. We landed on the opposite side of the river from the fort, and encamped for the night. Early the next morning the Indians took me over to the fort to see the white people that were there. It was then that my heart bounded to be liberated from the Indians and to be restored to my friends and my country. The white people were surprized to see me with the Indians, enduring the hardships of a savage life, at so early an age, and with so delicate a constitution as I appeared to possess. They asked me my name; where and when I was taken—and appeared very much interested on my behalf. They were continuing their inquiries, when my sisters became alarmed, believing that I should be taken from them, hurried me into their canoe and recrossed the river—took their bread out of the fire and fled with me, without stopping, till they arrived at the river Shenanjee. So great was their fear of losing me, or of my being given up in the treaty, that they never once stopped rowing till they got home.

Shortly after we left the shore opposite the fort, as I was informed by one of my Indian brothers, the white people came over to take me back; but after considerable inquiry, and having made diligent search to find where I was hid, they returned with heavy hearts. Although I had then been with the Indians something over a year, and had become considerably habituated to their mode of living, and attached to my sisters, the sight of white people who could speak English inspired me with an unspeakable anxiety to go home with them, and share in the blessings of civilization. My sudden departure and escape from them, seemed like a second captivity, and for a long time I brooded the thoughts of my miserable situation with almost as much sorrow and dejection as I had done those of my first sufferings. Time, the destroyer of every affection, wore away my unpleasant feelings, and I became as contented as before.

We tended our cornfields through the summer; and after we had harvested the crop, we again went down the river to the hunting ground on the Sciota, where we spent the winter, as we had done the winter before.

Early in the spring we sailed up the Ohio river, to a place that the Indians called Wiishto, where one river emptied into the Ohio on one side, and another on the other. At that place the Indians built a town, and we planted corn.

We lived three summers at Wiishto, and spent each winter on the Sciota. The first summer of our living at Wiishto, a party of Delaware Indians came up the river, took up their residence, and lived in common with us. They brought five white prisoners with them, who by their conversation, made my situation much more agreeable, as they could all speak English. I have forgotten the names of all of them except one, which was Priscilla Ramsay. She was a very handsome, good natured girl, and was married soon after she came to Wiishto to Capt. Little Billy's uncle, who went with her on a visit to her friends in the states. Having tarried with them as long as she wished to, she returned with her husband to Can-a-ah-tua, where he died. She, after his death, married a white man by the name of Nettles, and now lives with him (if she is living) on Grand River, Upper Canada.

Not long after the Delawares came to live with us, at Wiishto, my sisters told me that I must go and live with one of them, whose name was She-ninjee. Not daring to cross them, or disobey their commands, with a great degree of reluctance I went; and Sheninjee and I were married according to Indian custom.

Sheninjee was a noble man; large in stature; elegant in his appearance; generous in his conduct; courageous in war; a friend to peace, and a great lover of justice. He supported a degree of dignity far above his rank, and merited and received the confidence and friendship of all the tribes with whom he was acquainted. Yet, Sheninjee was an Indian. The idea of spending my days with him, at first seemed perfectly irreconcilable to my feelings: but his good nature, generosity, tenderness, and friendship towards me, soon gained my affection; and, strange as it may seem, I loved him!—To me he was ever kind in sickness, and always treated me with gentleness; in fact, he was an agreeable husband, and a comfortable companion. We lived happily together till the time of our final separation, which happened two or three years after our marriage, as I shall presently relate.

In the second summer of my living at Wiishto, I had a child at the time that the kernels of corn first appeared on the cob. When I was taken sick, Sheninjee was absent, and I was sent to a small shed, on the bank of the river, which was made of boughs, where I was obliged to stay till my husband returned. My two sisters, who were my only companions, attended me, and on the second day of my confinement my child was born; but it lived only two days. It was a girl: and notwithstanding the shortness of the time I possessed it, it was a great grief to me to lose it.

After the birth of my child, I was very sick, but was not allowed to go into the house for two weeks; when, to my great joy, Sheninjee returned, and I was taken in and as comfortably provided for as our situation would admit of. My disease continued to increase for a number of days; and I became so far reduced that my recovery was despaired of by my friends, and I concluded that my troubles would soon be finished. At length, however, my complaint took a favorable turn, and by the time that the corn was ripe I was able to get about. I continued to gain my health, and in the fall was able to go to our winter quarters, on the Sciota, with the Indians.

From that time, nothing remarkable occurred to me till the fourth winter of my captivity, when I had a son born, while I was at Sciota: I had a quick recovery, and my child was healthy. To commemorate the name of my much lamented father, I called my son Thomas Jemison.

In the spring, when Thomas was three or four moons [months] old, we returned from Sciota to Wiishto, and soon after set out to go to Fort Pitt, to dispose of our fur and skins, that we had taken in the winter, and procure some necessary articles for the use of our family.

I had then been with the Indians four summers and four winters, and had become so far accustomed to their mode of living, habits and dispositions, that my anxiety to get away, to be set at liberty, and leave them, had almost subsided. With them was my home; my family was there, and there I had many friends to whom I was warmly attached in consideration of the favors, affection and friendship with which they had uniformly treated me, from the time of my adoption. Our labor was not severe; and that of one year was exactly similar, in almost every respect, to that of the others, without that endless variety that is to be observed in the common labor of the white people. Notwithstanding the Indian women have all the fuel and bread to procure, and the cooking to perform, their task is probably not harder than that of white women, who have those articles provided for them; and their cares certainly are not half as numerous, nor as great. In the summer season, we planted, tended and harvested our corn, and generally had all our children with us; but had no master to oversee or drive us, so that we could work as leisurely as we pleased. We had no ploughs on the Ohio; but performed the whole process of planting and hoeing with a small tool that resembled, in some respects, a hoe with a very short handle.

Our cooking consisted in pounding our corn into samp or hommany, boiling the hommany, making now and then a cake and baking it in the ashes, and in boiling or roasting our venison. As our cooking and eating utensils consisted of a hommany block and pestle, a small kettle, a knife or two, and a few vessels of bark or wood, it required but little time to keep them in order for use.

Spinning, weaving, sewing, stocking knitting, and the like, are arts which have never been practised in the Indian tribes generally. After the revolutionary war, I learned to sew, so that I could make my own clothing after a poor fashion; but the other domestic arts I have been wholly ignorant of

At an early age, Mary Jemison was captured by the Shawnees and sold to the Senecas, with whom she spent all of her adult life. In her eighties she told her story to James Seaver, whose *Life of Mary Jemison* was a popular success. This illustration (New York, 1860; 4th ed.) was captioned: "Mary [Jemison] Being Arrayed in Indian Costume." *Courtesy of the Edward E. Ayer Collection, the Newberry Library.*

the application of, since my captivity. In the season of hunting, it was our business, in addition to our cooking, to bring home the game that was taken by the Indians, dress it, and carefully preserve the eatable meat, and prepare or dress the skins. Our clothing was fastened together with strings of deer skin, and tied on with the same.

In that manner we lived, without any of those jealousies, quarrels, and revengeful battles between families and individuals, which have been common in the Indian tribes since the introduction of ardent spirits amongst them.

The use of ardent spirits amongst the Indians, and the attempts which have been made to civilize and christianize them by the white people, has constantly made them worse and worse; increased their vices, and robbed them of many of their virtues; and will ultimately produce their extermination. I have seen, in a number of instances, the effects of education upon some of our Indians, who were taken when young, from their families, and placed at school before they had had an opportunity to contract many Indian habits, and there kept till they arrived to manhood; but I have never seen one of those but what was an Indian in every respect after he returned. Indians must and will be Indians, in spite of all the means that can be used for their cultivation in the sciences and arts.

One thing only marred my happiness, while I lived with them on the Ohio; and that was the recollection that I had once had tender parents, and a home that I loved. Aside from that consideration, or, if I had been taken in infancy, I should have been contented in my situation. Notwithstanding all that has been said against the Indians, in consequence of their cruelties to their enemies—cruelties that I have witnessed, and had abundant proof of—it is a fact that they are naturally kind, tender and peaceable towards their friends, and strictly honest; and that those cruelties have been practised, only upon their enemies, according to their idea of justice.

At the time we left Wiishto, it was impossible for me to suppress a sigh of regret on parting with those who had truly been my friends—with those whom I had every reason to respect. On account of a part of our family living at Genishau, we thought it doubtful whether we should return directly from Pittsburgh, or go from thence on a visit to see them.

Our company consisted of my husband, my two Indian brothers, my little son and myself. We embarked in a canoe that was large enough to contain ourselves and our effects, and proceeded on our voyage up the river. . . .

When we arrived at Genishau, the Indians of that tribe were making active preparations for joining the French, in order to assist them in retaking Fort Ne-a-gaw (as Fort Niagara was called in the Seneca language) from the British, who had taken it from the French in the month preceding. They marched off the next day after our arrival, painted and accoutred in all the habiliments of Indian warfare, determined on death or victory; and joined the army in season to assist in accomplishing a plan that had been previously concerted for the destruction of a part of the British army. The British feeling themselves secure in the possession of Fort Neagaw, and unwilling that their enemies should occupy any of the military posts in that quarter, determined to take Fort Schlosser, lying a few miles up the river from Neagaw, which they expected to effect with but little loss. Accordingly a detachment of soldiers, sufficiently numerous, as was supposed, was sent out to take it, leaving a strong garrison in the fort, and marched off, well prepared to effect their object. But on their way they were surrounded by the French and Indians, who lay in ambush to receive them, and were driven off the bank of the river into a place called the "Devil's Hole," together with their horses, carriages, artillery, and every thing pertaining to the army. Not a single man escaped being driven off, and of the whole number one only was fortunate enough to escape with his life. Our Indians were absent but a few days, and returned in triumph, bringing with them two white prisoners, and a number of oxen. Those were the first neat cattle that were ever brought to the Genesee flats.

The next day after their return to Genishau, was set apart as a day of feasting and frolicing, at the expence of the lives of their two unfortunate prisoners, on whom they purposed to glut their revenge, and satisfy their love for retaliation upon their enemies. My sister was anxious to attend the execution, and to take me with her, to witness the customs of the warriors, as it was one of the highest kind of frolics ever celebrated in their tribe, and one that was not often attended with so much pomp and parade as it was expected that would be. I felt a kind of anxiety to witness the scene, having never attended an execution, and yet I felt a kind of horrid dread that made my heart revolt, and inclined me to step back rather than support the idea of advancing. On the morning of the execution she made her intention of going to the frolic, and taking me with her, known to our mother, who in the most feeling terms remonstrated against a step at once so rash and unbecoming the true dignity of our sex:

"How, my daughter, (said she, addressing my sister,) how can you even think of attending the feast and seeing the unspeakable torments that those poor unfortunate prisoners must inevitably suffer from the hands of our warriors? How can you stand and see them writhing in the warriors' fire, in all the agonies of a slow, a lingering death? How can you think of enduring the sound of their groanings and prayers to the Great Spirit for sudden deliverance from their enemies, or from life? And how can you think of conducting to that melancholy spot your poor sister Dickewamis, (meaning myself,) who has so lately been a prisoner, who has lost her parents and brothers by the hands of the bloody warriors, and who has felt all the horrors of the loss of her freedom, in lonesome captivity? Oh! how can you think of making her bleed at the wounds which now are but partially healed? The recollection of her former troubles would deprive us of Dickewamis, and she would depart to the fields of the blessed, where fighting has ceased, and the corn needs no tending—where hunting is easy, the forests delightful, the summers are pleasant, and the winters are mild!—O! think once, my daughter, how soon you may have a brave brother made prisoner in battle, and sacrificed to feast the ambition of the enemies of his kindred, and leave us to mourn for the loss of a friend, a son and a brother, whose bow brought us venison, and supplied us with blankets!—Our task is quite easy at home, and our business needs our attention. With war we have nothing to do: our husbands and brothers are proud to defend us, and their hearts beat with ardor to meet our proud foes. Oh! stay then, my daughter; let our warriors alone perform on their victims their customs of war!"

This speech of our mother had the desired effect; we stayed at home and attended to our domestic concerns. The prisoners, however, were executed by having their heads taken off, their bodies cut in pieces and shockingly mangled, and then burnt to ashes!—They were burnt on the north side of Fall-brook, directly opposite the town which was on the south side, some time in the month of November, 1759.

I spent the winter comfortably, and as agreeably as I could have expected to, in the absence of my kind husband. Spring at length appeared, but Sheninjee was yet away; summer came on, but my husband had not found me. Fearful forebodings haunted my imagination; yet I felt confident that his affection for me was so great that if he was alive he would follow me and I should again see him. In the course of the summer, however, I received intelligence that soon after he left me at Yiskahwana he was taken sick and died at Wiishto. This was a heavy and an unexpected blow. I was now in my youthful days left a widow, with one son, and entirely dependent on myself for his and my support. My mother and her family gave me all the consolation in their power, and in a few months my grief wore off and I became contented.

In a year or two after this, according to my best recollection of the time, the King of England offered a bounty to those who would bring in the prisoners that had been taken in the war, to some military post where they might be redeemed and set at liberty.

John Van Sice, a Dutchman, who had frequently been at our place, and was well acquainted with every prisoner at Genishau, resolved to take me to Niagara, that I might there receive my liberty and he the offered bounty. I was notified of his intention; but as I was fully determined not to be redeemed at that time, especially with his assistance, I carefully watched his movements in order to avoid falling into his hands. It so happened, however, that he saw me alone at work in a corn-field, and thinking probably that he could secure me easily, ran towards me in great haste. I espied him at some distance, and well knowing the amount of his errand, run from him with all the speed I was mistress of, and never once stopped till I reached Gardow. He gave up the chase, and returned: but I, fearing that he might be lying in wait for me, stayed three days and three nights in an old cabin at Gardow, and then went back trembling at every step for fear of being apprehended. I got home without difficulty; and soon after, the chiefs in council having learned the cause of my elopement, gave orders that I should not be taken to any military post without my consent; and that as it was my choice to stay, I should live amongst them quietly and undisturbed. But, notwithstanding the will of the chiefs, it was but a few days before the old king of our tribe told one of my Indian brothers that I should be redeemed, and he would take me to Niagara himself. In reply to the old king, my brother said that I should not be given up; but that, as it was my wish, I should stay with the tribe as long as I was pleased to. Upon this a serious quarrel ensued between them, in which my brother frankly told him that sooner than I should be taken by force, he would kill me with his own hands!—Highly enraged at the old king, my brother came to my sister's house, where I resided, and informed her of all that had passed respecting me; and that, if the old king should attempt to take me, as he firmly believed he would, he would immediately take my life, and hazard the consequences. He returned to the old king. As soon as I came in, my sister told me what she had just heard, and what she expected without doubt would befal me. Full of pity, and anxious for my preservation, she then directed me to take my child and go into some high weeds at no great distance from the house, and there hide myself and lay still till all was silent in the house, for my brother, she said, would return at evening and let her know the final conclusion of the matter, of which she promised to inform me in the following manner: If I was to be killed, she said she would bake a small cake and lay it at the door, on the outside, in a place that she then pointed out to me. When all was silent in the house, I was to creep softly to the door, and if the cake could not be found in the place specified, I was to go in: but if the cake was there, I was to take my child and go as fast as I possibly could to a large spring on the south side of Samp's Creek, (a place that I had often seen,) and there wait till I should by some means hear from her.

Alarmed for my own safety, I instantly followed her advice, and went into the weeds, where I lay in a state of the greatest anxiety, till all was silent in the house, when I crept to the door, and there found, to my great distress, the little cake! I knew my fate was fixed, unless I could keep secreted till the storm was over; and accordingly crept back to the weeds, where my little Thomas lay, took him on my back, and laid my course for the spring as fast as my legs would carry me. Thomas was nearly three years old, and very large and heavy. I got to the spring early in the morning, almost overcome with fatigue, and at the same time fearing that I might be pursued and taken, I felt my life an almost insupportable burthen. I sat down with my child at the spring, and he and I made a breakfast of the little cake, and water of the spring, which I dipped and supped with the only implement which I possessed, my hand.

In the morning after I fled, as was expected, the old King came to our house in search of me, and to take me off; but, as I was not to be found, he gave me up, and went to Niagara with the prisoners he had already got into his possession.

As soon as the old King was fairly out of the way, my sister told my brother where he could find me. He immediately set out for the spring, and found me about noon. The first sight of him made me tremble with the fear of death; but when he came near, so that I could discover his countenance, tears of joy flowed down my cheeks, and I felt such a kind of instant relief as no one can possibly experience, unless when under the absolute sentence of death he receives an unlimited pardon. We were both rejoiced at the event of the old King's project; and after staying at the spring through the night, set out together for home early in the morning. When we got to a cornfield near the town, my brother secreted me till he could go and ascertain how my case stood; and finding that the old King was absent, and that all was peaceable, he returned to me, and I went home joyfully.

Not long after this, my mother went to Johnstown, on the Mohawk river, with five prisoners, who were redeemed by Sir William Johnson, and set at liberty.

When my son Thomas was three or four years old, I was married to an Indian, whose name was Hiokatoo, commonly called Gardow, by whom I had four daughters and two sons. I named my children, principally, after my relatives, from whom I was parted, by calling my girls Jane, Nancy, Betsey and Polly, and the boys John and Jesse. Jane died about twenty-nine years ago, in the month of August, a little before the great Council at Big-Tree, aged about fifteen years. My other daughters are yet living, and have families. . . .

An effusive versified account, "The Female Captive," treats Mary Jemison's life with more than poetic license. The author was Gordon M. Fisk (1825-1879), of Ludlow, Massachusetts, a newspaper editor and local poet, and it was "printed for M[oses] Baldwin, the Blind Man," to be peddled on the streets. Fisk romanticized "the tawny Indian race" which had "liv'd in peace" until the invasion of their lands by the white man. Seeking revenge, the Indians descend on the unsuspecting and unprotected Jemison family, taking Mary captive. Fisk's doggerel couplets jog on, recounting how "she lov'd the Indian style of life," and record her marriages, family difficulties, piety, and death.

SOURCE: Gordon M. Fisk, *Story of the Female Captive . . . a Poem . . .* (Palmer, Mass., 1844).

THE FEMALE CAPTIVE

In gone by years, when o'er this smiling land,
A lonely wilderness immense did stand—
When prowling beasts in eager search for prey,
Roam'd unmolested through the night and day,
Then liv'd in peace the tawny Indian race,
Who made these lands their choisest hunting-place—
Their smoking huts and shady council tree,
Gave evidence that they lived happily.
But when our fathers o'er the ocean came,
And left a kingdom great, and stamp'd with fame,
And built their cabins in the forest shade,
And on the red man's rights did much invade,
The dark-eyed savage raised his deadly arm,
And for revenge issued the dread alarm,—
The loud wild whoop throughout the forest rang,
And sullen war-song loud, the council sang.
In these dark early years, from strife remote,
A farmer dwelt in happiness devote,
His cheerful wife and smiling offspring dear,
Liv'd peacefully and undisturbed by fear.
One pleasant morning in the dawn of spring,
When nature smiling gay seem'd every thing,
This little group were at their day's employ,
With willing hands, and hearts that leap'd for joy,
When suddenly was heard the war-whoop sound,
While painted Indians did the house surround,
A neighbor there the warriors soon did slay,
And all the rest they captive led away.
Long was their march, o'er dismal hill and plain—
Fatigued, and suffering hunger, thirst and pain,
And when the second day's long march was done,
The trembling captives all were slain, but one.
This was a girl of only twelve years old,
Of whom a tale of sorrow shall be told,—
Her life was spared, and by them treated mild,
And in their mode adopted as their child.
Her hands were taught to plant and harvest corn,
To pound their meal, and warriors caps adorn.
At length, she lov'd the Indians' style of life,
And soon by one, was treasured as a wife,
She children had, but soon her husband, kind,

Fell sick, and died, and was to dust consign'd.
Her grief was great, but slowly wore away,
And she a second mate did soon obey,—
Her cares increas'd, she many children had,
Which grew mature, and caused her moments sad.
Her eldest son, in quarrel with the rest,
Butcher'd them coldly, as he would a beast,—
But he at length received his justice due,
For like his brothers, he was murdered too.
Years wore away, and she advanc'd in age,
But still in daily toils she did engage,—
Her husband died, and she was left alone,
But held a tract of land to call her own,—
And there she liv'd among her tawny kin,
Secure from harm, and from the battle's din,
Until the white men came and settled there,
And welcom'd her unto their willing care:
But with the red man's race she spent her days,
But sought the truth of God, and righteous ways,
And when *fourscore* and *ten* her years were made
Her mortal body in the tomb was laid.

A White Savage: "I Kill My First Man"

On May 16, 1870, an eleven-year-old boy by the name of Herman Lehmann was captured by Apache Indians. Within a few months he lost his white identity, becoming savage and cruel. When given the opportunity to escape, he refused because, in his own words, he "had learned to hate [his] own people," whose way of life he considered "effeminate." He killed an Apache medicine man, left the tribe, and joined the Comanches, with whom he lived until 1878 when they were confined to a reservation and he was forced to return to his white family. Although they welcomed him with kindness, Lehmann never readjusted to life among whites, preferring the company of Indians whenever possible. His captivity assumes special interest because he was the adopted son of the famous Comanche chief, Quannah Parker (c.1845-1911), whose mother was Cynthia Ann Parker (c.1827-1864), another white captive turned savage. (For her story, see James De Shields, *Cynthia Ann Parker . . .* [1886].) Lehmann died in 1932. His brother, Willie Lehmann, captured by the Apaches at the same time as Herman, died in 1951 at the age of ninety, the last surviving Indian captive.

A narrative of Herman Lehmann's captivity, called *Indianology* on the cover but *A Condensed History of the Apache and Comanche Indian Tribes* on the title page, was published in 1899 by Jonathan H. Jones. Lehmann was illiterate, and Jones wrote the narrative in the first person, presumably in the way Lehmann told it. This excerpt from *Indianology* reveals the extent and direction of Lehmann's Indianization. He delights in murder and torture, and he takes pride in dangling scalps from his belt.

It is difficult to isolate what factors determined the degree to which a captive became Indianized. At one end of the spectrum were captives like Hannah Duston, who resisted Indianization to the point of murdering her captors; at the other were Lehmann and Cynthia Ann Parker,

SOURCE: Jonathan H. Jones, *Indianology* (San Antonio, 1899). In 1927 J. Marvin Hunter published an expanded version of *Indianology* called *Nine Years Among the Indians*; A. C. Greene, *The Last Captive* (1972), combines both versions into a single narrative.

who not only accepted an Indian lifestyle but came to relish its more brutal ways. In *White into Red* (1973), J. Norman Heard, an expert on Indianization, concludes that the age when captured was in most but not all instances "the crucial factor" in determining the degree of assimilation. Another expert, James Axtell ("The White Indians of Colonial America," *William and Mary Quarterly* 32 [1975], pp. 55-88) argues that the Indians "chose their captives carefully so as to maximize the chances of acculturating them to Indian life," preferring women and children, whom they subjected to a ritualistic "educational process" which eased the trauma of adjustment.

CHAPTER IX.

I KILL MY FIRST MAN

"Three Mexicans camped with the squaws, and we soon gambled off and traded our horses to those Mexicans for guns, ammunition, blankets, etc. Sometimes we would give six or seven horses for one gun.

"Our sachem was not elected, but he was the bravest and most powerful, and went in front because he could, and the next in strength and power of endurance came second, etc. No Indian went unless he wanted to go, and the weakest was always found in the rear, and if he was not able to keep up, he was left unless he be wounded, then his comrades would protect him if it were not too risky.

"We stayed in camp about a month, killed mustangs, antelope, buffalo, deer, etc., enough to run the old warriors, the manikins and the women until we came back, and then we started on another stealing expedition.

"We only took the ponies we rode, each of us mounted on a separate pony, our guns primed and ammunition handy, besides a supply of bows and arrows.

"If a horse gave out, that Indian had to take it afoot until he could steal one, but if we got in a tight we took him up behind. We came south-east about one hundred and fifty miles and camped on a little ravine. Scouts were sent out and soon they returned and reported three men headed toward us. We all hid in ambush and made ready, but just as these men rode up we were discovered and fired upon, and one horse was killed. We vigorously returned the fire and they ran, but continued to fight. We caught one man and he spoke Spanish. We asked where his camp was and he told us it was over the mountain, but that it was deserted and that the men were all away chasing buffalo. The Indians left me to guard the prisoner, and they charged over the hill and on to camp, but instead of an easy capture, a volley of balls met them. There was a crowd in camp and they had fortified the place with rock. The Indians were repulsed and one wounded in the leg. The Indians came back and ordered me to murder my prisoner. He picked up a rock and hurled it at me; I dodged the missile and fired in the air but my arm grew steady, and I fired again, killing him instantly. I pounced upon him and soon his bloody scalp was dangling at my belt, and I was the proud recipient of Indian flattery.

"We continued our course and that night we came in contact with a company of men and had a little fight. We killed one white man and captured fifteen horses. I think this must have been near Ballinger. We came down to Pack Saddle in Llano County [Texas] and there had a terrible fight with four white men. We were in the roughs and so were the whites, so neither had the advantage, but we routed them in about a half hour. I think I wounded one of the white men severely. I had a good shot at him, but they all got away.

"We wended our way from there to House mountains, and there we captured a nice herd of horses, and this increased our drove to fifty. We went our same old route up the Llano river, but the rangers got on our trail and followed us up through Mason county, but we made for Kickapoo Springs [Concho County], but the rangers had changed horses and were giving us close chase. We changed horses often and rode cautiously and made our escape, but we were followed to the edge of the plains. We reached home safely and with all our horses, but the Mexicans had again joined our squaws, and this time they had plenty of mescal and corn whiskey, and tobacco in abundance. We all got drunk and one hundred and forty Indian warriors and sixty Mexicans went on a cattle raid. West of Fort Griffin, on the old trail, we ran into a big herd being driven to Kansas. There were about twenty hands with the cattle. We rushed up and opened fire. The cattle stampeded and the cowboys rode in an opposite direction. There were enough of us to surround the cattle and chase the boys. We soon gave the boys up and started for Mexico with the herd, but the second day we were overtaken by about forty white men, who tried to retake the cattle, and in the attempt two Mexicans and one Indian were killed—the Indian was shot through the neck—and we had four horses killed. We repulsed them and got possession of two of their dead, who were promptly scalped. I don't know what other losses they sustained. We went on southwest with the herd, and had about three thousand head when we reached the village. These we traded to Mexicans and immediately stampeded them. Some of these cattle were branded 'Hey.'

"We put the scalps of those boys on high poles and had a big feast and war dance. We slew forty beeves and roasted them all at once. We kept up a chant and dance around those scalps day and night. More Mexicans had come and replenished our stock of whiskey. We had a little disagreement—a debate—and in order to settle the rucus satisfactorily to all concerned, we killed two Mexicans and raised their scalps on poles. We drank all the whiskey, sobered up, ran off the Mexicans and kept all their trinkets, guns, ammunition, etc., but they got the most of the cattle, which was more than pay. Then we repented over the Mexican affair and hired them to make friends. We moved our village away out to the Sandy hills [Llano County] and spent some time hunting. There we found deer, antelope, musk-hogs and some few buffaloes.

"We sharpened our arrow spikes, mended our bows, brightened up our guns. Our arrows were made of a straight dogwood withe, with a feather in one end and a flint on the other. The Mexicans furnished us files with which to sharpen our arrows. We used whit-leather—or, as the Indians call it—'singers,' for our bow-strings. We poisoned several arrows and kept them in separate bundles.

"We started out south to make another run on the whites, and the first thing that broke the monotony of the raid and stirred up a little local interest, was several men near the Concho river [tributary of Colorado]. We shot at them and they fired on us. The battle was fierce, but both forces were drawn off in good order, and each side was permitted to care for their own dead and wounded. We lost three of the bravest Indians that ever smoked cigarettes. We put some sticks up in a big Live Oak tree, lay the dead up there (so that the wolves would not eat them) and covered them with blankets. All their guns, arrows and trinkets were wrapped up with them and their horses led under the tree and shot, so the Indians would be mounted and equipped when they reached the 'Happy Hunting Ground.'

"I don't know the loss of killed and wounded on the other side, but it must have been great for the fight was long and fierce and we saw nothing more of the whites.

"We came southeast to another river and espied a man walking 'round and 'round. The Indians crawled up, waylaid him and sent an arrow right through his breast. He stood there and spit up blood. The Indians let him suffer a little while and then dispatched him and carried along his scalp. This man must have been lost for he had nothing with which to fight, but he had some old rusty knives and bundles that looked somewhat worsted from the weather.

"Keeping our course we came upon some men working at rock quarries. One man was left to guard the camps. We surrounded them and fired twice at the guard and he ran and hid in the chaparral. The workmen made their escape through the thick undergrowth. We took possession of camps. We found only one horse, five 44-calibre, rim fire Winchesters, with belts full of cartridges, sugar, flour, salt and other things necessary for camp life. We strewed the ground with sugar, flour, meal and salt, destroyed the meat and demolished the wagon and everything else we could find that we could not carry along.

"We went south from there, as well as I remember, and saw some children playing in the field near a house. We slipped up close and made a run at the children and 'Snapping Turtle' grabbed at one child as he ran through the fence. The white man came out with a Winchester and shot Snapping Turtle through the side. We fought there for about two hours and tried to get revenge, but the man was brave and cautious and we never got a fair shot at him. We would not have fought if it had not been that he had crippled one of our men. There were cattle near the house branded broadaxe. We did not want cattle, we wanted blood and horses. We went a little further and rounded up nine good-looking horses. We sent these, the crippled Indian and two companions back to the village.

"We came a little further and saw a man making rails; we rushed at him; he threw down his axe, lost his hat, but how he did run! He reached his house in safety. We didn't care to tackle him there, but contented ourselves with taking his hat, axe, little sorrel pony and saddle. We rode up the hill and captured twelve head of horses, a big bay mule and a light sorrel mule. We then started for home by way of Kickapoo Springs and there we made ourselves the present of a nice drove of fat ponies. But scouts informed us that the hateful rangers were on our trail. We dreaded those fellows so we made for the plains, although this was not according to our programme, for we had anticipated a fortnight's hunt here. We traveled three days and nights without eating or sleeping. We well knew how sleepless and restless those rangers were and how unerring their aim when they got in a shot, so we out-rode them. The fourth day we came up on a big, old, fat jack[ass] some Mexicans had set free, so we butchered, roasted and ate him. He was very palatable after our three days' fast. We rested there and grazed our horses. Two days after we killed and ate a mustang. We thought we were entirely out of danger so we turned our fast horses loose and the most of the Indians rode mules, but I happened to be on a fast pony, but we were traveling leisurely along. We had started at daylight that morning and about a half hour by sun the rangers came upon us from the east. They had cautiously kept between us and the sun so they could not be seen. They were right at us ere we knew they were near. The chief ordered us to stand and fight, he said there was no hope in flight; but the warriors obeyed no orders but their own will and soon scattered."

PART FOUR

Behind the Frontier

An Antiquarian Records an Incident in the Deerfield Massacre

Its westward movement left behind the frontier a legacy of history which, by the 1830s, antiquarians and, soon after them, literary men began to explore. The distance between the dusty local pieties of an Elihu Hoyt and the epic grandeur of a Francis Parkman is considerable, but their treatment of Indian captivity indicates a common desire to recover the historic facts and to put them to good purpose. As the Indian was being relegated to the past or pushed to the South and West, the more settled societies also began to memorialize the captivity experience in their folklore and in the formulas and stereotypes of the mass media. Until this point, attention to the Indian captivity had been immediate and pragmatic. BEHIND THE FRONTIER, it had become historic.

The almost incidental, fragmentary references to the captivity of the Reverend John Williams and his family in Elihu Hoyt's *A Brief Sketch of the Settlement of Deerfield . . .* (1833) illustrate the efforts of local historians to preserve the past and seek some benefit from it. Throughout its early history, Deerfield, long the most northerly town on the Connecticut River, was subject to frequent Indian incursions. The town was the scene of two major massacres, one in 1675 and the other on February 29, 1704. It was during this latter siege that Williams, pastor of Deerfield since 1688, was taken captive. Like so many other victims of Queen Anne's War, he was forced to march to Canada. His wife, Eunice, too weak to travel, was killed along the way. Two sons and a daughter, also captured, survived the journey, but his two youngest

SOURCE: Elihu Hoyt, *A Brief Sketch of the First Settlement of Deerfield . . . Together with a Few of the Events Which Took Place There in Early Times . . .* (Greenfield, Mass., 1833).

children were killed during the attack. In 1706 Williams was ransomed and resumed his duties at Deerfield. His sons returned with him, but to Williams's great dismay his daughter converted to Roman Catholicism (see Swarton, pp. 31-39). For her story, see Clifton Johnson, *An Unredeemed Captive . . .* (1897). Williams died in 1729 at the age of sixty-six. His tombstone, like those of several other Deerfield captives, may still be seen in the Old Burying-Ground at Deerfield.

The destruction of Deerfield and the captivity of the Williams family were among the most publicized events in the history of colonial New England. Of an estimated 300 inhabitants, 47 were killed during the attack, and 112 were taken captive. Of these, 19 were slain on the way to Canada, 62 were eventually redeemed, and 31 never returned. Cotton Mather, a cousin of Mrs. Eunice Williams, published a letter written by Williams from Canada to his parishioners at Deerfield in an essay called *Good Fetch'd out of Evil . . .* (1706), and he urged Williams to write an account of what had befallen him. Williams wrote *The Redeemed Captive Returning to Zion . . .* (1707), a best seller and a classic of Puritan literature.

In the period before the Civil War, versions of the Williams captivity were printed in a variety of historical publications, evidence of a rapidly increasing interest in the American past, particularly the captive experience. Pedestrian antiquarians such as Elihu Hoyt used Indian captivity narratives to engender national pride by drawing public attention to the heroic exploits of pioneer ancestors. Accounts of Indian captivity appeared in Indian histories, military histories, ecclesiastical histories, and the journals of historical societies. The story of the Williams captivity, for example, was published in James Wimer's *Events in Indian History . . .* (1841), Henry White's *Indian Battles . . .* (c. 1859), and *The American Pioneer, a Monthly Periodical Devoted to the Objects of the Logan Historical Society* (1842-1843). It also appeared in Epaphras Hoyt's *Antiquarian Researches . . .* (1824) and was the subject of *The Deerfield Captive . . .* (1831), a book designed "for the instruction of the young."

The writer of the following sketch is desirous of preserving to posterity some account of the incidents which relate to the early settlement of the town [Deerfield, Mass.], with a view of handing it down to posterity; believing that it will gratify the feelings of those who are descendants of the early settlers of the place;—to them it may be a source of satisfaction to learn what privations and sufferings their ancestors endured. To those who are not immediate descendants from the sufferers, it may be some gratification to read of the exploits, the sufferings, the hairbreadth escapes which were the lot of those who first ventured to take a stand on the borders between civilized man, and the savage state. . . .

The Rev. John Williams, minister of the town, together with his wife and children, except his son Eleazer, were all either killed or taken prisoners. Two of his children were slain at the threshold of his own door. Mr. Williams was a son of Mr. Samuel Williams, of Roxbury, where he was born, Dec. 10th, 1664. He took his degree at Harvard College 1683; Settled in the ministry at Deerfield, May 1686, He married Eunice, daughter of the Rev. Eleazer Mather of Northampton. At the time of the attack on the town Mrs. Williams was weak and unable to travel; the next day after she was taken, in crossing the Green river, in the north part of what is now Greenfield, about six miles from her home she fell in the water, and was unable to proceed; her savage master thereupon sunk his tomahawk into her head, and she expired on the spot, and was left unburied. Her husband had requested his master to let him go to her assistance before she fell, but he refused to grant the request. Her remains were soon after found by some of the people of Deerfield and were brought in and decently interred. The tomb stones show the place where her remains rest, on which is the following Inscription: viz.—

"Here lyeth the body of Mrs. Eunice Williams, the vertues and desirable consort of the Rev. John Williams, and daughter of Rev. Eleazer and Mrs. Esther Mather of Northampton. She was born Aug. 2, 1664, and fell by the rage of the barbarous enemy, March 1, 1703—4."

"Proverb 31—28. Her children rise up and call her blessed."

Mr. Williams with his remaining children was carried into captivity where they endured much hardship; he eventually effected the redemption of all his children except his daughter Eunice, spoken of above. She married an Indian and lived in their habits and died in the Romish faith. Mr. Williams returned from captivity in November, 1706, after an absence of two and a half years; he landed at Boston, from Quebec, and was immediately waited on by a committee from his parish in Deerfield, with a request that he would return and continue his labors among his people, which invitation he accepted; and he preached there until his death which took place June 12th, 1729. He lived much respected, and died greatly lamented, by the people of his charge, and by all his friends and acquaintances. He was buried near by his first wife, and his tomb stones bear the following inscription: viz.—

"Here lyes the body of the Rev. John Williams, the beloved and faithful pastor of this place, who died on June 12, 1729, in the 65th year of his age."

"Rev. 14—13. Writes, blessed are the dead which die in the Lord."

Mr. Williams had three sons educated at Harvard College, and they were all eventually settled in the ministry as follows: viz.—

Eleazer, at Mansfield, Conn. Stephen, at Longmeadow, Mass. Wareham, at Waltham, Mass.

There are not now living in Deerfield any descendants from the Rev. John Williams, in a direct male line; but one of Mr. Williams' daughter's, by his second wife, married Doct. Thomas Williams of Roxbury, (now deceased,) who has one son settled at Deerfield. It is believed that there are many descendants of Rev. John Williams, in Connecticut and elsewhere. We have always understood that the Rev. Eleazer Williams left a family at Mansfield, and Rev. Stephen Williams at Longmeadow, some of whom we have seen. Rev. Wareham Williams of Waltham left a family, but we know little of them, except his son Samuel, who was a professor in Harvard University; he afterwards removed to Vermont, where he died, leaving posterity; some of them have recently visited Deerfield to view the place where their ancestors met with severe trials and sufferings. . . .

Washington Irving on John Colter's Race

John Colter—mountain man, Indian fighter, and explorer—had become one of the giants of western legend before the Civil War. When Washington Irving returned to the United States in 1832, having made his literary reputation with urbane and nostalgic sketches during a residence of seventeen years in Europe, he consciously sought to revitalize his American roots. He almost immediately undertook a tour of the western prairies of which he published an account which reveals a taste for the company of robust plainsmen and fur trappers and a hardihood unexpected in a dilettantish city man. John Jacob Astor read Irving's *Tour of the Prairies* (1835) and invited him to write a history of his great fur trading "enterprise" in the Northwest. The result was *Astoria* (1836) with its story of John Colter's captivity among the Blackfoot Indians at the headwaters of the Missouri, a people far different from the sentimentalized savages who appear in Irving's *The Sketch Book* (1819-1820).

Irving borrowed the story of Colter's captivity from *Travels in the Interior of America . . .* (1817) by John Bradbury, who heard it from Colter. Engrossing simply as a narrative of high adventure, it gains significance within Irving's context. This was the beginning of the period of Manifest Destiny. Whalers were penetrating the unknown territories of the Pacific at the same time that fur trappers in search of beaver pelts moved beyond the Rocky Mountains, and Irving could see each in terms of the other. Colter, like Daniel Boone, was "another of those heroes of the wilderness" whose "story deserves particular citation, as showing the hair-breadth adventures to which these solitary rovers . . . are exposed." But Irving compares the "type" of "western trapper" Colter represents to a "sailor" whose "past hazards only stimulate . . . to further risks." For Colter, "the vast prairie," like "the ocean," is "a boundless field of enterprise and exploit." Whereas the sailor crosses oceans, men like Colter make "vast internal voyages." Intrepid sailors

---

SOURCE: Washington Irving, *Astoria, or, Anecdotes of an Enterprise Beyond the Rocky Mountains* (Philadelphia, 1836).

pushed the course of empire to the eastern shores of America, men like Colter—and by implication men like John Jacob Astor—extend it to the Pacific coast and beyond. And like the oceans and the prairies, the "restless and predatory . . . savages" who "infest" the western territories are to be controlled so that empire can advance. Colter's story dramatizes but one instance of the "vindictive cruelty" and "implacable hostility" of Indians toward whites, a pattern of behavior which sanctioned the removal of the Indian by force.

Colter died in 1813, age unknown, but probably less than forty. He is best remembered as the discoverer of Yellowstone Park. For other nineteenth-century accounts of his captivity, see W. J. Snelling, *Tales of Travels West of the Mississippi . . .* (1830), *Indian Anecdotes and Barbarities . . .* (1837; see woodcut, p. 139), Thomas James, *Three Years Among the Indians and Mexicans . . .* (1846), and Frank Triplett, *Conquering the Wilderness . . .* (1883).

. . .The next morning early, as the party were yet encamped at the mouth of a small stream, they [Wilson Price Hunt expedition (1810-1812)] were visited by another of these heroes of the wilderness, one John Colter, who had accompanied Lewis and Clarke in their memorable expedition. He had recently made one of those vast internal voyages so characteristic of this fearless class of men, and of the immense regions over which they hold their lonely wanderings; having come from the head waters of the Missouri to St. Louis in a small canoe. This distance of three thousand miles he had accomplished in thirty days. Colter kept with the party all the morning. He had many particulars to give them concerning the Blackfeet Indians, a restless and predatory tribe, who had conceived an implacable hostility to the white men, in consequence of one of their warriors having been killed by Captain Lewis, while attempting to steal horses. Through the country infested by these savages the expedition would have to proceed, and Colter was urgent in reiterating the precautions that ought to be observed respecting them. He had himself experienced their vindictive cruelty, and his story deserves particular citation, as showing the hairbreadth adventures to which these solitary rovers of the wilderness are exposed.

Colter, with the hardihood of a regular trapper, had cast himself loose from the party of Lewis and Clarke in the very heart of the wilderness, and had remained to trap beaver alone on the head waters of the Missouri. Here he fell in with another lonely trapper, like himself, named Potts [John Potts, formerly of the Lewis and Clark expedition], and they agreed to keep together. They were in the very region of the terrible Blackfeet, at that time thirsting to revenge the death of their companion, and knew that they had to expect no mercy at their hands. They were obliged to keep concealed all day in the woody margins of the rivers, setting their traps after nightfall, and taking them up before daybreak. It was running a fearful risk for the sake of a few beaver skins; but such is the life of the trapper.

They were on a branch of the Missouri called Jefferson's Fork, and had set their traps at night, about six miles up a small river that emptied itself into the fork. Early in the morning they ascended the river in a canoe, to examine the traps. The banks on each side were high and perpendicular, and cast a shade over the stream. As they were softly paddling along, they heard the trampling of many feet upon the banks. Colter immediately gave the alarm of "Indians!" and was for instant retreat. Potts scoffed at him for being frightened by the trampling of a herd of buffaloes. Colter checked his uneasiness and paddled forward. They had not gone much further when frightful whoops and yells burst forth from each side of the river, and several hundred Indians appeared on either bank. Signs were made to the unfortunate trappers to come on shore. They were obliged to comply. Before they could get out of their canoe, a savage seized the rifle belonging to Potts. Colter sprang on shore, wrested the weapon from the hands of the Indian, and restored it to his companion, who was still in the canoe, and immediately pushed into the stream. There was the sharp twang of a bow, and Potts cried out that he was wounded. Colter urged him to come on shore and submit, as his only chance for life; but the other knew there was no prospect of mercy, and determined to die game. Levelling his rifle, he shot one of the savages dead on the spot. The next moment he fell himself, pierced with innumerable arrows.

The vengeance of the savages now turned upon Colter. He was stripped naked, and, having some knowledge of the Blackfoot language, overheard a consultation as to the mode of despatching him, so as to derive the greatest amusement from his death. Some were for setting him up as a mark, and having a trial of skill at his expense. The chief, however, was for nobler sport. He seized Colter by the shoulder, and demanded if he could run fast. The unfortunate trapper was too well acquainted with Indian customs not to comprehend the drift of the question. He knew he was to run for his life, to furnish a kind of human hunt to his persecutors. Though in reality he was noted among his brother hunters for swiftness of foot, he assured the chief that he was a very bad runner. His stratagem gained him some vantage ground. He was led by the chief into the prairie, about four hundred yards from the main body of savages, and then turned loose, to save himself if he could. A tremendous yell let him know that the whole pack of bloodhounds were off in full cry. Colter flew, rather than ran; he was astonished at his own speed; but he had six miles of prairie to traverse before he should reach the Jefferson fork of the Missouri; how could he hope to hold out such a distance with the fearful odds of several hundred to one against him! The plain too, abounded with the prickly pear, which wounded his naked feet.

Still he fled on, dreading each moment to hear the twang of a bow, and to feel an arrow quivering at his heart. He did not even dare to look round, lest he should lose an inch of that distance on which his life depended. He had run nearly half way across the plain when the sound of pursuit grew somewhat fainter, and he ventured to turn his head. The main body of his pursuers were a considerable distance behind; several of the fastest runners were scattered in the advance; while a swift-footed warrior, armed with a spear, was not more than a hundred yards behind him.

Inspired with new hope, Colter redoubled his exertions, but strained himself to such a degree, that the blood gushed from his mouth and nostrils, and streamed down his breast. He arrived within a mile of the river. The sound of footsteps gathered upon him. A glance behind showed his pursuer within twenty yards, and preparing to launch his spear. Stopping short, he turned round and spread out his arms. The savage, confounded by this sudden action, attempted to stop and hurl his spear, but fell in the very act. His spear stuck in the ground, and the shaft broke in his hand. Colter plucked up the pointed part, pinned the savage to the earth, and continued his flight. The Indians, as they arrived at their slaughtered companion, stopped to howl over him. Colter made the most of this precious delay, gained the skirt of cotton-wood bordering the river, dashed through it, and plunged into the stream. He swam to a neighboring island, against the upper end of which the driftwood had lodged in such quantities as to form a natural raft; under this he dived, and swam below water until he succeeded in getting a breathing place between the floating trunks of trees, whose branches and bushes formed a covert several feet above the level of the water. He had scarcely drawn breath after all his toils, when he heard his pursuers on the river bank, whooping and yelling like so many fiends. They plunged in the river, and swam to the raft. The heart of Colter almost died within him as he saw them, through the chinks of his concealment, passing and repassing, and seeking for him in all directions. They at length gave up the search, and he began to rejoice in his escape, when the idea presented itself that they might set the raft on fire. Here was a new source of horrible apprehension, in which he remained until night fall. Fortunately, the idea did not suggest itself to the Indians. As soon as it was dark, finding by the silence around that his pursuers had departed, Colter dived again, and came up beyond the raft. He then swam silently down the river for a considerable distance, when he landed, and kept on all night, to get as far as possible from this dangerous neighborhood.

By daybreak he had gained sufficient distance to relieve him from the terrors of his savage foes; but now new sources of inquietude presented themselves. He was naked and alone, in the midst of an unbounded wilderness; his only chance was to reach a trading post of the Missouri company, situated on a branch of the Yellowstone river. Even should he elude his

The story of John Colter's race, told by Washington Irving in *Astoria* (1836), was one of the more widely circulated escape narratives. This woodcut, captioned "Colter Pursued by the Indians," is from an anonymous anthology of *Indian Anecdotes and Barbarities* published the following year. *Courtesy of the Edward E. Ayer Collection, the Newberry Library.*

pursuers, days must elapse before he could reach this post, during which he must traverse immense prairies destitute of shade, his naked body exposed to the burning heat of the sun by day, and the dews and chills of the night season; and his feet lacerated by the thorns of the prickly pear. Though he might see game in abundance around him, he had no means of killing any for his sustenance, and must depend for food upon the roots of the earth. In defiance of these difficulties he pushed resolutely forward, guiding himself in his trackless course by those signs and indications known only to Indians and backwoodmen; and after braving dangers and hardships enough to break down any spirit but that of a western pioneer, arrived safe at the solitary post in question.

Such is a sample of the rugged experience which Colter had to relate of savage life; yet, with all these perils and terrors fresh in his recollection, he could not see the present band on their way to those regions of danger and adventure, without feeling a vehement impulse to join them. A western trapper is like a sailor; past hazards only stimulate him to further risks. The vast prairie is to the one what the ocean is to the other, a boundless field of enterprise and exploit. However he may have suffered in his last cruise, he is always ready to join a new expedition; and the more adventurous its nature, the more attractive is it to his vagrant spirit. . . .

George Bancroft on the MacCrea Abduction

In July 1777, a young woman named Jane MacCrea (sometimes McCrea, M'Crea, or M'Kray) left Fort Edward, New York, to join her fiancé, David Jones, a Tory officer in General Burgoyne's army. For some unknown reason, possibly because her long tresses would make an attractive trophy, she was abducted, murdered, and scalped by the Indians Jones had hired to escort her. The story of her fate is more intimately interwoven with the course of American history than any other captivity, for during the Revolutionary War American patriots exploited its pathos to stir up indignation against the British for failing to control their Indian troops. Since then it has inspired many a ballad, story, play, and picture, including Michel René Hilliard d'Auberteuil's *Miss McCrea; a Novel of the American Revolution* (1784); John Vanderlyn's painting, *The Death of Jane M'Crea;* and an episode in Joel Barlow's *Columbiad* (1807). It also provided a source for the death of Cora in Cooper's *The Last of the Mohicans* (see pp. 231-256).

This reference to the MacCrea abduction is taken from George Bancroft's *History of the United States* (1834-1885). Like Irving's version of the Colter narrative, it is a treatment of Indian captivity by a sophisticated historical scholar and influential public figure. Whenever Bancroft described a war in which Americans killed Indians, he included a captivity episode as a reminder that, with few exceptions, Indians were little better than barbarians whose "moral inflexibility" and intractable attachment to savage ways made their extermination a necessity. The MacCrea captivity fulfilled a double function. It called attention to the savagery of the Indians and of the British who encouraged it.

. . . Early in July, Burgoyne confessed to Germain [Lord George Germain (1716-1785), British secretary of state for the colonies] that, "were

SOURCE: George Bancroft, *History of the United States, from the Discovery of the American Continent* (New York, 1883-1885), vol. 5, p. 164. This edition is "The Author's Last Revision."

the Indians left to themselves, enormities too horrid to think of would ensue; guilty and innocent, women and infants, would be a common prey." The general, nevertheless, resolved to use them as instruments of "terror," and promised, after arriving at Albany, to send them "toward Connecticut and Boston," knowing full well that they were left to themselves by La Corne Saint-Luc, their leader, who was impatient of control in the use of the scalping-knife. Every day the savages brought in scalps as well as prisoners. On the twenty-seventh, Jane MacCrea, a young woman of twenty, betrothed to a loyalist in the British service and esteeming herself under the protection of British arms, was riding from Fort Edward to the British camp at Sandy Hill, escorted by two Indians. The Indians quarrelled about the reward promised on her safe arrival, and at a half-mile from Fort Edward one of them sunk his tomahawk in her skull. The incident was not of unusual barbarity; but this massacre of a betrothed girl on her way to her lover touched all who heard the story. Burgoyne, from fear of "the total defection of the Indians," pardoned the assassin. . . .

Francis Parkman on the Conspiracy of Pontiac

While still a sophomore at Harvard, Francis Parkman (1823-1893), a high-strung Boston Brahmin with an avid taste for the outdoors, mapped his life work. He would write "the story of what was then known as the 'Old French War,' the war that ended in the conquest of Canada." Shortly, his plan came "to include the whole course of the American conflict between France and England." It was an unusual ambition. The best historians, George Bancroft, for instance, thought of themselves as writers by avocation, and despite Bancroft's example, American history was not then looked upon as demanding much attention. Parkman began collecting material for his book when he was twenty-one. Its subject was the Indian uprising of 1763-1766 led by the Ottawa chief, Pontiac, actually the last phase of the "Old French War." From the outset, Parkman knew what he was about. Essentially a literary man with a flair for the dramatic, he was vigilant in his pursuit of the facts, whether those of the archive or of the western wilderness, and his grasp of the historical drama was firm. His preface to *The Conspiracy of Pontiac* (1851) began, "The conquest of Canada . . . changed the political aspects of the continent, prepared a way for the independence of the British colonies, rescued the vast tracts of the interior from the rule of military despotism, and gave them, eventually, to the keeping of an ordered democracy." The substance was of "momentous consequences" historically and epic in its literary possibilities. It also contained elements of the dramatic, romantic, and tragic, for, Parkman continued, it aimed "to portray the American forest and the American Indian at the period when both received their final doom." The return of the white captives by Pontiac's Indians, demanded under the truce terms of the

---

SOURCE: Francis Parkman, *The Conspiracy of Pontiac*, 6th ed. (Boston, 1870); Parkman states in the preface that new material "has been carefully collected, and is incorporated in the present edition."

British, was the last and perhaps the most poignant act in the historic, romantic drama Parkman wrote about the "Old French War."

Parkman himself was something of a captive. At the behest of his family, he read for a law degree, meanwhile collecting notes for his book on Pontiac and suffering from an attack of nerves and eye-strain. An opportunity to escape presented itself when a cousin invited him to go west on a hunting trip. In 1846 he left St. Louis and headed for the Rocky Mountains, taking all the risks, testing himself, and living on a day-to-day basis with Indians in what might fairly be called their uncorrupted savage state. His own description in the preface to *The Conspiracy of Pontiac* was, "In 1846, I visited various primitive tribes of the Rocky Mountains, and was, for a time, domesticated in a village of the western Dahcotah." Considering his precarious health, the hazards of the trail, and the manner in which he drove himself, he was lucky to have escaped unscathed. From these wanderings and observations he wrote his best-known book, *The California and Oregon Trail,* first published serially in *The Knickerbocker Review* beginning in 1847. It is not history, but a personal travel narrative, though history was being made at the time in the West, but it was an experience which made it possible for him later to write history that was compelling and vital. Terribly hampered by headaches and partial blindness, he began work on *Pontiac.*

The Seven Years' War (1756-1763) was a worldwide contest between France and England. For American colonists, it was a continuation of an almost uninterrupted border conflict, usually of minor concern in the larger imperial struggle, that had begun in 1689 with King William's War and was characterized by the horrors of Indian depredation. The border war preceding the European conflict erupted in America in 1754 and, with Pontiac's Rebellion, it continued beyond the formal end of hostilities signalized by the Treaty of Paris (1763). Under the terms of the treaty, France ceded Canada and its territories east of the Mississippi. Where the French had been easy in their relationships with the Indians, the English were insensitive and high-handed. They denied the Indians gunpowder and rum, and they encroached on their lands, More important, the Indians sensed "their final doom" and, writes Parkman, "led by a great and daring champion, they sought to avert it." Pontiac summoned a war council to organize an attack on the fort at Detroit, which he besieged when his efforts to invest it through guile were frustrated, and other Indian forces, with more success, attacked forts and settlements in the Ohio country and western Pennsylvania. Sent to relieve Fort Pitt (now Pittsburgh), Col. Henry Bouquet (1719-1765) defeated the Indians at Bushy Run, about twenty-six miles away, in August 1763. In the spring of 1764, at the head of a formidable column that included elements of the Royal American regiment, the Black Watch, and militia from Virginia and Pennsylvania, he marched from Fort Pitt to the Muskingum River through a wilderness that no such military force had ever before traversed. Here Bouquet encamped and awaited emissaries from the rebellious Delawares and Shawnees.

By the standards of the times, Bouquet was a compassionate man. Once, when it was reported to him that the white wife of an Indian chief returned as a war prisoner had run away with her Indian husband and child, he "requested that no pursuit should be made, as she was happier with her Chief than she would be if restored to her home." But the general occasion called for a firmness of which he was capable. He demanded the return of all white prisoners, including those who had been adopted into the tribes. Gen. Thomas Gage (1721-1787), military commander in chief of British forces in North America, gloated that Colonel Bouquet "Obliged them to deliver up even their Own Children born of white women." The reasons for Bouquet's severity are complex. The primary one was the demand of the American colonists that their captive kin be returned. But British purposes were also punitive, an effort to restrain the Indians from further rebellion through fear of reprisals. It was also the common belief that tribalized whites were often the most effective leaders of Indian opposition.

Parkman dramatizes the pathos of the redeemed captives. Yet, in the end, despite his sympathy, his romanticism, and his regret for the doom of "the American forest and the American Indian," he is of the party of progress. His vibrant language almost inadvertently reveals an ultimate prejudice. The children of the Indians and whites are "hybrid offspring." White prisoners are adopted into Indian tribes only after "the vengeance of the conquerors is sated; when they have shot, stabbed, burned, or beaten to death, enough to satisfy the shades of their departed relatives." Whites who chose the life of the Indian are bewitched by the "charms" of the wilderness which has "cast its magic" in a "spell," transforming them into outcasts. For Parkman, the wilderness was magic, but the magic was black.

The story Parkman tells about the old woman whose daughter, a returned captive, did not recognize her until Colonel Bouquet suggested that she "Sing the song you used to sing to her when a child," is still current in the folklore of western Pennsylvania. The captive was Regina Hartman, taken in October of 1755. Her family was from Württemberg, and the opening lines of the song, a German hymn, as preserved in a local history, were:

> Allein, und doch nicht ganze allein,
> Bin ich in meiner Einsamkeit.
>
> [Alone, and yet not all alone,
> Am I in my loneliness.]

Parkman also refers to children who "struggled lustily when consigned to the hands of their relatives," citing in his footnotes *A Narrative of the Captivity of John M'Cullough, Esq.,* reprinted in *Incidents of Border Warfare . . .* (1839) and elsewhere. The M'Cullough boy, age fourteen, had to be tied and guarded to prevent his escape to his Indian family, which he nonetheless managed under the cover of darkness. Parkman also refers in his notes to Mary Jemison (see pp. 110-123) as an example of a captive who "never lost her attachment to Indian life."

CHAPTER XXVII.
1764.

BOUQUET FORCES THE DELAWARES AND SHAWANOES TO SUE FOR PEACE.

. . . Bouquet continued his march down the valley of the Muskingum, until he reached a spot where the broad meadows, which bordered the river, would supply abundant grazing for the cattle and horses; while the terraces above, shaded by forest-trees, offered a convenient site for an encampment. Here he began to erect a small palisade work, as a depot for stores and baggage. Before the task was complete, a deputation of chiefs arrived, bringing word that their warriors were encamped, in great numbers, about eight miles from the spot, and desiring Bouquet to appoint the time and place for a council. He ordered them to meet him, on the next day, at a point near the margin of the river, a little below the camp; and thither a party of men was at once despatched, to erect a sort of rustic arbor of saplings and the boughs of trees, large enough to shelter the English officers and the Indian chiefs. With a host of warriors in the neighborhood, who would gladly break in upon them, could they hope that the attack would succeed, it behooved the English to use every precaution. A double guard was placed, and a stringent discipline enforced.

In the morning, the little army moved in battle order to the place of council. Here the principal officers assumed their seats under the canopy of branches, while the glittering array of the troops was drawn out on the meadow in front, in such a manner as to produce the most imposing effect on the minds of the Indians, in whose eyes the sight of fifteen hundred men under arms was a spectacle equally new and astounding. The perfect order and silence of the far-extended lines; the ridges of bayonets flashing in the sun; the fluttering tartans of the Highland regulars; the bright red uniform of the Royal Americans; the darker garb and duller trappings of the Pennsylvania troops, and the bands of Virginia backwoodsmen, who, in fringed hunting-frocks and Indian moccasons, stood leaning carelessly on their rifles,—all these combined to form a scene of military pomp and power not soon to be forgotten.

At the appointed hour, the deputation appeared. The most prominent among them were Kiashuta, chief of the band of Senecas who had deserted their ancient homes to form a colony on the Ohio; Custaloga, chief of the Delawares; and the head chief of the Shawanoes, whose name sets orthography at defiance. As they approached, painted and plumed in all their savage pomp, they looked neither to the right hand nor to the left, not deigning, under the eyes of their enemy, to cast even a glance at the military display around them. They seated themselves, with stern, impassive looks, and an air of sullen dignity; while their sombre brows betrayed the hatred still rankling in their hearts. After a few minutes had been consumed in the indispensable ceremony of smoking, Turtle Heart, a chief of the Delawares, and orator of the deputation, rose, bearing in his hand a bag containing the belts of wampum. Addressing himself to the English commander, he spoke as follows, delivering a belt for every clause of his speech:—

"Brother, I speak in behalf of the three nations whose chiefs are here present. With this belt I open your ears and your hearts, that you may listen to my words.

"Brother, this war was neither your fault nor ours. It was the work of the nations who live to the westward, and of our wild young men, who would have killed us if we had resisted them. We now put away all evil from our hearts; and we hope that your mind and ours will once more be united together.

"Brother, it is the will of the Great Spirit that there should be peace between us. We, on our side, now take fast hold of the chain of friendship; but, as we cannot hold it alone, we desire that you will take hold also, and we must look up to the Great Spirit, that he may make us strong, and not permit this chain to fall from our hands.

"Brother, these words come from our hearts, and not from our lips. You desire that we should deliver up your flesh and blood now captive among us; and, to show you that we are sincere, we now return you as many of them as we have at present been able to bring. [Here he delivered eighteen white prisoners, who had been brought by the deputation to the council.] You shall receive the rest as soon as we have time to collect them."

In such figurative terms, not devoid of dignity, did the Indian orator sue for peace to his detested enemies. When he had concluded, the chiefs of every tribe rose in succession, to express concurrence in what he had said, each delivering a belt of wampum and a bundle of small sticks; the latter designed to indicate the number of English prisoners whom his followers retained, and whom he pledged himself to surrender. In an Indian council, when one of the speakers has advanced a matter of weight and urgency, the other party defers his reply to the following day, that due time may be allowed for deliberation. Accordingly, in the present instance, the council adjourned to the next morning, each party retiring to its respective camp. But, when day dawned, the weather had changed. The valley of the Muskingum was filled with driving mist and rain, and the meeting was in consequence postponed. On the third day, the landscape brightened afresh, the troops marched once more to the place of council, and the Indian chiefs convened to hear the reply of their triumphant foe. It was not of a kind to please them. The opening words gave an earnest of what was to come; for Bouquet discarded the usual address of an Indian harangue: fathers, brothers, or children,—terms which imply a relation of friendship, or a desire to conciliate,—and adopted a sterner and more distant form.

"Sachems, war-chiefs, and warriors, the excuses you have offered are frivolous and unavailing, and your conduct is without defence or apology. You could not have acted as you pretend to have done through fear of the western nations; for, had you stood faithful to us, you knew that we would have protected you against their anger; and as for your young men, it was your duty to punish them, if they did amiss. You have drawn down our just resentment by your violence and perfidy. Last summer, in cold blood, and in a time of profound peace, you robbed and murdered the traders, who had come among you at your own express desire. You attacked Fort Pitt, which was built by your consent; and you destroyed our outposts and garrisons, whenever treachery could place them in your power. You assailed our troops—the same who now stand before you—in the woods at Bushy Run; and, when we had routed and driven you off, you sent your scalping-parties to the frontier, and murdered many hundreds of our people. Last July, when the other nations came to ask for peace, at Niagara, you not only refused to attend, but sent an insolent message instead, in which you expressed a pretended contempt for the English; and, at the same time, told the surrounding nations that you would never lay down the hatchet. Afterwards, when Colonel Bradstreet came up Lake Erie, you sent a deputation of your chiefs, and concluded a treaty with him; but your engagements were no sooner made than broken; and, from that day to this, you have scalped and butchered us without ceasing. Nay, I am informed that, when you heard that this army was penetrating the woods, you mustered your warriors to attack us, and were only deterred from doing so when you found how greatly we outnumbered you. This is not the only instance of your bad faith; for, since the beginning of the last war, you have made repeated treaties with us, and promised to give up your prisoners; but you have never kept these engagements, nor any others. We shall endure this no longer; and I am now come among you to force you to make atonement for the injuries you have done us. I have brought with me the relatives of those you have murdered. They are eager for vengeance, and nothing restrains them from taking it but my assurance that this army shall not leave your country until you have given them an ample satisfaction.

"Your allies, the Ottawas, Ojibwas, and Wyandots, have begged for peace; the Six Nations have leagued themselves with us; the great lakes and rivers around you are all in our possession, and your friends the French are in subjection to us, and can do no more to aid you. You are all in our power, and, if we choose, we can exterminate you from the earth; but the English are a merciful and generous people, averse to shed the blood even of their greatest enemies; and if it were possible that you could convince us that you sincerely repent of your past perfidy, and that we could depend on your good behavior for the future, you might yet hope for mercy and peace. If I find that you faithfully execute the conditions which I shall prescribe, I will not treat you with the severity you deserve.

"I give you twelve days from this date to deliver into my hands all the prisoners in your possession, without exception: Englishmen, Frenchmen, women, and children; whether adopted into your tribes, married, or living among you under any denomination or pretence whatsoever. And you are to furnish these prisoners with clothing, provisions, and horses, to carry them to Fort Pitt. When you have fully complied with these conditions, you shall then know on what terms you may obtain the peace you sue for."

This speech, with the stern voice and countenance of the speaker, told with chilling effect upon the awe-stricken hearers. It quelled their native haughtiness, and sunk them to the depths of humiliation. Their speeches in reply were dull and insipid, void of that savage eloquence, which, springing from a wild spirit of independence, has so often distinguished the forest orators. Judging the temper of their enemies by their own insatiable thirst for vengeance, they hastened, with all the alacrity of terror, to fulfil the prescribed conditions, and avert the threatened ruin. They dispersed to their different villages, to collect and bring in the prisoners; while Bouquet, on his part, knowing that his best security for their good faith was to keep up the alarm which his decisive measures had created, determined to march yet nearer to their settlements. Still following the course of the Muskingum, he descended to a spot near its confluence with its main branch, which might be regarded as a central point with respect to the surrounding Indian villages. Here, with the exception of the distant Shawanoe settlements, they were all within reach of his hand, and he could readily chastise the first attempt at deceit or evasion. The principal chiefs of each tribe had been forced to accompany him as hostages.

For the space of a day, hundreds of axes were busy at their work. The trees were felled, the ground cleared, and, with marvellous rapidity, a town sprang up in the heart of the wilderness, martial in aspect and rigorous in discipline; with storehouses, hospitals, and works of defence, rude sylvan cabins mingled with white tents, and the forest rearing its sombre rampart around the whole. On one side of this singular encampment was a range of buildings, designed to receive the expected prisoners; and matrons, brought for this purpose with the army, were appointed to take charge of the women and children among them. At the opposite side, a canopy of branches, sustained on the upright trunks of young trees, formed a rude council-hall, in keeping with the savage assembly for whose reception it was designed.

And now, issuing from the forest, came warriors conducting troops of prisoners, or leading captive children,—wild young barbarians, born perhaps among themselves, and scarcely to be distinguished from their own. Yet, seeing the sullen reluctance which the Indians soon betrayed in this ungrateful task, Bouquet thought it expedient to stimulate their efforts by sending detachments of soldiers to each of the villages, still retaining the chiefs in pledge for their safety. About this time, a Canadian officer, named Hertel, with a party of Caughnawaga Indians, arrived with a letter from Colonel Bradstreet, dated at Sandusky. The writer declared that he was unable to remain longer in the Indian country, and was on the point of retiring down Lake Erie with his army; a movement which, at the least, was of doubtful necessity, and which might have involved the most disastrous consequences. Had the tidings been received but a few days sooner, the whole effect of Bouquet's measures would probably have been destroyed, the Indians encouraged to resistance, and the war brought to the arbitration of a battle, which must needs have been a fierce and bloody one. But, happily for both parties, Bouquet now had his enemies firmly in his grasp, and the boldest warrior dared not violate the truce.

The messengers who brought the letter of Bradstreet brought also the tidings that peace was made with the northern Indians; but stated, at the same time, that these tribes had murdered many of their captives, and given up but few of the remainder, so that no small number were still within their power. The conduct of Bradstreet in this matter was the more disgraceful, since he had been encamped for weeks almost within gunshot of the Wyandot villages at Sandusky, where most of the prisoners were detained. Bouquet, on his part, though separated from this place by a journey of many days, resolved to take upon himself the duty which his brother officer had strangely neglected. He sent an embassy to Sandusky, demanding that the prisoners should be surrendered. This measure was in a great degree successful. He despatched messengers soon after to the principal Shawanoe village, on the Scioto, distant about eighty miles from his camp, to rouse the inhabitants to a greater activity than they seemed inclined to display. This was a fortunate step; for the Shawanoes of the Scioto, who had been guilty of atrocious cruelties during the war, had conceived the idea that they were excluded from the general amnesty, and marked out for destruction. This notion had been propagated, and perhaps suggested, by the French traders in their villages; and so thorough was the conviction of the Shawanoes, that they came to the desperate purpose of murdering their prisoners, and marching, with all the warriors they could muster, to attack the English. This plan was no sooner formed than the French traders opened their stores of bullets and gunpowder, and dealt them out freely to the Indians. Bouquet's messengers came in time to prevent the catastrophe, and relieve the terrors of the Shawanoes, by the assurance that peace would be granted to them on the same conditions as to the rest. Thus encouraged, they abandoned their design, and set out with lighter hearts for the English camp, bringing with them a portion of their prisoners. When about half-way on their journey, they were met by an Indian runner, who told them that a soldier had been killed in the woods, and their tribe charged with the crime. On hearing this, their fear revived, and with it their former purpose. Having collected their prisoners in a meadow, they surrounded the miserable wretches, armed with guns, war-clubs, and bows and arrows, and prepared to put them to death. But another runner arrived before the butchery began, and, assuring them that what they had heard was false, prevailed on them once more to proceed. They pursued their journey without farther interruption, and, coming in safety to the camp, delivered the prisoners whom they had brought.

These by no means included all of their captives, for nearly a hundred were left behind, because they belonged to warriors who had gone to the Illinois to procure arms and ammunition from the French; and there is no authority in an Indian community powerful enough to deprive the meanest warrior of his property, even in circumstances of the greatest public exigency. This was clearly understood by the English commander, and he therefore received the submission of the Shawanoes, at the same time compelling them to deliver hostages for the future surrender of the remaining prisoners.

Band after band of captives had been daily arriving, until upwards of two hundred were now collected in the camp; including, as far as could be ascertained, all who had been in the hands of the Indians, excepting those belonging to the absent warriors of the Shawanoes. Up to this time, Bouquet had maintained a stern and rigorous demeanor; repressing his natural clemency and humanity, refusing all friendly intercourse with the Indians, and telling them that he should treat them as enemies until they had fully complied with all the required conditions. In this, he displayed his knowledge of their character; for, like all warlike savages, they are extremely prone to interpret lenity and moderation into timidity and indecision; and he who, from good-nature or mistaken philanthropy, is betrayed into yielding a point which he has before insisted on, may have deep cause to rue it. As their own dealings with their enemies are not leavened with such humanizing ingredients, they can seldom comprehend them; and to win over an Indian foe by kindness should only be attempted by one who has already proved clearly that he is able and ready to subdue him by force.

But now, when every condition was satisfied, such inexorable rigor was no longer demanded; and, having convoked the chiefs in the sylvan council-house, Bouquet signified his willingness to receive their offers of peace.

"Brother," began the Indian orator, "with this belt of wampum I dispel the black cloud that has hung so long over our heads, that the sunshine of peace may once more descend to warm and gladden us. I wipe the tears from your eyes, and condole with you on the loss of your brethren who have perished in this war. I gather their bones together, and cover them deep in the earth, that the sight of them may no longer bring sorrow to your hearts; and I scatter dry leaves over the spot, that it may depart for ever from memory.

"The path of peace, which once ran between your dwellings and mine, has of late been choked with thorns and briers, so that no one could pass that way; and we have both almost forgotten that such a path had ever been.

I now clear away all such obstructions, and make a broad, smooth road, so that you and I may freely visit each other, as our fathers used to do. I kindle a great council fire, whose smoke shall rise to heaven, in view of all the nations; while you and I sit together and smoke the peace-pipe at its blaze."

. . .

From the hard formalities and rigid self-control of an Indian council-house, where the struggles of fear, rage, and hatred were deep buried beneath a surface of iron immobility, we turn to scenes of a widely different nature; an exhibition of mingled and contrasted passions, more worthy the pen of the dramatist than that of the historian; who, restricted to the meagre outline of recorded authority, can reflect but a feeble image of the truth. In the ranks of the Pennsylvania troops, and among the Virginia riflemen, were the fathers, brothers, and husbands of those whose rescue from captivity was a chief object of the march. Ignorant what had befallen them, and doubtful whether they were yet among the living, these men had joined the army, in the feverish hope of winning them back to home and civilization. Perhaps those whom they sought had perished by the slow torments of the stake; perhaps by the more merciful hatchet; or perhaps they still dragged out a wretched life in the midst of a savage horde. There were instances in which whole families had been carried off at once. The old, the sick, or the despairing, had been tomahawked, as useless encumbrances; while the rest, pitilessly forced asunder, were scattered through every quarter of the wilderness. It was a strange and moving sight, when troop after troop of prisoners arrived in succession—the meeting of husbands with wives, and fathers with children, the reunion of broken families, long separated in a disastrous captivity; and, on the other hand, the agonies of those who learned tidings of death and horror, or groaned under the torture of protracted suspense. Women, frantic between hope and fear, were rushing hither and thither, in search of those whose tender limbs had, perhaps, long since fattened the cubs of the she-wolf; or were pausing, in an agony of doubt, before some sunburnt young savage, who, startled at the haggard apparition, shrank from his forgotten parent, and clung to the tawny breast of his adopted mother. Others were divided between delight and anguish: on the one hand, the joy of an unexpected recognition; and, on the other, the misery of realized fears, or the more intolerable pangs of doubts not yet resolved. Of all the spectators of this tragic drama, few were obdurate enough to stand unmoved. The roughest soldiers felt the contagious sympathy, and softened into unwonted tenderness.

Among the children brought in for surrender, there were some, who, captured several years before, as early, perhaps, as the French war, had lost every recollection of friends and home. Terrified by the novel sights around them, the flash and glitter of arms, and the strange complexion of the pale-faced warriors, they screamed and struggled lustily when consigned to the hands of their relatives. There were young women, too, who had become the partners of Indian husbands; and who now, with all their hybrid offspring, were led reluctantly into the presence of fathers or brothers whose images were almost blotted from their memory. They stood agitated and bewildered; the revival of old affections, and the rush of dormant memories, painfully contending with more recent attachments, and the shame of their real or fancied disgrace; while their Indian lords looked on, scarcely less moved than they, yet hardening themselves with savage stoicism, and standing in the midst of their enemies, imperturbable as statues of bronze. These women were compelled to return with their children to the settlements; yet they all did so with reluctance, and several afterwards made their escape, eagerly hastening back to their warrior husbands, and the toils and vicissitudes of an Indian wigwam.

Day after day brought renewals of these scenes, deepening in interest as they drew towards their close. A few individual incidents have been recorded. A young Virginian, robbed of his wife but a few months before, had volunteered in the expedition with the faint hope of recovering her; and, after long suspense, had recognized her among a troop of prisoners, bearing in her arms a child born during her captivity. But the joy of the meeting was bitterly alloyed by the loss of a former child, not two years old, captured with the mother, but soon taken from her, and carried, she could not tell whither. Days passed on; they could learn no tidings of its fate, and the mother, harrowed with terrible imaginations, was almost driven to despair; when, at length, she discovered her child in the arms of an Indian warrior, and snatched it with an irrepressible cry of transport.

When the army, on its homeward march, reached the town of Carlisle, those who had been unable to follow the expedition came thither in numbers, to inquire for the friends they had lost. Among the rest was an old woman, whose daughter had been carried off nine years before. In the crowd of female captives, she discovered one in whose wild and swarthy features she discerned the altered lineaments of her child; but the girl, who had almost forgotten her native tongue, returned no sign of recognition to her eager words, and the old woman bitterly complained that the daughter, whom she had so often sung to sleep on her knee, had forgotten her in her old age. Bouquet suggested an expedient which proves him a man of feeling and perception. "Sing the song that you used to sing to her when a child." The old woman obeyed; and a sudden start, a look of bewilderment, and a passionate flood of tears, removed every doubt, and restored the long-lost daughter to her mother's arms.

The tender affections by no means form a salient feature in the Indian character. They hold them in contempt, and scorn every manifestation of them, yet, on this occasion, they would not be repressed, and the human heart betrayed itself, though throbbing under a breastplate of ice. None of the ordinary signs of emotion, neither tears, words, nor looks, declared how greatly they were moved. It was by their kindness and solicitude, by their attention to the wants of the captives, by their offers of furs, garments, the choicest articles of food, and every thing which in their eyes seemed luxury, that they displayed their sorrow at parting from their adopted relatives and friends. Some among them went much farther, and asked permission to follow the army on its homeward march, that they might hunt for the captives, and supply them with better food than the military stores could furnish. A young Seneca warrior had become deeply enamoured of a Virginian girl. At great risk of his life, he accompanied the troops far within the limits of the settlements; and, at every night's encampment, approaching the quarters of the captives as closely as the sentinels would permit, he sat watching, with patient vigilance, to catch a glimpse of his lost mistress.

The Indian women, whom no idea of honor compels to wear an iron mask, were far from emulating the frigid demeanor of their lords. All day they ran wailing through the camp; and, when night came, the hills and woods resounded with their dreary lamentations.

The word *prisoner,* as applied to captives taken by the Indians, is a misnomer, and conveys a wholly false impression of their situation and treatment. When the vengeance of the conquerors is sated; when they have shot stabbed, burned, or beaten to death, enough to satisfy the shades of their departed relatives, they usually treat those who survive their wrath with moderation and humanity; often adopting them to supply the place of lost brothers, husbands, or children, whose names are given to the successors thus substituted in their place. By a formal ceremony, the white blood is washed from their veins; and they are regarded thenceforth as members of the tribe, faring equally with the rest in prosperity or adversity, in famine or abundance. When children are adopted in this manner by Indian women, they nurture them with the same tenderness and indulgence which they extend, in a remarkable degree, to their own offspring; and such young women as will not marry an Indian husband are treated with a singular forbearance, in which superstition, natural temperament, and a sense of right and justice may all claim a share. The captive, unless he excites suspicion by his conduct, or exhibits peculiar contumacy, is left with no other restraint than his own free will. The warrior who captured him, or to whom he was assigned in the division of the spoil, sometimes claims, it is true, a certain right of property in him, to the exclusion of others; but this claim is soon forgotten, and is seldom exercised to the inconvenience of the captive, who has no other prison than the earth, the air, and the forest. Five hundred miles of wilderness, beset with difficulty and danger, are the sole bars to his escape, should he desire to effect it; but, strange as it may appear, this wish is apt to expire in his heart, and he often remains to the end of his life a contented denizen of the woods.

Among the captives brought in for delivery were some bound fast to prevent their escape; and many others, who, amid the general tumult of joy and sorrow, sat sullen and scowling, angry that they were forced to abandon the wild license of the forest for the irksome restraints of society. Thus to look back with a fond longing to inhospitable deserts, where men, beasts, and Nature herself, seem arrayed in arms, and where ease, security, and all that civilization reckons among the goods of life, are alike cut off, may appear to argue some strange perversity or moral malformation. Yet such has been the experience of many a sound and healthful mind. To him who has once tasted the reckless independence, the haughty self-reliance, the sense of irresponsible freedom, which the forest life engenders, civilization thenceforth seems flat and stale. Its pleasures are insipid, its pursuits wearisome, its conventionalities, duties, and mutual dependence alike tedious and disgusting. The entrapped wanderer grows fierce and restless, and pants for breathing-room. His path, it is true, was choked with difficulties, but his body and soul were hardened to meet them; it was beset with dangers, but these were the very spice of his life, gladdening his heart with exulting self-confidence, and sending the blood through his veins with a livelier current. The wilderness, rough, harsh, and inexorable, has charms more potent in their seductive influence than all the lures of luxury and sloth. And often he on whom it has cast its magic finds no heart to dissolve the spell, and remains a wanderer and an Ishmaelite to the hour of his death. . . .

Henry David Thoreau on Hannah Duston's Captivity

Although his philosophy of history differs from that of Irving, Bancroft, or Parkman, Henry David Thoreau (1817-1862) agreed that history should be well written and that historical events should be made to reveal their philosophical import. He includes an account of the captivity of Hannah Duston (also Dustun, Dustin, or, as Thoreau spells it, Dustan) in his journal, *A Week on the Concord and Merrimack Rivers* (1849), to illustrate a sense of the abiding presence of evil and the penetration of the past into the present.

Violent and dramatic, the Duston captivity provokes moral speculation. Hannah Duston and her nurse, Mary Neff, were taken captive by Abenaki Indians in 1697 during King William's War. In the camp with the two women was another captive, a boy named Samuel Lennardson, who had been taken during a raid on Worcester a year and a half earlier. In making her escape and in retaliation for the murder of her newborn infant, Hannah Duston tomahawked her captors while they were sleeping, and she took their scalps for a bounty offered by the Massachusetts General Court. Cotton Mather had heard the narrative either directly from her or from her pastor, John Rolfe.

Different versions of this popular story reflect changing American attitudes toward violence, Indians, and femininity. Mather applauded Hannah Duston's heroism, seeing in it God's providence. In "A Mother's Revenge," a short sketch in his *Legends of New England . . .* (1831), John Greenleaf Whittier attributes her behavior to temporary insanity brought on by the death of her baby and the presumed deaths of her entire family, a view also enunciated by Timothy Dwight, who included an account of the Duston captivity in his *Travels in New England and New York . . .* (1821). Nathaniel Hawthorne, who likewise wrote a short sketch about Hannah Duston, finds her barbaric and embarrassingly unfeminine (see "The Duston Family," pp. 224-230).

SOURCE: Henry David Thoreau, *A Week on the Concord and Merrimack Rivers* (Boston, 1849).

Thoreau withholds censure. What Hannah represents is more important than what she did. She is both a victim of natural depravity and the performer of a depraved act. On the surface, Hannah Duston's captivity reveals racial injustice on the parts of both Indians and whites. At a more profound level, it represents a tendency toward barbarism which Thoreau hints is discernible in all of human history. By narrating part of Hannah Duston's captivity in the present tense, Thoreau suggests an interaction between past and present, emphasized through the association he makes between his trip on the Merrimack River and that by which Hannah Duston and her fellow captives escape the Indians. Allusions to the apples of Eden accentuate the suggestion that the evil in which Hannah is enmeshed is a condition of the universe. Thoreau mentions the "apple-tree" three times as he tells the Duston story, and he observes that "This seems a long time ago, yet it happened since Milton wrote his Paradise Lost." But he puts past events at a distance from the present by immediately adding that though they took place recently, their "antiquity is not the less for that." So the note on which he ends is ambiguous. The fruit of the apple tree has been eaten by the living, and it may or may not be untainted.

A footnote is irresistible. When Hannah Duston returned, the bounty on scalps had expired. Her husband, Thomas Duston, petitioned the General Court to reinstate the bounty, or at least to award his wife a compensation for the service she had rendered the community by slaying the Indians whose scalps she took. His petition was evidently effective, for the General Court awarded £25 to Hannah and £12 10s each to Mary Neff and Samuel Lennardson. Mrs. Duston also received a £50 reward from the governor of Maryland, and in later life she was allotted a pension for her services as an Indian killer.

THURSDAY

. . . On the thirty-first day of March, one hundred and forty-two years before this [1839], probably about this time in the afternoon, there were hurriedly paddling down this part of the river, between the pine woods which then fringed these banks, two white women and a boy, who had left an island at the mouth of the Contoocook before daybreak. They were slightly clad for the season, in the English fashion, and handled their paddles unskilfully, but with nervous energy and determination, and at the bottom of their canoe lay the still bleeding scalps of ten of the aborigines. They were Hannah Dustan, and her nurse, Mary Neff, both of Haverhill, eighteen miles from the mouth of this river, and an English boy, named Samuel Lennardson, escaping from captivity among the Indians. On the 15th of March previous, Hannah Dustan had been compelled to rise from childbed, and half-dressed, with one foot bare, accompanied by her nurse, commence an uncertain march, in still inclement weather, through the snow and the wilderness. She had seen her seven elder children flee with their father, but knew not of their fate. She had seen her infant's brains dashed out against an apple-tree, and had left her own and her neighbors' dwellings in ashes. When she reached the wigwam of her captor, situated on an island in the Merrimack, more than twenty miles above where we now are, she had been told that she and her nurse were soon to be taken to a distant Indian settlement, and there made to run the gauntlet naked. The family of this Indian consisted of two men, three women, and seven children, beside an English boy, whom she found a prisoner among them. Having determined to attempt her escape, she instructed the boy to inquire of one of the men, how he should despatch an enemy in the quickest manner, and take his scalp. "Strike 'em there," said he, placing his finger on his temple, and he also showed him how to take off the scalp. On the morning of the 31st she arose before daybreak, and awoke her nurse and the boy, and taking the Indians' tomahawks, they killed them all in their sleep, excepting one favorite boy, and one squaw who fled wounded with him to the woods. The English boy struck the Indian who had given him the information on the temple, as he had been directed. They then collected all the provision they could find, and took their master's tomahawk and gun, and scuttling all the canoes but one, commenced their flight to Haverhill, distant about sixty miles by the river. But after having proceeded a short distance, fearing that her story would not be believed if she should escape to tell it, they returned to the silent wigwam, and taking off the scalps of the dead, put them into a bag as proofs of what they had done, and then retracing their steps to the shore in the twilight, recommenced their voyage.

Early this morning this deed was performed, and now, perchance, these tired women and this boy, their clothes stained with blood, and their minds racked with alternate resolution and fear, are making a hasty meal of parched corn and moose-meat, while their canoe glides under these pine roots whose stumps are still standing on the bank. They are thinking of the dead whom they have left behind on that solitary isle far up the stream, and of the relentless living warriors who are in pursuit. Every withered leaf which the winter has left seems to know their story, and in its rustling to repeat it and betray them. An Indian lurks behind every rock and pine, and their nerves cannot bear the tapping of a woodpecker. Or they forget their own dangers and their deeds in conjecturing the fate of their kindred, and whether, if they escape the Indians, they shall find the former still alive. They do not stop to cook their meals upon the bank, nor land, except to carry their canoe about the falls. The stolen birch forgets its master and does them good service, and the swollen current bears them swiftly along with little need of the paddle, except to steer and keep them warm by exercise. For ice is floating in the river; the spring is opening; the muskrat and the beaver are driven out of their holes by the flood; deer gaze at them from the bank; a few faint-singing forest birds, perchance, fly across the river to the northernmost shore; the fish-hawk sails and screams overhead, and geese fly over with a startling clangor; but they do not observe these things, or they speedily forget them. They do not smile or chat all day. Sometimes they pass an Indian grave surrounded by its paling on the bank, or the frame of a wigwam, with a few coals left behind, or the withered stalks still rustling in the Indian's solitary cornfield on the interval. The birch stripped of its bark, or the charred stump where a tree has been burned down to be made into a canoe, these are the only traces of man,—a fabulous wild man to us. On either side, the primeval forest stretches away uninterrupted to Canada or to the "South Sea"; to the white man a drear and howling wilderness, but to the Indian a home, adapted to his nature, and cheerful as the smile of the Great Spirit.

While we loiter here this autumn evening, looking for a spot retired enough, where we shall quietly rest to-night, they thus, in that chilly March evening, one hundred and forty-two years before us, with wind and current favoring, have already glided out of sight, not to camp, as we shall, at night, but while two sleep one will manage the canoe, and the swift stream bear them onward to the settlements, it may be, even to old John Lovewell's [hero of Lovewell's Fight, 1725] house on Salmon Brook to-night.

According to the historian [Cotton Mather], they escaped as by a miracle all roving bands of Indians, and reached their homes in safety, with their trophies, for which the General Court paid them fifty pounds. The family of Hannah Dustan all assembled alive once more, except the infant whose brains were dashed out against the apple-tree, and there have been many who in later times have lived to say that they had eaten of the fruit of that apple-tree.

This seems a long while ago, and yet it happened since Milton wrote his *Paradise Lost*. But its antiquity is not the less great for that, for we do not regulate our historical time by the English standard, nor did the English by the Roman, nor the Roman by the Greek. . . .

The Legend of Murderer's Creek

For his enormously successful textbooks, William Holmes McGuffey (1800-1873) sought readings attractive enough to hold a child's attention but which, at the same time, could teach lessons in morality and history and also reading, spelling, grammar, and pronunciation. The legend of "Murderer's Creek" fits these purposes. It teaches that friendship and trust are qualities worth dying for and that bravery and self-sacrifice transcend the boundaries of sex or race. And almost incidentally, it is a lesson in colonial history calculated to instill national pride.

McGuffey reprinted "Murderer's Creek" from *The Child's Picture Book of Indians* (1833), collating it with the original in James Kirke Paulding's *The New Mirror for Travellers* (1828), a satire on fashionable summer resorts in New York's Hudson River region. A truncated version of the tale also appeared in Paulding's novel, *Koningsmarke, the Long Finne* (1823). There is a stream in Orange County, New York, which to this day is called Murderer's Creek. Local legends of settlers waylaid by Indians are associated with it, but there was no mention of a Stacy family until Paulding.

McGuffey's *Eclectic Readers* shaped the moral and cultural development of millions of American schoolchildren. By 1860, more than 122 million copies had been printed. His benevolent attitude toward Indians contrasts with that of his father, Alexander McGuffey, an Indian fighter who, during the 1790s, had served in the Ohio country under Generals Arthur St. Clair and "Mad Anthony" Wayne.

SOURCE: *McGuffey's Newly Revised Eclectic Third Reader* (Cincinnati, Ohio, 1846).

LESSON XXX.

1. Ex-tinct', having no one of their number left alive.
Tac'-it, (pro. *tae-it*), silent.
4. Im-port'-u-nate, pressing, urging.
7. En-croach'-ment, pushing in upon the property or rights of another. [ty.
Mas'-er-cre, to murder with cruel-
9. Grav'-i-ty, seriousness, or solemn dignity. [made fast.
10. Moor'-ed, confined by anchors.
11. Re-frain'-ed, kept from.
13. Ap-pri'-sing, giving notice to.
15. Tom'-a-hawk, an Indian hatchet.
17. Trait'-or, one who sells the interests of his country to an enemy.
In-vinc'-i-ble, unconquerable.
21. Shroud'-ed, covered up.
22. Sac'-ri-fice, destruction incurred for the good of another.
Firm'-ness, strength of purpose.
Suf-fice', to be enough.

MURDERER'S CREEK.

PRONOUNCE correctly. Cen-tu-ry, not *cen-ter-y:* beau-ti-ful, not *beau-ti-fl:* hus-band, not *hus-bund:* par-tic-u-lar, not *per-tic-i-lar:* chil-dren, not *chil-durn*: in-ter-ro-ga-ted; not *in-ter-rer-ga-ted*: ag-o-ny, not *ag-er-ny*: mo-ment, not *mo-munt:* sac-ri-fice, not *sa-cri-fis.*

1. A LITTLE more than a century ago, the beautiful region, watered by this stream, was possessed by a small tribe of Indians, which has long since become extinct, or incorporated with some other savage nation of the west. Three or four hundred yards from the stream, a white family, of the name of Stacy, had established itself in a log-house, by tacit permission of the tribe, to whom Stacy had made himself useful, by his skill in a variety of little arts, highly estimated by the savages.

2. In particular, a friendship subsisted between him and an old Indian, called Naoman, who often came to his house, and partook of his hospitality. The Indians seldom forgive injuries, or forget benefits. The family consisted of Stacy, his wife, and two children, a boy and a girl, the former five, the latter three years old.

3. One day, Naoman came to Stacy's log-hut, in his absence, lighted his pipe, and sat down. He looked very serious, sometimes sighed deeply, but said not a word. Stacy's wife asked him what was the matter? if he was sick? He shook his head, sighed, but said nothing, and soon went away.

4. The next day, he came again, and behaved in the same manner. Stacy's wife began to think strange of this, and related it to her husband, who advised her to urge the old man to an explanation, the next time he came. Accordingly, when he repeated his visit, the day after, she was more importunate than usual.

5. At last, the old Indian said, "I am a red man, and the pale-faces are our enemies: why should I speak?" "But my husband and I are your friends; you have eaten salt with us a thousand times, and my children have sat on your knee as often. If you have any thing on your mind, tell it to me."

6. "It will cost me my life, if it is known, and the white-faced women are not good at keeping secrets," replied Naoman. "Try me, and see." "Will you swear, by your Great Spirit, that you will tell none but your husband?" "I have none else to tell." "But will you swear?" "I do swear, by our Great Spirit, that I will tell none but my husband." "Not if my tribe should kill you for not telling?" "Not if your tribe *should* kill me for not telling."

7. Naoman then proceeded to tell her, that, owing to some encroachments of the white people below the mountains, his tribe had become irritated, and were resolved, that night, to massacre all the white settlers within their reach; that she must send for her husband, inform him of the danger, and as secretly and speedily as possible, take their canoe, and paddle with all haste, over the river to Fishkill for safety. "Be quick, and do nothing that may excite suspicion," said Naoman.

8. The good wife sought her husband, who was down on the river fishing, told him the story, and, as no time was to be lost, they proceeded to their boat, which was unluckily filled with water. It took some time to clear it out, and, meanwhile, Stacy recollected his gun, which had been left behind. He proceeded to the house, and returned with it. All this took up time, and precious time it proved to this poor family.

9. The daily visits of old Naoman, and his more than ordinary gravity, had excited suspicion in some of the tribe, who had, accordingly, paid particular attention to the movements of Stacy. One of the young Indians, who had been kept on the watch, seeing the whole family about to take to the boat, ran to the little Indian village, about a mile off, and gave the alarm.

10. Five Indians collected, ran down to the river where their canoes were moored, jumped in, and paddled after Stacy, who, by this time, had got some distance out into the stream. They gained on him so fast, that twice he dropped his paddle, and took up his gun.

11. But his wife prevented his shooting, by telling him that, if he fired, and they were afterward overtaken, they would meet with no mercy from the Indians. He accordingly refrained, and plied his paddle, till the sweat rolled in big drops down his forehead. All would not do; they were overtaken within a hundred yards of the shore, and carried back, with shouts and yells of triumph.

12. When they came on shore, the Indians set fire to Stacy's house, and dragged himself, his wife, and children, to their village. Here the principal old men, and Naoman among them, assembled to deliberate on the affair.

13. The chief men of the council stated, that some of the tribe had, undoubtedly, been guilty of treason, in apprising Stacy and his family of the

designs of the tribe, whereby they took the alarm, and well nigh escaped. He proposed to examine the prisoners, to learn who gave the information.

14. The old men assented to this, and Naoman among the rest. Stacy was first interrogated by one of the old men, who spoke English, and interpreted to the others. Stacy refused to betray his informant.

15. His wife was then questioned, while, at the same moment, two Indians stood threatening the two children with tomahawks, in case she did not confess. She attempted to evade the truth, by declaring she had a dream the night before, which alarmed her, and that she had persuaded her husband to fly.

16. "The Great Spirit never deigns to talk in dreams to a white face," said the old Indian. "Woman, thou hast two tongues and two faces. Speak the truth, or thy children shall surely die." The little boy and girl were then brought close to her, and the two savages stood over them, ready to execute their bloody orders.

17. "Wilt thou name," said the old Indian, "the red man who betrayed his tribe? I will ask thee three times." The mother answered not. "Wilt thou name the traitor? This is the second time." The poor mother looked at her husband, and then at her children, and stole a glance at Naoman, who sat smoking his pipe with invincible gravity.

18. She wrung her hands, and wept, but remained silent. "Wilt thou name the traitor? 'T is the third and last time." The agony of the mother waxed more bitter; again she sought the eye of Naoman, but it was cold and motionless.

19. A pause of a moment awaited her reply, and the tomahawks were raised over the heads of the children, who besought their mother not to let them be murdered.

20. "Stop," cried Naoman. All eyes were turned upon him. "Stop," repeated he in a tone of authority. "White woman, thou hast kept thy word with me to the last moment. I am the traitor. I have eaten of the salt, warmed myself at the fire, shared the kindness of these Christian white people, and it was I that told them of their danger.

21. "I am a withered, leafless, branchless trunk: cut me down, if you will: I am ready." A yell of indignation sounded on all sides. Naoman descended from the little bank where he sat, shrouded his face with his mantle of skins, and submitted to his fate. He fell dead at the feet of the white woman, by a blow of the tomahawk.

22. But the sacrifice of Naoman, and the firmness of the Christian white woman, did not suffice to save the lives of the other victims. They perished; how, it is needless to say; and the memory of their fate has been preserved in the name of the pleasant stream, on whose banks they lived and died, which, to this day, is called "Murderer's Creek."

PAULDING.

QUESTIONS.—What is the subject of this lesson? For whom did Naoman have a particular regard? How did he show affection for them, in this case? How did Stacy attempt to escape? What was the result? What did Naoman confess? What did the Indians do to him? What do you think of Naoman's conduct? Which is better, to do harm, or to suffer harm?

In the last sentence, what part of speech is *which*? What is its antecedent? Why is it called a *relative*? To what is it nominative? Which are the verbs in that sentence? Which of them is in the infinitive mode? Why is this mode called *infinitive*? See Pinneo's Primary Grammar, Mode.

The Ballad of "The White Captive"

The American ballad about Amanda, a white girl heroically rescued from death at the stake by the Indian chief, Albin, illustrates the popularity of the Indian captivity narratives among the folk, for whom they became the substance of tales, legends, and songs. The origin and authenticity of "The White Captive" are uncertain. Phillips Barry *(Bulletin of the Folk-Song Society of the Northeast* 8 [1934], pp. 19-24) claims to have found its source in a poem titled "Olban, or, the White Captive," published in the *Columbian Sentinel* of Boston in 1818. Other critics (Vance Randolph and Floyd C. Shoemaker, *Ozark Folksongs* [Columbia, Mo., 1946-1950], vol. 4, p. 118; Robert E. Pike, *Journal of American Folklore* 56 [1943], p. 137) maintain that it dates back to one of the early Indian wars, that the incidents described in the ballad probably occurred somewhere along the upper Merrimack River in the vicinity of Lincoln, New Hampshire, and that "Young Albin" is the Indian chief Metallak, last of the Coo-ash-aukes, who died in Stewartstown, New Hampshire, in 1847, at 120 years of age. According to Pike, Metallak was "known to have been deposed from his chieftainship for having saved a white captive from torture."

In any event, the situation parallels that of Cooper's noble Indians who sacrifice themselves for white captives, and the origin of the ballad is of less importance than its popularity among the literate and the folk. In folk versions it exists in variants collected from parts of the country as far distant as Maine, Florida, Missouri, Texas, and Utah; it appears under such different titles as "Olban, or, the White Captive," "Amanda, the Captive," "Young Albin," "Her White Bosom Bare," and even a confused variant known as "The White-Bosomed Bear," in which the heroine "Amandrew" was captured and "lay bound with a white-bosomed bear" until rescued by "young Album the chief."

The two versions here reprinted show changes which took place in the ballad as it was adapted to folk culture in different places at different times. "The White Captive" is from Vermont; "Bright Amanda" is from Utah. In Utah, "Young Alvin" is "chief of the Utes," the Indians gather around a "campfire" instead of a "watch fire," and Amanda is abducted up "the great Bear River" instead of "the Merrimac." The most striking difference of the western version is that it lacks the conciliatory note on which the eastern version ends. Free from the dangers of Indian warfare, the folk in Vermont could romanticize the Indians and pronounce peaceful benedictions. In Utah, Indian uprisings occurred as late as the 1880s.

THE WHITE CAPTIVE

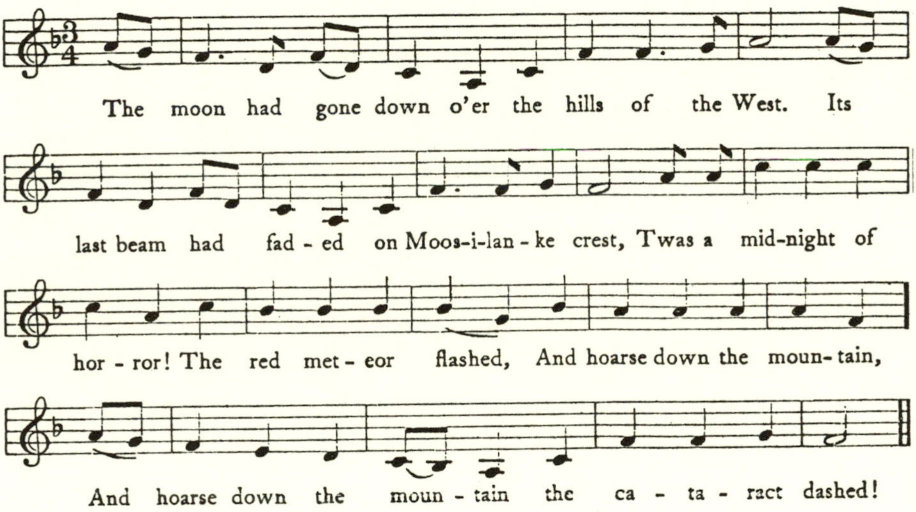
The moon had gone down o'er the hills of the West. Its
last beam had fad - ed on Moos-i-lan - ke crest, Twas a mid-night of
hor - ror! The red met - eor flashed, And hoarse down the moun- tain,
And hoarse down the moun - tain the ca - ta - ract dashed!

The moon had gone down o'er the hills of the West;
Its last beam had faded on Moosilauk crest.
'Twas a midnight of horror! the red meteor flashed,
And hoarse down the mountain the cataract dashed!

At intervals came, 'mid the hollow wind's sigh,
The hoot of the owl, and the catamount's cry,
The howl of the wolf from its lone granite cell,
And the crash of the dead forest tree as it fell.

SOURCE: Helen Flanders, Elizabeth Ballard, *et al.*, *New Green Mountain Songster* (New Haven: Yale University Press, 1939), pp. 256-258, from a manuscript in the family papers of the late Perrin B. Fisk, formerly minister of the Congregational Church in Springfield, Vermont, contributed by his daughter, Mrs. Grace Fisk Bartlett, of Cabot, Vermont, and printed in the Springfield, Massachusetts, *Sunday Union*, December 31, 1933. The melody was written down by Mrs. Bartlett.

Amanda, the pride of her village and home,
Far, far up the Merrimac waters had come,
In war led a captive, unfriended, forlorn,
Her feet bathed in blood, and her garments all torn.

At the foot of a hemlock the wild game was flung;
Above, from its branches, the rude armor hung;
From battle and plunder the warriors reposed,—
The toils of the day, which the evening had closed.

Ere blushes of morning again should return,
In torture Amanda was destined to burn!
She courted the vengeance and wrath of her foes,
And sighed for the hour when her sufferings should close.

The watch fire was lighted, and fanned by the breeze,
Its light shone around on the evergreen trees;
And fiercer the look of the plumed savage seemed,
As the light on his features of bronze dimly gleamed.

The pile was constructed,—its red embers flared;
Amanda was bound, and her white bosom bared;
Around her stood waiting the merciless throng,
Impatient to join in the war-dance and song.

Young Albin, the chief of the warriors, drew near,
With the eye of the eagle, the foot of the deer,
And a soul that would scorn from a foeman to crave
A sigh for his suffering,—a tear o'er his grave.

One moment he hung on the charms of the fair,
Her bright hazel eye now uplifted in prayer,
Her dark raven locks, which in ringlets below
Half hid from the gazer her bosom of snow.

"Forbear!" cried the chieftain, "Your torture forbear!
Amanda shall live! By my wampum I swear!
Tonight, if a victim must burn at the tree,
Young Albin, your leader, your victim shall be."

To rescue Amanda, as forward he rushed,
The revelry ceased, and all tumult was hushed,
And mute stood the circle of warriors around
As Albin the cords of Amanda unbound.

On Pemigewasset, at dawning of day,
Their birchen canoe was seen gliding away,
As swift as the wild duck that swam by its side,
In silence their bark down the river did glide.

At dusk of the evening a white cot was seen,
The smoke curling blue o'er the willowy green,
A moment of parting was seen on the shore,
And Albin, the warrior, was heard of no more.

Amanda returned to her village and home,
And Albin once more to his warriors has gone [come?].
And long may the banner of peace o'er them wave—
Amanda the captive, and Albin the brave!

BRIGHT AMANDA

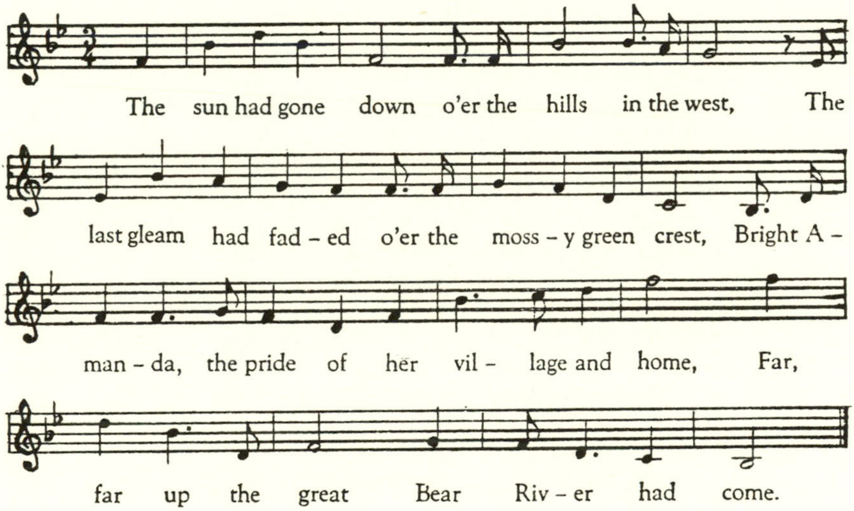
The sun had gone down o'er the hills in the west, The
last gleam had fad – ed o'er the moss – y green crest, Bright A –
man – da, the pride of her vil – lage and home, Far,
far up the great Bear Riv – er had come.

The sun had gone down o'er the hills in the west,
The last gleam had faded o'er the mossy green crest,
Bright Amanda, the pride of her village and home,
Far, far up the great Bear River had come.

At the foot of the mountain bright Amanda did sigh,
At the hoot of the owl or the catamount cry.

SOURCE: Lester A. Hubbard, *Ballads and Songs from Utah* (Salt Lake City: University of Utah Press, 1961), pp. 98-99. Sung by Milas E. Wakefield of Ogden, Sept. 12, 1948. He said: "I learned this from Nan Luce, now named Leonard, who sang it at a social on Christmas Eve in Huntington about 1889. She was dressed as an Indian girl." The melody was transcribed by Kenly W. Whitelock.

At the howl of the wolf in his own quiet cell,
Or the crash of some dry forest tree as it fell.

The campfire was kindled and fanned by the breeze,
The red embers shone through the evergreen trees,
All beauties of nature and charms of the fair,
Bright Amanda was bound all heartbroken there.

In was brought the captive all friendless and forlorn,
With her face bathed in tears and her garments were torn,
How fierce were the looks of those wild savage fiends,
As the light on their features in tranquils did gleam.

The campfire was kindled, the red torches glared,
The light shone upon her features so fair,
But around that crowd no mercy was shown,
All impatient to join in the war dance and song.

And before the blush of the morn shall return,
Bright Amanda in torture you're destined to burn,
She read of her fate in the face of her foes,
And sighed for the time when her suffering might close.

Young Alvin, the leader of the warriors, drew near,
With an eye like an eagle, a step like a deer,
With a soul that yearned her fair features to save,
Gave a sigh for her suffering and a tear for her grave.

One moment he gazed on her features so fair,
Her dark hazel eyes uplifted in prayer,
And her long waving tresses in ringlets did flow,
Which hid from his gaze her white bosom of snow.

"Forbear," cried the leader, "ye traitors, forbear,
This maiden shall live by the scalp that I wear,
And if there's a victim to burn at the tree,
Young Alvin, your leader, that victim shall be."

Then quick to the arms of Amanda he rushed,
The rabble was ceased, the tumult was hushed.
How mute were the warriors encircled around
As young Alvin the cords of Amanda unbound.

Then swift as the arrows that whizzed by their side,
They mounted and rode to the dark rolling tide.
No word of parting was heard at the shore,
And young Alvin, their leader, was heard of no more.

At the blush of the morn, at the dawn of the day,
A birch-bark canoe was seen gliding away.
As swift as the wild duck down the river does glide,
Together they sailed down the dark rolling tide.

At the dusk of the evening a white cot was seen,
The blue smoke was curling amid willows so green,
How great were the joys of Amanda on shore
To see her dear father and mother once more.

Young Alvin stood near them to see them embrace,
With his heart overjoyed and tears rolled down his face,
And all that he asked was for shelter and food
From the parents of Amanda to the chief of the Utes.

Folktales About the Escapes of Tim Murphy

Most folktales about Indian captivity emphasize the ingenuity of captives who used Yankee wit to escape. These tales accumulated around certain conspicuous figures, transforming them into folk heroes whose fame derived in large measure from this convergence. One such hero was Tim Murphy, known in New York state as the "Savior of the Schoharie" because of his legendary exploits there as scout, soldier, and Indian fighter.

The facts of Murphy's life have been obscured by time and legend. The son of Irish immigrants, Murphy was born in Minisink, New Jersey, in 1751. Six years later the Murphy family is said to have moved to Pennsylvania where Tim grew up and married. Tradition holds that while he was away on a trip, Murphy's wife and children were massacred by Indians. Tradition also holds that when Murphy returned he vowed to spend the rest of his days hunting down and killing Indians. In the process he is said to have become as savage and vindictive as his enemies. He conforms to the type of "Indian-hater" whom Judge James Hall described in *Legends of the West . . .* (1832) and who became a memorable character in William Montgomery Bird's *Nick of the Woods* (1837) and Melville's *The Confidence-Man* (1857). Murphy fought in the Revolutionary War and, according to tradition, killed Gen. Simon Fraser, Burgoyne's most important subordinate. Many of Murphy's exploits took place in the area where his contemporary, Mary Jemison (see pp. 110-123), lived, and Murphy is mentioned in her narrative. Murphy roamed the hills of western New York until his death in 1818.

The following anecdotes are only a few of the clever escapes credited to Murphy. Each is based on a motif attached to other American folk heroes as well. The first tale resembles one told in Concord, New Hampshire, about Daniel Abbott, a local hero. Variants of the second story have been told about Tom Quick, Daniel Boone, and the Dutch pioneer, Peter Vrooman. The third story is a classic "trickster tale." Variants have been collected in Maine, New Hampshire, New York, Pennsylvania, Illinois, Kentucky, Arkansas, and Missouri; it has been associated with such American heroes as Daniel Boone, Davy Crockett, and Jim Bridger.

For further tales about Tim Murphy, see William Sigby, *The Life and Adventures of Timothy Murphy* (1839), Emelyn E. Gardner, *Folklore from the Schoharie Hills* (1937), Harold W. Thompson, *Body, Boots and Britches* (1941), and Tristram P. Coffin, *Uncertain Glory* (1971).

I

Timothy Murphy killed a good many Indians in his day. He was a smart man and he knew how to fool them. One day when he was skating he saw some Indians pretty close to him on the bank. All of a sudden he couldn't skate. He would go a little ways and fall down. Then he'd pick himself up, go a little further, and—down he'd go again. He kept this up, while the Indians laughed and laughed at him for not being able to skate. When he had put quite a distance between himself and the Indians, all of a sudden he skated away like sixty, leaving the Indians behind him.

SOURCE: Collected in 1940 for Harold Thompson by his student, Laura Settle, from her father, C. Jay Settle, who heard it from Charles Adams, a resident of Schoharie County, New York. Harold Thompson File, New York State Historical Society.

II

One autumn Tim Murphy with his large family left his home in the valley for a winter residence on the mountain-top, whence he could more easily command the movements of his Indian enemies. When it came time in the spring to sow wheat on his valley farm, Tim started to go down the mountain, with a drag on one shoulder and seven skipple of wheat on the other. Suddenly a party of Indians burst out of the brush. There was no hope of escape for Murphy, except to leap from a precipitous cliff which projected from part of the summit. So, without stopping to think twice or to say his

SOURCE: Emelyn E. Gardner, "Folk-Lore from Schoharie County, New York," *Journal of American Folklore* 27 (1914), p. 305. Collected by Emelyn Gardner from Alonzo Parslow of Blenheim, New York, "an aged man of Irish ancestry."

prayers, burdened as he was, he took the leap, and struck upon a projecting cliff a hundred feet below. So great was the force with which he landed, that he sank into the rock up to his knees. The Indians, supposing him killed, made no attempt either to follow him or to await his coming in the valley. Murphy, keeping still until he was quite sure that he had nothing to fear from them, went down into the valley, where he borrowed a pick and shovel, and came back and dug himself out. Then he went about his business unmolested, and put in a crop which yielded him eighty skipple for every one he put in.

III

Some Indians came upon Tim Murphy one day as he was splitting logs. He asked them to help him by pulling the two halves of the log apart and free his wedge. When they all had their hands in the crack, he pulled out his wedge and caught their fingers so they couldn't get away. Then he killed them all.

SOURCE: Collected in 1940 for Harold Thompson by his student, Laura Settle, from her father, C. Jay Settle, who heard it from Mrs. Ella Engle, a resident of Schoharie County, New York. Harold Thompson File, New York State Historical Society.

Daniel Boone and the Indians

Indian captivity contributed to the making of literary legend about such American heroes as Daniel Boone. The Boone legend spread not orally but through the medium of print. Stories about Boone originate with "The Adventures of Col. Daniel Boon," a bogus autobiography based rather loosely on the life of a Kentucky pioneer by the name of Boone, written and published by John Filson in *The Discovery, Settlement and Present State of Kentucky* (1784). According to the Filson account, Boone discovered Kentucky, almost single-handedly fought off Indian attacks, and was the greatest of America's frontier heroes.

Differences between the following excerpts from Filson's *Adventures* and Timothy Flint's *Biographical Memoir of Daniel Boone . . .* (1833) show how Indian captivity was used to shape the Boone legend. Boone's exploits as an Indian captive grew with the legend. Filson devotes a bland and brief paragraph to the captivity of Boone and John Stewart among the Shawnee Indians in 1769. He mentions the incident almost routinely. Flint, on the other hand, romanticizes the episode by expatiating on the beauties of the landscape and its potential for white habitation and by emphasizing the stamina and guile by which Boone and Stewart effected their escape. He did the same with Filson's account of Boone's rescue of his daughter, Jemima, and her companions kidnapped by Indians in July 1776 and with his capture and adoption by Blackfish, a Shawnee chief, in 1778.

The literary legend of Boone was influenced by more genuine American folk heroes like Tim Murphy (pp. 171-173). His literary descendants are legion (see Cooper, pp. 231-256).

I

. . . In the decline of the day, near Kentucke river, as we ascended the brow of a small hill, a number of Indians rushed out of a thick cane-brake upon us, and made us prisoners. The time of our sorrow was now arrived, and the scene fully opened. The Indians plundered us of what we had, and kept us in confinement seven days, treating us with common savage usage. During this time we discovered no uneasiness or desire to escape, which made them less suspicious of us; but in the dead of night, as we lay in a thick cane brake by a large fire, when sleep had locked up their senses, my situation not disposing me for rest, I touched my companion and gently awoke him. We improved this favourable opportunity, and departed, leaving them to take their rest, and speedily directed our course towards our old camp, but found it plundered, and the company dispersed and gone home. About this time my brother, Squire Boon, with another adventurer, who came to explore the country shortly after us, was wandering through the forest, determined to find me, if possible, and accidentally found our camp. . . .

SOURCE: John Filson, "The Adventures of Col. Daniel Boon," in *The Discovery, Settlement and Present State of Kentucke* (Wilmington, Del., 1784).

II

. . . In order to extend the means of gaining more exact information with regard to this beautiful country, the party divided, and took different directions. Boone and Stewart formed one division, and the remaining three the other. The two former had as yet seen few thick forests. The country was much of it of that description, now known by the name of "Barrens," or open woods, which had the appearance of having been planted out with trees at wide and regular distances from each other, like those of an orchard, allowing the most luxuriant growth of cane, grass, or clover beneath them. They now passed a wide and deep forest, in which the trees were large and thick. Among them were many of the laurel tribe, in full verdure in mid winter. Others were thick hung with persimmons, candied by the frost, nutritive, and as luscious as figs. Others again were covered with winter grapes. Every thing tended to inspire them with exalted notions of the natural resources of the country, and to give birth to those extravagant romances, which afterwards became prevalent, as descriptions of Kentucky. Such were Finley's [John Finley, a Virginia trader who persuaded Boone to explore Kentucky] accounts of it—views which went abroad, and created even in Europe an impression of a kind of new El Dorado, or rather rural paradise. Other and very different scenes, in no great length of time, disenchanted the new paradise, and presented it in the sober traits of truth.

They were never out of sight of buffaloes, deer, and turkeys. At night-fall they came in view of Kentucky river, and admired in unsated astonishment, the precipices three hundred feet high, at the foot of which, as in a channel

SOURCE: Timothy Flint, *Biographical Memoir of Daniel Boone . . .* (Cincinnati, 1833).

cut out of the solid limestone, rolled the dark waters of the beautiful stream. A lofty eminence was before them. Thinking it would afford them a far view of the meanderings of the river, they ascended it. This expectation was realized. A large extent of country stretched beneath them. Having surveyed it, they proposed to commence their return to rejoin their companions. As they were leisurely descending the hill, little dreaming of danger, the Indian yell burst upon their ears. A numerous party of Indians sprang from the cane-brake, surrounded, vanquished, and bound them, before they had time to have recourse to their arms. The Indians proceeded to plunder them of their rifles, and every thing in their possession but the most indispensable articles of dress. They then led them off to their camp, where they confined them in such a manner as effectually to prevent their escape.

Not knowing a word of the speech of their captors, who knew as little of theirs, they were wholly ignorant of what fate awaited them. The Indians next day marched them off, rapidly towards the north, compelling them to travel at a rate which was excessively annoying to captives in their predicament—manacled, in momentary apprehension of death, and plunging deeper into the wilderness in advancing towards the permanent abode of their savage masters. It was well for them that they were more athletic than the savages, equally capable of endurance, and alike incapable of betraying groans, fear, or even marks of regret in their countenance. They knew enough of savage modes to be aware that the least indications of weariness, and inability to proceed, would have brought the tomahawk and scalping knife upon their skulls, weapons, with which they were thus early supplied from Detroit. They therefore pushed resolutely on, with cheerful countenances, watching the while with intense earnestness, to catch from the signs and gestures of the Indians, what was their purpose in regard to their fate. By the second day, they comprehended the words of most frequent recurrence in the discussion, that took place respecting them. Part, they perceived, were for putting them to death, to prevent their escape. The other portion advocated their being adopted into the tribe, and domesticated. To give efficacy to the counsels of these last, the captives not only concealed every trace of chagrin, but dissembled cheerfulness, and affected to like their new mode of life; and seemed as happy, and as much amused, as the Indians themselves.

Fortunately, their previous modes of life, and in fact their actual aptitudes and propensities wonderfully qualified them, along with their reckless courage and elasticity of character, to enact this difficult part with a success, which completely deceived the Indians, and gave the entire ascendency to the advice of those who proposed to spare, and adopt them into their tribe. Lulled by this semblance, the captors were less and less strict in their guard. On the seventh night of their captivity, the savages, having made a great fire, and fed plentifully, all fell into a sound sleep, leaving their prisoners, who affected to be as deeply asleep as themselves, wholly unguarded.

It need hardly be said, that the appearance of content they had worn, was mere outward show; and that they slept not. Boone slowly and cautiously raised himself to a sitting posture, and thus remained a few moments to mark, if his change of position had been observed. One of the sleepers turned in his sleep. Boone instantly dropped back to his recumbent posture and semblance of sleep. So he remained fifteen minutes, when he once more raised himself, and continued sitting for some time, without noting a movement among the slumberers around him. He then ventured to communicate his purpose to his companions.

The greatest caution was necessary to prevent disturbing the savages, as the slightest noise would awake them, and probably bring instant death upon the captives. Stewart succeeded in placing himself upon his feet without any noise. The companions were not far apart, but did not dare to whisper to each other the thought that occurred alike to both—that, should they escape without rifles and ammunition, they must certainly die of hunger. The place where their rifles stood had been carefully noted by them, and by groping their way with the utmost care, they finally reached them. Fortunately, the equipments, containing the usual supply of powder and ball, were near the rifles. The feelings with which Boone and Stewart stole forth from the circle of their captors may be imagined. They made their way into the woods through the darkness, keeping close together for some time, before they exchanged words.

It was not far from morning when they began their attempt at escape; but they had made considerable progress from the Indian encampment before the dawn. They took their course with the first light, and pursued it the whole day, reaching their camp without meeting with any incident. As the sun was declining, forms were seen approaching the camp in the distance. The uncertain light in which they were first visible, rendered it impossible for Boone and Stewart to determine whether they were whites or Indians; but they grasped their rifles, and stood ready for defence. The forms continued to approach cautiously, and slowly, until they were within speaking distance. Boone then hailed them with the challenge, "Who comes there?" The delight may be imagined with which Boone and Stewart heard the reply of "White men and friends!" "Come on then," said Boone. The next moment he found himself in the arms of his brother, who, accompanied by a single companion, had left North Carolina, and made his way all the distance from the Yadkin to the Cumberland. They had been wandering many days in the woods, in pursuit of Boone and his party, and had thus providentially fallen upon them. . . .

The Christian Hermit

The *Narrative of the Massacre, by the Savages, of the Wife and Children of Thomas Baldwin . . .* (New York, 1836) is probably a fabrication. The main feature of this edition of the pamphlet, which has a subsection on Daniel Boone and an additional and quite unrelated captivity narrative, is that it appears to have been written for entertainment, religious enlightenment, and the profit of the publisher. A close friend of Boone, Baldwin emigrates with him from North Carolina to Kentucky, witnesses the extinction of his family at the hands of "savage monsters," but escapes from the Indians himself to live out the rest of his life in solitude. Bible in hand, he devoutly advises the rare visitor that "Dark are the ways of Providence while we are wrapt up in mortality, but convinced there is a God, we must hope and believe that all is right."

In fiction, fact, and folklore there were two extreme responses available to a man who had survived the massacre of his family by the Indians. He might become an "Indian-hater," turned by his blasting experience into a man more savage than the Indians he swears, in vengeance, to destroy; or he might accept his loss as a chastening from the hands of a just but inscrutable God. The folk figure, Tim Murphy (pp. 171-173), is such an Indian-hater. The most complex literary example is Col. John Moredock in Herman Melville's novel, *The Confidence-Man.* Colonel Moredock sees Indians as diabolic for having destroyed his family and becomes diabolic himself as he seeks to destroy them, but, as destroyer of diabolic creatures, he is in some inverse way carrying out the work of the Lord. This shared religious mission brings Thomas Baldwin, "the *Christian philosopher,*" and Melville's Moredock together. But Moredock is intense and complex, worthy of comparison with one of Cotton Mather's "illustrious, wonderful providences" (see Swarton, pp. 31-

---

SOURCE: *Narrative of the Massacre, by the Savages, of the Wife and Children of Thomas Baldwin, Who, Since the Melancholy Period of the Destruction of His Unfortunate Family, Has Dwelt Entirely Alone, in a Hut of His Own Construction, Secluded from Human Society, in the Extreme Western Part of the State of Kentucky . . .* (New York, 1836).

39). Baldwin's religion is sentimental pietism. Though providence is invoked, the massacre of the Baldwin family does not seem providential in a Puritan sense. Rather, a secular explanation, revenge for Baldwin's participation in a punitive attack on an Indian village, is given for their destruction. One suspects that the publisher was exploiting two conventions, the softer religiosity into which Puritan severity had declined, combined with the shock of sterotypical Indian horrors. The illustrative material in the pamphlet bears this out. The cover (see p. 184) displays an aged Baldwin, bearded like a biblical patriarch, holding his Bible and quoting a biblical consolation. On the other side, a double-page plate (see p. 183) shows the "Massacre of Baldwin Family by the Savages!" No detail is spared from a burning at the stake in the background to a scalping in the foreground. This unsubtle attempt to be all things to all men is further evidenced in the depiction of the Indians. They are hideously savage, an overt argument that the Indian must be assimilated or obliterated. Yet, as a counter, there is a good Indian who helps Baldwin escape and who later brings him sad tidings about the fate of his lost child.

The appeal of the Baldwin narrative is enhanced by associating him with Daniel Boone, an association which is not borne out in any of the Boone biographies. Boone is seen in a fuller light than usual. Aside from his traditional feats and a quotation which implies that he is a divine "instrument ordained to settle the wilderness," Boone is also spotted for what the historic record indicates he really was, a speculator with a "thirst for cheap and uncultivated lands."

The commercial success and fictional nature of this captivity narrative seem confirmed by its existence in various forms, some with a slightly different emphasis. A first edition, published in New York in 1835 by Martin and Wood, has only a short reference to Boone at the end and lacks the unrelated captivity, a romantic episode in which an army officer rescues his "intended" from an infatuated Indian who wishes, in Fenimore Cooper fashion, "to make her his squaw." A plagiary entitled *A Narrative of the Horrid Massacre by the Indians, of the Wife and Children of the Christian Hermit . . .* (St. Louis, 1840) points up even more Indian barbarities and "the folly of attempting to civilize the savage." An analogue, *Narrative of the Extraordinary Life of . . . John Conrad Shafford, . . . the Dutch Hermit . . .* (New York, 1840), has a Canadian setting and emphasizes "the most shameful treatment" of Shafford's daughter but is close to the Baldwin captivity and is illustrated with a woodcut of a bearded ancient holding his Bible and garbed in a robe like a medieval monk.

The narrative, then, crude and unpretentious though it is, has a range of cultural applications. Near the end, the traveler who visits the hermit expresses hope that Baldwin's pious example "will prove profitable to the reader." He then suggests that it might, in addition, depict "the many difficulties that attended those, who . . . first attempted to explore and form settlements in the western wilds." Finally, waving the banner of Manifest Destiny, he asserts that it exemplifies the American "spirit of enterprise."

In the extreme western part of the State of Kentucky, quite remote from any other inhabitant, there now dwells one of the most eccentric, and, apparently, one of the most contented and happy characters, that the western country affords. The true name of this extraordinary person, is THOMAS BALDWIN, although better known in the neighborhood in which he dwells, by that of "the *Christian Philosopher;*" a title which cannot be considered ill applied to one who has drank so deep of the cup of sorrow, and borne his afflictions with so great a share of christian fortitude and resignation. It was in the latter part of November last, (1835) that the writer, in an excursion to the west, was induced, by the solicitation of a christian friend, to visit this venerable Patriarch (now in the 86th year of his age) in his secluded retreat. His humble, weather-beaten habitation, composed of rough materials, is one of his own construction, and where, as he stated, he had, with the exception of a few months, dwelt entirely alone, since the melancholy period when every member of his family (with one exception) fell victims to the ferocity of the merciless savages. His own relation of the murderous deed, together with other interesting particulars of his early adventures (which he freely and concisely imparted to the writer) are, in substance, as follows:. . .

It was at about this period, that the savages obtained the information that peace had taken place between the United States and Great Britain, and that the troops of the former were next to be employed in effecting their extermination—this had a good effect, insomuch that they expressed a willingness to bury the hatchet, and no longer disturb the peace of their white neighbors, if they could be permitted to rebuild their settlements, and their squaws suffered therein to remain unmolested, while they were engaged in hunting as formerly; proposals which were readily acceded to by the whites, and so strong did the savages feign a disposition on their part strictly to adhere thereto, that the former too soon threw themselves off their guard, and some of them, imprudently to remove to greater distances from their fortified settlements—the land (then wild and uncultivated) in the vicinity of the small spot which I now improve, being not only rich and fertile, but abounding with game, I was like others, so much disposed to confide in the professions of friendship of the savages, as then to select this spot as the permanent residence of my family, although less than one mile distant from an Indian settlement. My Indian neighbors appeared however pacifically disposed, for several months after my removal, when, unfortunately, in one of my excursions, meeting with a savage from a distant settlement, by whom I was not only recognized as one of Colonel [George Rogers] Clark's party (who had assisted in destroying their villages) but one from whom on that occasion, he, as he hinted, strongly suspected that he had received a wound, the destruction of myself and family were by him no doubt at that moment determined on! as, three days after, a little after sunrise, my family were alarmed by the discovery of a savage, frightfully painted and armed with tomahawk and scalping knife, secreted in some thick brush, within a few rods of my house—as soon as discovered, he gave the war whoop, which was probably a signal to nine or ten others, who at that moment rushed from a neighboring forest, and who, with a horrible shout, approached my dwelling with uplifted tomahawks. I was at that instant employed within, and my poor affrighted family had scarcely time to close the door, when their savage foes were pounding and demanding entrance thereat—although they soon succeeded with their tomahawks in cutting a passage sufficiently large to admit of an entrance one at a time, yet, fearing probably of meeting with too warm a reception from those within, they preferred and adopted other means to dislodge us; unfortunately, the roof of my dwelling being composed of pine slabs, overlaid with straw and dry bark, they communicated fire thereto, which burned with such rapidity, as to leave us no other alternative than either to remain where we were, and become the victims of the devouring flames, or by attempting to escape therefrom, fall into the hands of the savages, from whom we had but little mercy to expect!—as but a moment's time was left us to decide, the latter was preferred. My family at that time was composed of myself, wife and three children (two sons and a daughter.) I was the last to leave the house, being engaged in reloading my rifle, yet had a clear and melancholy view of the fate of each unfortunate member of my family as they rushed from the flames; which presented a spectacle, heart-rending in the extreme to a husband and parent, who could afford them no assistance! My oldest son, armed with a hatchet, was the first to attempt to escape, and by dashing out the brains of the savage who first laid hold of him, succeeded in clearing his way, but was closely pursued by others, and made prisoner of; and his younger brother, in attempting to follow his example, was knocked down, and while one of the merciless wretches was engaged in tearing off his scalp, he was despatched by a blow from another! My beloved companion, his mother, shared a similar fate! and my little daughter (but eleven years of age) who left the house at the same time with her poor mother, was seized by another of the savage monsters, and while apparently in the very act of raising his tomahawk to despatch her, she fell on her knees and entreated for mercy! Believing that she was about to share a similar fate of the others, and feeling determined that it should be at the expense of the life of him into whose hands she had fallen, I levelled my rifle at the head of the barbarian, which (fortunately for me perhaps) missed fire! fortunately I say, for had it taken effect, I should in all probability have been doomed to endure tortures, similar to those which were afterward inflicted on my unfortunate son! My house was now completely enwrapt in flames and could no longer afford me a shelter, and as the savages were in a measure obscured by a thick body of smoke produced thereby, seemed at the instant to offer me some and the only chance to effect my escape by flight, and as no time was to be lost, I hastily threw off my coat and waistcoat, threw my loaded rifle into the flames, and sprang forth, and succeeded in outrunning several of them, but becoming exhausted, I was laid hold of by a stout savage, who (with his tomahawk raised ready to despatch me if I advanced a step further) demanded my surrender, to which I reluctantly acceded! I was immediately thereupon strongly pinioned, and led a short distance from where lay the slaughtered remains of my poor wife and child—in a few moments after my surviving son and daughter were brought to the same spot, and where we were compelled to remain, without being permitted to exchange a word with each other, until the blood-thirsty wretches had finished packing up the most valuable of my effects which they had saved from the flames.

Having to their satisfaction succeeded, in not only destroying the lives of two innocent unoffending victims, but in the total destruction of my late peaceful dwelling, together with most of its contents, the fruits of many years industry, they took up their line of march in a direction west, compelling myself and two children to accompany them. They travelled with considerable speed until they reached, as I have since ascertained, a distance of twelve miles, when they came to a halt, and for what purpose, we were too soon made acquainted—it was to consult and agree in what manner they should inflict the greatest torture on my poor son, in retaliation for the death of the savage who had fallen by his hands! The mode finally agreed upon was to burn him alive, at a stake, after their usual manner of putting to death a great portion of their prisoners. Preparations were accordingly made; one end of a stake of about twelve feet in length was driven into the ground, and to which my poor ill-fated son was bound; some dry brush was next gathered and thrown around him, and piled to the height of his breast, and to which fire was then communicated, when their savage dance to and fro around the stake, attended with terrific yells, commenced!—What at this moment were my feelings, and those of my little daughter, who were both compelled to stand and witness the shocking scene, I shall not attempt to describe,—parents alone can best judge! For half an hour my ears were pierced with the dreadful shrieks and dying groans of my poor child, in the course of which I twice fainted, and was brought to by the water thrown in my face by his tormenters; and who, to increase my distress, by their gestures gave me to understand that I was reserved for still greater torments; this was communicated to me by the savage to whom I have alluded, as being in all probability the instigator of the fatal and unprovoked attack on my innocent family—who, during the sufferings of my son, repeatedly cast on me a fiendlike frown, pointing at the same time to the wound on his head, which he believed was inflicted by me. In little more than half an hour from the time that fire was communicated to the brush by which my son was enveloped, he ceased to breathe; nor could I but feel thankful that his sufferings were at an end. . . .

A busy fold-out with a detailed caption illustrated the *Narrative of the Massacre . . . of the Wife and Children of Thomas Baldwin,* sometimes known as "the Christian Hermit." The caption reads: "The scenes which the above Plate is designed to represent (as described by Baldwin) are—Fig. 1 his House in Flames—2 a Savage in the act of Tomahawking Mrs. B. (his wife.)—3 his youngest child (a daughter eleven years of age) on her knees intreating a Savage to spare her life—4 two Savages, one in the act of tomahawking and the other in that of scalping his oldest son—5 Baldwin (the elder) intercepted and taken captive in his attempt to escape by flight—6 the Savages burning his second son at a stake, around which they are dancing to and fro in savage triumph—7 the Savages returning (with the unfortunate Baldwin and his only surviving child, captives) to their settlement." *Courtesy of the Everett D. Graff Colleciton, the Newberry Library.*

Thomas Baldwin, the Christian Hermit," as shown on the title page, Bible in hand. The caption reads: "Great, indeed, have been my afflictions; but, as it was the will of Heaven, I ought not to murmur, but to say like him, whose afflictions were still greater, 'the Lord gave and has taken away, and blessed be his name.'" *Courtesy of the Everett D. Graff Collection, the Newberry Library.*

"Thus, kind sir, have I so far complied with your request, as to indulge you with a short narrative of the deep afflictions to which I was subjected in the early part of my life: and should you now wish to know from what source I have been able to obtain consolation and support in the midst of my sorrows, I would point you to that sacred book"—the old gentleman here pointing to an octavo Bible lying upon his table, and which bore the marks of having been faithfully read—"from that" he continued, "I think I have obtained that comfort, and drawn that instruction, in my most sorrowful moments, which no human being could impart. It has taught me not only the way to eternal life, but has taught me that the many sore afflictions of which it has pleased my blessed Father in Heaven to make me the subject, was intended for my spiritual good! It has taught me that I ought not in the hour of adversity, to depend too much on the arm of flesh; but that my trust should be in Him alone, who is mighty to save. . . ."

Sal Fink: "How She Cooked Injuns"

The Indian captivity experience appeared in a variety of forms—literary, quasi-literary, and nonliterary. It was also made to serve a variety of purposes. But its tonal range was usually restricted to the tragic, horrific, pathetic, moralistic, pietistic, or romantic. There was, however, an area of exception. Along the frontier, where wild tales were told, where boasters outdid one another with their bragging, and where man, woman, and beast were bigger than life, it was possible for the Indian captivity to be comic. A body of comic story-telling flourished before the Civil War in the backwoods region well below the Mason-Dixon Line and bounded by the Mississippi Valley, known as the Old Southwest. Essentially oral and folkloristic, it became the basis for hundreds of robust sketches published in the newspapers of the region, sporting magazines, cheap paperbacks, and almanacs. These sketches were crudely realistic and locally colorful, and they captured distinctive aspects of the American character and scene that had not been previously set down. They often centered on the extravagant, sometimes virtually mythic accomplishments of historic figures who were in the process of becoming legendary. Davy Crockett is one such figure. Mike Fink (c. 1770-c.1823)—sharpshooter, trapper, and the most famous keelboatman on the western waterways—was another. He is said to have had a daughter named Sal who was worthy of her sire.

Sal Fink's encounter with the Indians was published in the *Crockett Almanac* for the year 1854 under the main title, "Sal Fink, the Mississippi Screamer." The first two issues of these almanacs, for the years 1835 and 1836, were published in Nashville, Tennessee, with the copyright taken in Crockett's name. After his death, they were published in various eastern cities.

The popularity of the *Crockett Almanacs* was largely due to the lively filler material supplied by journalists who adapted whatever was at hand. No precise source has been found for Sal Fink's captivity, but she is a sister to "The Farmer's Cursed Wife" who, in the folk ballad (Child

---

SOURCE: "Sal Fink, the Mississippi Screamer," from *Crockett's Almanac, 1854. Containing Life, Manners and Adventures in the Backwoods, and Rows, Sprees, and Scrapes on the Western Waters* (Philadelphia, New York, Boston, Baltimore: Fisher & Brother, 1854).

The *Crockett Almanacs* featured Old Southwestern Humor. This portrait of Sal Fink, Mike's daughter, accompanied a frontier anecdote entitled, "How She Cooked Injuns." *Courtesy of American Antiquarian Society.*

278), escaped from Hell because she was too much for the Devil, and the grisly prank Sal plays on her captors is similar to the practical joke in Poe's "Hop Frog," a tale about a court jester who avenges an insult by setting his enemies afire.

Sal Fink, of course, is not the only female captive who was equal to the occasion. Though exuberantly comic, she is the equivalent of the complex, tragic Hannah Duston (see pp. 156-159, 224-230). For comedy has its tragic underside, especially along the frontier.

SAL FINK, THE MISSISSIPPI SCREAMER
HOW SHE COOKED INJUNS

I dar say you've all on you, if not more, frequently heerd this great she human crittur boasted of, an' pointed out as *"one o' the gals"*—but I tell you what, stranger, you have never really set your eyes on *"one of the gals,"* till you have seen Sal Fink, the Mississippi screamer, whose miniature pictur I here give, about as nat'ral as life, but not half as handsome—an' if thar ever was a gal that desarved to be christened *"one o' the gals,"* then this gal was that gal—and no mistake.

She fought a duel once with a thunderbolt, an' came off without a singe, while at the fust fire she split the thunderbolt all to flinders, an' gave the pieces to Uncle Sam's artillerymen, to touch off their cannon with. When a gal about six years old, she used to play see-saw on the Mississippi snags, and arter she war done she would snap 'em off, an' so cleared a large district of the river. She used to ride down the river on an alligator's back, standen upright, an' dancing *Yankee Doodle,* and could leave all the steamers behind. But the greatest feat she ever did, positively outdid anything that ever was did.

One day when she war out in the forest, making a collection o' wild cat skins for her family's winter beddin, she war captered in the most all-sneaken manner by about fifty Injuns, an' carried by 'em to Roast flesh Hollow, whar the blood drinkin wild varmints detarmined to skin her alive, sprinkle a leetle salt over her, an' devour her before her own eyes; so they took an' tied her to a tree, to keep till mornin' should bring the rest o' thar ring-nosed sarpints to enjoy the fun. Arter that, they lit a large fire in the Holler, turned the bottom o' thar feet towards the blaze, Injun fashion, and went to sleep to dream o' thar mornin's feast; well, after the critturs got into a somniferous snore, Sal got into an all-lightnin' of a temper, and burst all the ropes about her like an apron string! She then found a pile o' ropes, took and tied all the Injun's heels together all round the fire,—then fixin a cord to the shins of every two couple, she, with a suddenachous jerk, that made the intire woods tremble, pulled the intire lot o' sleepin' red-skins into that ar great fire, fast together, an' then sloped like a panther out of her pen, in the midst o' the tallest yellin, howlin, scramblin and singin', that war ever seen or heerd on, since the great burnin' o' Buffalo prairie!

MOCCASIN BILL, a Dime Novel

On the eve of the Civil War, at a time of national dissension, the New York firm of Beadle and Adams, publishers of ten-cent game books and songsters, embarked on a venture which changed the literary taste of America. Erastus Beadle (1821-1894), founder of the company, sought a form of entertainment which would appeal to a wide cross-section of Americans, young and old, rich and poor, northern and southern, and which would be exciting and yet, at least as he initially planned it, morally and culturally uplifting. The medium he created was the dime novel, named for its format and price.

Pocket-size and paper-bound, dime novels were totally without literary pretence. Hireling writers produced them by the hundreds. They rarely exceeded thirty thousand words, and an experienced professional could grind one out within twenty-four hours. Calculated to inspire patriotism, their content was almost always American, and their setting was usually in the West or at least the unexplored American wilderness, often at the time of the Revolutionary War. Their heroes and heroines resembled stock characters in folklore, Old Southwestern Humor, and the frontier romances of Cooper, Simms, and Bird. Solitary hunters patterned after Leatherstocking were commonplace, and plots were predictable, but the dime novel was packed with adventure, bravado, and a violence which bordered on the sadistic. When success brought competition from rival publishing houses and readers began to tire of formulaic plots, the dime novels became increasingly gaudy and violent, and special series were issued to cater to the tastes of various audiences. A "Dime Library" (1877-1905) was designed for adult readers and a "Half-Dime Library" (1877-1905) for the presumably emptier heads and pockets of children, while the original "Dime Novel Series" (1860-1885) was purveyed to young and old.

Paul Bibbs's *Moccasin Bill; or, Cunning Serpent the Ojibwah . . .* (1873) reveals a typical instance of the Indian captivity, a standard plot

SOURCE: Paul Bibbs, *Moccasin Bill; or, Cunning Serpent the Ojibwah, a Romance of Big Stone Lake* (New York, 1873).

Lurid covers advertised the contents of dime novels. The cover of *Moccasin Bill* shows the abduction of Laura Hautville by Cunning Serpent. Her brother, Moccasin Bill, and her lover, an Indianized white captive named Deerfoot, pursue.

device in many dime novels, especially during the 1860s and 1870s, when they featured frontier themes. Like Natty Bumppo (see Cooper, pp. 231-256), Moccasin Bill is a solitary trapper who, like Tim Murphy (pp. 171-173), hates Indians. In his youth, he had witnessed the massacre of his parents and the abduction of his sister, Laura Hautville, by a sinister Ojibwah Indian, "Cunning Serpent," and he never forgave the Indian race for this unfortunate incident. Years later, a famine forces the Ojibwahs to return captives in exchange for food and supplies. Although most of the captives are so thoroughly Indianized that the whites at first mistake them for Indians, Laura Hautville has almost miraculously retained her white identity in spite of eighteen years of hardship, brightened only by the hope of an eventual reunion with her brother and by her love for Deerfoot, a white captive who appears to be an Indian. The remainder of the novel consists of captures, escapes, and recaptures reminiscent of Cooper's *The Last of the Mohicans.* Cunning Serpent abducts Laura. Moccasin Bill sets out to the rescue but is preceded by Deerfoot, who battles with Cunning Serpent and flees with Laura. In a final episode, Laura and Deerfoot are married, and the novel ends with a paragraph extolling the virtues of western trappers: "There is not an American youth living who has not, at one time or another, been interested in the life of a trapper; and if any who reads this story ever goes to the Far North-west, he will not need a better friend or surer guide than Moccasin Bill."

Whatever else they may have been, dime novels like *Moccasin Bill* were extremely popular. Beadle advertised his first, *Malaeska, or the Indian Wife of the White Hunter* (1860) by Ann Sophia Stephens, as "a dollar book for a dime," and it sold 65,000 copies within a few months. When Edward Sylvester Ellis's *Seth Jones; or, the Captives of the Frontier* was released the same year, its sales soon soared to 300,000. First printings were usually 60,000 copies, and it was a rare dime novel that was not reprinted. By the 1880s the exploits of train robbers and detectives superseded Indians and trappers, and having increased in shuddery fascination but declined in redeeming social value, dime novels fell into a low repute from which they never recovered. They lingered on into the twentieth century until supplanted by the nickelodeon, motion pictures, comic books, radio, and television—media which they influenced.

Dime novels like *Moccasin Bill* provided color and romance for millions of Americans, and they reinforced traditional values at a time when they had come into question. Hard work and virtue were rewarded, at least in dime novels, and whether villain or hero, characters were rugged, self-reliant, and in control of their own destinies. Like the *McGuffey Readers* (pp. 160-164), dime novels made the distinction between good and evil perfectly clear. In the chapters from *Moccasin Bill* reprinted here, Laura tells her brother, Moccasin Bill, about her captivity and is subsequently recaptured by Cunning Serpent, who overhears a romantic conversation between her and Deerfoot and, out of jealousy, plots Deerfoot's death.

CHAPTER VII.

LAURA HAUTVILLE'S HISTORY.

That night, seated in a small apartment in the fort, lighted by a huge log fire at one end of it, were Henry [Moccasin Bill] and Laura Hautville. The arm of the brother was around his beautiful sister's waist, and he listened with rapt attention to each word that fell from her lips. Young as he was when they were parted, he had never forgotten her, and as each year of his life went by, he had yearned to see her more and more, though sometimes the thought that she was dead would take possession of him. So, too, it was with her. She was older than he, and the details of that dreadful tragedy upon the river she had never forgotten.

"Laura," said her brother, "you must have had a sad time of it, since last I saw you?"

"Sad? Oh, yes," she replied. "That is no name for what I suffered. It was only the hope of again seeing you that often kept me alive. Yes, sooner than again fall into the hands of these savages—and especially one—I would hurl myself from a high cliff!"

"Fear not, sister. You are safe here."

"Would you like to hear my history, Henry?"

"Nothing would please me better."

"You shall hear it, then.

"When the Indian who bore me from you lifted me into his canoe, I felt as if I could jump into the river, so terrible did his face look and seem. I could not cry, for I was far too terrified for that. When we reached the shore he took me out and hid the canoe in some bushes. Then he seized me in his arms and ran like a frightened deer into the forest.

"On, on he carried me until he came to a stream of water, which he at once entered and then waded down the stream for fully a mile. Then stepping out upon the bank, he carried me to a cave that was not far off. He scraped together some leaves, upon which he laid me. There, in English, he told me to go asleep. Of course this was out of the question, and for the first time, I began to weep. But the Indian pointed to his tomahawk, and I was fain to stop on the instant.

"In half an hour or so from the time we entered the cave, it was with feelings of great relief that I saw the Indian leave me. Soon after, feeling terribly tired, I fell asleep. When I awoke it was night. Just outside the cave was burning a fire, and over it the Indian was cooking meal. When this was done he came and offered me a piece, and feeling very hungry, I did not refuse it. This seemed to please him, and after that he spoke in a far kinder tone to me. He gave me a drink of water from a leathern canteen, and then he prepared to leave the place. He took me in his arms again and carried me along at a rapid pace.

"The night was a beautiful one. The moon was shining brightly, with not a cloud to dim a single star. To my surprise the Indian proceeded toward the river where we had left it that afternoon. The canoe was in the bushes just as he had left it. He placed me in it, then stepped inside himself and pushed off from the shore. He headed the canoe up the stream, keeping near the shore and paddling rapidly. Feeling tired, I laid down in the bottom of the canoe and fell asleep. I slept for hours, for when I awoke the east was becoming streaked with gray, accompanied with a wind, which chilled me through and through. We had been on the water all night and I knew we were miles away from the spot from which we had started the night before.

"Soon after the rising of the sun the Indian headed the canoe ashore, and I was very glad of being allowed a chance of exercising my limbs again. The Indian collected a pile of dried sticks and leaves and then kindled them into a blaze. At a short distance from this he kindled another fire, and then a third some distance from the second. The spot where we landed had a few trees growing close to the river, but behind these the prairie stretched far as the eye could reach. The fires the savage had kindled were signals, though at that time I did not understand it.

"The Indian kept the fires burning for at least two hours; then he produced some jerked beef. Giving me part of this, he ate the remainder himself and then lay down on the ground and was soon asleep. How I longed to escape, but I knew that, even if I could succeed in doing so, a far more terrible fate awaited me—that of starvation.

"The Indian slept until it was afternoon. The moment he awoke he rose to his feet and gazed out upon the prairie. I followed his example, and my eyes fell upon a line of dark objects far away. They were Indians, and mounted. They were stringing over the prairie like wolves, and coming directly toward us. It was a splendid sight, Henry—those horses as they galloped over the prairie, with long manes and lithe limbs!

"In a short time they reached us, and with a quick jerk of the bridle they brought their steeds to a stand-still. For a few moments they and my captor conversed together, then I was suddenly seized and placed upon one of the horses, beside a young, and not bad-looking Indian. My captor—whose name you know is Cunning Serpent—took his seat on one of the spare horses the prairie Indians ever carry along with them when upon a journey, and in less than a minute the whole troop was again in motion, heading in the direction whence they had just come. My Indian rode like a Centaur, and despite the situation I was in, that prairie ride was a delightful one. The savages headed north, and they rode at a rapid pace until sundown.

"By this time we had arrived at the extremity of another forest, through which a stream of reddish water was coursing its way. It was the Red River of the North.

"The next morning Cunning Serpent produced another canoe, and after we had embarked he paddled down the stream. For four days did we journey thus, and early on the morning of the fifth day the Indian ran the canoe into a wide creek, up which he proceeded for nearly three miles. Suddenly he ceased to paddle for a moment, and gave forth a loud whoop. Scarcely had it died from his lips when it was answered by a hundred others. The next moment a spot of ground free from trees, and occupied by two hundred lodges, came into view. It was a singular sight, and I am not equal to the task of describing it.

"I instantly became the target of three hundred pairs of eyes. For a long while they surveyed me, as if I had been some great curiosity; then I was placed in the care of a horrible looking old hag, who took me to her lodge.

"Time went by and I grew to be a big girl. The Indian girls were kind to me, and learned me to embroider and make leggins and moccasins. At the same time I learned the pleasant news that I was to be, some day, the wife of a great chief.

"With but one exception, the warriors were kind to me, and gave me the name of the White Lily. That one exception was a young warrior, who, from the first day I saw the village, had evinced a dislike for me. This he took care to show on every occasion, and I was in constant dread of him. He was by far the best-looking man in the village, and was called Deerfoot.

"One day, some eight years after my capture, I was in the forest, gathering wild-flowers. Suddenly I heard a light foot step behind me. I turned round, and, to my horror, Deerfoot was before me.

"White Lily,' he said, 'do not fear me. I am your friend.' To my surprise, he spoke in English, the first time I had heard that tongue spoken for a long, long time.

"'Listen to me,' he continued, 'I, like you, am not an Indian. I was captured when ten years of age, and have been living with them ever since. Would you not like to escape?'

"He put the question so suddenly that I knew not how to reply.

" 'I shall do so,' he quickly added, 'at the first opportunity, and, if you desire it, I will take you with me. It is for this very reason that I have never appeared friendly toward you, for, had I done so, we would have been closely watched, and that would hinder my plans. But I must not linger here. We may be seen. Remember, White Lily, that I am openly your enemy, but secretly your friend.'

"With these words, he disappeared silently through the bushes, and I was alone. But wily as Deerfoot was, our interview must have been seen. I was treated as before, with the exception that I was never again allowed to go far from the village, and even then I was under the strict watch of some of the Indian girls.

"This scene I have just related took place in the spring. Late that fall an Indian runner came into the village with the news that a large body of Sioux were on the war-path, and that their presence at our village was not to be unexpected. Of course, this intelligence was received with the wildest excitement. The head chief immediately held a council, after which nearly all of the warriors immediately returned to their lodges. In less than an hour they issued forth again. The ocher and vermilion had been washed from their faces, and streaks of black placed in their stead. This was the war-paint.

"Their appearance was greeted with unearthly shrieks and yells from the squaws, who loudly commanded them, also, to bring back the scalps of their enemies to appease the wrath within them. The warriors answered not a word, but, one following the footsteps of the other, they strode silently away into the forest, leaving the village guarded by the boys and a few old men. Had Deerfoot been with me, I should have certainly endeavored to escape; but he was not; he was gone with the war-party.

"The warriors were absent four days, then they returned. They had ambushed the advancing Sioux and a terrible conflict took place, in which the head-chief and the second were killed. But our party were victorious and they took many scalps. On their return the squaws went forth to meet them, and when some learned they had lost a husband, some a brother or father, loud shrieks rent the air. They demanded the scalps of their slain enemies, and as these were handed them, their cries of grief changed into exclamations of joy and exultation.

"Among those who returned was Deerfoot. He was the only one whose belt did not carry a scalp. Indianized as he was, he had not got down to that. During the conflict with the Sioux, Cunning Serpent, by his bravery, had attracted the notice of the tribe toward himself, and, as their head-chief was no more, he was unanimously proclaimed to be their chief—the position he now occupies.

"Years went by. Last fall the crops of the Indians, suffering for want of rain, died out. The sagacity of Cunning Serpent told him a famine must be the result. Having no corn, of course they were unable to make their winter's store of pemmican, which, for weeks in winter, is an Ojibwah's sole subsistence. Accordingly, to my joy, I was informed secretly by Deerfoot that it was the intention of the tribe to move southward. This was indeed gratifying news. Being near to civilized parts, I expected to easily effect my escape, an expectation, dear brother, which has been more than realized. Yes, in one hour, I have regained both freedom and my brother. . . ."

CHAPTER XI.

AN EVENTFUL NIGHT.

That day proved to be one of those balmy winter days which, in the latitude of which I write, so often succeeds a cold snap—days as mild as those of spring itself.

Indeed, it proved a God-send to the settlers, who, after a terrible walk of fifteen miles, found themselves that night in St. James.

The settlers received them with a hearty welcome, and, ere long the homeless ones were feeling comfortable, under the circumstances. Fearing an attack from the savages, the settlers of St. James had made the utmost of preparations for its defense. In fact, with its model block-house, it could have repulsed double or treble the amount of Indians which attacked Blue Creek. Two cannons, which, from old age, would have been considered as useless on a field of battle, had been purchased by the pioneers, and they were mounted on the parapet, ready, on an instant's warning, to commence action.

That night, the twilight had scarcely deepened into darkness, when a young Indian—to all appearances—suddenly debouched from the forest, and with hasty footsteps approached the block-house. When near the stockade, he was accosted by one of the villagers, who was performing the duties of a sentry:

"Who are you?"

"I am called by the red-skins, Deerfoot."

"You look like an Indian," replied the sentry, "but your voice is that of a white. Which are you?"

"I am a white—by both birth and nature. But I wish to ask you a question. Among the settlers who arrived here this evening, did you notice a female who was dressed like an Ojibwah squaw, and in fawn-skin?"

"I did. I noticed, in particular, her beauty."

"Yes, yes. Well, I wish to speak to her."

"Will it be agreeable to her?"

Deerfoot smiled. He answered:

"I can answer for that. Besides, I bring with me news of importance."

The sentry scanned the speaker closely for a few moments; then, calling to some one who was near to take his place for a few moments, he walked toward the fort in search of Laura Hautville.

Before long, the man returned, accompanied, not by White Lily, but by her brother—Henry Hautville. The two advanced toward the stockade gate with hasty steps.

"Where is the Indian?" demanded Hautville.

"Here sir," said the sentry, pointing to Deerfoot.

"You inquired for my sister, I believe?" said the young man, turning toward Deerfoot.

"I asked to see the White Lily—or Laura Hautville, whichever name you please to call her by," was the answer.

"Well, why do you wish to see her?"

There was no response.

"You do not answer."

"You are not the person I sent for," replied Deerfoot, firmly, yet in a respectful tone.

"Very well. Perhaps you have no objections against stepping into the fort?"

"None whatever, sir, I assure you."

The two proceeded together toward the fort. Entering, Deerfoot was led into a room lighted by a huge fire, and a candle, upon a rude wooden table. On entering, Henry fastened the door, a circumstance which did not escape the notice of Deerfoot, although he said nothing.

"Who are you?" demanded Hautville.

"Why?"

"Why? Red-skin, answer my question!"

"Red-skin, you call me!" answered Deerfoot, slightly losing his temper. "Sir, I am as white as you are."

Saying this, he pulled up the sleeve of his hunting-shirt, and bared an arm white and beautiful in its proportions. This surprised Hautville, and he said, in a changed tone:

"You are, as you said, white. Still, why may not you be some agent of that savage, Cunning Serpent?"

"Your sister—if such the White Lily be—can answer that question."

For a few moments after hearing this, Henry Hautville was silent. He then said:

"I will bring my sister. Wait."

He unbolted the door, and left the room, soon to return with his sister. As she entered, and her eyes fell upon Deerfoot, a deep blush overspread her face, and she advanced and held forth her hand. Turning to her brother, she said:

"Henry, here is Deerfoot—he whom I spoke of when I gave you my history."

Forgetting his late dislike toward Deerfoot, Henry walked forward, grasped him by the hand and said:

"Let us be friends."

A few moments later, he quitted the room. The night was a warm one for winter, and the lovers—for such they were—not wishing to be overheard by listeners, quitted the fort. They passed through the gate and forward to the edge of the clearing. Here they lingered for upward of an hour, and then Deerfoot prepared to leave her.

"Forget not what I have said, Laura. Cunning Serpent is a fiend, and he will use every part his subtle imagination possesses to obtain possession of you again. Good-bye, for the present."

He wound his arms around her, and then walked away. He did not immediately enter the forest, but crossing the clearing, walked along the river's bank up the stream.

She watched him with a beating heart until he had disappeared, then, heaving a sigh, she prepared to leave the spot. But before she could do so, a noise from behind startled her, and at the same instant a hand clutched her arm. She turned, suspecting for a moment that it might be her brother. But no. The moon's light was streaming down through the trees, and standing before her was the form of Cunning Serpent. His grim visage said that he had heard all they had spoken. She tried to put on a show of fearlessness, but failed, trembling in every limb.

"Come," said the savage, still retaining possession of her arm; "I did not think that the White Lily would so easily be caught."

"Villain!" returned she, addressing him in his own tongue, "release my arm."

"The White Lily is once more mine," he continued, without noticing her words. "She loves Deerfoot, but, ugh! he shall fall ere another moon has come. I heard all."

"Red devil!" she exclaimed, making a desperate but futile effort to release herself. "*You* threaten Deerfoot. You are mad! He is brave, where you fear a wolf; strong, while you are like a woman; noble, while you are like that after which you are called."

The contempt with which this was said was not without its effect upon the savage, but he said nothing. A deep scowl sat rigidly on his face, and after a moment's hesitation, with a celerity of movement known only to a savage, he seized her in his arms. A scream of terror escaped her, but before its echoes had died away, she was being borne swiftly into the cover of the deep forest. On, on the terrible savage ran—two things serving to keep him on the move. One was, the prize he had coveted and was now in possession of—the other, the certainty of being pursued.

In something less than two hours, the savage, for the first time, came to a halt. He had arrived at an Indian village, not large, but sufficiently so to protect him from any open attack of all the whites in the immediate neighborhood. He placed his captive in one of the lodges, occupied by only an old hag, whom he advised to keep a sharp look-out, that his captive did not escape. Then, in a single movement, he turned to leave the lodge, and at the same time confronted the young girl.

"Let the White Lily not try to escape," he said. "Cunning Serpent will now find her lover—the nimble Deerfoot. She shall soon behold him. Ha! ha! Soon."

Laura sprung forward—sprung forward, as if to implore the savage to listen to her a moment. But he must have known her intention, for he executed a quick movement which placed him outside the lodge, where she was not likely to follow him. Yes, he was gone.

She threw herself down upon the earth and moaned bitterly. Not for herself—not for her own dreadful position—not with the thought that she was in the power of the fiend whose prisoner she was; but with the dreadful knowledge that the demon was upon her lover's track, and, unaware of the enemy he had made, would not fail to be struck.

"Oh, Deerfoot!" she moaned, in the language of her childhood; "would to Heaven you knew as much as I do. Then you might escape. But cunning is more than a match for bravery, and you must fall."

The old hag heard these words, but not knowing their import, said nothing, only watched the young captive with a jealous eye.

Let us follow the chief.

Immediately after quitting the lodge, he walked toward a spot where were assembled a number of savages. Stepping still when he had arrived near them, he said:

"Warriors! Cunning Serpent sees your weapons. They are sharp. He sees your paint. It is red. We know why this is. To-night we were to attack the pale-faces; but this must not be. Your actions ask the reason. Braves, we have been betrayed."

A howl of anger met this declaration; and a score of voices demanded the betrayer's name.

"You know him," continued Cunning Serpent. "It is he who did not join my warriors, a few days back, when we took so many scalps, and who complained, like a woman, of having a spirit within him that made him sick. It was a lie! He did not want to fight the pale-faces. More than that—to-night I saw him go to the fort of our enemies. Why? To warn them that we were upon their track. He is a traitor. What shall be his doom?"

As if with one accord, a score of voices proclaimed:

"The stake! The stake!"

"You know his name," added the chief. "Deerfoot!"

Warriors rushed madly over the village, hunting for the man the words of Cunning Serpent had raised their anger against. But he was not to be found. He was not in the village. But he would return, they thought; and with angered mien, they awaited his coming.

A Cowboy Captured by Indians

Nat Love was born a slave in 1854 on a plantation in Tennessee. After the Civil War he headed west and worked as a hired hand for the cattle trains departing from Texas, Arizona, and New Mexico for Kansas, Colorado, Wyoming, and the Dakotas. When the cattle industry declined, Love became a railroad porter. The account of his capture by Indians is taken from *The Life and Adventures of Nat Love Better Known in the Cattle Country as "Deadwood Dick"* . . . (1907).

During the heyday of the cattle industry (1866-1896), something like a quarter to a third of the estimated 35,000 cowboys in the West were black. They were a mainstay of the industry, yet by 1907 the existence of black cowboys had been for the most part forgotten, largely because western novels like Owen Wister's *The Virginian* (1902) made the cowboy into an America hero, and it was the white stereotype which they fostered, not historical fact, that dominated the American mind. Moreover, at the time, most white Americans were unwilling to accept black heroes of any sort.

Love displays almost superhuman daring, strength, and ingenuity. He probably modelled his narrative after legends about frontier heroes like Boone (pp. 174-177) and Crockett. He emphasizes his associations with such figures as Bat Masterson, Jesse and Frank James, Kit Carson, Buffalo Bill, and Billy the Kid. Love may also have patterned his narrative after the lurid dime novels in which Indian captivity plays a prominent part (pp. 200-208). The House of Beadle and Adams published

---

SOURCE: *The Life and Adventures of Nat Love Better Known in the Cattle Country as "Deadwood Dick" by Himself. A True History of Slavery Days, Life on the Great Cattle Ranges and on the Plains of the "Wild and Woolly" West, Based on Facts, and Personal Experiences of the Author* (Los Angeles, 1907).

ninety-seven dime novels about a western hero named "Deadwood Dick." Many people claimed to be the original "Deadwood," but a subtitle of the first novel in the series, which seems to refer to the color of the hero's clothes, may well suggest the color of the person who is its hero. The title is: *Deadwood Dick, the Prince of the Road; or, the Black Rider of the Black Hills* (1877). Love claimed to have earned the nickname of "Deadwood Dick" during a shooting and roping contest in Deadwood, South Dakota.

Love does not designate the tribal affiliation of the Indians who captured him. Both Apache and Pima tribes lived near the Gila River in Arizona, where he was captured, but the evidence suggets that "Yellow Dog's tribe" was Pima. Apaches usually killed their captives, while Pimas adopted them. That many of the Indians mentioned are part black also points to the Pimas since Apaches feared and hated blacks.

CHAPTER XIV.

I AM CAPTURED BY THE INDIANS AND ADOPTED INTO THE TRIBE

It was a bright, clear fall day, October 4, 1876, that quite a large number of us boys started out over the range hunting strays which had been lost for some time. We had scattered over the range and I was riding along alone when all at once I heard the well known Indian war whoop and noticed not far away a large party of Indians making straight for me. They were all well mounted and they were in full war paint, which showed me that they were on the war path, and as I was alone and had no wish to be scalped by them I decided to run for it. So I headed for Yellow Horse Canyon and gave my horse the rein, but as I had considerable objection to being chased by a lot of painted savages without some remonstrance, I turned in my saddle every once in a while and gave them a shot by way of greeting, and I had the satisfaction of seeing a painted brave tumble from his horse and go rolling in the dust every time my rifle spoke, and the Indians were by no means idle all this time, as their bullets were singing around me rather lively, one of them passing through my thigh, but it did not amount to much. Reaching Yellow Horse Canyon, I had about decided to stop and make a stand when one of their bullets caught me in the leg, passing clear through it and then through my horse, killing him. Quickly falling behind him I used his dead body for a breast work and stood the Indians off for a long time, as my aim was so deadly and they had lost so many that they were careful to keep out of range.

But finally my ammunition gave out, and the Indians were quick to find this out, and they at once closed in on me, but I was by no means subdued, wounded as I was and almost out of my head, and I fought with my empty gun until finally overpowered. When I came to my senses I was in the Indians' camp.

My wounds had been dressed with some kind of herbs, the wound in my breast just over the heart was covered thickly with herbs and bound up. My nose had been nearly cut off, also one of my fingers had been nearly cut off. These wounds I received when I was fighting my captors with my empty gun. What caused them to spare my life I cannot tell, but it was I think partly because I had proved myself a brave man, and all savages admire a brave man and when they captured a man whose fighting powers were out of the ordinary they generally kept him if possible as he was needed in the tribe.

Then again Yellow Dog's tribe was composed largely of half breeds, and there was a large percentage of colored blood in the tribe, and as I was a colored man they wanted to keep me, as they thought I was too good a man to die. Be that as it may, they dressed my wounds and gave me plenty to eat, but the only grub they had was buffalo meat which they cooked over a fire of buffalo chips, but of this I had all I wanted to eat. For the first two days after my capture they kept me tied hand and foot. At the end of that time they untied my feet, but kept my hands tied for a couple of days longer, when I was given my freedom, but was always closely watched by members of the tribe. Three days after my capture my ears were pierced and I was adopted into the tribe. The operation of piercing my ears was quite painful, in the method used, as they had a small bone secured from a deer's leg, a small thin bone, rounded at the end and as sharp as a needle. This they used to make the holes, then strings made from the tendons of a deer were inserted in place of thread, of which the Indians had none. Then horn ear rings were placed in my ears and the same kind of salve made from herbs which they placed on my wounds was placed on my ears and they soon healed.

The bullet holes in my leg and breast also healed in a surprisingly short time. That was good salve all right. As soon as I was well enough I took part in the Indian dances. One kind or another was in progress all the time. The war dance and the medicine dance seemed the most popular. When in the war dance the savages danced around me in a circle, making gestures, chanting, with every now and then a blood curdling yell, always keeping time to a sort of music provided by stretching buffalo skins tightly over a hoop.

When I was well enough I joined the dances, and I think I soon made a good dancer. The medicine dance varies from the war dance only that in the medicine dance the Indians danced around a boiling pot, the pot being filled with roots and water and they dance around it while it boils. The medicine dance occurs about daylight.

I very soon learned their ways and to understand them, though our conversation was mostly carried on by means of signs. They soon gave me to understand that I was to marry the chief's daughter, promising me 100 ponies to do so, and she was literally thrown in my arms; as for the lady she seemed perfectly willing if not anxious to become my bride. She was a beautiful woman, or rather girl; in fact all the squaws of this tribe were good looking, out of the ordinary, but I had other notions just then and did not want to get married under such circumstances, but for prudence sake I seemed to enter into their plans, but at the same time keeping a sharp lookout for a chance to escape. I noted where the Indians kept their horses at night, even picking out the handsome and fleet Indian pony which I meant to use should opportunity occur, and I seemed to fall in with the Indians' plans and seemed to them so contented that they gave me more and more freedom and relaxed the strict watch they had kept on me, and finally in about thirty days from the time of my capture my opportunity arrived.

My wounds were now nearly well, and gave me no trouble. It was a dark, cloudy night, and the Indians, grown careless in their fancied security, had relaxed their watchfulness. After they had all thrown themselves on the ground and the quiet of the camp proclaimed them all asleep I got up and crawling on my hands and knees, using the greatest caution for fear of making a noise, I crawled about 250 yards to where the horses were picketed, and going to the Indian pony I had already picked out I slipped the skin thong in his mouth which the Indians use for a bridle, one which I had secured and carried in my shirt for some time for this particular purpose, then springing to his back I made for the open prairie in the direction of the home ranch in Texas, one hundred miles away. All that night I rode as fast as my horse could carry me and the next morning, twelve hours after I left the Indians camp I was safe on the home ranch again. And my joy was without bounds, and such a reception as I received from the boys. They said they were just one day late, and if it hadn't been for a fight they had with some of the same tribe, they would have been to my relief. As it was they did not expect to ever see me again alive. But that they know that if the Indians did not kill me, and gave me only half a chance I would get away from them, but now that I was safe home again, nothing mattered much and nothing was too good for me.

It was a mystery to them how I managed to escape death with such wounds as I had received, the marks of which I will carry to my grave and it is as much a mystery to me as the bullet that struck me in the breast just over the heart passed clear through, coming out my back just below the shoulder. Likewise the bullet in my leg passed clear through, then through my horse, killing him.

Those Indians are certainly wonderful doctors, and then I am naturally tough as I carry the marks of fourteen bullet wounds on different part of my body, most any one of which would be sufficient to kill an ordinary man, but I am not even crippled. It seems to me that if ever a man bore a charm I am the man, as I have had five horses shot from under me and killed, have fought Indians and Mexicans in all sorts of situations, and have been in more tight places than I can number. Yet I have always managed to escape with only the mark of a bullet or knife as a reminder. The fight with the Yellow Dog's tribe is probably the closest call I ever had, and as close a call as I ever want.

The fleet Indian pony which carried me to safety on that memorable hundred mile ride, I kept for about five years. I named him "The Yellow Dog Chief." And he lived on the best the ranch afforded, until his death which occurred in 1881, never having anything to do except an occasional race, as he could run like a deer. I thought too much of him to use him on the trail and he was the especial pet of every one on the home ranch, and for miles around.

I heard afterwards that the Indians pursued me that night for quite a distance, but I had too much the start and besides I had the fastest horse the Indians owned. I have never since met any of my captors of that time. As they knew better than to venture in our neighborhood again. My wound healed nicely, thanks to the good attention the Indians gave me. My captors took everything of value I had on me when captured. My rifle which I especially prized for old associations sake; also my forty fives, saddle and bridle, in fact my whole outfit leaving me only the few clothes I had on at the time.

My comrades did not propose to let this bother me long, however, because they all chipped in and bought me a new outfit, including the best rifle and revolvers that could be secured, and I had my pick of the ranch horses for another mount. During my short stay with the Indians I learned a great deal about them, their ways of living, sports, dances, and mode of warfare which proved of great benefit to me in after years. The oblong shields they carried were made from tanned buffalo skins and so tough were they made that an arrow would not pierce them although I have seen them shoot an arrow clean through a buffalo. Neither will a bullet pierce them unless the ball hits the shield square on, otherwise it glances off.

All of them were exceedingly expert with the bow and arrow, and they are proud of their skill and are always practicing in an effort to excel each other. This rivalry extends even to the children who are seldom without their bows and arrows.

They named me Buffalo Papoose, and we managed to make our wants known by means of signs. As I was not with them a sufficient length of time to learn their language, I learned from them that I had killed five of their number and wounded three while they were chasing me and in the subsequent fight with my empty gun. The wounded men were hit in many places, but they were brought around all right, the same as I was. After my escape and after I arrived home it was some time before I was again called to active duty, as the boys would not hear of me doing anything resembling work, until I was thoroughly well and rested up. But I soon began to long for my saddle and the range.

And when orders were received at the ranch for 2000 head of cattle, to be delivered at Dodge City, Kansas, I insisted on taking the trail again. It was not with any sense of pride or in bravado that I recount here the fate of the men who have fallen at my hand.

It is a terrible thing to kill a man no matter what the cause. But as I am writing a true history of my life, I cannot leave these facts out. But every man who died at my hands was either seeking my life or died in open warfare, when it was a case of killing or being killed.

PART FIVE

Beyond the Frontier

The Frontiers of Fantasy

A Surprising Account, of the Captivity and Escape of Philip M'Donald, and Alexander M'Leod, of Virginia . . . (1786) is indeed surprising, for it is a captivity which takes place wholly within the realm of the imagination. It stands somewhere between the literature of travel fantasy, a genre which goes back to the time of Lucian's *True History* (c.200 A.D.), and the fantastic extrapolations of the science fiction of today.

However, this narrative is a landmark in another way. The literature BEHIND THE FRONTIER was basically an historic response to the Indian captivity experience. It followed events closely, if not in literal detail, at least in the sense that they conveyed emotional immediacy. *A Surprising Account* inaugurates the literature BEYOND THE FRONTIER, a literature which transcended the factual, creating an imaginative experience from the historical tradition. This narrative describes the fantastic adventures of two Revolutionary War soldiers. They claim to have been waylaid by "a monstrous creature in human shape" who takes them to his tribe, a utopian civilization located on a Pacific island some two thousand miles in circumference. The "monstrous creatures" speak Hebrew, abhor violence, and are committed to justice and egalitarianism. From "ancient records," the soldiers discover that their civilization originated in Asia but was cut off from the homeland "soon after the flood." The captives live happily with the tribe and would have remained had a storm not driven them to sea while they were sailing to a neighboring island in search of exotic fruit.

This strange little narrative was published at a time when fiction was considered frivolous if not morally detrimental. For entertainment,

---

SOURCE: *A Surprising Account, of the Captivity and Escape of Philip M'Donald, and Alexander M'Leod, of Virginia. From the Chickkemogga Indians, and of Their Great Discoveries in the Western World. From June 1779, to January 1786, When They Returned in Health to Their Friends, After an Absence of Six Years and a Half. Written by Themselves.* (Bennington, Vt., 1786).

eighteenth-century audiences read "true accounts" of adventure and disaster, but, as the popularity of this narrative reveals (it had at least eight editions before 1800), a story need only appear to be based on fact. To ease the way from fact to fancy, the narrative begins with a captivity in the Ohio River Valley by Chickkemogga Indians. The beginning, while fictitious, seems plausible, and would have seemed even more so to contemporary readers familiar with Indian captivity narratives. "Chickkemogga," strange as it looks, is merely a variant spelling of "Chickamauga," the name given to a band of Cherokee Indians who espoused the British cause during the Revolution and afterwards remained hostile toward Americans. When they escape, the narrators are in the vicinity of a large body of inland water, probably Lake Michigan, which they cross in a canoe. Knowing little about this region, readers would have been constrained to accept the fantasy its unknown author spun.

The fantasy is akin to several popular books and legends. The "monstrous creature in human shape" recalls legends popular during the nineteenth century and still circulated today about "Bigfoot," a homonoid said to roam the western wilderness. It also resembles the Patagonian giants described by Isaac Morris in *A Narrative of the Dangers and Distresses Which Befel . . . the Crew, Belonging to the "Wager" . . .* (London, 1751). The Morris narrative had already inspired *The Life, Extraordinary Adventures, Voyages, and Surprizing Escapes of Capt. Neville Frowde . . .* (London, 1773), a novel attributed to Edward Kimber which resembles the M'Donald and M'Leod narrative in its fanciful exaggerations. That the "creatures" speak Hebrew can be attributed to books like James Adair's *History of the American Indians . . .* (1775) which posited a similarity between Hebrew and certain Indian dialects and argued on the basis of this similarity that the Indians were descended from the Lost Tribes of Israel. The "fruit" which "resembles a rich cake" is probably a reference to the breadfruit which was discovered by Captain James Cook in Hawaii in 1778 and was the object of Lt. William Bligh's ill-fated expedition to the South Seas aboard the *Bounty* in1789. The large Pacific island on which the creatures live conforms to the popular belief that California was an island. Most of all, the narrative recalls Jonathan Swift's fantasy, *Gulliver's Travels* (1726).

The excerpt which follows begins at the point in the narrative when M'Donald and M'Leod are captured by the "monstrous creature."

. . . Here we must mention with admiration, the surprizing benificence of Deity, in replenishing the earth with every necessary and even luxurious growth of nature, for the sustenance of his dependent creatures. Here we found a fine well watered country, beautiful to behold, the trees were exceeding high and large, at a great distance from each other, and so little underbrush that a man may easily have cleared an acre in two days. The wild fruits were excellent, and the spontaneous growths of the earth were beyond all description luxuriant. We had not travelled far in the level country, before we reached a large plain kind of track, free from every sort of vegitation, and resembling a road in America: on seeing this, we concluded we must be near some sort of inhabitants, but as we were uncertain of what sort they may be it made us tremble with apprehension. We lifted up our hearts and voices to heaven for protection, and relying on the mercyful care of providence determined to prosecute our journey along the beaten path untill we arrived at some place of dwelling for human beings; we had not been long traveling, in the road before mentioned, when we distinctly heard a human voice at a small distance from us, and by the sound, we were led to conclude, the speaker was not of the indian tribes with whom we had been acquainted. We stopped for some time, irresolute and undetermined whether to proceed or to retire; when a tremendous voice assailed our ears,- and suddenly a monstrous creature in human shape, but nearly twelve feet in height, jumped from a rock into the road, and taking us both up, almost dead with fear, into his hand, exclaimed, in the Hebrew language, what creatures can these be!

We were not partly recovered from our fright, and seeing no appearance of malignity in the aspect of our possessor, we carefully turned ourselves round & took hold of the long shaggy hair of his outside garment to keep us from falling, and then ventured to address him in the language of his exclamation, and beg him not to kill us. He was pleased beyond measure to hear us speak, and told us to apprehend no danger from him, for he belonged to a race of beings that never intentionally did harm to any creature.

We were greatly relieved from our fears by this declaration, and after about an hour's travel, upon rising a high hill we discovered a large regular built city before us, in appearance, but when we came to it our astonishment was greatly encreased. The houses were exceedingly beautiful and lofty though consisting of but two stories, and the people appeared exceedingly loving and tractable.

It was only a little village as they informed us, about ten English miles in length, and the same in breadth, and contained about five hundred families.

Mr. M'Donnald having been educated at the University of Edinburgh, could understand their language perfectly well, and communicated to them the history of Europe, at which they were much surprised. In return they informed us, that they had ancient records which we might see, if we pleased.

In examining the records, we discovered that they were originally from Asia, and most probably separated from that continent soon after the flood. They have a tradition among them that a long time ago, their progenitors were miraculously planted by the being they adore, on the happy spot they at present possess, (which is a fertile island, according to our computation, two thousand miles in circumference). That they were prohibited by their religion from war, and that murder and infidelity were equally unknown among them.

They address their praises to the sun, as the representative of the being they adore; for which purpose the whole village were summoned together at the rising and setting of that planet. When with united voices, and a solemn attention beyond what we had ever seen before, they performed their ceremonies.

These people are strangers to the use of flesh, and all kinds of spirituous liquors; they live to a great age, and though vastly numerous, they populate so slow that it is very rare three children belong to one family. We saw some people among them above an hundred years old, according to their reckoning, and their days are nearly twice the length of ours.

We were sent soon after we were found, to the high priest or king of their nation, who attended with great pleasure the recital of our principles of religion, and the divine precepts of the scripture, but when we informed him of the quarrels among christians, and their shedding so much blood to support their different sectaries, his astonishment was greater than can be conceived, and in his public declamations he often took occasion to return thanks that the vices of christians were unknown to them as to practice.

We could have spent our lives among this people contentedly, and never should have thought of seeking for another home, but Providence had ordered otherwise, and our return to our native home after a long absence was effected by accident as follows.

On a little uninhabited island, about three leagues from the main, grows a sort of fruit of which the inhabitants of the main are exceeding fond, and which, when dried, in taste, nearly resembles rich cake: the produce of this island is collected annually by the king's orders, and distributed throughout his dominions. The water craft made use of in this business, is very large and strong built boats, conveniently fixed for the purpose, & covered with a deck to prevent the fruit from getting wet. The annual produce of this island is computed to be equal to one half the bread consumed by the inhabitants in a year. And as the inhabitants are exceeding fond of milk with their cake, (of which they have great plenty) it forms a very considerable part of their living.

We had been among these hospitable people so long that all their cares became ours, and we partook of all their amusements. We were with the party employed on the island business, and had nearly compleated our loading when a violent storm arose, which occasioned some of the boats to break their landfasts, and as none of the natives were in the boat with us, we were driven at the mercy of the winds and waves, and were soon out of sight of land. The storm beginning to encrease, we lashed our helm down, and went below. The wind now raged with great violence, and the rain poured from the clouds in such torrents as to oblige us to shut ourselves up close, the storm continuing with unremitted fury for several days, during which we lost our rudder and mast.

We were driven in this situation twenty-eight days without any prospect of relief. We put up our earnest supplications to heaven for assistance, and returned unfeigned thanks for the signal interpositions of providence in our behalf. It was early in the morning of the twenty-ninth day, while we were at our devotions, that we discovered a ship to the south of us, and steering towards us. Tho we had never hoped to see Europeans again, our joy at this discovery cannot be easily conceived or described. The ship proved to be a Russian frigate, just returning from a voyage of discoveries in the South Seas, who took us on board and treated us with great humanity. Our fruit was of a kind they had not seen in their voyage, and on our arrival at St. Petersburgh, we received a handsome price for our cargo, and a strong invitation to sail in her Imperial Majesty's service in quest of the island we described, but our impatience to see our friends prompted us to equip ourselves for our voyage to America. We according left Petersburgh on board an English vessel bound to London, from whence we set sail for America in a few days after, and by the blessing of Heaven arrived safe in Virginia on the fourth of January 1786, after an absence of above six years and a half.

The Pocahontas Plays

Several plays about Indian captivity were written and staged during the first half of the nineteenth century, when American playwrights were struggling to create a national dramatic tradition. The presence of Indian characters on stage was a distinctively American novelty. Dressed in exotic costume, Indians provided magnificent stage pageantry. Indian captivity itself could be exploited for its pathos, and it afforded an opportunity to depict American history on stage. Most of the captivity plays are lost and are known only from handbills and other contemporary references, but among those that have survived is a series of productions about John Smith and Pocahontas, known as "the Pocahontas plays."

The following selection is reprinted from James Nelson Barker's *The Indian Princess; or, La Belle Sauvage* (1808), a play based on the account of John Smith's captivity given in his *Generall Historie of Virginia.* Barker treats the Pocahontas story with a dignity appropriate to her theatrical debut. Pocahontas is depicted as a princess, and her father, Powhatan, is a noble king, the equal of England's King James. When she falls in love with John Rolfe, Pocahontas speaks elegant blank verse. *The Indian Princess* inspired a series of imitations which culminated in a satire by John Brougham titled *An Original Aboriginal Erratic Operatic Semi-Civilized and Demi-Savage Extravaganza, Being a Per-Version of Ye Trewe and Wonderfulle Hystorie of Ye Renowned Princesse, Po-ca-hon-tas: or, the Gentle Savage* (1855). By the 1850s the novelty that audiences once found in the Pocahontas plays was a subject for burlesque.

Yet Barker's influence on the history of American drama should not be underestimated. Throughout his career, he encouraged American playwrights to use American subjects. *The Indian Princess* was the first play about Indians by an American author to be produced. In 1817 Barker returned to the subject of Indian captivity with *The Armourer's Escape,* based on the famous captivity at Nootka Sound of the American

---

SOURCE: James Nelson Barker, *The Indian Princess; or, La Belle Sauvage* (Philadelphia, 1808). First performed in Philadelphia on April 6, 1808, at the Chestnut Street Theatre.

seaman, John Jewitt, who, to the delight of his audience, played himself in the leading role.

Other plays on the Pocahontas theme include George Washington Custis's *Pocahontas; or, the Settlers of Virginia* (1830), Robert Dale Owen's *Pocahontas* (1837), Charlotte Barnes Conner's *Forest Princess* (1848), and *Pocahontas*, an undated play by Samuel Byers which was apparently never performed.

ACT II, SCENE 1

Inside the palace at Werocomoco. Powhatan *in state,* Grimosco [Indian priest], &c., *his wives, and warriors, ranged on each side. Music.*

Pow. My people, strange beings have appeared among us; they come from the bosom of the waters, amid fire and thunder; one of them has our war-god delivered into our hands: behold the white being!

Music. Smith *is brought in; his appearance excites universal wonder;* Pocahontas *expresses peculiar admiration.*

Poc. O Nima [an Indian attendant]! is it not a God!

Pow. Miami [an Indian prince], though thy years are few, thou art experienced as age; give us thy voice of counsel.

Mia. Brothers, this stranger is of a fearful race of beings; their barren hunting grounds lie beneath the world, and they have risen, in monstrous canoes, through the great water, to spoil and ravish from us our fruitful inheritance. Brothers, this stranger must die; six of our brethren have fall'n by his hand. Before we lay their bones in the narrow house, we must avenge them: their unappeased spirits will not go to rest beyond the mountains; they cry out for the stranger's blood.

Nan [Nantaquas, Powhatan's son]. Warriors, listen to my words; listen, my father, while your son tells the deeds of the brave white man. I saw him when 300 of our fiercest chiefs formed the war-ring around him. But he defied their arms; he held lightning in his hand. Wherever his arm fell, there sunk a warrior: as the tall tree falls, blasted and riven, to the earth, when the angry Spirit darts his fires through the forest. I thought him a god; my feet grew to the ground; I could not move!

Poc. Nima, dost thou hear the words of my brother?

Nan. The battle ceased, for courage left the bosom of our warriors; their arrows rested in their quivers; their bowstrings no longer sounded; the tired chieftains leaned on their war-clubs, and gazed at the terrible stranger, whom they dared not approach. Give an ear to me, king: 'twas then I held out the hand of peace to him, and he became my brother; he forgot his arms, for he trusted to his brother; he was discoursing wonders to his friend, when our chiefs rushed upon him, and bore him away. But oh! my father, he must not die; for he is not a war captive; I promised that the chain of friendship should be bright between us. Chieftains, your prince must not falsify his word; father, your son must not be a liar!

Poc. Listen, warriors; listen, father; the white man is my brother's brother!

Grim. King! when last night our village shook with the loud noise, it was the Great Spirit who talk'd to his priest; my mouth shall speak his commands: King, we must destroy the strangers, for they are not our God's children; we must take their scalps, and wash our hands in the white man's blood, for he is an enemy to the Great Spirit.

Nan. O priest, thou hast dreamed a false dream; Miami, thou tellest the tale that is not. Hearken, my father to my true words! the white man is beloved by the Great Spirit; his king is like you, my father, good and great; and he comes from a land beyond the wide water, to make us wise and happy!

Powhatan deliberates. Music.

Pow. Stranger, thou must prepare for death. Six of our brethren fell by thy hand. Thou must die.

Poc. Father, O father!

Sm. Had not your people first beset me, king,
I would have prov'd a friend and brother to them;
Arts I'd have taught, that should have made them gods,
And gifts would I have given to your people,
Richer than red men ever yet beheld.
Think not I fear to die. Lead to the block.
The soul of the white warrior shall shrink not.
Prepare the stake! amidst your fiercest tortures,
You'll find its fiery pains as nobly scorned,
As when the red man sings aloud his death-song.

Poc. Oh! shall that brave man die!

Music. The king motions with his hand, and Smith is led to the block.

Mi. (to executioners) Warriors, when the third signal strikes, sink your tomahawks in his head.

Poc. Oh, do not, warriors, do not! Father, incline your heart to mercy; he will win your battles, he will vanquish your enemies. *(1st signal)* Brother, speak! save your brother! Warriors, are you brave? preserve the brave man! *(2nd signal)* Miami, priest, sing the song of peace; ah! strike not, hold! mercy!

Music. The 3d signal is struck, the hatchets are lifted up: when the princess, shrieking, runs distractedly to the block, and presses Smith's head to her bosom.

White man, thou shalt not die; or I will die with thee!

Music. She leads Smith to the throne, and kneels.

My father, dost thou love thy daughter? listen to her voice; look upon her tears: they ask for mercy to the captive. Is thy child dear to thee, my father? Thy child will die with the white man.

Plaintive music. She bows her head to his feet. Powhatan, after some deliberation, looking on his daughter with tenderness, presents her with a string of white wampum. Pocahontas, with the wildest expression of joy, rushes forward with Smith, presenting the beads of peace.

Captive! thou art free!—

Music. General joy is diffused—Miami and Grimosco only appear discontented. The prince Nantaquas congratulates Smith. The princess shows the most extravagant emotions of rapture.

Sm. O woman! angel sex! where'er thou art,
Still art thou heavenly. The rudest clime
Robs not thy glowing bosom of it's nature.
Thrice blessed lady, take a captive's thanks!
(he bows upon her hand.)

Poc. My brother!
(music. Smith expresses his gratitude.)

Nan. Father, hear the design that fills my breast. I will go among the white men; I will learn their arts; and my people shall be made wise and happy.

Poc. I too will accompany my brother.

Mi. Princess!—

Poc. Away, cruel Miami; you would have murdered my brother!—

Pow. Go, my son; take thy warriors, and go with the white men. Daughter, I cannot lose thee from mine eyes; accompany thy brother but a little on his way. Stranger, depart in peace; I entrust my son to thy friendship.

Sm. Gracious sir,
He shall return with honours and with wonders;
My beauteous sister! noble brother come!

Music. Exeunt, on one side, Smith, princess, Nantaquas, Nima, and train. On the other, king, priest, Miami, &c. The two latter express angry discontent.

YAMOYDEN, a Narrative Poem

The long narrative poem, *Yamoyden, a Tale of the Wars of King Philip . . .* (1820) was written by two precocious authors, James W. Eastburn (1797-1819) and Robert C. Sands (1799-1832). It will doubtless surprise modern readers to learn that for a time it was one of the most popular books in America. Eastburn, who died before the poem was completed, was studying for the Episcopal ministry at Bristol, Rhode Island, near Mount Hope where King Philip (d. 1676) lived.

The poem, however, is less about King Philip than the misfortunes of Yamoyden, a fictional Nipnet chief, and Nora, his Puritan wife. Disowned by whites and Indians, Yamoyden takes his wife and child to an island near Mount Hope, intending to shield them from the dangers of King Philip's War. To draw Yamoyden into the conflict, Philip arranges the abduction of Nora and her child so that Yamoyden will think they have been killed by the Puritans. This information is betrayed to the Puritans, who recapture Nora and return her to her unforgiving father. The poem concludes with a battle in which Philip is killed. During the battle, Yamoyden intercedes to save Nora's father and is himself killed, but only after a tearful reunion with his wife, who dies promptly from grief. The passage quoted here is a central episode in the poem, Nora's capture by Philip's braves and her recapture by the Puritans.

Eastburn and Sands based *Yamoyden* on several then well-known books, including William Hubbard's *A Narrative of the Troubles with the Indians in New-England . . .* (1677), Cotton Mather's *Magnalia Christi Americana . . .* (1702), and Thomas Church's *Entertaining Passages Relating to Philip's War . . .* (1716). They portray the Indians as the innocent victims of white bigotry. Nora's captivity is the result of anger aroused by incessant Puritan encroachments on Indian lands. This attitude is common to much of the imaginative literature about Indian captivity during the nineteenth century, when artists could view the Indian from a distance and in verse, drama, fiction, and the visual arts lament his passing. Earlier poems like John Mayhem's *Gallic Perfidy*

SOURCE: James W. Eastburn and Robert C. Sands, *Yamoyden, a Tale of the Wars of King Philip . . .* (New York, 1820).

. . . (1758) and the anonymous *Returned Captive* . . . (1787) condemn Indians for their savagery.

Yamoyden was praised by the historian John Palfrey (1796-1881) in the *North American Review* for its American subject matter. It is the literary progenitor of books about Indians, including Longfellow's *The Song of Hiawatha* (1855) and the novels of Cooper and William Gilmore Simms. Cooper's *The Wept of Wish-ton-Wish* (1829), with its captures, restorations, and recaptures and the deaths of its star-crossed Indian and his white wife, repeats the conclusion of *Yamoyden.*

XVIII.

There is a trampling in the wood;—
The mat, the cabin's entrance rude,
Shakes;—it was no dream of fear,—
Behold an Indian's face appear;—
He stands within the cot,—and three
Come scowling in his company.
Ask not what terrors o'er her past,
As fixed as stood the patriarch's wife,
When the forbidden glance she cast,
And lightning rooted her aghast,
Leaving a mock of life,—
Gazing she sate, in silent dread,
Till sight was gone, and thought was dead:
Yet close and closer still, she prest
The sleeping infant on her breast;
A mother's instinct quick was left,
Of other sign of life bereft.

XIX.

But when she felt an iron grasp
Tearing that infant from her clasp,
Her piercing scream the forest rent,
And all despair's high strength was sent
Gathering around her heart;
"O mercy, Jesus! save my child!"
She cried in tones so sadly wild,
The WAMPANOAG, fierce and bold,
Shrunk from his purpose, and his hold
Relaxed with sudden start.
Her spoiler's dusky brow she scanned,—
Yet struggling from his ruthless hand
Her wailing child to tear,—

As one would mark the madman's eye,
When a fearful precipice was nigh,
And he had grasped him there.
She met his glances, stern and keen,
Such might the hungry wolf's have been,—
Whose spoils now swathed him round;—
And in his front all bare and bleak,
And in his high, scar-riven cheek,
No line of mercy found.
A rapid look surveyed the rest;—
In vain to them despair may cling!
Ah! sooner mantling verdure blest
On the bald thundercliff shall spring!

XX.

The mother from her child is torn,—
A cry that rent her heart forlorn,
Their murderous triumph told;
Then kind oblivion came to save
From madness; dark, as is the grave,
Dreamless and void and cold.
One bears her senseless in his arms,
Another stills the babe's alarms;
Then through the forest's tangled way,
Swift and straight, toward the bay
Their path the Indians hold.
Each stepping where the first had gone,
'Twas but as the mark of one.
So noiseless was their cautious tread,
The wakeful squirrel overhead
Knew not that aught beneath him sped.
No bough recoiled as on they broke,
Scarce rustling leaf their impress spoke.

XXI.

From the first blush who judges man,
Must ill his Maker's image scan:
The traveller in the boundless lands,
Where the fair west its stores expands,
Oft marks, with cheerful green unblent,
High piled to heaven the bleak ascent,
As scathed and blasted by the fire,
That fell from the Almighty's ire.

But as along the vale he sweeps,
More gently swell the fir-clad steeps,
Till all the sunny mountain rise,
With golden crown amid the skies.
Not the swarth skin, nor rude address
Bespeak the bosom's dreariness;—
Happy, if thus the evil brain
Bore stampt the outward curse of Cain!

XXII.

Slowly from NORA'S wandering soul,
Oblivion's mists of midnight roll,
And, as she woke, to view again
Uncertain horror's spectral train,
Dashing waves were murmuring near,
Rode the bright moon high and clear:
The plunderers crost a shelving glade;
Around the forest's mass of shade
Rose darkling; and before, the bay
Was quivering with the silver ray.
Dim memory rose; an Indian eye
Watched its first dawning earnestly.
Strange was the face that, frank and bold,
Spoke a heart cast in gentler mould.
He bore the waking lady up
And lingered last of all the group;
Nor e'er at superstition's shrine,
Did votary mark the fire divine,
When wavering in its golden vase,
With feeling more intense,
Than o'er her wan and death-like face,—
Like morning blushing o'er the snow,—
The warrior watched the beaming glow
Of lost intelligence.

XXIII.

He pointed, where his comrade bore
Her infant in his arms, before.
His gaze with melting ruth was fraught,
And that uncertain peril taught
A language to his look:
Of needful silence in that hour,
Of rescue near from saviour power

And faithful aid it spoke.
But still they sped toward the wave,
And he whose glance had sworn to save,
Yet often eyed the circling wood
Where only gloom and mystery brood.
The rippling tides, the insects shrill,
At times the plaining whip-poor-will,
In melancholy concord wake;
But other sound was none, to break
The wild suspense of hope and fear;
There was no sign of rescue near.
Fair shone the moon; but there gleamed no ray
Of hope in her calm and pearly way;
Bright rolled the expanding floods below,
But there shone no promise in their flow;
The hues serene of nature's rest
But agonized her anxious breast.

XXIV.

Nearer and nearer to the shore,
Their prize the hurrying party bore;—
The bank is gained; its brake amid,
Their light canoe was closely hid.
While cautious its descent they guide,
To the calm bosom of the tide,
Their comrade, lingering yet above,
Gazed anxiously around to prove
His silent promise true;—
But not a sound is heard, nor sign
Is there of aid; the giant pine
Its gloomy limbs unmoving bears,
And still the silent forest wears
Its sad and solemn hue.

XXV.

'Tis launched,—they beckon him to haste;
One glance he threw, and hope has past,
No more could NORA brook to wait,
In passiveness, uncertain fate.
She shrieked,—far rung the loud alarm,—
And as she struggled from his arm
To break, whose faint resistance made
A moment's brief delay,

An Indian leapt to lend his aid;
But, ere he touched the trembling maid,
Even in his middle way,—
Loud from the wood a gunshot rung,
Straight from earth the NIPNET sprung,
Then, with but one mortal pain,
Dead he sunk upon the plain.
Again, again the volleys pour,
And NORA saw and heard no more.

XXVI.

She woke; the ground was wet with blood,—
Her Indian saviour o'er her stood;
Around her she discovered then,
The faces of her countrymen.
"Where is my child?" they answer not;—
Her dusky guardian's eye she sought;—
O'er his high cheek of rugged mould,
The moon-beam glistened, clear and cold;
A crystal tear was starting bright,
And glittering with the pale, pure light;—
"Where is my child? in mercy, say?"
He pointed to the expanding bay;—
There was no speck on its azure sheet,
No trace in the waters smooth and fleet,—
As if furrowing keel had ploughed them never,—
And she knew her child was gone for ever. . . .

Nathaniel Hawthorne's "The Duston Family"

In March 1836, Nathaniel Hawthorne (1804-1864) became editor of *The American Magazine of Useful and Entertaining Knowledge*, a position he held only six months because it turned out to consist of literary drudgery. His assignment was to fill out a periodical which featured engravings (see illustration, p. 227). Usually, he wrote paraphrases and summaries of material from other publications, but sometimes he included more original work. One such instance is his retelling of the tale of the Duston (variously spelled: see Thoreau, pp. 156-159) captivity. Hawthorne's source was the historian and divine, Cotton Mather, who gave him his facts and occasion for acid comment on Puritan bigotry. Though he makes Hannah Duston the clear center of his sketch, he does so by placing her within the framework of a character of quite different qualities, her husband, Goodman Duston. Typically, Hawthorne exploits the affirmative connotations of his quaint, Puritan honorific.

Their respective characters move in opposite directions as the story unfolds. Initially, Hannah Duston is a "good woman" in a "helpless state." In the end she has become a "bloody old hag," a "raging tigress." Goodman Duston, at first uncertain and inept, eventually proves to be a "tender hearted, yet valiant man," and there is a hint, when he leaves his wife to succor their children, that he senses the potential of her character. But the essence of the matter is that he preserves and she destroys. Within the tradition of Puritan typology, Cotton Mather associated Hannah Duston with the Old Testament heroine, Jael, who slew the Canaanite general while he slept (Judges 4:17-22). Hannah Duston is prefigurative for Hawthorne, too. In *The Marble Faun* (1861), he will link Jael to Miriam, his dark heroine. She paints a portrait of Jael that captures her "heroic face and lofty beauty," but with a "certain wayward quirk of her pencil . . . [she] converted the heroine into a vulgar murderess." What Hawthorne projects here is woman as a danger to man.

The story has other Hawthorne touches. There is, for example, a facetious tone at the beginning in the reference to Hannah Duston's

---

SOURCE: "The Duston Family," *The American Magazine of Useful and Entertaining Knowledge* 2 (May 1836), pp. 395-397.

fecundity, a tone which turns sour indeed when we see her taking the scalps of children. In short, Hawthorne was engrossed by the ironies and moral questions of the Duston captivity: when is it moral to kill, especially to kill children, Christian children (though Catholic), and to receive payment for it? Hawthorne, uneasily serving out his time, found himself overtaken by what Melville was later to call, in the biblical phrase, his fascination with "the power of blackness."

Hawthorne was to return to the subject of Indian captivity when he wrote his masterpiece, *The Scarlet Letter* (1850). The adultery of Hester Prynne takes place in a period of her husband's prolonged absence. Unknown to her, he has been "held in bonds among the heathen-folk," that is, the Indians. On the day that Hester is condemned to stand on the scaffold publicly displaying the scarlet emblem of her sin, her husband is brought to Boston by his Indian captor "to be redeemed." Thereafter, he assumes the name Roger Chillingworth and the role of physician, for during "his Indian captivity . . . he had gained much knowledge of the properties of native herbs and roots." In fact, it is said that he "had enlarged his medical attainments by joining in the incantations of the savage priests." At this point Hawthorne makes the Indian captivity more than a plot device. He had initially described Chillingworth as "clad in a strange disarray of civilized and savage costume," outward indication of the profound effect of his Indianizing experience, and he plays ironically with events and words. In the vocabulary of the captivity narrative, Chillingworth is brought to Boston "to be redeemed," but his captivity, in a spiritual sense, does not move him toward redemption. Like Hannah Duston, he becomes a savage and a demon.

Goodman Duston and his wife, somewhat less than a century and a half ago, dwelt in Haverhill, at that time a small frontier settlement in the province of Massachusetts Bay. They had already added seven children to the King's liege subjects in America; and Mrs. Duston about a week before the period of our narrative, had blessed her husband with an eighth. One day in March, 1698, when Mr. Duston had gone forth about his ordinary business, there fell out an event, which had nearly left him a childless man, and a widower besides. An Indian war party, after traversing the trackless forest all the way from Canada, broke in upon their remote and defenceless town. Goodman Duston heard the war whoop and alarm, and, being on horseback, immediately set off full speed to look after the safety of his family. As he dashed along, he beheld dark wreaths of smoke eddying from the roofs of several dwellings near the road side; while the groans of dying men,—the shrieks of affrighted women, and the screams of children, pierced his ear, all mingled with the horrid yell of the raging savages. The poor man trembled yet spurred on so much the faster, dreading that he should find his own cottage in a blaze, his wife murdered in her bed, and his little ones tossed into the flames. But, drawing near the door, he saw his seven elder children, of all ages between two years and seventeen, issuing out together, and running down the road to meet him. The father only bade them make the best of their way to the nearest garrison, and, without a moment's pause, flung himself from his horse, and rushed into Mrs. Duston's bedchamber.

The good woman, as we have before hinted, had lately added an eighth to the seven former proofs of her conjugal affection; and she now lay with the infant in her arms, and her nurse, the widow Mary Neff, watching by her bedside. Such was Mrs. Duston's helpless state, when her pale and breathless husband burst into the chamber, bidding her instantly to rise and flee for her life. Scarcely were the words out of his mouth, when the Indian yell was heard: and staring wildly out of the window, Goodman Duston saw that the blood-thirsty foe was close at hand. At this terrible instant, it appears that the thought of his children's danger rushed so powerfully upon his heart, that he quite forgot the still more perilous situation of his wife; or, as is not improbable, he had such knowledge of the good lady's character, as afforded him a comfortable hope that she would hold her own, even in a contest with a whole tribe of Indians. However that might be, he seized his gun and rushed out of doors again, meaning to gallop after his seven children, and snatch up one of them in his flight, lest his whole race and generation should be blotted from the earth, in that fatal hour. With this idea, he rode up behind them, swift as the wind. They had, by this time, got about forty rods from the house, all pressing forward in a group; and though the younger children tripped and stumbled, yet the elder ones were not prevailed upon, by the fear of death, to take to their heels and leave these poor little souls to perish. Hearing the tramp of hoofs in their rear, they looked round, and espying Goodman Duston, all suddenly stopped. The little ones stretched out their arms; while the elder boys and girls, as it were, resigned their charge into his hands; and all the seven children seemed to say.—'Here is our father! Now we are safe!'

But if ever a poor mortal was in trouble, and perplexity, and anguish of spirit, that man was Mr. Duston! He felt his heart yearn towards these seven poor helpless children, as if each were singly possessed of his whole affections; for not one among them all, but had some peculiar claim to their dear father's love. There was his first-born; there, too, the little one who, till within a week past, had been the baby; there was a girl with her mother's features, and a boy, the picture of himself, and another in whom the looks of both parents were mingled; there was one child, whom he loved for his mild, quiet, and holy disposition, and destined him to be a minister; and another, whom he loved not less for his rough and fearless spirit, and who, could he live to be a man, would do a man's part against these bloody Indians. Goodman Duston looked at the poor things, one by one; and with yearning fondness, he looked at them all, together; then he gazed up to Heaven for a

Hawthorne's magazine sketch, "The Duston Family," paints the redoubtable Hannah in dark colors but portrays her husband affirmatively. The illustration shows Goodman Duston defending their children. The caption reads: "The Escape of the Duston Family." *Courtesy of the Edward E. Ayer Collection, the Newberry Library.*

moment, and finally waved his hand to his seven beloved ones. 'Go on, my children,' said he, calmly. 'We will live or die together!'

He reined in his horse, and caused him to walk behind the children, who, hand in hand, went onward, hushing their sobs and wailings, lest these sounds should bring the savages upon them. Nor was it long, before the fugitives had proof that the red devils had found their track. There was a curl of smoke from behind the huge trunk of a tree—a sudden and sharp report echoed through the woods—and a bullet hissed over Goodman Duston's shoulder, and passed above the children's heads. The father, turning half round on his horse, took aim and fired at the skulking foe, with such effect as to cause a momentary delay of the pursuit. Another shot—and another—whistled from the covert of the forest; but still the little band pressed on, unharmed; and the stealthy nature of the Indians forbade them to rush boldly forward, in the face of so firm an enemy as Goodman Duston. Thus he and his seven children continued their retreat, creeping along, as Cotton Mather observes, 'at the pace of a child of five years old,' till the stockades of a little frontier fortress appeared in view, and the savages gave up the chase.

We must not forget Mrs. Duston, in her distress. Scarcely had her husband fled from the house, ere the chamber was thronged with the horrible visages of the wild Indians, bedaubed with paint and besmeared with blood, brandishing their tomahawks in her face, and threatening to add her scalp to those that were already hanging at their girdles. It was, however, their interest to save her alive, if the thing might be, in order to exact a ransom. Our great-great-grandmothers, when taken captive in the old times of Indian warfare, appear, in nine cases out of ten, to have been in pretty much such a delicate situation as Mrs. Duston; notwithstanding which, they were wonderfully sustained through long, rough, and hurried marches, amid toil, weariness, and starvation, such as the Indians themselves could hardly endure. Seeing that there was no help for it, Mrs. Duston rose, and she and the widow Neff, with the infant in her arms, followed their captors out of doors. As they crossed the threshold, the poor babe set up a feeble wail; it was its death cry. In an instant, an Indian seized it by the heels, swung it in the air, dashed out its brains against the trunk of the nearest tree, and threw the little corpse at the mother's feet. Perhaps it was the remembrance of that moment, that hardened Hannah Duston's heart, when her time of vengeance came. But now, nothing could be done, but to stifle her grief and rage within her bosom, and follow the Indians into the dark gloom of the forest, hardly venturing to throw a parting glance at the blazing cottage, where she had dwelt happily with her husband, and had borne him eight children—the seven, of whose fate she knew nothing, and the infant, whom she had just seen murdered.

The first day's march was fifteen miles; and during that, and many succeeding days, Mrs. Duston kept pace with her captors; for, had she lagged behind, a tomahawk would at once have been sunk into her brains. More than one terrible warning was given her; more than one of her fellow captives,—of whom there were many,—after tottering feebly, at length sank upon the ground; the next moment, the death groan was breathed, and the scalp was reeking at an Indian's girdle. The unburied corpse was left in the forest, till the rites of sepulture should be performed by the autumnal gales, strewing the withered leaves upon the whitened bones. When out of danger of immediate pursuit, the prisoners, according to Indian custom, were divided among different parties of the savages, each of whom were to shift for themselves. Mrs. Duston, the widow Neff, and an English lad, fell to the lot of a family, consisting of two stout warriours, three squaws, and seven children. These Indians, like most with whom the French had held intercourse, were Catholics; and Cotton Mather affirms, on Mrs. Duston's authority, that they prayed at morning, noon, and night, nor ever partook of food without a prayer; nor suffered their children to sleep, till they had prayed to the christian's God. Mather, like an old hard-hearted, pedantic bigot, as he was, seems trebly to exult in the destruction of these poor wretches, on account of their Popish superstitions. Yet what can be more touching than to think of these wild Indians, in their loneliness and their wanderings, wherever they went among the dark, mysterious woods, still keeping up domestic worship, with all the regularity of a household at its peaceful fireside.

They were travelling to a rendezvous of the savages, somewhere in the northeast. One night, being now above a hundred miles from Haverhill, the red men and women, and the little red children, and the three pale faces, Mrs. Duston, the widow Neff, and the English lad, made their encampment, and kindled a fire beneath the gloomy old trees, on a small island in Contocook river. The barbarians sat down to what scanty food Providence had sent them, and shared it with their prisoners, as if they had all been the children of one wigwam, and had grown up together on the margin of the same river within the shadow of the forest. Then the Indians said their prayers—the prayers that the Romish priests had taught them—and made the sign of the cross upon their dusky breasts, and composed themselves to rest. But the three prisoners prayed apart; and when their petitions were ended, they likewise lay down, with their feet to the fire. The night wore on; and the light and cautious slumbers of the red men were often broken, by the rush and ripple of the stream, or the groaning and moaning of the forest, as if nature were wailing over her wild children; and sometimes, too, the little red skins cried in sleep, and the Indian mothers awoke to hush them. But, a little before break of day, a deep, dead slumber fell upon the Indians. 'See,' cries Cotton Mather, triumphantly, 'if it prove not so!'

Uprose Mrs. Duston, holding her own breath, to listen to the long, deep breathing of her captors. Then she stirred the widow Neff, whose place was by her own, and likewise the English lad; and all three stood up, with the doubtful gleam of the decaying fire hovering upon their ghastly visages, as they stared round at the fated slumberers. The next instant, each of the three captives held a tomahawk. Hark! that low moan, as of one in a troubled dream—it told a warriour's death pang! Another!—Another!—and the third half-uttered groan was from a woman's lips. But, Oh, the children! Their skins are red; yet spare them, Hannah Duston, spare those seven little ones, for the sake of the seven that have fed at your own breast. 'Seven,' quoth Mrs. Duston to herself. 'Eight children have I borne—and where are the seven, and where is the eighth!' The thought nerved her arm; and the copper coloured babes slept the same dead sleep with their Indian mothers. Of all that family, only one woman escaped, dreadfully wounded, and fled shrieking into the wilderness! and a boy, whom, it is said, Mrs. Duston had meant to save alive. But he did well to flee from the raging tigress! There was little safety for a red skin, when Hannah Duston's blood was up.

The work being finished, Mrs. Duston laid hold of the long black hair of the warriours, and the women, and the children, and took all their ten scalps, and left the island, which bears her name to this very day. According to our notion, it should be held accursed, for her sake. Would that the bloody old hag had been drowned in crossing Contocook river, or that she had sunk over head and ears in a swamp, and been there buried, till summoned forth to confront her victims at the Day of Judgment; or that she had gone astray and been starved to death in the forest, and nothing ever seen of her again, save her skeleton, with the ten scalps twisted round it for a girdle! But, on the contrary, she and her companions came safe home, and received the bounty on the dead Indians, besides liberal presents from private gentlemen, and fifty pounds from the Governour of Maryland. In her old age, being sunk into decayed circumstances, she claimed, and, we believe, received a pension, as a further price of blood.

This awful woman, and that tender hearted, yet valiant man, her husband, will be remembered as long as the deeds of old times are told round a New England fireside. But how different is her renown from his!

The Captivity of the Munro Sisters from James Fenimore Cooper's THE LAST OF THE MOHICANS

The theme of Indian captivity is best known today from the historical romances of James Fenimore Cooper (1789-1851). The Leatherstocking saga records the life and prodigious adventures of a woodsman, Natty Bumppo, who embodies the virtues of the white race kept pure by his bond with nature. He is a plebeian hero and a childless wanderer, but his literary offspring flourish in sophisticated art forms and even more so in the mass media. Cooper's *Leatherstocking Tales* are the literary high point of the captivity tradition. This selection is from *The Last of the Mohicans* (1826), probably the most famous and certainly the busiest of the Leatherstocking series. Along with much else, it describes the captivity of Cora and Alice by the evil Indian, Magua, who has abducted them to avenge an insult he received from their father, Colonel Munro, the British commander at Fort William Henry on Lake George, New York. Natty Bumppo, also called "La Longue Carabine" and "Hawkeye" in this novel, and the noble Indians, Chingachgook and Uncas, rescue them just as they are about to be tortured because Cora has refused to marry Magua. The action takes place in 1757 near Fort William Henry a few days before the garrison is massacred by the French and Indians under General Montcalm.

What Cooper knew about Indians and Indian captivity he learned at secondhand. His daughter, Susan Fenimore Cooper, reports that he

---

SOURCE: James Fenimore Cooper, *The Last of the Mohicans; a Narrative of 1757 . . .* (Philadelphia, 1826).

read captivity narratives. *The Last of the Mohicans* is based on accounts of Indian captivity in such narratives as Jonathan Carver's *Travels Through the Interior Parts of North-America . . .* (1778), David Humphrey's *An Essay on the Life of the Honorable Major-General Israel Putnam . . .* (1788), and the Reverend John Heckewelder's *History, Manners, and Customs, of the Indian Nations . . .* (1818). Natty Bumppo owes his origin to frontiersmen like Daniel Boone (see pp. 174-177) and Tim Murphy (see pp. 171-173); and Cora owes something to Jane MacCrea (see Bancroft, pp. 141-142).

As a writer, Cooper stood at the edge of the American literary frontier, with the European novelistic tradition behind him and unknown territory ahead. He saw rich possibilities in the captivity tradition. Captivity narratives could be exploited for their suspense, pathos, and horror. Better still, the subject matter was indigenous. If the structure was European, the content was uniquely American. But Cooper was a social critic as well as a literary craftsman and patriot. For example, beneath the pattern of escape and pursuit which Indian captivity brings to *The Last of the Mohicans,* there is subtle evidence of racial tensions. Although Uncas loves Cora, they cannot marry, for his Indian blood may never mix with hers, especially because Cora is herself the product of an interracial union. Her mother was part black, so Cora's marriage to Uncas would constitute a double offense against established racial taboos. Only the patrician Major Duncan Heyward and the delicate, pure-blooded Alice Munro may marry, and the future of America rests with their progeny.

CHAPTER IX

"Be gay securely;
Dispel, my fair, with smiles, the tim'rous clouds,
That hang on thy clear brow."
Death of Agrippina.

. . . "They are gone, Cora!" he whispered; "Alice, they are returned whence they came, and we are saved! To heaven, that has alone delivered us from the grasp of so merciless an enemy, be all the praise!"

"Then to heaven will I return my thanks!" exclaimed the younger sister, rising from the encircling arms of Cora, and casting herself, with enthusiastic gratitude, on the naked rock to her knees; "to that heaven who has spared the tears of a gray-headed father; has saved the lives of those I so much love—"

Both [Duncan] Heyward, and the more tempered Cora, witnessed the act of involuntary emotion with powerful sympathy, the former secretly believing that piety had never worn a form so lovely, as it had now assumed in the youthful person of Alice. Her eyes were radiant with the glow of her grateful feelings; the flush of her beauty was again seated on her cheeks, and her whole soul seemed ready and anxious to pour out its thanksgivings, through the medium of her eloquent features. But when her lips moved, the words they should have uttered appeared frozen by some new and sudden chill. Her bloom gave place to the paleness of death; her soft and melting eyes grew hard, and seemed contracting with horror; while those hands, which she had raised, clasped in each other, towards heaven, dropped in horizontal lines before her, the fingers pointing forward in convulsed motion. Heyward turned the instant she gave a direction to his suspicions, and, peering just above the ledge which formed the threshold of the open outlet of the cavern, he beheld the malignant, fierce, and savage features of le Renard Subtil [Magua].

In that moment of horrid surprise, the self-possession of Heyward did not desert him. He observed by the vacant expression of the Indian's countenance, that his eye, accustomed to the open air, had not yet been able to penetrate the dusky light which pervaded the depth of the cavern. He had even thought of retreating beyond a curvature in the natural wall, which might still conceal him and his companions, when, by the sudden gleam of intelligence that shot across the features of the savage, he saw it was too late, and that they were betrayed.

The look of exultation and brutal triumph which announced this terrible truth, was irresistibly irritating. Forgetful of every thing but the impulses of his hot blood, Duncan [Heyward] levelled his pistol and fired. The report of the weapon made the cavern bellow like an eruption from a volcano, and when the smoke, it vomited, had driven away before the current of air which issued from the ravine, the place so lately occupied by the features of his treacherous guide was vacant. Rushing to the outlet, Heyward caught a glimpse of his dark figure, stealing around a low and narrow ledge, which soon hid him entirely from his sight.

Among the savages, a frightful stillness succeeded the explosion, which had just been heard bursting from the bowels of the rock. But when le Renard raised his voice in a long and intelligible whoop, it was answered by a spontaneous yell from the mouth of every Indian within hearing of the sound. The clamorous noises again rushed down the island, and before Duncan had time to recover from the shock, his feeble barrier of brush was scattered to the winds, the cavern was entered at both its extremities, and he and his companions were dragged from their shelter, and borne into the day, where they stood surrounded by the whole band of the triumphant Hurons.

CHAPTER X.

"I fear we shall outsleep the coming morn,
As much as we this night have overwatched!"
Midsummer's Night Dream.

THE instant the first shock of this sudden misfortune had abated, Duncan began to make his observations on the appearance and proceedings of their captors. Contrary to the usages of the natives in the wantonness of their success, they had respected, not only the persons of the trembling sisters, but his own. The rich ornaments of his military attire, had indeed been repeatedly handled by different individuals of the tribe, with eyes expressing a savage longing to possess the baubles, but before the customary violence could be resorted to, a mandate, in the authoritative voice of the large warrior already mentioned, stayed the uplifted hand, and convinced Heyward that they were to be reserved for some object of particular moment.

While, however, these manifestations of weakness were exhibited by the young and vain of the party, the more experienced warriors continued their search throughout both caverns, with an activity that denoted they were far from being satisfied with those fruits of their conquest, which had already been brought to light. Unable to discover any new victim, these diligent workers of vengeance soon approached their male prisoners, pronouncing the name of "la Longue Carabine [Natty]," with a fierceness that could not easily be mistaken. Duncan affected not to comprehend the meaning of their repeated and violent interrogatories, while his companion was sparred the effort of a similar deception, by his ignorance of French. Wearied, at length, by their importunities, and apprehensive of irritating his captors by too stubborn a silence, the former looked about him in quest of Magua, who might interpret his answers to those questions which were, at each moment, becoming more earnest and threatening.

The conduct of this savage had formed a solitary exception to that of all his fellows. While the others were busily occupied in seeking to gratify their childish passion for finery, by plundering even the miserable effects of the scout, or had been searching, with such blood-thirsty vengeance in their looks, for their absent owner, le Renard had stood at a little distance from the prisoners, with a demeanour so quiet and satisfied, as to betray, that he, at least, had already effected the grand purpose of his treachery. When the eyes of Heyward first met those of his recent guide, he turned them away, in horror, at the sinister though calm look he encountered. Conquering his disgust, however, he was able, with an averted face, to address his successful enemy:

"Le Renard Subtil is too much of a warrior," said the reluctant Heyward, "to refuse telling an unarmed man what his conquerors say."

"They ask for the hunter who knows the paths through the woods," returned Magua, in his broken English, laying his hand, at the same time, with a ferocious smile, on the bundle of leaves, with which a wound on his own shoulder was bandaged; "la Longue Carabine! his rifle is good, and his eye never shut; but, like the short gun of the white chief, it is nothing against the life of le Subtil!"

"Le Renard is too brave to remember the hurts he has received in war, or the hands that gave them!"

"Was it war, when the tired Indian rested at the sugar tree, to taste his corn! who filled the bushes with creeping enemies! who drew the knife! whose tongue was peace, while his heart was coloured with blood! Did Magua say that the hatchet was out of the ground, and that his hand had dug it up?"

As Duncan dare not retort upon his accuser, by reminding him of his own premeditated treachery, and disdained to deprecate his resentment by any words of apology, he remained silent. Magua seemed also content to rest the controversy, as well as all further communication, there, for he resumed the leaning attitude against the rock, from which, in his momentary energy, he had arisen. But the cry of "la Longue Carabine," was renewed, the instant the impatient savages perceived that the short dialogue was ended.

"You hear," said Magua, with stubborn indifference; "the red Hurons call for the life of the 'long rifle,' or they will have the blood of them that keep him hid!"

"He is gone—escaped; he is far beyond their reach."

Renard smiled with cold contempt, as he answered:

"When the white man dies, he thinks he is at peace; but the red men know how to torture even the ghosts of their enemies. Where is his body? Let the Hurons see his scalp!"

"He is not dead, but escaped."

Magua shook his head incredulously, and added—

"Is he a bird, to spread his wings; or is he a fish, to swim without looking at the sun! The white chief reads in his books, and believes the Hurons are fools!"

"Though no fish, the 'long rifle' can swim. He floated down the stream when the powder was all burnt, and when the eyes of the Hurons were behind a cloud."

"And why did the white chief stay?" demanded the still incredulous Indian. "Is he a stone, that goes to the bottom, or does the scalp burn his head?"

"That I am not a stone, your dead comrade, who fell into the falls, might answer, were the life still in him," said the provoked young man, using, in his anger, that boastful language which was most likely to excite the admiration of an Indian. "The white man thinks none but cowards desert their women."

Magua muttered a few words, inaudibly, between his teeth, before he continued, aloud—

"Can the Delawares swim, too, as well as crawl in the bushes? Where is 'le Gros Serpent [Chingachgook]'?"

Duncan, who perceived by the use of these Canadian appellations, that his late companions were much better known to his enemies than to himself, answered, reluctantly: "He also is gone down with the water."

" 'Le Cerf Agile [Uncas]' is not here?"

"I know not whom you call the 'nimble deer,' said Duncan, gladly profiting by any excuse to create delay.

"Uncas," returned Magua, pronouncing the Delaware name with even greater difficulty than he spoke his English words. " 'Bounding elk' is what the white man says when he calls to the young Mohican [Uncas]."

"Here is some confusion in names between us, le Renard," said Duncan, hoping to provoke a discussion. "Daim is the French for deer, and cerf for stag; élan is the true term, when one would speak of an elk."

"Yes," muttered the Indian, in his native tongue; "the pale faces are prattling women! they have two words for each thing, while a red skin will make the sound of his voice speak for him." Then changing his language, he continued, adhering to the imperfect nomenclature of his provincial instructers, "The deer is swift, but weak; the elk is swift, but strong; and the son of 'le serpent' is 'le cerf agile.' Has he leaped the river to the woods?"

"If you mean the younger Delaware, he too is gone down with the water."

As there was nothing improbable to an Indian, in the manner of the escape, Magua admitted the truth of what he had heard, with a readiness that afforded additional evidence how little he would prize such worthless captives. With his companions, however, the feeling was manifestly different.

The Hurons had awaited the result of this short dialogue with characteristic patience, and with a silence, that increased, until there was a general stillness in the band. When Heyward ceased to speak, they turned their eyes, as one man, on Magua, demanding, in this expressive manner, an explanation of what had been said. Their interpreter pointed to the river, and made them acquainted with the result, as much by the action as by the few words he uttered. When the fact was generally understood, the savages raised a frightful yell, which declared the extent of their disappointment. Some ran furiously to the water's edge, beating the air with frantic gestures, while others spat upon the element, to resent the supposed treason it had committed against their acknowledged rights as conquerors. A few, and they not the least powerful and terrific of the band, threw lowering, sullen looks, in which the fiercest passion was only tempered by habitual self-command, at those captives who still remained in their power; while one or two even gave vent to their malignant feelings by the most menacing gestures, against which neither the sex, nor the beauty of the sisters, was any protection. The young soldier made a desperate, but fruitless, effort to spring to the side of Alice, when he saw the dark hand of a savage twisted in the rich tresses, which were flowing in volumes over her shoulders, while a knife was passed around the head from which they fell, as if to denote the horrid manner in which it was about to be robbed of its beautiful ornament. But his hands were bound, and at the first movement he made, he felt the grasp of the powerful Indian, who directed the band, pressing his shoulder like a vice. Immediately conscious how unavailing any struggle against such an overwhelming force must prove, he submitted to his fate, encouraging his gentle companions, by a few low and tender assurances, that the natives seldom failed to threaten more than they performed.

But, while Duncan resorted to these words of consolation, to lull the apprehensions of the sisters, he was not so weak as to deceive himself. He well knew that the authority of an Indian chief was so little conventional, that it was oftener maintained by his physical superiority, than by any moral supremacy he might possess. The danger was, therefore, magnified exactly in proportion to the number of the savage spirits by which they were surrounded. The most positive mandate from him, who seemed the acknowledged leader, was liable to be violated, at each moment, by any rash hand that might choose to sacrifice a victim to the manes of some dead friend or relative. While, therefore, he sustained an outward appearance of calmness and fortitude, his heart leaped into his throat, whenever any of their fierce captors drew nigher than common to the helpless sisters, or fastened one of their sullen wandering looks on those fragile forms, which were so little able to resist the slightest assault.

His apprehensions were however greatly relieved, when he saw that the leader had summoned his warriors to himself in council. Their deliberations were short, and it would seem, by the silence of most of the party, the decision unanimous. By the frequency with which the few speakers pointed in the direction of the encampment of Webb [Thomas Webb (c. 1724-1796), British officer], it was apparent they dreaded the approach of danger from that quarter. This consideration probably hastened their determination, and quickened the subsequent movements.

During this short conference, Heyward finding a respite from his greatest fears, had leisure to admire the cautious manner in which the Hurons had made their approaches, even after hostilities had ceased.

It has already been stated, that the upper half of the island was a naked rock, and destitute of any other defences than a few scattering logs of drift wood. They had selected this point to make their descent, having borne the canoe through the wood, around the cataract, for that purpose. Placing their arms in the little vessel, a dozen men, clinging to its sides, had trusted themselves to the direction of the canoe, which was controlled by two of the most skilful warriors, in attitudes, that enabled them to command a view of the dangerous passage. Favoured by this arrangement, they touched the head of the island, at that point which had proved so fatal to their first adventurers, but with the advantages of superior numbers, and the possession of fire arms. That such had been the manner of their descent, was rendered quite apparent to Duncan, for they now bore the light bark from the upper end of the rock, and placed it in the water, near the mouth of the outer cavern. As soon as this change was made, the leader made signs to the prisoners to descend and enter.

As resistance was impossible, and remonstrance useless, Heyward set the example of submission, by leading the way into the canoe, where he was soon seated with the sisters, and the still wondering David [Gamut, a music master, also captured]. Notwithstanding the Hurons were necessarily ignorant of the little channels among the eddies and rapids of the stream, they knew the common signs of such a navigation too well, to commit any material blunder. When the pilot chosen for the task of guiding the canoe had taken his station, the whole band plunged again into the river, the vessel glided down the current, and in a few moments the captives found themselves on the south bank of the stream, nearly opposite to the point where they had struck it, the preceding evening.

Here was held another short but earnest consultation, during which, the horses, to whose panic their owners ascribed their heaviest misfortune, were led from the cover of the woods, and brought to the sheltered spot. The band now divided. The great chief, so often mentioned, mounting the charger of Heyward, led the way directly across the river, followed by most of his people, and disappeared in the woods, leaving the prisoners in charge of six savages, at whose head was le Renard Subtil. Duncan witnessed all their movements with renewed uneasiness.

He had been fond of believing, from the uncommon forbearance of the savages, that he was reserved as a prisoner, to be delivered to Montcalm. As the thoughts of those who are in misery seldom slumber, and the invention is never more lively, than when it is stimulated by hope, however feeble and remote, he had even imagined that the parental feelings of Munro were to be made instrumental in seducing him from his duty to the king. For though the French commander bore a high character for courage and enterprise, he was also thought to be expert in those political practices, which do not always respect the nicer obligations of morality, and which so generally disgraced the European diplomacy of that period.

All those busy and ingenious speculations were now annihilated by the conduct of his captors. That portion of the band who had followed the huge warrior, took the route towards the foot of Horican, and no other expectation was left for himself and companions, than that they were to be retained as hopeless captives by their savage conquerors. Anxious to know the worst, and willing, in such an emergency, to try the potency of his wealth, he overcame his reluctance to speak to Magua. Addressing himself to his former guide, who had now assumed the authority and manner of one who was to direct the future movements of the party, he said, in tones as friendly and confiding as he could assume—

"I would speak to Magua, what is fit only for so great a chief to hear."

The Indian turned his eyes on the young soldier, scornfully, as he answered—

"Speak, then; trees have no ears!"

"But the red Hurons are not deaf; and counsel that is fit for the great men of a nation, would make the young warriors drunk. If Magua will not listen, the officer of the king knows how to be silent."

The savage spoke carelessly to his comrades, who were busied, after their awkward manner, in preparing the horses for the reception of the sisters, and moved a little to one side, whither, by a cautious gesture, he induced Heyward to follow.

"Now speak," he said; "if the words are such as Magua should hear."

"Le Renard Subtil has proved himself worthy of the honourable name given to him by his Canada fathers," commenced Heyward; "I see his wisdom, and all that he has done for us, and shall remember it, when the hour to reward him arrives. Yes, yes! Renard has proved that he is not only a great chief in council, but one who knows how to deceive his enemies!"

"What has Renard done?" coldly demanded the Indian.

"What! has he not seen that the woods were filled with outlying parties of the enemies, and that the serpent could not steal through them without being seen? Then, did he not lose his path, to blind the eyes of the Hurons? Did he not pretend to go back to his tribe, who had treated him ill, and driven him from their wigwams, like a dog? And, when we saw what he wished to do, did we not aid him, by making a false face, that the Hurons might think the white man believed that his friend was his enemy? Is not all this true? And when le Subtil had shut the eyes and stopped the ears of his nation by his wisdom, did they not forget that they had once done him wrong, and forced him to flee to the Mohawks? And did they not leave him on the south side of the river, with their prisoners, while they have gone foolishly on the north? Does not Renard mean to turn like a fox on his footsteps, and carry to the rich and gray headed Scotchman [Munro], his daughters? Yes, yes, Magua, I see it all, and I have already been thinking how so much wisdom and honesty should be repaid. First, the chief of William Henry will give as a great chief should, for such a service. The medal of Magua will no longer be of tin, but of beaten gold; his horn will run over with powder; dollars will be as plenty in his pouch, as pebbles on the shore of Horican; and the deer will lick his hand, for they will know it to be vain to fly from before the rifle he will carry! As for myself, I know not how to exceed the gratitude of the Scotchman, but I—yes, I will—"

"What will the young chief, who comes from towards the sun, give?" demanded the Huron, observing that Heyward hesitated in his desire to end the enumeration of benefits with that which might form the climax of an Indian's wishes.

"He will make the fire-water from the islands in the salt lake, flow before the wigwam of Magua, swifter than yon noisy Hudson, until the heart of the Indian shall be lighter than the feathers of the humming-bird, and his breath sweeter than the wild honeysuckle."

Le Renard had listened with the deepest silence, as Heyward slowly proceeded in this subtle speech. When the young man mentioned the artifice he supposed the Indian to have practised on his own nation, the countenance of the listener was veiled in an expression of cautious gravity. At the allusion to the injury which Duncan affected to believe had driven the Huron from his native tribe, a gleam of such ungovernable ferocity flashed from the other's eyes, as induced the adventurous speaker to believe he had struck the proper chord. And by the time he reached the part where he so artfully blended the thirst of vengeance with the desire of gain, he had, at least, obtained a command of the deepest attention of the savage. The question put by le Renard had been calm, and with all the dignity of an Indian; but it was quite apparent, by the thoughtful expression of the listener's countenance, that the answer was most cunningly devised. The Huron mused a few moments, and then laying his hand on the rude bandages of his wounded shoulder, he said, with some energy—

"Do friends make such marks?"

"Would 'la Longue Carabine' cut one so light on an enemy?"

"Do the Delawares crawl upon those they love like snakes, twisting themselves to strike?"

"Would 'le Gros Serpent' have been heard by the ears of one he wished to be deaf?"

"Does the white chief burn his powder in the faces of his brothers?"

"Does he ever miss his aim, when seriously bent to kill?" returned Duncan, smiling with well acted disdain.

Another long and deliberative pause succeeded these sententious questions and ready replies. Duncan saw that the Indian hesitated. In order to complete his victory, he was in the act of recommencing the enumeration of the rewards, when Magua made an expressive gesture, and said—

"Enough; le Renard is a wise chief, and what he does will be seen. Go, and keep the mouth shut. When Magua speaks, it will be the time to answer."

Heyward, perceiving that the eyes of his companion were warily fastened on the rest of the band, fell back immediately, in order to avoid the appearance of any suspicious confederacy with their leader. Magua approached the horses, and affected to be well pleased with the diligence and ingenuity of his comrades. He then signed to Heyward to assist the sisters into their saddles, for he seldom deigned to use the English tongue, unless urged by some motive of more than usual moment.

There was no longer any plausible pretext for further delay, and Duncan was obliged, however reluctantly, to comply. As he performed this office, he whispered his reviving hopes in the ears of the trembling maidens, who, through dread of encountering the savage countenances of their captors, seldom raised their eyes from the ground. The mare of David had been taken with the followers of the large chief; in consequence, its owner, as well as Duncan, were compelled to journey on foot. The latter did not, however, so much regret this circumstance, as it might enable him to retard the speed of the party—for he still turned his longing looks in the direction of fort Edward, in the vain expectation of catching some sound from the quarter of the forest, which might denote the approach of speedy succour.

When all were prepared, Magua made the signal to proceed, advancing in front, to lead the party in his own person. Next followed David, who was gradually coming to a true sense of his condition, as the effects of the wound became less and less apparent. The sisters rode in his rear, with Heyward at their side, while the Indians flanked the party, and brought up the close of the march, with a caution that seemed never to tire.

In this manner they proceeded in uninterrupted silence, except when Heyward addressed some solitary word of comfort to the females, or David gave vent to the moanings of his spirit, in piteous exclamation, which he intended should express the humility of his resignation. Their direction lay towards the south, and in a course nearly opposite to the road to William Henry. Notwithstanding this apparent adherence in Magua to the original determination of his conquerors, Heyward could not believe his tempting bait was so soon forgotten; and he knew the windings of an Indian path too well, to suppose that its apparent course led directly to its object, when artifice was at all necessary. Mile after mile was, however, passed through the boundless woods in this painful manner, without any prospect of a termination to their journey. Heyward watched the sun, as he darted his meridian rays through the branches of the trees, and pined for the moment when the policy of Magua should change their route to one more favourable to his hopes. Sometimes he fancied that the wary savage, despairing of passing the beleaguering army of Montcalm, in safety, was holding his way towards a well known border settlement, where a distinguished officer of the crown, and a favoured friend of the Six Nations, held his large possessions, as well as his usual residence. To be delivered into the hands of Sir William Johnson [British Indian agent], was far preferable to being led into the wilds of Canada; but in order to effect even the former, it would be necessary to traverse the forest for many weary leagues, each step of which was carrying him further from the scene of the war, and, consequently, from the post, not only of honour, but of duty.

Cora alone remembered the parting injunctions of the scout, and whenever an opportunity offered, she stretched forth her arm to bend aside the twigs that met her hands. But the vigilance of the Indians rendered this act of precaution both difficult and dangerous. She was often defeated in her purpose, by encountering the dark glances of their watchful eyes, when it became necessary to feign an alarm she did not feel, and occupy the limb, by some gesture of feminine apprehension. Once, and once only, was she completely successful; when she broke down the bough of a large sumach, and, by a sudden thought, let her glove fall at the same instant. This sign intended for those that might follow, was observed by one of her conductors, who restored the glove, broke the remaining branches of the bush in such a manner, that it appeared to proceed from the struggling of some beast in its branches, and then laid his hand on his tomahawk, with a look so significant, that it put an effectual end to these stolen memorials of their passage.

As there were horses, to leave the prints of their footsteps, in both bands of the Indians, this interruption cut off any probable hopes of assistance being conveyed through the means of their trail.

Heyward would have called out twenty times to their leader, and ventured a remonstrance, had there been any thing encouraging in the gloomy reserve of the savage. But Magua, during all this time, seldom turned to look at his followers, and never spoke. With the sun for his only guide, or aided by such blind marks as are only known to the sagacity of a native, he held his way along the barrens of pine, through occasional little fertile vales, across brooks and rivulets, and over undulating hills, with the accuracy of instinct, and nearly with the directness of a bird. He never seemed to hesitate. Whether the path was hardly distinguishable, whether it disappeared, or whether it lay beaten and plain before him, made no sensible difference in his speed or certainty. It seemed as though fatigue could not affect him. Whenever the eyes of the wearied travellers rose from the decayed leaves over which they trode, his dark form was to be seen glancing among the stems of the trees in front, his head immoveably fastened in a forward position, with the light plume on its crest, fluttering in a current of air, made solely by the swiftness of his own motion.

But all this diligence and speed was not without an object. After crossing a low vale, through which a gushing brook meandered, he suddenly rose a hill, so steep and difficult of ascent, that the sisters were compelled to alight, in order to follow. When the summit was gained, they found themselves on a level spot, but thinly covered with trees, under one of which Magua had thrown his dark form, as if willing and ready to seek that rest, which was so much needed by the whole party.

CHAPTER XI.

—"Cursed be my tribe,
If I forgive him."—*Shylock.*

THE Indian had selected for this desirable purpose, one of those steep, pyramidal hills, which bear a strong resemblance to artificial mounds, and which so frequently occur in the valleys of the American states. The one in question was high, and precipitous; its top flattened, as usual; but with one of its sides more than ordinarily irregular. It possessed no other apparent advantages for a resting place, than in its elevation and form, which might render defence easy, and surprise nearly impossible. As Heyward, however, no longer expected that rescue, which time and distance now rendered so improbable, he regarded these little peculiarities with an eye devoid of interest, devoting himself entirely to the comfort and condolence of his feebler companions. The Narragansets were suffered to browse on the branches of the trees and shrubs, that were thinly scattered over the summit of the hill, while the remains of their provisions were spread under the shade of a beech, that stretched its horizontal limbs like a vast canopy above them.

Notwithstanding the swiftness of their flight, one of the Indians had found an opportunity to strike a straggling fawn with an arrow, and had borne the more preferable fragments of the victim, patiently on his shoulders, to the stopping place. Without any aid from the science of cookery, he was immediately employed, in common with his fellows, in gorging himself with this digestable sustenance. Magua alone sat apart, without participation in the revolting meal, and apparently buried in the deepest thought.

This abstinence, so remarkable in an Indian, at length attracted the notice of Heyward. The young man willingly believed that the Huron deliberated on the most eligible manner to elude the vigilance of his associates, in order to possess himself of the promised bribe. With a view to assist his plans by any suggestion of his own, and to strengthen the temptation, he left the beech, and straggled, as if without an object, to the spot where le Renard was seated.

"Has not Magua kept the sun in his face long enough to escape all danger from the Canadians?" he asked, as though no longer doubtful of the good intelligence established between them; "and will not the chief of William Henry be better pleased to see his daughters before another night may have hardened his heart to their loss, and will make him less liberal in his reward?"

"Do the pale faces love their children less in the morning than at night?" asked the Indian, coldly.

"By no means," returned Heyward, anxious to recall his error, if he had made one; "the white man may, and does often, forget the burial place of his fathers; he sometimes ceases to remember those he should love, and has promised to cherish: but the affection of a parent for his child is never permitted to die."

"And is the heart of the white-headed chief soft, and will he think of the babes that his squaws have given him? He is hard to his warriors, and his eyes are made of stone!"

"He is severe to the idle and wicked, but to the sober and deserving he is a leader, both just and humane. I have known many fond and tender parents, but never have I seen a man whose heart was softer towards his child. You have seen the gray-head in front of his warriors, Magua, but I have seen his eyes swimming in water, when he spoke of those children who are now in your power!"

Heyward paused, for he knew not how to construe the remarkable expression that gleamed across the swarthy features of the attentive Indian. At first it seemed as if the remembrance of the promised reward grew vivid in his mind, as he listened to the sources of parental feeling which were to assure its possession; but as Duncan proceeded, the expression of joy became so fiercely malignant, that it was impossible not to apprehend it proceeded from some passion even more sinister than avarice.

"Go," said the Huron, suppressing the alarming exhibition in an instant, in a death-like calmness of countenance; "go to the dark-haired daughter, and say, Magua waits to speak. The father will remember what the child promises."

Duncan, who interpreted this speech to express a wish for some additional pledge that the promised gifts should not be withheld, slowly and reluctantly repaired to the place where the sisters were now resting from their fatigue, to communicate its purport to Cora.

"You understand the nature of an Indian's wishes," he concluded, as he led her towards the place where she was expected, "and must be prodigal of your offers of powder and blankets. Ardent spirits are, however, the most prized by such as he; nor would it be amiss to add some boon from your own hand, with that grace you so well know how to practise. Remember, Cora, that on your presence of mind and ingenuity, even your life, as well as that of Alice, may in some measure depend."

"Heyward, and yours!"

"Mine is of little moment; it is already sold to my king, and is a prize to be seized by any enemy who may possess the power. I have no father to expect me, and but few friends to lament a fate, which I have courted with the unsatiable longings of youth after distinction. But, hush; we approach the Indian. Magua, the lady, with whom you wish to speak, is here."

The Indian rose slowly from his seat, and stood for near a minute silent and motionless. He then signed with his hand for Heyward to retire, saying, coldly—

"When the Huron talks to the women, his tribe shut their ears."

Duncan still lingering, as if refusing to comply, Cora said, with a calm smile—

"You hear, Heyward, and delicacy at least should urge you to retire. Go to Alice, and comfort her with our reviving prospects."

She waited until he had departed, and then turning to the native, with all the dignity of her sex, in her voice and manner, she added: "What would le Renard say to the daughter of Munro?"

"Listen," said the Indian, laying his hand firmly upon her arm, as if willing to draw her utmost attention to his words; a movement that Cora as firmly, but quietly repulsed, by extricating the limb from his grasp—"Magua was born a chief and a warrior among the red Hurons of the lakes; he saw the suns of twenty summers make the snows of twenty winters run off in the streams, before he saw a pale-face; and he was happy! Then his Canada fathers came into the woods, and taught him to drink the fire-water, and he became a rascal. The Hurons drove him from the graves of his fathers, as they would chase the hunted buffalo. He ran down the shores of the lakes, and followed their outlet to the 'city of cannon.' There he hunted and fished, till the people chased him again through the woods into the arms of his enemies. The chief, who was born a Huron, was at last a warrior among the Mohawks!

"Something like this I had heard before," said Cora, observing that he paused to suppress those passions which began to burn with too bright a flame, as he recalled the recollection of his supposed injuries.

"Was it the fault of le Renard that his head was not made of rock? Who gave him the fire-water? who made him a villain? 'Twas the pale-faces, the people of your own colour."

"And am I answerable that thoughtless and unprincipled men exist, whose shades of countenance may resemble mine?" Cora calmly demanded of the excited savage.

"No; Magua is a man, and not a fool; such as you never open their lips to the burning stream; the Great Spirit has given you wisdom!"

"What then have I to do, or say, in the matter of your misfortunes, not to say of your errors?"

"Listen," repeated the Indian, resuming his earnest attitude; "when his English and French fathers dug up the hatchet, le Renard struck the war-post of the Mohawks, and went out against his own nation. The pale-faces have driven the red-skins from their hunting grounds, and now, when they fight, a white man leads the way. The old chief of Horican, your father, was the great captain of our war party. He said to the Mohawks do this, and do that, and he was minded. He made a law, that if an Indian swallowed the fire-water, and came into the cloth wigwams of his warriors, it should not be forgotten. Magua foolishly opened his mouth, and the hot liquor led him into the cabin of Munro. What did the gray-head? let his daughter say."

"He forgot not his words, and did justice, by punishing the offender," said the undaunted maiden.

"Justice!" repeated the Indian, casting an oblique glance of the most ferocious expression at her unyielding countenance; "is it justice to make evil, and then punish for it! Magua was not himself; it was the fire-water that spoke and acted for him! but Munro did not believe it. The Huron chief was tied up before all the pale-faced warriors, and whipped with sticks, like a dog."

Cora remained silent, for she knew not how to palliate this imprudent severity on the part of her father, in a manner to suit the comprehension of an Indian.

"See!" continued Magua, tearing aside the slight calico that very imperfectly concealed his painted breast; "here are scars given by knives and bullets—of these a warrior may boast before his nation; but the gray-head has left marks on the back of the Huron chief, that he must hide, like a squaw, under this painted cloth of the whites."

"I had thought," resumed Cora, "that an Indian warrior was patient, and that his spirit felt not, and knew not, the pain his body suffered?"

"When the Chippewas tied Magua to the stake, and cut this gash," said the other, laying his finger proudly on a deep scar on his bosom, "the Huron laughed in their faces, and told them, women struck so light! His spirit was then in the clouds! But when he felt the blows of Munro, his spirit lay under the birch. The spirit of a Huron is never drunk; it remembers for ever!"

"But it may be appeased. If my father has done you this injustice, show him how an Indian can forgive an injury, and take back his daughters. You have heard from Major Heyward—"

Magua shook his head, forbidding the repetition of offers he so much despised.

"What would you have," continued Cora, after a most painful pause, while the conviction forced itself on her mind, that the too sanguine and generous Duncan had been cruelly deceived by the cunning of the savage.

"What a Huron loves—good for good; bad for bad!"

"You would then revenge the injury inflicted by Munro, on his helpless daughters. Would it not be more like a man to go before his face, and take the satisfaction of a warrior?"

"The arms of the pale-faces are long, and their knives sharp!" returned the savage, with a malignant laugh; "why should le Renard go among the muskets of his warriors, when he holds the spirit of the gray-head in his hand?"

"Name your intention, Magua," said Cora, struggling with herself to speak with steady calmness. "Is it to lead us prisoners to the woods, or do you contemplate even some greater evil? Is there no reward, no means of palliating the injury, and of softening your heart? At least, release my gentle sister, and pour out all your malice on me. Purchase wealth by her safety, and satisfy your revenge with a single victim. The loss of both his daughters might bring the aged man to his grave, and where would then be the satisfaction of le Renard?"

"Listen," said the Indian again. "The light eyes can go back to the Horican, and tell the old chief what has been done, if the dark-haired woman will swear, by the Great Spirit of her fathers, to tell no lie."

"What must I promise?" demanded Cora, still maintaining a secret ascendancy over the fierce passions of the native, by the collected and feminine dignity of her presence.

"When Magua left his people, his wife was given to another chief; he has now made friends with the Hurons, and will go back to the graves of his tribe, on the shores of the great lake. Let the daughter of the English chief follow, and live in his wigwam for ever."

However revolting a proposal of such a character might prove to Cora, she retained, notwithstanding her powerful disgust, sufficient self-command to reply, without betraying the least weakness.

"And what pleasure would Magua find in sharing his cabin with a wife he did not love; one who would be of a nation and colour different from his own? It would be better to take the gold of Munro, and buy the heart of some Huron maid with his gifts and generosity."

The Indian made no reply for near a minute, but bent his fierce looks on the countenance of Cora, in such wavering glances, that her eyes sunk with shame, under an impression, that, for the first time, they had encountered an expression that no chaste female might endure. While she was shrinking within herself, in dread of having her ears wounded by some proposal still more shocking than the last, the voice of Magua answered, in its tones of deepest malignancy—

"When the blows scorched the back of the Huron, he would know where to find a woman to feel the smart. The daughter of Munro would draw his water, hoe his corn, and cook his venison. The body of the gray-head would sleep among his cannon, but his heart would lie within reach of the knife of le Subtil."

"Monster! well dost thou deserve thy treacherous name!" cried Cora, in an ungovernable burst of filial indignation. "None but a fiend could meditate such a vengeance! But thou overratest thy power! You shall find it is, in truth, the heart of Munro you hold, and that it will defy your utmost malice!"

The Indian answered this bold defiance by a ghastly smile, that showed an unaltered purpose, while he motioned her away, as if to close their conference, for ever. Cora, already regretting her precipitation, was obliged to comply; for Magua instantly left the spot, and approached his gluttonous comrades. Heyward flew to the side of the agitated maiden, and demanded the result of a dialogue, that he had watched at a distance with so much interest. But unwilling to alarm the fears of Alice, she evaded a direct reply, betraying only by her countenance her utter want of success, and keeping her anxious looks fastened on the slightest movements of their captors. To the reiterated and earnest questions of her sister, concerning their probable destination, she made no other answer, than by pointing towards the dark groupe, with an agitation she could not control, and murmuring, as she folded Alice to her bosom—

"There, there; read our fortunes in their faces; we shall see! we shall see!"

The action, and the choked utterance of Cora, spoke more impressively than any words, and quickly drew the attention of her companions on that spot, where her own was riveted with an intenseness, that nothing but the importance of the stake could create.

When Magua reached the cluster of lolling savages, who, gorged with their disgusting meal, lay stretched on the earth, in a sort of brutal indulgence, he commenced speaking with the utmost dignity of an Indian chief. The first syllables he uttered, had the effect to cause his listeners to raise themselves in attitudes of respectful attention. As the Huron used his native language, the prisoners, notwithstanding the caution of the natives had kept them within the swing of their tomahawks, could only conjecture the substance of his harangue, from the nature of those significant gestures with which an Indian always illustrates his eloquence.

At first, the language, as well as the action of Magua, appeared calm and deliberative. When he had succeeded in sufficiently awakening the attention of his comrades, Heyward fancied, by his pointing so frequently toward the direction of the great lakes, that he spoke of the land of their fathers, and of their distant tribe. Frequent indications of applause escaped the listeners, who, as they uttered the expressive "hugh!" looked at each other in open commendation of the speaker. Le Renard was too skilful to neglect his advantage. He now spoke of the long and painful route by which they had left those spacious hunting grounds and happy villages, to come and battle against the enemies of their Canadian fathers. He enumerated the warriors of the party; their several merits; their frequent services to the nation; their wounds, and the number of the scalps they had taken. Whenever he alluded to any present, (and the subtle Indian neglected none,) the dark countenance of the flattered individual gleamed with exultation, nor did he even hesitate to assert the truth of the words, by gestures of applause and confirmation. Then the voice of the speaker fell, and lost the loud, animated tones of triumph with which he had enumerated their deeds of success and victory. He described the cataract of Glenn's [Glens Falls, N.Y.]; the impregnable position of its rocky island, with its caverns, and its numerous encircling rapids and whirlpools; he named the name of 'la Longue Carabine,' and paused until the forest beneath them had sent up the last echo of a loud and long yell, with which the hated appellation was received. He pointed toward the youthful military captive, and described the death of a favourite warrior, who had been precipitated into the deep ravine by his hand. He not only mentioned the fate of him who, hanging between heaven and earth, had presented such a spectacle of horror to the whole band, but he acted anew the terrors of his situation, his resolution and his death, on the branches of a sapling; and, finally, he rapidly recounted the manner in which each of their friends had fallen, never failing to touch upon their courage, and their most acknowledged virtues. When this recital of events was ended, his voice once more changed, and became plaintive, and even musical, in its low, soft, guttural sounds. He now spoke of the wives and children of the slain; their destitution; their misery, both physical and moral; their distance; and, at last, of their unavenged wrongs. Then suddenly lifting his voice to a pitch of terrific energy, he concluded, by demanding—

"Are the Hurons dogs, to bear this? Who shall say to the wife of Menowgua, that the fishes have his scalp, and that his nation have not taken revenge! Who will dare meet the mother of Wassawattimie, that scornful woman, with his hands clean! What shall be said to the old men, when they ask us for scalps, and we have not a hair from a white head to give them! The women will point their fingers at us. There is a dark spot on the names of the Hurons, and it must be hid in blood!—"

His voice was no longer audible in the burst of rage, which now broke into the air, as if the wood, instead of containing so small a band, was filled with their nation. During the foregoing address, the progress of the speaker was too plainly read by those most interested in his success, through the medium of the countenances of the men he addressed. They had answered his melancholy and mourning, by sympathy and sorrow; his assertions, by gestures of confirmation; and his boastings, with the exultation of savages. When he spoke of courage, their looks were firm and responsive; when he alluded to their injuries, their eyes kindled with fury; when he mentioned the taunts of their women, they dropped their heads in shame; but when he pointed out their means of vengeance, he struck a chord which never failed to thrill in the breast of an Indian. With the first intimation that it was within their reach, the whole band sprang upon their feet, as one man, and giving utterance to their rage for a single instant, in the most frantic cries, they rushed upon their prisoners in a body, with drawn knives and uplifted tomahawks. Heyward threw himself between the sisters and their enemies, the foremost of whom he grappled with a desperate strength that for a moment checked his violence. This unexpected resistance gave Magua time to interpose, and with rapid enunciation and animated gestures, he drew the attention of the band again to himself. In that language he knew so well how to assume, he diverted his comrades from their instant purpose, and invited them to prolong the misery of their victims. His proposal was received with acclamations, and executed with the swiftness of thought.

Two powerful warriors cast themselves together on Heyward, while another was occupied in securing the less active singing-master. Neither of the captives, however, submitted without a desperate though fruitless struggle. Even David hurled his assailant to the earth; nor was Heyward secured, until the victory over his companion enabled the Indians to direct their united force to that object. He was then bound and fastened to the body of the sapling, on whose branches Magua had acted the pantomime of the falling Huron. When the young soldier regained his recollection, he had the painful certainty before his eyes, that a common fate was intended for the whole party. On his right was Cora, in a durance similar to his own, pale and agitated, but with an eye, whose steady look still read the proceedings of their enemies. On his left, the withes which bound her to a pine, performed that office for Alice which her trembling limbs refused, and alone kept her lovely but fragile form from sinking to the ground. Her hands were clasped before her in prayer, but instead of looking upward to that power which alone could rescue them, her unconscious looks wandered to the countenance of Duncan, with a species of infantile dependency. David had contended; and the novelty of the circumstance held him silent, in deliberation, on the propriety of the unusual occurrence.

The vengeance of the Hurons had now taken a new direction, and they prepared to execute it, with all that barbarous ingenuity, with which they were familiarized by the practice of centuries. Some sought knots, to raise the blazing pile; one was riving the splinters of pine, in order to pierce the flesh of their captives with the burning fragments; and others bent the tops of two saplings to the earth, in order to suspend Heyward by the arms between the recoiling branches. But the vengeance of Magua sought a deeper and a more malignant enjoyment.

While the less refined monsters of the band prepared, before the eyes of those who were to suffer, these well known and vulgar means of torture, he approached Cora, and pointed out, with the most malign expression of countenance, the speedy fate that awaited her—

"Ha!" he added, "what says the daughter of Munro? Her head is too good to find a pillow in the wigwam of le Renard; will she like it better when it rolls about this hill, a plaything for the wolves? Her bosom cannot nurse the children of a Huron; she will see it spit upon by Indians!"

"What means the monster!" demanded the astonished Heyward.

"Nothing!" was the firm but mild reply. "He is a savage, a barbarous and ignorant savage, and knows not what he does. Let us find leisure, with our dying breath, to ask for him penitence and pardon."

"Pardon!" echoed the fierce Huron, mistaking, in his anger, the meaning of her words; "the memory of an Indian is longer than the arm of the pale-faces; his mercy shorter than their justice! Say; shall I send the yellow-hair to her father, and will you follow Magua to the great lakes, to carry his water, and feed him with corn?"

Cora beckoned him away, with an emotion of disgust she could not control.

"Leave me," she said, with a solemnity that for a moment checked the barbarity of the Indian; "you mingle bitterness in my prayers, and stand between me and my God!"

The slight impression produced on the savage was, however, soon forgotten, and he continued pointing, with taunting irony, towards Alice.

"Look! the child weeps! She is young to die! Send her to Munro, to comb his gray hairs, and keep the life in the heart of the old man."

Cora could not resist the desire to look upon her youthful sister, in whose eyes she met an imploring glance, that betrayed the longings of nature.

"What says he, dearest Cora?" asked the trembling voice of Alice. "Did he speak of sending me to our father?"

For many moments the elder sister looked upon the younger, with a countenance that wavered with powerful and contending emotions. At length she spoke, though her tones had lost their rich and calm fulness, in an expression of tenderness, that seemed maternal.

"Alice," she said, "the Huron offers us both life—nay, more than both; he offers to restore Duncan—our invaluable Duncan, as well as you, to our friends—to our father—to our heart-stricken, childless father, if I will bow down this rebellious, stubborn pride of mine, and consent—"

Her voice became choked, and clasping her hand, she looked upward, as if seeking, in her agony, intelligence from a wisdom that was infinite.

"Say on," cried Alice; "to what, dearest Cora? Oh! that the proffer were made to me! to save you, to cheer our aged father! to restore Duncan, how cheerfully could I die!"

"Die!" repeated Cora, with a calmer and a firmer voice, "that were easy! Perhaps the alternative may not be less so. He would have me," she continued, her accents sinking under a deep consciousness of the degradation of the proposal, "follow him to the wilderness; to go to the habitations of the Hurons; to remain there: in short, to become his wife! Speak then, Alice; child of my affections! sister of my love! And you too, Major Heyward, aid my weak reason with your counsel. Is life to be purchased by such a sacrifice? Will you, Alice, receive it at my hands, at such a price? And *you*, Duncan; guide me; control me between you; for I am wholly yours."

"Would I!" echoed the indignant and astonished youth. "Cora! Cora! you jest with our misery! Name not the horrid alternative again; the thought itself is worse than a thousand deaths."

"That such would be *your* answer, I well knew!" exclaimed Cora, her cheeks flushing, and her dark eyes once more sparkling with the glow of the lingering but momentary emotions of a woman. "What says my Alice? for her will I submit without another murmur."

Although both Heyward and Cora listened with painful suspense and the deepest attention, no sounds were heard in reply. It appeared as if the delicate and sensitive form of Alice had shrunk into itself, as she listened to this proposal. Her arms had fallen lengthwise before her, with the fingers moving in slight convulsions; her head dropped upon her bosom, and her whole person seemed suspended against the tree, looking like some beautiful emblem of the wounded delicacy of her sex, devoid of animation, and yet keenly conscious. In a few moments, however, her head began to move slowly, in a sign of deep, unconquerable disapprobation, and by the time the flush of maiden pride had diffused itself over her fine features, and her eye had lighted with the feelings which oppressed her, she found strength to murmur—

"No, no, no; better that we should die, as we have lived, together!"

"Then die!" shouted Magua, hurling his tomahawk with violence at the unresisting speaker, and gnashing his teeth with a rage that could no longer be bridled, at this sudden exhibition of firmness in the one he believed the weakest of the party. The axe cleaved the air in front of Heyward, and cutting some of the flowing ringlets of Alice, buried itself, and quivered in the tree above her head. The sight maddened Duncan to desperation. Collecting all his energies in one effort, he snapped the twigs which bound him, and rushed upon another savage, who was preparing, with loud yells, and a more deliberate aim, to repeat the blow. They encountered, grappled, and fell to the earth together. The naked body of his antagonist, afforded Heyward no means of holding his adversary, who glided from his grasp, and rose again with one knee on his chest, pressing him down with the weight of a giant. Duncan already saw the knife gleaming in the air, when a whistling sound swept past him, and was rather accompanied, than followed, by the sharp crack of a rifle. He felt his breast relieved from the load it had endured; he saw the savage expression of his adversary's countenance change to a look of vacant wildness, and then the Indian fell prostrate and dead, on the faded leaves by his side.

Thomas Cole Paints the Death of Cora

Fenimore Cooper and Thomas Cole (1801-1848) were kindred spirits. They stood together on the frontier of American art at the point where imaginative perception was first projected in a sophisticated complex way, and they sensed that American culture was being shaped by the relationship between the spacious natural setting of the New World and the rich historical heritage of European civilization. Thoughtful men concerned with the destiny of their young country, they sought appropriate forms to convey their visions and native historical traditions to serve as a context for the fresh ideas that the existence of America was generating. Cole wrote in an "Essay on American Scenery" (1835) that "American scenes are not destitute of historical and legendary associations . . ." but he also observed that "the most distinctive, and perhaps the most impressive, characteristic of American scenery is its wildness." For Cole, the Indian was integral to the American scene, a figure embodying America's history and wildness, and white captivity was the most traumatic action on the landscape. Cooper agreed.

The cultural soil was thin, however. They had to scratch hard for a usable past, and it did not produce new art forms. Cooper accepted the structure of the British novel, and Cole painted landscapes and allegories in the tradition of the European masters. But both men discovered in the American wilderness significant compensation for the lack of historical density and new forms. Cooper was something of a painter with words, typically giving his readers a series of dramatic scenes strung on a chain of flight and pursuit. Cole, for his part, had a literary bent. His paintings told stories, not simply his allegorical series such as *The Course of Empire* (1836) which portrays the rise and fall of great civilizations (by inference American civilization among them), but his naturalistic Hudson River landscapes, which, like Cooper's word-pictures of the wilderness, are symbolic. For Cooper and Cole, the wilderness was quite literally awe-inspiring. Divinity was immanent in Nature, and American destiny was to be read in landscape.

Cooper greatly admired Cole's *The Course of Empire.* He called it "a grand epic poem" and used it in his utopian novel, *The Crater* (1847), as an analogue to sustain his sociohistorical observations. Cole, within a year of its publication, painted three scenes based on Cooper's *The Last of the Mohicans.* Two of them were different versions of Cora Munro, the commandant's daughter, captured by the evil Magua when Fort William Henry fell to the French, kneeling in supplication before Tamenund (Chief Tammany). One was commissioned by the Baltimore Art Collector Robert Gilmor and is now owned by the New York Historical Association of Cooperstown. The other, painted for Daniel Wadsworth, is in the Wadsworth Atheneum at Hartford, Connecticut. A third painting is reproduced here. It depicts the outcome of Tamenund's decision to award Cora, by right of capture, to Magua. This decision leads to a resumption of the chase in an effort to free Cora, and thus to the climax of the novel.

After a specified truce period, Leatherstocking and the good Indians set out in pursuit of Cora and Magua. Uncas, the last of the Mohicans, who is in love with Cora, takes the lead. They follow Magua and his white captive through the obscure passages of a cavern that opens onto a precipice. From above Uncas sees Magua and hears the voice of Cora:

> "I will go no further," cried Cora, stopping unexpectedly on a ledge of rocks, that overhung a deep precipice, at no great distance from the summit of the mountain. "Kill me if thou wilt, detestable Huron; I will go no further."
>
> The supporters of the maiden raised their ready tomahawks with the impious joy that fiends are thought to take in mischief, but Magua stayed the uplifted arms. The Huron chief, after casting the weapons he had wrested from his companions over the rock, drew his knife, and turned to his captive, with a look in which conflicting passions fiercely contended.
>
> "Woman," he said, "choose; the wigwam or the knife of le Subtil [Magua]!"
>
> Cora regarded him not, but dropping on her knees, she raised her eyes and stretched her arms toward heaven, saying, in a meek and yet confiding voice—
>
> "I am thine! do with me as thou seest best!"
>
> "Woman," repeated Magua, hoarsely, and endeavoring in vain to catch a glance from her serene and beaming eye, "choose!"
>
> But Cora neither heard nor heeded his demand. The form of the Huron trembled in every fibre, and he raised his arm on high, but dropped it again with a bewildered air, like one who doubted. Once more he struggled with himself and lifted the keen weapon again—but just then a piercing cry was heard above them, and Uncas appeared, leaping frantically, from a fearful height, upon the ledge. Magua recoiled a step; and one of his assistants, profiting by the chance, sheathed his own knife in the bosom of Cora.

Detail showing the death of Cora from an oil painting by Thomas Cole of *A Scene from THE LAST OF THE MOHICANS* (1827). *Courtesy of the University of Pennsylvania.*

The Huron sprang like a tiger on his offending and already retreating countryman, but the falling form of Uncas separated the unnatural combatants. Diverted from his object by this interruption, and maddened by the murder he had just witnessed, Magua buried his weapon in the back of the prostrate Delaware [Uncas], uttering an unearthly shout as he committed the dastardly deed. But Uncas arose from the blow, as the wounded panther turns upon his foe, and struck the murderer of Cora to his feet, by an effort in which the last of his failing strength was expended. Then, with a stern and steady look, he turned to le Subtil, and indicated, by the expression of his eye, all that he would do, had not the power deserted him. The latter seized the nerveless arm of the unresisting Delaware, and passed his knife into his bosom three several times, before his victim, still keeping his gaze riveted on his enemy with a look of inextinguishable scorn, fell dead at his feet [Chapter 32].

An Indian's Love Lyric

Like *The Last of the Mohicans* (pp. 231-256) and *Yamoyden* (pp. 218-223), "The Stolen White Girl" is about Indian captivity and love that transcends race. It commands attention because it was written by an Indian and expresses an Indian viewpoint. Known as Chess-quat-a-lawny, or "Yellow Bird" in English, its author, John Rollin Ridge, was born on tribal lands in Georgia in 1827. His father, John Ridge, was a Cherokee chief, and his grandfather, Major Ridge, a distinguished Indian orator. Despite the disapproval of many tribesmen, both John Ridge and Major Ridge signed a treaty at New Echota, Cherokee Nation, in 1835, which consented to the relocation of the tribe west of the Mississippi River. On June 22, 1839, shortly after moving their families to the Western Cherokee lands, John Ridge was assassinated, in the presence of his wife and children, by a faction of the Cherokee Nation which viewed his participation in the relocation procedures as traitorous. Major Ridge was later ambushed and murdered by the same faction.

Although he lived most of his life among whites, John Rollin Ridge always considered himself an Indian, and throughout his career as journalist, editor, scholar, and reformer, he championed his people. He may have had no firsthand experience with white captives himself, but he was surely familiar with the subject through other Indians. More important, though, he understood the loneliness of exile among another people. His mother, Sarah Bird Northrup, a white woman, was rejected by her family and friends when she married an Indian. Ridge's own wife, Elizabeth Wilson, was also white, and she caused somewhat of an uproar when she married an Indian and moved away to live with his tribe.

Like the "half-breed" in the poem, Ridge had, in a sense, "stolen" his bride. Their love was, as Ridge puts it, all the more "pleasing and rare" because of the racial and cultural "contrast between them." The poem is a sentimental, autobiographical projection, expressing hope

---

SOURCE: John Rollin Ridge, *Poems* (San Francisco, 1868), pp. 72-74.

for the union of the white bride and her dark lover. They are united by a scarcely veiled sexual bond and protected by the Indian's belted knife—the mention of which hints at the uncertainty of the situation. The rather obvious imagery of the interplay of light and shadow suggests that reconciliation is little more than a hope and a prayer. This is literally the form of the last stanza. We are left with the fate of the lovers, and what they represent, in doubt. Yet Ridge has given his subject an unusual turn. This becomes evident when his poem is compared with Fenimore Cooper's highly charged literary treatment of a romantic relationship between a white woman and an Indian in *The Last of the Mohicans.* Marriage is out of the question, even that of a princely Indian like Uncas to a woman like Cora, whose blood lines are dubious. Such a marriage would be contrary to the racial conventions of the white culture. Furthermore, for Cooper, Cora represents white civilization, and her marriage to an Indian, who represents the virtues of pristine nature, would subvert these virtues. Cooper feared Indianization because it appeared to threaten the affirmative qualities he symbolized in Uncas and Cora. Ridge saw Indianization at least as a hope, and the final stanza of invocation admits the possibility of divine approval for his lovers.

Ridge remained an outcast. In 1849, he became involved in an argument which ended in the murder of another Indian, an enemy of his family. Fearing the consequences, Ridge fled, first to Missouri and later to California, where, against his wishes, he remained until his death in 1867.

As a poet and literary figure, Ridge gained renown during his lifetime. He wrote the *Life and Adventures of Jaoquin Murietta* (1854) and "Mount Shasta," a poem about California which was much praised during its day and is still reprinted. After his death, his wife collected and published a small volume of his verse.

THE STOLEN WHITE GIRL

THE prairies are broad, and the woodlands are wide
And proud on his steed the wild half-breed may ride,
With the belt round his waist and the knife at his side.
And no white man may claim his beautiful bride.

Though he stole her away from the land of the whites,
Pursuit is in vain, for her bosom delights
In the love that she bears the dark-eyed, the proud,
Whose glance is like starlight beneath a night-cloud.

Far down in the depths of the forest they'll stray,
Where the shadows like night are lingering all day;
Where the flowers are springing up wild at their feet,
And the voices of birds in the branches are sweet.

Together they'll roam by the streamlets that run,
O'ershadowed at times then meeting the sun—
The streamlets that soften their varying tune,
As up the blue heavens calm wanders the moon!

The contrast between them is pleasing and rare;
Her sweet eye of blue, and her soft silken hair,
Her beautiful waist, and her bosom of white
That heaves to the touch with a sense of delight;

His form more majestic and darker his brow,
Where the sun has imparted its liveliest glow—
An eye that grows brighter with passion's true fire,
As he looks on his loved one with earnest desire.

Oh, never let Sorrow's cloud darken their fate,
The girl of the "pale face," her Indian mate!
But deep in the forest of shadows and flowers,
Let Happiness smile, as she wings their sweet hours.

Erastus Dow Palmer Captures a White Captive in Marble

Erastus Dow Palmer (1817-1904), a skilled carpenter of Utica, New York, taught himself the art of cutting cameo portraits, moving on to sculpture when the detailed work of shell carving caused him severe eyestrain. "White Captive" (1858) is his most famous statue. Palmer had no formal training. His school was nature, and he avoided the influence of the academy, neoclassical traditions, and imported styles. He did not go abroad until late in his career, after he had already achieved professional success. But he was not simply a realist or a nationalist. In an essay entitled "Philosophy of the Ideal" (1856), he expressed the opinion that "no work in sculpture, however well wrought out physically, results in excellence, unless it rests upon, and is sustained by the dignity of a moral or intellectual intention." The realistic portrayal of the human figure, though perhaps beautiful, is artistically unjustified unless it conveys a story that is edifying, and the melodramatic moment alone is insufficient; even such a moment as the marmoreal captive awaiting a fate worse than death has to convey a moral tale. Or to be more accurate, it must obviously suggest one.

It is said that while Palmer shaped "White Captive," his wife read aloud to him, often from the romances of Fenimore Cooper. Certainly, for the public which would acclaim his statue, its subject was familiar and clearly American. The statue was also a literary provocation. To write out its story or to poetize it proved irresistible. Thus, an article in the *Atlantic Monthly*, appearing under the caption "Art," begins with a traditional formula that tales have employed for beginning, and only after he has told his story can the reviewer get on with his proper business. The reviewer claimed "genuine greatness" for "White Captive" because, he felt, it "is original, it is faithful, it is American; our women may look upon it, and say, 'She is one of us,' with more satisfaction than the Greek women could have derived from the Venus de' Medici, with its insignificant head and its impossible spine." In his *Book of the Artists* (1867), the critic Henry T. Tuckerman, who delighted in sculpture with moral messages and native themes, pronounced his approbation, heightened by a quotation from a poem which hailed "White Captive" when she was first displayed in New York: "The subject is thoroughly American, the head is a type of native female beauty, and the statue is not less interesting in an historical than harmonious and expressive in an artistic point of view:

> Ye who believe Humanity, when shorn
> Of all the moral guards that shield our life,
> Despoiled and outraged, powerless, forlorn—
> No inward armor hath to meet the strife;—
> Gaze on her gentlest offspring naked here,
> And girt with savage foes; the soft wrists bound,
> The breath suspended in the grasp of fear;
> And from the feet which consecrate the ground,
> Up to the virgin lips and earnest brow,
> Behold her soul triumphant! Nerves may quail
> And fibres quiver,—yet a beauty now,
> Transcending nature, thrills those features pale,
> As, through her anguish, Love and Faith we see
> Not vainly strive to set the captive free."

James Jackson Jarves, a connoisseur and cosmopolitan, voiced the minority opinion. In *The Art-Idea* (1864), he asserted that "Palmer has much to learn from classical art," and, with a force and frankness rare among Victorian art critics, he described "White Captive" as "a petulant, pouty girl, vulgar in face and form, apparently the copy of a very indifferent model, with so materialistic a treatment on the surface of the marble as to suggest *meat* and immodesty." He preferred "Venus de' Medici."

Once on a time a maiden dwelt with her father,—they two, and no more,—in a rude log-cabin on the skirts of a grand old Western forest,—majestic mountains behind them, and the broad, free prairie in front.

Cut off from all Christian companionship and the informing influences of civilized arts, all their news was of red men and of game, their entertainments the ever-varying moods of Nature, their labors of the rudest, their dangers familiar, their solacements simple and solitary. Alone the sturdy hunter beat the woods all day, on the track of panthers, bears, and deer; alone, all day, his pretty daughter kept the house against perils without and despondency within,—the gun and the broom alike familiar to her hand.

Commissioned to illumine the murk[y] wilderness around her with the glow of her Christian loveliness and faith, Nature had touched her with inspirations of refinement, with a culture as unconscious as the growing of the grass, and the clear intuitions of a spiritual life full of heaven-born inclinations. Nature, too, had endowed her with fine lines of beauty, attitudes of

---

SOURCE: "Palmer's 'White Captive,'" *Atlantic Monthly* (Jan. 1860), vol. 5, pp. 108-109.

Erastus Dow Palmer's "White Captive" (1858). *Courtesy of the Metropolitan Museum of Art.*

grace, movements of dignity and love, and all the charmfulness that had learned its shapes from flowers and its arts from birds. Nature's officers, the elements, had bestowed on her each his appropriate gift,—the Air its crispness, the Earth its variety, the Sun its brightness and its ruddy glow, the very Water from the well its freshness and its fluent forms; the stars repeated their friendliness in her eyes, the grass dimpled her pliant feet, the breeze tossed her brown hair in triumphs of the unstudied becoming, and from the wildness all about her she had her wit and her delightful ways; Morning lent her her cheerfulness, Evening her pensiveness, and Night her soul.

But Night, that had given her the Christian soul, true and wise, self-reliant and aspiring, brought also the surprise and the peril that should put it to the proof; for once, when the hunter was belated on his path, and sudden midnight had caught him beyond the mountain, far from the rest of his hearth and the song of his darling, came the red Pawnees, a treacherous crew,—doubly godless because ungrateful, who had broken the hunter's bread and slept on the hunter's blanket,—and laid waste his hearth, and stole away his very heart. For they dragged her many a fearful mile of darkness and distraction, through the black woods, and over the foreboding river, and into the grim recesses of the rocks; and there they stripped her naked, and bound her to a stake, as the day was breaking. But the Christian heart was within her, and the Christian soul upheld her, and the Christian's God was by her side; and so she stood, and waited, and was brave.

And here still she stands, as the sculptor's soul sat down before her, in a vision of faith and tenderness, to receive her image,—stands and waits for the pity and the help of you and me, her brothers and her lovers. . . .

. . . Horror possesses her, but indignation also; she is terrified, but brave; she shrinks, but she repels; and while all her beautiful body trembles and retreats, her countenance confronts her captors, and her steady gaze forbids them. "Touch me not!" she says, with every shuddering limb and every tensely-braced muscle, with lineaments all eloquent with imperious disgust,—"Touch me not!"

Her lips quiver, and tears are in her eyes, (we do not forget that it is of marble we are speaking,—there *are* tears in her eyes,) but they only linger there; she is not weeping now; her chin trembles, and one of her hands is convulsively clenched,—but it is with the anguish of her sore besetting, not the spasm of mortal fear. Though Heaven and Earth, indeed, might join to help her, we yet know that the soul of the maiden will help itself,—that her hope clings fast, and her courage is undaunted, and her faith complete.

Among her thronged emotions we look in vain for shame. Her nakedness is a coarse chance of her overwhelming situation, for which she is no more concerned than for her galled wrists or her dishevelled hair. What is it to such a queen as she, that the eyes of grinning brutes are blessed by her perfect beauties? . . .

"The Escape" from Herman Melville's TYPEE

The doctrine of Manifest Destiny was an almost religious belief for Americans in the nineteenth century. It held that they were a chosen people, divinely sanctioned to populate the vast territories of the New World, and it provided the justification for obtaining western lands, whether bought, as in the case of the Louisiana Purchase (1803), or annexed, as in the case of Texas (1845), or conquered, as in the case of the lands taken from Mexico (1848). In all cases, the aboriginal inhabitants were in opposition to progress, and the Indian captivity narratives are a by-product of this opposition. The story of continental expansion by white civilization to the coast of California is well known. Less well known, but likewise an application of the doctrine of Manifest Destiny, was American expansion into the Pacific Ocean. During the War of 1812, Captain David Porter, commanding the *Essex*, showed the American flag for the first time in the Pacific. In 1813 he seized Nukuhiva, in the Marquesas Islands, in the name of the United States and attempted to subdue the native tribes, among them the reputedly savage Typees. Congress declined this annexation, but it is notable as the first instance of outright American imperialism beyond the continental limits of the United States. More peaceful scientific expeditions by the Navy followed, but of far greater significance (at least from the standpoints of economics and literature) was the penetration into the Pacific of the American whaling fleet.

For a venturesome young American in the age of Manifest Destiny, two opportunities were open. He might go west, seeking his fortune on the land frontier, or he might go to sea. The New Yorker, Herman Melville (1819-1891), explored the possibilities of Illinois in 1840, was disappointed, and the next year embarked as an ordinary seaman on the whaling ship *Acushnet*, out of Fairhaven, Massachusetts, bound for the Pacific. He returned late in 1844, his pockets empty but his head full of sailor's yarns about South Sea island savages whose daughters were enticing beyond compare, handsome sailors and abusive officers in the

SOURCE: Herman Melville, *Typee, a Peep at Polynesian Life* (New York, 1846).

United States Navy, and white whales as monstrous and unhuntable as the grizzly bears of the West. In 1846 he published his first book, *Typee*, partially titled "Narrative of a Four Months' Residence Among the Natives of a Valley of the Marquesas Islands." It is based on his captivity and escape from a Marquesan tribe. It is an equivalent, or at least a variation, of an Indian captivity narrative of the American western frontier.

The facts are that Melville and a shipmate, Richard Tobias Greene, the "Toby" of the narrative, jumped ship at Nukuhiva on July 9, 1842. They went inland, traversing difficult terrain, to the brink of a precipitous valley they believed inhabited by a gentle, friendly people. Upon descending, they found themselves captives of the Typees, supposed man-eaters whose recollections of Captain Porter gave them reason to dislike American sailors. Somewhere along the way, Melville had injured his leg, and when it grew worse, Greene was released so that he could seek medical aid. Melville was held in captivity, lame and uneasy regarding his prospects, but generally his circumstances were interesting and pleasant. He was eventually rescued by an Australian whaler, the *Lucy Ann*, signed on, and continued his adventures, but he did not hear from Greene until after he had published *Typee*. Later editions print "a natural sequel to the adventure," validating Melville, based on information "related to the author by Toby himself."

Melville's fictionalized version of his captivity experience, like the experience itself, conforms to the Indian captivity archetype in its obvious particulars. At the same time, it raises some of the more subtle issues of the Indian narratives, and in Melville's hands they become moral issues artistically posed. The most crucial are the values of civilization versus primitivism, appearance versus reality, and guilt versus innocence. The narrator finds life among the Typees Edenic, but their cannibalism is literally a threat. Metaphorically it is also a threat, for he is in danger of being consumed by an alien culture. The issue is Indianization (see John Tanner, pp. 97-109). So he rejects the attractions of the primitive life, personified in the charming Fayaway, and makes a break for the boat that has come to his rescue. He is pursued on into the sea by a pack of howling "savages" led by an "enraged chief" armed with a "tomahawk." He escapes by dashing a boat-hook into the throat of the chief. Like Hannah Duston (see pp. 156-159, 224-230), he has momentarily become a savage.

Melville's narrator makes a nice distinction in his choice of language. The Typees who seek to prevent his escape are "savages." The Polynesians who are members of the rescue party are "our natives" or "the Kannaka" ("man"). Thus, there are good Indians and bad Indians, but, more profoundly, the narrator's words betray an ambivalence toward the primitive. The logical consequence in terms of Manifest Destiny is that bad Indians may be killed and primitive societies are expendable.

Language as an indicator of the equation of American Indian and Polynesian may be confirmed in one of the more curious items in the

Hacks who wrote penny dreadfuls and literary artists like Melville and Poe described Pacific island natives as if they were American Indians. The *Narrative of the Capture . . . of Mrs. Eliza Fraser* on a Pacific island near New Guinea shows natives with Indian headdress, armed with tomahawks and bow and arrows, burning a shipwrecked sailor at the stake. *Courtesy of the Edward E. Ayer Collection, the Newberry Library.*

captivity canon. In May 1835, a British ship in passage from Sidney to Singapore was wrecked on a reef near the Torres Straits between Australia and New Guinea. The crew was captured by "savages," described as black, and several survivors, including the captain, Samuel Frazer, were tortured and murdered. After a hideous ordeal, the captain's wife, Eliza Ann, was rescued and brought to London, where she immediately told her story to the solicitous Lord Mayor. It was printed in the London *Courier* of August 19, 1837, and certainly elsewhere. On October 5 following, it was reprinted from the *Courier* in *The Army and Navy Chronicle,* published in Washington, D.C. The Seminole War, then raging in Florida, had created renewed interest in Indian captivities (see Mason, pp. 85-89), and an enterprising printer, apparently with an American reprint from a London paper as his source, produced a sensational confection for the penny dreadful market: *Narrative of the Capture, Sufferings, and Miraculous Escape of Mrs. Eliza Fraser . . .* (New York, 1837). His "savages" are "of a dark copper color" and are specifically termed "Indians." Their women are "squaws" and one of their children is called a "young papoose." Their weapons include "tomahawks," and they use an "Indian canoe." Mrs. Fraser tells us that she was "compelled to take up her abode in a wigwam and to become the adopted wife of one of the chiefs," but just before the marriage act was consummated she was "providentially rescued." What was originally a British narrative of shipwreck in the Pacific is recast for a mass audience in the United States so that it conforms to the trite patterns and American stereotypes found in the Indian captivity narratives. Inevitably, these patterns included the notion that the Pacific was yet another American frontier.

CHAPTER XXXIV.

THE ESCAPE.

Nearly three weeks has elapsed since the second visit of Marnoo, and it must have been more than four months since I entered the valley, when one day about noon, and whilst everything was in profound silence, Mow-Mow, the one-eyed chief, suddenly appeared at the door, and leaning forward towards me as I lay directly facing him, said in a low tone, "Toby pemi ena" (Toby has arrived here). Gracious heaven! What a tumult of emotions rushed upon me at this startling intelligence! Insensible to the pain that had before distracted me, I leaped to my feet, and called wildly to Kory-Kory who was reposing by my side. The startled islanders sprang from their mats; the news was quickly communicated to them; and the next moment I was making my way to the Ti [tribal meetinghouse] on the back of Kory-Kory [a guard and companion], and surrounded by the excited savages.

All that I could comprehend of the particulars which Mow-Mow rehearsed to his auditors as we proceeded, was that my long-lost companion had arrived in a boat which had just entered the bay. These tidings made me most anxious to be carried at once to the sea, lest some untoward circumstance should prevent our meeting; but to this they would not consent, and continued their course towards the royal abode. As we approached it, Mehevi [the paramount chief] and several chiefs showed themselves from the piazza, and called upon us loudly to come to them.

As soon as we had approached, I endeavored to make them understand that I was going down to the sea to meet Toby. To this the king objected, and motioned Kory-Kory to bring me into the house. It was in vain to resist; and in a few moments I found myself within the Ti, surrounded by a noisy group engaged in discussing the recent intelligence. Toby's name was frequently repeated, coupled with violent exclamations of astonishment. It seemed as if they yet remained in doubt with regard to the fact of his arrival, and at every fresh report that was brought from the shore they betrayed the liveliest emotions.

Almost frenzied at being held in this state of suspense, I passionately besought Mehevi to permit me to proceed. Whether my companion had arrived or not, I felt a presentiment that my own fate was about to be decided. Again and again I renewed my petition to Mehevi. He regarded me with a fixed and serious eye, but at length yielding to my importunity, reluctantly granted my request.

Accompanied by some fifty of the natives, I now rapidly continued my journey; every few moments being transferred from the back of one to another, and urging my bearer forward all the while with earnest entreaties. As I thus hurried forward, no doubt as to the truth of the information I had received ever crossed my mind. I was alive only to the one overwhelming idea, that a chance of deliverance was now afforded me, if the jealous opposition of the savages could be overcome.

Having been prohibited from approaching the sea during the whole of my stay in the valley, I had always associated with it the idea of escape. Toby too—if indeed he had ever voluntarily deserted me—must have effected his flight by the sea; and now that I was drawing near to it myself, I indulged in hopes which I had never felt before. It was evident that a boat had entered the bay, and I saw little reason to doubt the truth of the report that it had brought my companion. Every time therefore that we gained an elevation, I looked eagerly around, hoping to behold him.

In the midst of an excited throng, who by their violent gestures and wild cries appeared to be under influence of some excitement as strong as my own, I was now borne along at a rapid trot, frequently stooping my head to avoid the branches which crossed the path, and never ceasing to implore those who carried me to accelerate their already swift pace.

In this manner we had proceeded about four or five miles, when we were met by a party of some twenty islanders, between whom and those who accompanied me ensued an animated conference. Impatient of the delay occasioned by this interruption, I was beseeching the man who carried me to proceed without his loitering companions, when Kory-Kory, running to my side, informed me, in three fatal words, that the news had all proved false—that Toby had not arrived—"Toby owlee permi." Heaven only knows how, in the state of mind and body I then was, I ever sustained the agony which this intelligence caused me; not that the news was altogether unexpected; but I had trusted that the fact might not have been made known until we should have arrived upon the beach. As it was, I at once foresaw the course the savages would pursue. They had only yielded thus far to my entreaties, that I might give a joyful welcome to my long-lost comrade; but now that it was known he had not arrived, they would at once oblige me to turn back.

My anticipations were but too correct. In spite of the resistance I made, they carried me into a house which was near the spot, and left me upon the mats. Shortly afterwards several of those who had accompanied me from the Ti, detaching themselves from the others, proceeded in the direction of the sea. Those who remained—among whom were Marheyo [Kory-Kory's father], Mow-Mow, Kory-Kory, and Tinor [Kory-Kory's mother]—gathered about the dwelling, and appeared to be awaiting their return.

This convinced me that strangers—perhaps some of my own countrymen—had for some cause or other entered the bay. Distracted at the idea of their vicinity, and reckless of the pain which I suffered, I heeded not the assurances of the islanders, that there were no boats at the beach, but starting to my feet endeavored to gain the door. Instantly the passage was blocked up by several men, who commanded me to resume my seat. The fierce looks of the irritated savages admonished me that I could gain nothing by force, and that it was by entreaty alone that I could hope to compass my object.

Guided by this consideration, I turned to Mow-Mow, the only chief present whom I had been much in the habit of seeing, and carefully concealing my real design, tried to make him comprehend that I still believed Toby to have arrived on the shore, and besought him to allow me to go forward to welcome him. To all his repeated assertions, that my companion had not been seen, I pretended to turn a deaf ear: while I urged my solicitations with an eloquence of gesture which the one-eyed chief appeared unable to resist. He seemed indeed to regard me as a froward child, to whose wishes he had not the heart to oppose force, and whom he must consequently humor. He spoke a few words to the natives, who at once retreated from the door, and I immediately passed out of the house.

Here I looked earnestly round for Kory-Kory; but that hitherto faithful servitor was nowhere to be seen. Unwilling to linger even for a single instant when every moment might be so important, I motioned to a muscular fellow near me to take me upon his back: to my surprise he angrily refused. I turned to another, but with a like result. A third attempt was as unsuccessful, and I immediately perceived what had induced Mow-Mow to grant my request, and why the other natives conducted themselves in so strange a manner. It was evident that the chief had only given me liberty to continue my progress towards the sea, because he supposed that I was deprived of the means of reaching it.

Convinced by this of their determination to retain me a captive, I became desperate; and almost insensible to the pain which I suffered, I seized a spear which was leaning against the projecting eaves of the house, and supporting myself with it, resumed the path that swept by the dwelling. To my surprise, I was suffered to proceed alone; all the natives remaining in front of the house, and engaging in earnest conversation, which every moment became more loud and vehement; and to my unspeakable delight I perceived that some difference of opinion had arisen between them; that two parties, in short, were formed, and consequently that in their divided counsels there was some chance of my deliverance.

Before I proceeded a hundred yards I was again surrounded by the savages, who were still in all the heat of argument, and appeared every moment as if they would come to blows. In the midst of this tumult old Marheyo came to my side, and I shall never forget the benevolent expression of his countenance. He placed his arm upon my shoulder, and emphatically pronounced the only two English words I had taught him—"Home" and "Mother." I at once understood what he meant, and eagerly expressed my thanks to him. Fayaway [an island nymph] and Kory-Kory were by his side, both weeping violently; and it was not until the old man had twice repeated the command that his son could bring himself to obey him, and take me again upon his back. The one-eyed chief opposed his doing so, but he was overruled, and, as it seemed to me, by some of his own party.

We proceeded onwards, and never shall I forget the ecstasy I felt when I first heard the roar of the surf breaking upon the beach. Before long I saw the flashing billows themselves through the opening between the trees. Oh glorious sight and sound of ocean! with what rapture did I hail you as familiar friends! By this time the shouts of the crowd upon the beach were distinctly audible, and in the blended confusion of sounds I almost fancied I could distinguish the voices of my own countrymen.

When we reached the open space which lay between the groves and the sea, the first object that met my view was an English whale-boat, lying with her bow pointed from the shore, and only a few fathoms distant from it. It was manned by five islanders, dressed in short tunics of calico. My first impression was that they were in the very act of pulling out from the bay; and that, after all my exertions, I had come too late. My soul sunk within me: but a second glance convinced me that the boat was only hanging off to keep out of the surf; and the next moment I heard my own name shouted out by a voice from the midst of the crowd.

Looking in the direction of the sound, I perceived, to my indescribable joy, the tall figure of Karakoee, an Oahu Kannaka, who had often been aboard the "Dolly," while she lay in Nukuheva. He wore the green shooting-jacket with gilt buttons, which had been given to him by an officer of the Reine Blanche—the French flag-ship—and in which I had always seen him dressed. I now remembered the Kannaka had frequently told me that his person was tabooed in all the valleys of the island, and the sight of him at such a moment as this filled my heart with a tumult of delight.

Karakoee stood near the edge of the water with a large roll of cotton-cloth thrown over one arm, and holding two or three canvas bags of powder, while with the other hand he grasped a musket, which he appeared to be proffering to several of the chiefs around him. But they turned with disgust from his offers, and seemed to be impatient at his presence, with vehement gestures waving him off to his boat, and commanding him to depart.

The Kannaka, however, still maintained his ground, and I at once perceived that he was seeking to purchase my freedom. Animated by the idea, I called upon him loudly to come to me; but he replied, in broken English, that the islanders had threatened to pierce him with their spears, if he stirred a foot towards me. At this time I was still advancing, surrounded by a dense throng of the natives, several of whom had their hands upon me, and more than one javelin was threateningly pointed at me. Still I perceived clearly that many of those least friendly towards me looked irresolute and anxious.

I was still some thirty yards from Karakoee when my farther progress was prevented by the natives, who compelled me to sit down upon the ground, while they still retained their hold upon my arms. The din and tumult now became tenfold, and I perceived that several of the priests were on the spot, all of whom were evidently urging Mow-Mow and the other chiefs to prevent my departure; and the detestable word "Roo-ne! Roo-ne!" which I had heard repeated a thousand times during the day, was now shouted out on every side of me. Still I saw that the Kannaka continued his exertions in my favor—that he was boldly debating the matter with the savages, and was striving to entice them by displaying his cloth and powder, and snapping the lock of his musket. But all he said or did appeared only to augment the clamors of those around him, who seemed bent upon driving him into the sea.

When I remembered the extravagant value placed by these people upon the articles which were offered to them in exchange for me, and which were so indignantly rejected, I saw a new proof of the same fixed determination of purpose they had all along manifested with regard to me, and in despair, and reckless of consequences, I exerted all my strength, and shaking myself free from the grasp of those who held me, I sprang upon my feet and rushed towards Karakoee.

The rash attempt nearly decided my fate; for, fearful that I might slip from them, several of the islanders now raised a simultaneous shout, and pressing upon Karakoee, they menaced him with furious gestures, and actually forced him into the sea. Appalled at their violence, the poor fellow, standing nearly to the waist in the surf, endeavored to pacify them; but at length, fearful that they would do him some fatal violence, he beckoned to his comrades to pull in at once, and take him into the boat.

It was at this agonizing moment, when I thought all hope was ended, that a new contest arose between the two parties who had accompanied me to the shore; blows were struck, wounds were given, and blood flowed. In the interest excited by the fray, every one had left me except Marheyo, Kory-Kory, and poor dear Fayaway, who clung to me, sobbing indignantly. I saw that now or never was the moment. Clasping my hands together, I looked imploringly at Marheyo, and moved towards the now almost deserted beach. The tears were in the old man's eyes, but neither he nor Kory-Kory attempted to hold me, and I soon reached the Kannaka, who had anxiously watched my movements; the rowers pulled in as near as they dared to the edge of the surf; I gave one parting embrace to Fayaway, who seemed speechless with sorrow, and the next instant I found myself safe in the boat, and Karakoee by my side, who told the rowers at once to give way. Marheyo and Kory-Kory, and a great many of the women, followed me into the water, and I was determined, as the only mark of gratitude I could show, to give them the articles which had been brought as my ransom. I handed the musket to Kory-Kory, with a rapid gesture which was equivalent to a "Deed of Gift;" threw the roll of cotton to old Marheyo, pointing as I did so to poor Fayaway, who had retired from the edge of the water and was sitting down disconsolate on the shingles; and tumbled the powder-bags out to the nearest young ladies, all of whom were vastly willing to take them. This distribution did not occupy ten seconds, and before it was over the boat was under full way; the Kannaka all the while exclaiming loudly against what he considered a useless throwing away of valuable property.

Although it was clear that my movements had been noticed by several of the natives, still they had not suspended the conflict in which they were engaged, and it was not until the boat was above fifty yards from the shore that Mow-Mow and some six or seven other warriors rushed into the sea and hurled their javelins at us. Some of the weapons passed quite as close to us as was desirable, but no one was wounded, and the men pulled away gallantly. But although soon out of the reach of the spears, our progress was extremely slow; it blew strong upon the shore, and the tide was against us; and I saw Karakoee, who was steering the boat, give many a look towards a jutting point of the bay round which we had to pass.

For a minute or two after our departure, the savages, who had formed into different groups, remained perfectly motionless and silent. All at once the enraged chief showed by his gestures that he had resolved what course he would take. Shouting loudly to his companions, and pointing with his tomahawk towards the headland, he set off at full speed in that direction, and was followed by about thirty of the natives, among whom were several of the priests, all yelling out "Roo-ne! Roo-ne!" at the very top of their voices. Their intention was evidently to swim off from the headland and intercept us in our course. The wind was freshening every minute, and was right in our teeth, and it was one of those chopping angry seas in which it is so difficult to row. Still the chances seemed in our favor, but when we came within a hundred yards of the point, the active savages were already dashing into the water, and we all feared that within five minutes' time we should have a score of the infuriated wretches around us. If so our doom was sealed, for these savages, unlike the feeble swimmers of civilized countries, are, if anything, more formidable antagonists in the water than when on the land. It was all a trial of strength; our natives pulled till their oars bent again, and the crowd of swimmers shot through the water despite its roughness, with fearful rapidity.

By the time we had reached the headland, the savages were spread right across our course. Our rowers got out their knives and held them ready between their teeth, and I seized the boat-hook. We were all aware that if they succeeded in intercepting us they would practise upon us the manœuvre which has proved so fatal to many a boat's crew in these seas. They would grapple the oars, and seizing hold of the gunwale, capsize the boat, and then we should be entirely at their mercy.

After a few breathless moments I discerned Mow-Mow. The athletic islander, with his tomahawk between his teeth, was dashing the water before him till it foamed again. He was the nearest to us, and in another instant he would have seized one of the oars. Even at the moment I felt horror at the act I was about to commit; but it was no time for pity or compunction, and with a true aim, and exerting all my strength, I dashed the boat-hook at him. It struck him just below the throat, and forced him downwards. I had no time to repeat my blow, but I saw him rise to the surface in the wake of the boat, and never shall I forget the ferocious expression of his countenance.

Only one other of the savages reached the boat. He seized the gunwale, but the knives of our rowers so mauled his wrists, that he was forced to quit his hold, and the next minute we were past them all, and in safety. The strong excitement which had thus far kept me up, now left me, and I fell back fainting into the arms of Karakoee.

* * *

The circumstances connected with my most unexpected escape may be very briefly stated. The captain of an Australian vessel, being in distress for men in these remote seas, had put into Nukuheva in order to recruit his ship's company; but not a single man was to be obtained; and the barque was about to get under weigh, when she was boarded by Karakoee, who informed the disappointed Englishman that an American sailor was detained by the savages in the neighboring bay of Typee; and he offered, if supplied with suitable articles of traffic, to undertake his release. The Kannaka had gained his intelligence from Marnoo, to whom, after all, I was indebted for my escape. The proposition was acceded to; and Karakoee, taking with him five tabooed natives of Nukuheva, again repaired aboard the barque, which in a few hours sailed to that part of the island, and threw her main-top-sail aback right off the entrance to the Typee bay. The whale-boat, manned by the tabooed crew, pulled towards the head of the inlet, while the ship lay "off and on" awaiting its return.

The events which ensued have already been detailed, and little more remains to be related. On reaching the "Julia" I was lifted over the side, and my strange appearance and remarkable adventure occasioned the liveliest interest. Every attention was bestowed upon me that humanity could suggest. But to such a state was I reduced, that three months elapsed before I recovered my health.

The mystery which hung over the fate of my friend and companion Toby has never been cleared up. I still remain ignorant whether he succeeded in leaving the valley, or perished at the hands of the islanders.

Bibliographical Note

There is no exhaustive bibliography of Indian captivity narratives. R.W.G. Vail, *The Voice of the Old Frontier* (Philadelphia: University of Pennsylvania Press, 1949) contains an indispensable annotated bibliography of all narratives, citing their different editions, published before 1800 in America and abroad. A list of the hundreds of narratives in the Edward E. Ayer Collection of the Newberry Library can be found in *Narratives of Captivity Among the Indians of North America* (Chicago: Newberry Library, 1912) and a *Supplement* (Newberry, 1928) compiled by Clara A. Smith. Dorothy Forbis Behen, "The Captivity Story in American Literature, 1577-1826: An Examination of Written Reports in English, Authentic and Fictitious, of the Experiences of the White Men Captured by the Indians North of Mexico" (Ph.D. diss., University of Chicago, 1952) and Louise K. Barnett, *The Ignoble Savage: American Literary Racism, 1790-1890* (Westport, Conn.: Greenwood, 1975) have bibliographies which include novels and short stories about Indian captivity published in America during the eighteenth and early nineteenth centuries. For a list of plays about Indian captivity, see Arthur Hobson Quinn, *A History of American Drama from the Beginning to the Civil War* (New York: Appleton-Century-Crofts, 1923; rev. ed., 1951). While far from complete, these works together provide a basic bibliography.

Most of the narratives published in America before 1800 can be obtained from the Readex Microprint Edition of Early American Imprints, produced under the direction of Clifford K. Shipton of the American Antiquarian Society. Works in this collection are arranged according to the numbers in Charles Evans, *American Bibliography* (1903-1934). In addition to the Newberry Library, other libraries housing noteworthy collections are the Library of Congress, the Boston Public Library, the Rosenbach Museum, the Huntington Library, the American Antiquarian Society, the Library Company of Philadelphia, and the university libraries of Harvard, Brown, Texas, Yale, Kansas, Rochester, and the University of California at Berkeley. Twentieth-century anthologies such as Howard Peckham, *Captured by Indians* (New Brunswick: Rutgers University Press, 1954), Frederick Drimmer, *Scalps and Tomahawks* (New York: Coward-McCann, 1961), and, for the more academically oriented, Richard VanDerBeets, *Held Captive by Indians* (Knoxville, Tenn.: University of Tennessee Press, 1973) will interest readers who do not have access to the major libraries, want to read more narratives than are contained in the present collection, but do not want to purchase reprints of single items, many of which are available. The narratives in Peckham, *Captured by Indians* and Drimmer, *Scalps and Tomahawks* have been edited and rewritten for a popular audience. Those in VanDerBeets, *Held Captive by Indians* are reprinted in full and without alterations. Wilcomb E. Washburn of the Smithsonian Institution has begun the process of editing 311 narratives for a facsimile reprint project sponsored by the Garland Publishing Company in conjunction with the Newberry Library, which will supply the majority of the copy-texts.

Scholarship on Indian captivity narratives is remarkably varied. Historical studies include Emma Lewis Coleman, *New England Captives Carried to Canada* (Portland, Me.: Southworth Press, 1925); Dorothy A. Dondore, "White Captives Among the Indians," *New York History* 13 (1932), pp. 292-300; Jason Almus Russell, "The Narratives of the Indian Captivities," *Education* 51 (1930), pp. 84-88; James Axtell, "The White Indians of Colonial America," *The William and Mary Quarterly* 32 (1975), pp. 55-88; Richard VanDerBeets, " 'A Thirst for Empire': The Indian Captivity Narrative as Propaganda," *Research Studies* 40 (1972), pp. 207-215; Kathryn Whitford, "Hannah Dustin: The Judgement of History," *Essex Institute Historical Collections* 108 (1972), pp. 304-325; and Robert Arner, "The Story of Hannah Duston: Cotton Mather to Thoreau," *American Transcendental Quarterly* 18 (1973), pp. 19-23. For ethnological, anthropological, and psychological studies, see John R. Swanton, "Notes on the Mental Assimilation of Races," *Journal of the Washington Academy of Sciences* 16 (1926), pp. 493-502; Nathaniel Knowles, "The Torture of Captives by the Indians of Eastern North America," *Proceedings of the American Philosophical Society* 82 (1940), pp. 151-225; Erwin H. Ackernecht, " 'White Indians': Psychological and Physiological Peculiarities of White Children Abucted and Reared by North American Indians," *Bulletin of the History of Medicine* 15 (1944), pp. 15-36; C.-Marius Barbeau, "Indian Captivities," *Proceedings of the American Philosophical Society* 94 (1950), pp. 522-548; Dwight L. Smith, "Shawnee Captivity Ethnography," *Ethnohistory* 2 (1955), pp. 29-41; A. Irving Hallowell, "American Indians, White and Black: The Phenomenon of Transculturation," *Current Anthropology* 4 (1963), pp. 519-531; and J. Norman Heard, *White into Red: A Study of the Assimilation of White Persons Captured by Indians* (Metuchen, N.J.: Scarecrow Press, 1973). For the relation of folklore to the Indian captivity genre, see Rayna D. Green, "Traits of Indian Character: The 'Indian' Anecdote in American Vernacular Tradition," *Southern Folklore Quarterly* 39 (1975), pp. 233-262. For an analysis and her "The Only Good Indian: The Image of the Indian in American

Vernacular Tradition" (Ph.D. diss., Indiana University, 1973). For an analysis of how folklore about Indian captivity shaped the Boone legend, see Kent Ladd Steckmesser, "The Hero of the American West in History and Legend" (Ph.D. diss., University of Chicago, 1960) and Richard Slotkin, "Emergence of a Myth: John Filson's 'Daniel Boone Narrative' and the Literature of the Indian Wars, 1638-1848" (Ph.D. diss., Brown University, 1967). Phoebe S. Allen finds similarities in structure, style, and content in her comparative study, "The Double Exposure of Texas Captives," *Western Folklore* 32 (1973), pp. 249-261. Dawn L. Gherman's "From Parlour to Tepee: The White Squaw on the American Frontier" (Ph.D. diss., University of Massachusetts, 1975) contains an analysis of how women are depicted in the captivity narratives.

Literary scholarship falls into two categories. The first approaches captivity narratives in terms of their mythic and archetypal significance. Studies in this category are Phillips D. Carleton, "The Indian Captivity," *American Literature* 15 (1943), pp. 169-180; Leslie Fiedler, *The Return of the Vanishing American* (New York: Stein and Day, 1968); James Meade, "The 'Westerns' of the East: Narratives of Indian Captivity from Jeremiad to Gothic Novel" (Ph.D. diss., Northwestern University, 1971); Elémire Zolla, *The Writer and the Shaman* (New York: Harcourt, Brace, Jovanovich, 1973); Richard VanDerBeets, "The Indian Captivity Narrative: An American Genre" (Ph.D. diss., University of the Pacific, 1973) and "The Indian Captivity Narrative as Ritual," *American Literature* 43 (1972), pp. 548-562; and Richard Slotkin, *Regeneration Through Violence* (Middletown, Conn.: Wesleyan University Press, 1973). A second category identifies the captivity narratives as a literary tradition which influenced the development of a national literature by infusing it with American themes and settings. Studies from this latter perspective are Albert Keiser, *The Indian in American Literature* (New York: Oxford University Press, 1933); Roy Harvey Pearce, "The Significances of the Captivity Narrative," *American Literature* 19 (1947), pp. 1-20; Alexander Cowie, *The Rise of the American Novel* (New York: American Book Company, 1948); Behen, "The Captivity Story in American Literature"; Henri Petter, *The Early American Novel* (Columbus, Ohio: Ohio State University Press, 1971); Richard VanDerBeets, "A Surfeit of Style: The Indian Captivity Narrative as Penny Dreadful," *Research Studies* 39 (1971), pp. 297-306; VanDerBeets, "Cooper and the 'Semblance of Reality': A Source for *The Deerslayer*," *American Literature* 42 (1971), pp. 544-546; David Minter, "By Dens of Lions: Notes on Stylization in Early Puritan Captivity Narratives," *American Literature* 45 (1973), pp. 335-347; James A. Levernier, "Indian Captivity Narratives: Their Functions and Forms" (Ph.D. diss., University of Pennsylvania, 1975); Barnett, *The Ignoble Savage;* and David T. Haberly, "Women and Indians: *The Last of the Mohicans* and the Captivity Tradition," *American Quarterly* 28 (1976), pp. 431-441. John

Seelye's study of the origins of American culture, *Prophetic Waters: The River in American Life and Literature* (New York: Oxford University Press, 1977), emphasizes personal narratives, including John Smith's and Mary Rowlandson's, and comments acutely on the captivity genre.

Works helpful in understanding the historical and cultural context in which the Indian captivity narratives were written are so numerous that only a few of the more significant can be mentioned here. Angie Debo, *A History of the Indians of the United States* (Norman, Okla.: University of Oklahoma Press, 1970) and Wilcomb E. Washburn, *The Indian in America* (New York: Harper and Row, 1975) provide a comprehensive view of Indian history and its effect on American culture. The orientation of Francis Jennings is evident in his title, *The Invasion of America: Indians, Colonialism, and the Cant of Conquest* (Norton: New York, 1976). An incisive analysis of changing American attitudes toward the Indian from colonial times through the present can be found in Roy Harvey Pearce, *The Savages of America: A Study of the Indian and the Idea of Civilization* (Baltimore, Md.: The Johns Hopkins Press, 1953; rev. ed., 1965). In *The American Indian Wars* (New York: Harper and Brothers, 1960), John Tebbel and Keith Jennison survey the events, causes, and consequences of the major Indian wars. Detailed ethnological and historical information about the Indian tribes of North America can be found in John R. Swanton, *The Indian Tribes of North America*, Smithsonian Institution Bureau of American Ethnology Bulletin 145 (Washington, D.C., 1952), and Frederick Webb Hodge, *Handbook of American Indians North of Mexico* (New York: Pageant Books, 1959). For studies of European preconceptions about the Indian during the period of colonization, see Lee Huddleston, *Origins of the American Indians: European Concepts, 1492-1729* (Austin, Texas: University of Texas Press, 1967) Edward Dudley and Maximillian Novak, eds., *The Wild Man Within* (Pittsburgh: University of Pittsburgh Press, 1972), and Gary B. Nash, "The Image of the Indian in the Southern Colonial Mind," *The William and Mary Quarterly* 29 (1972), pp. 197-230.

Index

Abbott, Daniel, 172
Abenaki Indians, 61, 156
Account of a Beautiful Young Lady . . . , An, xxvii
Account of the Captivity of Elizabeth Hanson . . . , An, xx
Acushnet, 264
Adair, James, 210
Adams, Charles, 172
Adams, John Quincy, xxiv
"Adventure of a Young British Officer Among the Abenakee Savages," 61
"Adventures of Col. Daniel Boon, The," xxvii, 174; selection from, 175. *See also* Boone, Daniel
Affecting History of the Dreadful Distresses of Frederick Manheim's Family, 64; illustration from, 70
Affecting Narrative of the Captivity and Sufferings of Mrs. Mary Smith. . . , An, xxii, 64-65, 76, 97; selection from, 65-75
Alabama, 65
Algonquin Indians, 29
Almanacs, 60-61, 186-188; illustration from, 187; selections from, 61-63, 188
Almon, John, 50
American Magazine of Useful and Entertaining Knowledge, The, 224; illustration from, 227; selection from, 225-230
American Pioneer, The, xxiv, 132
American Revolution. *See* Revolutionary War
American Whig Review, The, xxiv
Anthropophagi, xv. *See also* cannibalism
Antiquarian Researches. . . , 132
Apache Indians, xxii, xxiii, 124, 201
Arcadia, xv, xvi. *See also* utopias
Arizona, 200, 201
Arkansas, 172
Armourer's Escape, The, 214, 215
Army and Navy Chronicle, The, 267
Art-Idea, The, 261
Asia, 209
Astor, John Jacob, 135, 136
Astoria, 90
Astoria, 135-136; selection from, 136-140. *See also* Irving, Washington
Atkinson, Gen. Henry, 78, 83
Atlantic Monthly, 260; selection from, 261-263
Attitudes toward Indians: British, xv-xix, 3, 12, 32, 47, 141, 144; Catholic, xvi-xix, 3, 23-24; Eastern, xxiv-xxvii, 85, 90, 131, 166, 218; French, xv-xvi, 3, 23-24, 47, 144; Puritan, xvi-xix, 3, 24, 32, 40; Quaker, xvi-xix, 40; Spanish, xv-xvi, 3-4, 41, 61; Western, xxiv, 90, 131, 136, 166
Australia, 267
Axtell, James, 125

Baldwin, Elmer, 76
Baldwin, Moses, 121
Ballads, xxiv, xxvi, xxx, 141, 165-166; selection of, 166-170
Ballads and Songs from Utah: selection from, 168-170
Ballard, Elizabeth, 166
Bancroft, George, xxv, 141, 156, 232; selection by, 141-142. *See also* MacCrea, Jane
Barker, James Nelson, xxvii, 214; selection by, 215-217. *See also* Pocahontas Plays
Barlow, Arthur, xvi
Barlow, Joel, 141
Barnett, Louis K., xiv
Barrow, Robert, 40, 42, 43
Barry, Phillips, 165
Bartlett, Grace Fisk, 166
Battles, Indian-Anglo. *See* massacres; wars
Beadle, Erastus, 189, 191. *See also* Beadle and Adams; dime novels

Beadle and Adams, 189-191. *See also* dime novels
Beverly, Mass., 31, 34
Bibbs, Paul, 189; selection by, 192-199. *See also* dime novels
Bickerstaff's Boston Almanack, 61. *See also* almanacs
Bickerstaff's Genuine Boston Almanack, 60-61; selection from, 61-63. *See also* almanacs
"Bigfoot," 210
"Billy the Kid." *See* Bonner, William F.
Biographical Memoir of Daniel Boone, xxvii, 174; selection from, 175-177. *See also* Boone, Daniel
Bird, Robert Montgomery, xxvii, 171, 189
Blackfish (Shawnee chief), 174
Blackfoot Indians, 104, 135, 136, 137
Black Hawk (Sauk chief), xxiv, 76-77, 83
Black Hawk's War, xxii, 76
Black Hills, 91
Blacks, xxix, 200-201; selection about, 201-205
Black Watch, The, 144
Bleecker, Ann Eliza, xxvii-xxviii
Blenheim, N.Y., 172
Bligh, Lt. William, 210
Body, Boots and Britches, 172
Bonner, William F., 200
Book of the Artists, 260-261
Boone, Daniel, 172, 178, 179; and John Colter, 135; and Leatherstocking, xxviii, 232; and Nat Love, 200; selections about, 175-177. *See also* folk heroes; folklore; legends
Boone, Jemima, 174
Boston, Mass., 31, 39, 61, 133, 142, 143
Bounty, 210
Bouquet, Col. Henry, xxiii, 144-145; selection about, 146-155
Boyd, Lt. William, 111
Brackenridge, Hugh Henry, xxii
Bradbury, John, 135
Braddock's Defeat, 111
Bradford, William, xvii
Bradstreet, Col. John, 147, 148, 150
Brant, Joseph (Mohawk chief), 111
Brazil, 4
Breadfruit, 210
Bressani, Father Francis Joseph, xviii, xix, 23-24; selection by, 24-30
Breve Relatione d'Alcune Missioni. . . , 23
Bridger, Jim, xxvi, 172
Brief and True Report of the New-Found Land of Virginia, A, 70
Brief Sketch of the First Settlement of Deerfield, A, 131; selection from, 132-134. *See also* Deerfield, Mass.; Hoyt, Elihu; Williams, Rev. John
"Bright Amanda," 166, 168-170. *See also* ballads
British: attitudes toward French, 32, 47; attitudes toward Indians, xv-xix, 3, 12, 24, 32, 40, 141, 144; attitudes toward native Irish, xvii; bounty for American scalps, xxi, 50, 51; propaganda directed against, xxi, 50-51, 141; refusal of, to relinquish forts, 51; use of Indian allies, xxi, 50-51
Broadsides, xxii, 85-86; example of, 87-89
Brougham, John, 214. *See also* Pocahontas Plays
Brown, Charles Brockden, xxvii, xxviii
Brown, Thomas, xx
Buffalo, description of, 57-58
Buffalo Bill. *See* Cody, William F.
Bulletin of the Folk-Song Society of the Northeast, 165
Burgoyne, Gen. John, 141-142, 171
Butler, John, 111
Byers, Samuel, 215. *See also* Pocahontas Plays

Cabeza de Vaca, Nuñez, xvi, 4
Cabot, John, xvii
California and Oregon Trail, The, 144. *See also*, Parkman, Francis
Canada, xiii, 3, 23, 31, 35, 39, 47, 53, 96, 114, 131, 132, 143, 144, 159, 225
Cannibalism, xv, 25, 27, 42, 47, 48-49, 80, 265
Captivity: affirmative portrayal of, xviii, xxi, xxiii, xxiv-xxv, 96-97, 110-111, 121, 145-146, 166, 218, 257-258; Catholic attitude toward, xiii, xvi-xix, 24; as cultural metaphor, xxx; in dime novels, 189-191, 200; folklore about, xiv, xxiv, xxvi-xxvii, 131, 165-166, 171-172, 174, 178, 186, 189; in imaginative literature, xxvii-xxx, 209-210, 218-219, 224-225, 231-232, 264-267; among Polynesians, xxii, xxix, 264-267; Puritan view of, xvii-xix, 24, 31-32, 40, 41; Quaker view of, xiii, xvii-xix, 40; visual arts and, xiv, 12, 253-256, 260-263
"Captivity and Sufferings of Mrs. Mason," xxiii, 85-86; selection from, 87-89

Captivity narratives: in almanacs, xxiii, 60, 186; anthologies of, xxiii, xxv, 70; as broadsides, xxiii, 85-86; as children's literature, xxvi, 132, 189; comedy in, xiv, 186-188; definition of, xiv; fantasy in, xxvii, 209-210; folklore and, xxiv, xxvi-xxvii, 131, 165-166, 171-172, 174, 178, 186, 189; as history, 131-132, 135-136, 141, 143-146, 156-157; about Indianized captives, xxi, xxiii, 65, 96-97, 110-111, 121, 124-125, 144-146, 257-258, 265; in *Jesuit Relations*, 23-24; market for, xiii, xxii, 23, 50, 64, 76, 85, 90, 98, 179, 189, 191; and novels, xiv, xxvii-xxx, 189-191, 219, 225, 231-232, 264-267; number of, xiv; as penny dreadfuls, xxii, 64-65, 76-77, 178-179; plagiariasm among, 56, 64, 179; as plays, xiv, xxvii, 12, 214-215; as poetry, xxvii, 12, 121, 218-219, 257-258; as propaganda, xix-xxiii, 47, 50-51, 60, 64-65, 76-77, 85-86, 90, 141, 179; publication and distribuiton of, xxiii, 23, 41, 50, 60, 85-86, 90, 98, 179, 189, 191; rarity of, xxiii, 86; as religious documents, xvii-xx, 22-23, 31-32, 40-41, 178-179; secularization of, xix-xxiii, 47; sensationalism in, xxii, 47, 50-51, 55, 60, 64, 76, 111, 179; setting of, xxii; significance of, to scholars, 24, 55-56; and visual arts, xiv, 12, 253-256, 260-263
Captivity of the Oatman Girls. . . , xxii
Capture and Escape. . . , The, xxii, 90
Carlisle, Pa., 153
Carson, Kit, 200
Carver, Jonathan, 56, 232
Casco Bay, Me., xviii, 31, 33, 34
Cassen, George, 14, 15
Catholicism. *See* Jesuits; Roman Catholicism
Cattle industry, 200
Caughnawaga Indians, 150
Cayoga Indians, 110
Champlain, Lake, 26
Champlain, Samuel de, xvi, 24
Charles V (king of Spain), 3
Chateaubriand, François René de, xxiv
Cherokee Indians, xxiii, 63, 93, 210, 257. *See also* Ridge, John Rollin
Cherokee: Nation, 257; Removal, xxiii
Cherry Valley Massacre, 111
Chess-quat-a-law-ny. *See* Ridge, John Rollin
Chickamauga Indians, 210
Chickasaw Indians, 63, 65
Chickkemogga Indians. *See* Chickamauga Indians
Chief Joseph (Nez Perce chief), xxiv
Children's literature, xxvi, 160. *See also* McGuffey, William Holmes; *McGuffey's Readers*
Chippewa Indians, 246
Choctaw Indians, 65
"Christian Philosopher," 178, 180; illustration of, 184; selection about, 180-185
Church, Thomas, 218
Civil War, 60, 132, 135, 186, 189, 200
Clark, Col. George Rogers, 180
Clark, William. *See* Lewis and Clark Expedition
Cody, William F., 200
Coffin, Tristram P., 172
Colden, Cadwallader, 97
Cole, Thomas, 253-254; painting by, 255
Colorado, 200
Colorado River, 127
Columbiad, 141
Columbian Magazine, 61
Columbian Sentinel, 165
Columbia River, 90
Colter, John, 135-136; illustration of, 139; selection about, 136-140
Comanche Indians, xxii, 124
Concord, N.H., 172
Condensed History of the Apache and Comanche Tribes, A. *See Indianology*
Confidence-Man, The, 171, 178. *See also* Indian-hater; Melville, Herman
Connecticut, 133, 142, 254
Connecticut River, 131
Conner, Charlotte Barnes, 215. *See also* Pocahontas Plays
Conquering the Wilderness. . . , 136
Conspiracy of Pontiac, The, xxv-xxvi, xxix, xxx, 143-146; selection from, 146-155. *See also* Parkman, Francis
Cook, Captain James, 210
Cooper, James Fenimore, xiv, xxv, xxvii, xxviii-xxix, xxx, 56, 141, 165, 174, 179, 189, 191, 219, 231-232, 253-254, 258, 260; selections by, 232-252, 254-256
Cooper, Susan Fenimore, 231
Cortez, Hernando, 4
Cou-ash-auke Indians, 165
Course of Empire, The, 253, 254
Cowboys, 200-202; selection about, 201-205

Crater, The, xxix, 254
Crawford, Col. William, 51, 111
Crazy Horse (Sioux chief), xxiv
Creek Indians, 64, 65
Crèvecoeur, Michel Guillaume Jean de, 97
Croatan Indians, xvi
Crockett, Davy, xxvi, 172, 186, 200
Crockett Almanacs, 186; illustration from, 187; selection from, 188. *See also* almanacs
Cruger, Lt. Col. John, 61
Cuba, 3, 5
Cumberland River, 60
Custer, Gen. George Armstrong, 90
Curtis, George Washington, 215. *See also* Pocahontas Plays
Cynthia Ann Parker. . . , 124

Dakotah Indians, 146
Dakota Territory, 90, 200
Dare, Virginia, xvi
d'Auberteuil, Michel René Hilliard, 141
Deadwood, S.D., 201
Deadwood Dick, 201
Deadwood Dick. *See* Love, Nat
Death of Jane M'Crea, The, 141
de Bry, Theodore, xv, 70
Decennium Luctuosum. . . , xix
Deerfield, Mass., xxiv, 131-134. *See also* Deerfield Massacre; Williams, Rev. John
Deerfield Captive. . . , The, xxvi, 132. *See also* children's literature
Deerfield Massacre, xxiv, 131-134
Delaware Indians, xxiii, 114, 144, 146, 147, 236
De Shields, James, 124
De Soto, Hernando, 3, 6, 10-11
Detroit, Mich., xxi, 50, 98, 144, 176
Dickenson, Jonathan. *See* Dickinson, Jonathan
Dickinson, Jonathan, xvi-xvii, xviii, xix, 40-41; selection by, 41-43
Dime novels, xiv, xxvii, xxx, 90, 189-191, 200-201; illustration from, 190; selection from, 192-199
Discovery, Settlement and Present State of Kentucky, The, 174; selection from, 175. *See also* Boone, Daniel; Filson, John
Dodge, John, xxi, 50-51; selection by, 51-54
Dodge City, Kan., 205
Drake, Samuel Gardner, xxiv, xxv, 3
Drake, Sir Francis, xv
Drayton, Michael, xvi
Dustan, Hannah. *See* Duston, Hannah
Dustin, Hannah. *See* Duston, Hannah
Duston, Hannah, xix, xxiv, 124, 156-157, 188, 265; selections about, 157-159, 225-230
Duston, Thomas, 157, 224; selection about, 225-230
"Duston Family, The," 156, 224-225; illustration of, 227; selection from, 225-230
Dwight, Timothy, 156

Eastburn, James, xxvii, 218; selection by, 219-223
Eastburn, Robert, xx
Edgar Huntly, xxviii
El Dorado, 175
Eliot, Reverend John, xvii
Ellis, Edward Sylvester, 191
Elvas, Gentleman of. *See* Gentleman of Elvas
Emry, Thomas, 14, 15, 19
Engle, Ella, 173
Entertaining Passages Relating to Philip's War. . . , 218
Erie, Lake, 147, 148
Essay for the Recording of Illustrious Providences. . . , 31
"Essay on American Scenery," 253
Essay on the Life of the Honorable Major-General Israel Putnam. . . , An, 232
Essex, 264
Events in Indian History. . . , 132

Fairhaven, Mass., 264
Faithful Narrative of the Many Dangers and Sufferings . . . of Robert Eastburn. . . , A, xx
"Farmer's Cursed Wife, The," 186, 188
Fauquier, Lt. Gov. Francis, xxiii
"Female Captive, The," 121-123
Filson, John, xxvii, 174; selection by, 175. *See also* Boone, Daniel
Fink, Mike, xiv, 186
Fink, Sal, xiv, 186-188; illustration of, 187; selection about, 188. *See also* almanacs; Old Southwestern Humor
Finley, John, 175
Fisk, Gordon M., 121; selection by, 122-123
Flanders, Helen, 166
Fleming, William and Elizabeth, xx, xxi
Flint, Timothy, xxvii, 174; selection by, 175-177

Florida, xvii, xxii, 3, 4, 6, 40, 41, 60, 62, 65, 85, 87, 165
Folk ballads. *See* ballads
Folk heroes, xxvi-xxvii, 135-136, 171-172, 174, 178-179, 186, 200; selections about, 172-173, 175-177
Folklore, xiv, xxiv, xxvi-xxvii, 131, 165-166, 171-172, 174, 178, 186, 189; selections about, 166-170, 172-173, 175-177. *See also* legends
Folktales, xxvi-xxvii, 165, 171-172, 174; selections of, 172-173
Forest Princess, 215. *See also* Pocahontas Plays
Forts: Casco, 32; Chicago, 82; Edward, 141, 142; Griffin, 126; Laramie, 90, 91; Massachusetts, 47, 48-49; Mims, 65; Niagara, xxi, 117, 118, 120, 121, 148; Pitt, 61, 62, 112, 113, 144, 148, 149; Richelieu, 24; Sully, 90; William Henry, 56, 231, 241, 243, 254
Fox Indians, 76-77, 83
Fraser, Gen. Simon, 171
Frazer, Captain Samuel, 267; illustration of, 266
Frazer, Eliza Ann, 267; illustration of, 266
French: attempts of, to convert captives, 32; attitude toward British, 47; attitude toward Indians, xv-xvi, 3, 24, 144; bounty for British scalps, xx; British attitude toward, 32, 47; propaganda directed against, xx-xxi, 47, 50; use of Indian allies, xv-xvi, 47, 144
French and Indian Cruelty. . . , xx
French and Indian Wars, xii, xx, 31, 32, 47, 50, 97, 110, 131, 143-144, 156
Frobisher, Martin, xv

Galena, Ill., 82
Gallic Perfidy, 218
Gardner, Emelyn, 172; selection by, 172-173
Generall Historie of Virginia. . . , xvi, 12, 13, 14, 214; illustration from, 13; selection from, 14-19. *See also* Pocahontas; Smith, Captain John
Genesee River Valley, 110
Gentleman of Elvas, xvi, 3
George, Lake, 231
Georgia, 257
Germain, Lord George, 141
Geronimo (Apache chief), xxiv
Gettysburg, Pa., 110
Gila River, 201
Gilmor, Robert, 254
Girty, Simon, 51
Glens Falls, N.Y., 248
God's Protecting Providence. . . , xix, 40-41; selection from, 41-43
Good Fetch'd out of Evil. . . , 132
Gothic novel, xxviii
Great and Small Voyages, xv
Great Lakes, 64. *See also* names of individual lakes
Greene, A. C., 124
Greene, Richard Tobias, 265
Gulf of Mexico, 64
Gulliver's Travels, 210
Gyles, John, xx, xxi

Hakluyt, Richard, xvi, 3
Hall, Frances and Almira (*also* Sylvia and Rachel), xxii, 76-77, 97; selection about, 77-84; illustration of, 79
Hall, Judge James, 171
Hamilton, Henry, 50, 51
Hanson, Elizabeth, xx
Harbison, Massy, xxii
Hariot, Thomas, 70
Harmar, Gen. Josiah, xxii
Hartford, Conn., 254
Hartman, Regina, 145
Haverhill, Mass., 157, 158, 225
Hawaii, 210
Hawthorne, Nathaniel, 156, 224-225; selection by, 225-230
Heard, J. Norman, 125
Hebrew language, Indians who speak, 209, 210
Heckewelder, Rev. John, 232
Hedgehog; description of, 58
Hiokatoo (Seneca chief), 111, 121
Historie of Cambria, The, 61
History, Manners, and Customs, of the Indian Nations. . . , 232
History of American Literature, 60
Hitory of La Salle County, Illinois, 76
History of the American Indians. . . , 210
History of the Five Indian Nations of Canada. . . , 97
History of the United States (Bancroft), xxv, 141; selection from, 141-142
Hofland, Barbara, xxvi
Hooker, Thomas, xix
Hope, Mount, 218
"Hop Frog" (by Poe), 188

House of Beadle and Adams. *See* Beadle and Adams; dime novels
Hoyt, Elihu, xxiv, 131-132; Selection by, 132-134
Hoyt, Epaphras, 168
Hubbard, Lester A., 168
Hubbard, William, 218
Hudson River, 160, 253
Humbolt, Nev., xxiv
Humiliations Follow'd with Deliverances. . . , xix, 31
Hummingbird, description of, 58-59
Humphrey, David, 232
Hunt, Wilson Price, 136
Hunter, J. Marvin, 124
Huron, Lake, 51, 103, 104
Huron Indians, 23, 24, 26, 27, 29, 233, 237, 238, 240, 244, 246, 248, 250

Illinois, xxiv, 50, 70, 77, 82, 83, 150, 172
Incidents of Border Life. . . , xxiv
Incidents of Border Warfare. . . , 145
Independence, Mo., 90
Indian agent, 50; selection about, 51-54
Indian Anecdotes and Barbarities. . . , xxiii, 136; illustration from, 139
Indian Battles. . . , xxiv, 132
Indian Captivities, 3; selection from, 4-11
Indian captivity. *See* captivity
Indian captivity narratives. *See* captivity narratives
"Indian-hater," stereotype of, 171, 178
Indian history, xxiv-xxv, 132
Indianization. *See* Indianized captives
Indianized captives: attitude of, toward whites, xxiii, 124; narratives about, xxiii, xxiv-xxv, 65, 97; numbers of, xxiii, 97; objectivity of, 110; Parkman's attitude toward, xxv-xxvi, 145-146; portrayal of, in fiction, 191, 225, 265; price paid by, 98, 265; selections about, 99-109, 111-123, 125-128, 146-155; types of, xxiii, 124-125
Indianology, xxiii, 124
Indian Princess, The, xxvii, 214; selection from, 215-217. *See also* Pocahontas Plays
Indians: affirmative portrayal of, xiv, xvi, xxi, xxiii, xxiv-xxv, 65, 90, 97-98, 110-111, 121, 145-146, 165, 166, 179, 218, 257-258; and British allies, xxi, 47, 51, 141, 210; cannibalism among, xv, 25, 27, 42, 47, 48-49, 265; Catholic attitude toward, xvii, 3, 23-24; Eastern view of, xxiv-xxvii, 85, 90, 131, 166, 218; European preconceptions about, xv; and French allies, xx-xxi, 23, 31-32, 47, 50, 144; origins of, xv, 210; and Spanish allies, 41, 60; stereotypes of, xv-xxiii, xxiv, xxviii, 3-4, 12, 24, 32, 64, 76, 90, 131, 136, 166, 179, 191; wars of, xxii, xxiii, xxiv, xxv, 23, 31, 50-51, 64-65, 76-77, 85, 90, 111, 131-132, 143-144, 157, 165, 166, 218, 231, 254, 267; Welsh-speaking, 61, 62; Western view of, xxiv, 90, 131, 136, 166
Indian tribes. *See* names of individual tribes
Iroquois. . . , The, xxv
Iroquois Confederacy, 110
Iroquois Indians, xxv, 24
Irving, Washington, xxix, xxx, 135-136, 156; selection by, 136-140

Jackson, Andrew, xxiii, xxiv, 65
Jackson, Helen Hunt, 90
Jamaica, 40
James, Edwin, 97
James, Frank and Jesse, 200
James, Thomas, 136
James River, 14
Jamestown, Va., xvi, 15, 16, 19
Jarves, James Jackson, 261
Jemison, Mary, xxiii, xxv, 65, 110-111, 146, 171; illustration of, 116; selections about, 111-123. *See also* Indianized captives
Jesuit Relations, The, xix, 23-24; selection from, 24-30
Jesuit Relations and Allied Documents, The, 23
Jesuits, xiii, xviii, xix, 3, 23-24
Jewitt, John, 214-215
Jobese Indians, 40
Johns, Jane, xxii
Johnson, Sir William, 121, 241
Johonnot, Jackson, xxii
Jones, David, 141
Jones, Jonathan H., xxiii, 124; selection by, 125-128
Journal of American Folklore, 165; selection from, 172-173
Journal of the Captivity of Jean Lowry. . . , A, xxi
Journal of William Scudder. . . , The, 51

Kansas, 90, 126, 200, 205
Kaskaskia, 50. *See also* Illinois
Kelly, Fanny, xxii, 90-91; illustration of, 95; selection by, 91-96
Kennebeck River, 33
Kentucky, 83, 172, 174, 175, 178, 180
Kentucky River, 175
Kickapoo Indians, 65
Kimber, Edward, 210
King George's War, 47. *See also* French and Indian Wars
King Philip (Wampanoag chief), 218
King Philip's War, xviii, xxv, xxvii, 218
King William's War, 31, 32, 47, 97, 144, 156. *See also* French and Indian Wars
Kinnan, Mary, 51
Knickerbocker Review, The, 144
Koningsmarke, the Long Finne, 160

Lake of the Woods, 104
Lakes. *See* names of individual lakes
Larimer, Sarah, xxii, 90
La Salle County, Ill., 76
Last Captive, The, 124
Last of the Mohicans, The, xiv, 56, 141, 191, 231, 254, 257, 258; selections from, 232-252, 254-256. *See also* Cooper, James Fenimore
Laudonnière, René, xv
Leatherstocking Tales, xxviii-xxix, 231-232; influence of, on dime novels, 189, 191; Parkman's attitude toward, xxv-xxvi; selections from, 232-252, 254-256. *See also* Cooper, James Fenimore; *Last of the Mohicans*
Lee, Nelson, xxii
Legends, xxvi-xxvii, 135, 160, 165, 174; selections about, 136-140, 161-164, 166-170, 175-177. *See also* folk heroes; folklore
Legends of New England. . ., 156
Legends of the West. . ., 171
Lehmann, Herman, xxiii, 110, 124-125; selection about, 125-128. *See also* Indianized captives
Lehmann, Willie, 124
Le Mote, Capt., 51
Lennardson, Samuel, 156, 157
Letters from an American Farmer. . ., 97
Lewis, Jane, xxii
Lewis, Meriweather. *See* Lewis and Clark Expedition
Lewis and Clark Expedition, 136
Life and Adventures of Jaoquin Murietta, 258
Life and Adventures of Nat Love. . ., 200-201; selection from, 201-205
Life and Adventures of Timothy Murphy, The, 172
Life, Extraordinary Adventures, Voyages, and Surprizing Escapes of Capt. Neville Frowde. . ., The, 210
Lincoln, Abraham, 77
Lincoln, N.H., 165
Little Big Horn, Battle of, 90
Lloyd, Humphrey, 61
Local history: captivity narrative as, xxiv, 76, 131-132; selection from, 132-134
London *Courier*, 267
Longfellow, Henry Wadsworth, 219
Long Tribes of Israel, xv, 210
Loudon, Archibald, xxiii
Louisiana, 63
Louisiana Purchase, 264
Love, Nat, 200-201; selection by, 201-205. *See also* blacks
Lovewell, John, 159
Lovewell's Fight, 159
Lowry, Jean, xxi
Lucian, 209
Lucy Ann, 265
Ludlow, Mass., 121

MacCrea, Jane, 141, 232; selection about, 141-142. *See also* Bancroft, George; Cole, Thomas; Cooper, James Fenimore; *Last of the Mohicans*
M'Crea, Jane. *See* MacCrea, Jane
M'Cullough, John, 145
M'Donald, Philip, xiv, xxvii, 209-210; selection about, 210-213
McGuffey, Alexander, 160
McGuffey, William Holmes, 160. *See also McGuffey's Readers*
McGuffey's Readers, xxvi, 160, 191; selection from, 161-164. *See also* children's literature
Machilimakanac. *See* Mackinac Island
Mackinac Island, 51, 52
M'Kray, Jane. *See* MacCrea, Jane
M'Leod, Alexander, xiv, xxvii, 209-210; selection about, 210-213
Madoc. *See* Prince Madoc
Magnalia Christi Americana. . ., xix, 31, 218;

selection from, 32-39. *See also* Puritan; special providences
Maine, 165, 172
Malaeska, 191. *See also* dime novels
Manifest Destiny, xvii, 135, 179, 264, 265
Marble Faun, The, 225
Mardi, xxix
Marquesas Islands, 264, 265
Maryland, 157, 230
Mason, Mrs., xxiii, 85-86, 97; selection about, 87-89. *See also* broadsides
Mason-Dixon Line, 186
Massachusetts, xvii, 31, 55, 132, 133, 264
Massachusetts Bay, 225
Massachusetts General Court, 156, 157, 159
Massacres: Braddock's Defeat, 111; Cherry Valley, 111; Deerfield, xxiv, 131-134; Fort Mims, 65; Fort William Henry, 56, 231, 241, 243, 253, 254; Wyoming, 111. *See also* wars (Anglo-Indian)
Masterson, William Barclay "Bat," 200
Mather, Cotton, 159, 178, 218; attitude of, toward captivity, xix, xxiv, 31-32, 156; attitude of, toward Indians, xvii, xviii, 32; Hawthorne's opinion of, 224, 228, 229; selection by, 32-39
Mather, Increase, xvii, 31
Mayhem, John, 218-219
Melville, Herman, xiv, xxvii, xxix, xxx, 178, 225, 264-265, 267; selection by, 267-274
Memoirs of Charles Dennis Rousoe d'Eres. . . , 55-56; selection from, 56-59
Memoirs of . . . John Gyles. . . , xx
Merrimack River, 158, 165, 166, 167
Metallak (Coo-ash-auke chief), 165
Mexico, 4, 5, 55, 62, 126, 264
Michigan, xxiv
Michigan, Lake, 51, 210
Military history, xxiv, 132
Miller, Anna C., xxv
Milton, John, 157, 159
Minisink, N.J., 171
Minnesota, 97
Mississippi, 64-65
Mississippi River, xxii, 4, 5, 60, 62, 63, 76, 85, 144, 257
Miss McCrea, 141
Missouri, 90, 165, 172, 258
Missouri Company, 138
Missouri River, 63, 135, 136, 137, 139
Moccasin Bill, 189-191; cover of, 190; selection from, 192-199. *See also* dime novels
Mohawk Indians, 110, 111, 239
Mohawk River, 121
Montaigne, Michel Eyquem de, xv
Montana, 91
Montcalm, Gen. Louis Joseph de, 231, 238, 241
Montreal, 32, 53
Moose, description of, 58
Morris, Isaac, 210
"Mother's Revenge, A," 156. *See also* Duston, Hannah
"Mount Shasta," 258
"Murderer's Creek," 160; selection from, 161-164
Murphy, Tim, xxvi, 171-172, 178, 232; selection about, 172-173. *See also* folk heroes; folklore
Muskingum River, 144, 146, 147, 149

Naper, Capt. Joseph, 82
Narragansett Indians, 243
Narrative of My Captivity Among the Sioux Indians. . . , xxii, 90-91; selection from, 91-96; illustration from, 95
Narrative of the Captivity and Adventure of John Tanner. . . , A, xxiii, xxiv, 97-98; selection from, 98-109
Narrative of the Captivity and Providential Escape of Mrs. Jane Lewis. . . , A, xxii
Narrative of the Captivity of John M'Cullough. . . , A, 145
Narrative of the Capture and Providential Escape of Misses Frances and Almira Hall . . . , xxii, 76-77, 86; illustration from, 79; selection from, 77-84
Narrative of the Capture and Treatment of John Dodge. . . , A, xxi, 50-51; selection from, 51-54
Narrative of the Capture of Certain Americans at Westmorland. . . , A, xxi
Narrative of the Capture, Sufferings, and Miraculous Escape of Mrs. Eliza Fraser. . . , 267; illustration from, 266
Narrative of the Dangers and Distresses Which Befel . . . the Crew, Belonging to the "Wager". . . , A, 210
Narrative of the Extraordinary Life of . . . John Conrad Shafford. . . , 179
Narrative of the Horrid Massacre by the

Indians, of the Wife and Children of the Christian Hermit . . . , A, 179
Narrative of the Life and Sufferings of Mrs. Jane Johns . . . , A, xxii
Narrative of the Life of Mrs. Mary Jemison . . . , A, xxiii, 110-111; illustration from, 116; selection from, 111-112
Narrative of the Massacre, by the Savages, of the Wife and Children of Thomas Baldwin. . . , 178-179; illustrations from, 183, 184; selection from, 180-185
Narrative of the Sufferings and Surprizing Deliverances of William and Elizabeth Fleming. . . , A, xx, xxi
Narrative of the Sufferings of Massy Harbison. . . , A, xxii
"Narrative of the Tragical Death of Mrs. Darius Barber. . . ," 86. *See also* broadsides
Narrative of the Troubles with the Indians in New-England. . . , A, 218
Narratives of a Late Expedition Against the Indians. . . , 51
Narváez, Panfilo de, 3, 4, 5
Natchez, Miss., 60, 64, 67
Neff, Mary, 156, 157, 226, 228, 229
New Amsterdam, 23
New Echota. *See* Cherokee Nation
New England, xvii, xix, xxvi, 39, 40
New Englands Trials, 12
New France, xvi, 23
New Green Mountain Songster, selection from, 166-168
New Guinea, 267
New Hampshire, 165, 172
New Jersey, 171
New Mexico, 200
New Mirror for Travellers, The, 160
New Spain, 4
New York (state), xxii, 110, 141, 160, 171, 172, 231, 260
New York State Historical Society, 172, 173
Niagara River, 56
Nick of the Woods, 171
Ninety Six, 63
Nine Years Among the Indians, 124
Nipnet Indians, 218
Nootka Sound, 214
North American Review, xxviii, 219
North Carolina, 177, 178
Northrup, Sarah Bird, 257
Northwest Passage, 14
Norton, Rev. John, xx, 47, 50; selection by, 48-49
Novel of sensibility, xxvii-xxviii
Nukuhiva, 264, 265, 271

Oatman sisters, xxii
Oglala Sioux. *See* Sioux Indians
Ohio, 50
Ohio River, xxii, 61, 112, 114, 115, 117, 210
Ohio Territory, xxii, 144, 160
Ojibwa Indians, 97, 98, 99, 104, 105, 148, 191, 195, 196
Olden Time, The, xxiv
Old Southwest, 60, 186
Old Southwestern Humor, 186-188; illustration from, 187; selection from, 188
Oneida Indians, 110
Onondaga Indians, 110
Orange County, N.Y., 160
Oregon Trail, xxix, 90
Original Aboriginal Erratic Operatic . . . Extravaganza. . . , An, 214. *See also* Pocahontas Plays
Ortiz, Juan, xiii, xvi; selection about, 4-11
Ottawa Indians, 98, 99, 143, 148
Owen, Robert Dale, 215. *See also* Pocahontas Plays
Ozark Folksongs, 165

Painting, xiv, 12, 141, 253-254; selection from, 255. *See also* visual arts
Palfrey, John, 219
Palmer, Erastus Dow, xxx, 260-261; selection by, 262
Panther, Abraham (*pseud.*), xxvii
Papal bull. *See Sublimus Deus*
Paradise Lost, 157, 159
Parker, Cynthia Ann, 124
Parker, Quannah (Comanche chief), 124
Parkman, Francis, xxix-xxx, 90, 131, 143-146; attitude of, toward Indianized captives, xxv-xxvi, 145-146; opinion of, about Cooper, xxv-xxvi; selection by, 146-155
Parslow, Alonzo, 172
Particular History of the Five Year French and Indian War . . . , A, xxiv
Passe, Simon van de, 13
Patagonia, 210
Paul III (pope), xvi
Paulding, James Kirke, 160, 163; selection by, 161-163

Pawnee Indians, xxix, 263
Peacock, 61
Peace of 1783, 60
Penn, William, xvi
Pennsylvania, xxii, 43, 110, 144, 145, 171, 172
Penny dreadfuls, xxii-xxiii, 64-65, 76-77, 97, 179, 266; selections of, 66-75, 77-84, 180-185
Perils of the Ocean and Wilderness. . . , 23; selection from, 24-30
Philadelphia, Pa., 40, 214
Philosophes, xxiv
"Philosophy of the Ideal," 260
Pierre, xxix
Pike, Robert E., 165
Pilgrims, xvii
Pima Indians, 201
Pittsburgh, Pa., 53, 117, 144
Plain Narrative of the Uncommon Sufferings and Remarkable Deliverance of Thomas Brown. . . , A, xx
Plains Indians, xxii
Plays, xiv, xxvii, 12, 214-215; Selection of, 215-217. *See also* Pocahontas Plays
Pocahontas, xxvii, 3, 12, 14, 214-215; selections about, 14-19, 215-217; portrait of, from *Generall Historie*, 13
Pocahontas (Byers), 215
Pocahontas (Custis), 215
Pocahontas (Owen), 215
Pocahontas Plays, xxvii, 214-215; selection from, 215-217
Poe, Edgar Allan, xxvii, 188, 266
Poems (Ridge), 257-258; selection from, 258-259
Poetry, xiv, 12, 121, 257-258; selections of, 122-123, 219-223, 258-259
Polynesians, depicted as Indians, xxii, xxix, 265-267
Pontiac (Ottawa chief), xxiii, 76, 143-146. *See also* Parkman, Francis
Porcupine. *See* hedgehog
Powhatan, 13, 18-19, 214
Prince Madoc (of Wales), 61
Pritts, Joseph, xxiv
Propaganda, xii, xix-xxiii, 47, 50-51, 55, 60, 64-65, 76-77, 85-86, 90, 141, 179; selections which contain, 48-49, 51-54, 61-63, 65-75, 77-84, 87-89, 91-96
Pulp thrillers. *See* penny dreadfuls
Puritan: attitude toward captivity, xiii, xvii-xix, 31-32, 40, 41; attitude toward Catholics, xx-xxi; attitude toward French, xx-xxi, 32; attitude toward Indians, xvii-xix, xxv, 32, 40

Quaker: attitude toward captivity, xii, xvii-xix, 40; attitude toward Indians, xvi-xvii, 40
Quebec, 30, 36, 39, 47, 55, 133
Queen Anne (of England), 12
Queen Anne's War, 47, 131. *See also* French and Indian Wars
Quick, Tom, xxvi, 172. *See also* folk heroes
Quinn, Arthur Hobson, xiv

Rainy Lake, 104
Raleigh, Sir Walter, xvi
Ramona, 90
Randolph, Vance, 165
Rattlesnake, description of, 59
Red Cloud (Sioux chief), xxiv
Redeemed Captive. . . , The (Norton), xx, 47; selection from, 48-49
Redeemed Captive. . . , The (Williams), xviii, 132
Red River, 62, 63, 98, 104, 108, 109
Relation . . . (Cabeza de Vaca), xvi, 4
Remarkable Adventures of Jackson Johonnot. . . , The, xxii
Remembrancer. . . , The, 50
Returned Captive . . . , 219
Revolutionary War, xiii, xxi, 47, 50-51, 61, 110, 115, 141, 171, 189, 209, 210
Reynolds, Gov. John, 78
Rhode Island, 218
Ridge, John Rollin, 257-258; selection by, 258-259
"Rip Van Winkle," xxx
Rivers. *See* names of individual rivers
Roanoke, xvi
Robinson, Jehu, 14, 15, 19
Rolfe, John, 13, 214
Rolfe, Rev. John, 156
Roman Catholic: attitude toward captivity, xiii, xvi-xix, 3, 23-24; attitude toward Indians, 23-24
Roman Catholicism: effect of, on captives, 32, 132; effect of, on Indians, 23-24; propaganda against, xx-xxi
Rousoe d'Eres, Charles Dennis, 55-56; selection by, 56-59

Rowlandson, Mary, xv, xvii-xviii, xxv
Royal Americans, 144, 146

St. Augustine, Fla., 41, 88
St. Clair, Gen. Arthur, xxii, 160
St. Johns River, 8
St. Louis, Mo., 76, 83, 136, 144
St. Petersburg, 213
Sands, Robert C., xxvii, 218; selection by, 219-223
Sandusky, Ohio, 50, 111, 150
Sauk Indians, xxiv, 76, 77, 83
Sault Ste. Marie, 98, 103
"Savior of the Schoharie." *See* Murphy, Tim
Scalping, xx, xxi, 76, 157, 179
Scanyawtauragahrooote Indians, 55-56, 57
Scarlet Letter, The, 225
Scene from THE LAST OF THE MOHICANS, A (painting by Cole), 253-256; illustration of, 255. *See also* visual arts
Schoharie, N.Y., 171, 172, 173
Schioolcraft, Henry Rowe, xxv, 98
Schoolcraft, James, 98
Science fiction, 209; selection which foreshadows, 210-213
Scioto River, 112, 113, 115, 150
Scott, Sir Walter, xxvii
Scudder, William, 51
Sculpture, xiv, 12, 260-261; selection, 262. *See also* visual arts
Seaver, James, 110-111; selection by, 111-121. *See also* Jemison, Mary
Selection of Some of the Most Interesting Narratives of Outrages Committed by the Indians. . . , A, xxiii
Seminole Indians, xxiii, 85
Seminole Wars, xxii, xxiii, 85, 87, 267
Seneca Indians, 110, 111, 116, 117, 146, 154
Seth Jones, 191
Settle, Laura, 172, 173
Seven Cities of Cibola, 4
Seven Years' War, xx, 47, 110, 144. *See also* French and Indian Wars
Shakespeare, William, xv
Shawnee Indians, xxiii, 64, 97, 110, 116, 144, 146, 149, 150, 151, 174
Shea, John Dawson Gilmary, 23; selection by, 24-30
Shilling shockers. *See* penny dreadfuls
Shoemaker, Floyd C., 165
Shoshone Indians, xxiv
Sidney, Australia, 267
Sigby, William, 172
Simms, William Gilmore, xxvii, 189, 219
Singapore, 267
Sioux Indians, xxii, xxiv, 90, 92, 104, 194, 195
Sitting Bull (Sioux chief), xxiv
Six Nations, 148, 241
Sketch Book, The, 135
Smith, Captain John, xiii, xiv, xvi, xxvii, 12, 14, 214-215; selection by, 14-19; selection about, 215-217. *See also* Pocahontas; Pocahontas Plays
Smith, Mary, xxi, 64-65, 76, 97; selection about, 65-75
Snelling, W. J., 136
Society of Friends, xix, 41. *See also* Quaker
Society of Jesus. *See* Jesuits; Roman Catholicism
Song of Hiawatha, The, 219
Sorel, Canada, 23
South Carolina, 61, 63
South Dakota, 201
South Seas, xxii, xxix, 159, 264
Sovereignty and Goodness of God. . . , The, xv
Spanish: attitude of, toward Americans, 60; attitude of, toward British, 41; attitude of, toward Indians, xv-xvi, 34, 41, 60; British attitude toward, 41
Special providences, xviii-xix, 31, 32, 178
Spencer, Mass., 55
Spiritual autobiography, xix, 32
Springfield Sunday Union, 166
Staden, Hans, 4
Stephens, Ann Sophia, 191. *See also* dime novels
Stereotypes of Indians: British, xv-xix, 3, 12, 24, 32, 40, 141; in dime novels, xxviii, 189-191; Eastern, xxiv-xxvii, 90, 131, 166, 218; in folklore, xxvi, 165-166, 170-171; French, xvi, 3, 24, 144; in penny dreadfuls, xxii-xxiii, 64-65, 76-77, 97, 179; Spanish, xvi, 3-4; Western, xxiv, 90, 136, 166
Stewart, Isaac, 54, 60-61; selection by, 61-63
Stewart, John, 174, 175-177
Stewartstown, N.H., 165
Stolen Boy, The, xxvi. *See also* children's literature
"Stolen White Girl, The," 257-258; text of, 258-259

Story of the Female Captive, 121; selection from, 122-123
Stratton, R. B., xxii
Sublimus Deus, xvi
Sullivan, Gen. John, 61, 111
Surprising Account, of the Captivity and Escape of Philip M'Donald, and Alexander M'Leod. . . , A., xiv, xxvii, 209-210; selection from, 210-213
Susquehanna River, xxi
Swarton, Hannah, xiv, xv, xviii, xix, 24, 31-32, 132, 178; selection by, 32-39
Swarton, Marie, 32
Swift, Jonathan, 210

Tales of Travels West of the Mississippi. . . , 136
Tampa Bay, Fla., 3
Tanner, John, xxiii, xxiv, 65, 97-98, 110, 265; selection by, 98-109. *See also* Indianized captives
Tecumseh (Shawnee chief), xxii, 64, 76
Tempest, The, xv
Tennessee, 65, 200
Tennessee River, 60
Texas, 126, 165, 200, 264
Texas, Annexation of, 264
Thompson, Harold W., 172
Thoreau, Henry David, xxiv, 156-157; selection by, 157-159
Three Years Among the Comanches. . . , xxii
Three Years Among the Indians and the Mexicans. . . , 136
Thwaites, Reuben Gold, 23
Tompson, Benjamin, xvii
Tories, 51, 61, 111, 144. *See also* Revolutionary War
Torres Straits, 267
"To the Virginian Voyage," xvi
Tour of the Prairies, 135
Transcendentalism, xxiv
Travel fantasy, 209; selection which resembles, 210-213
Travels in New England and New York. . . , 156
Travels in the Interior of America. . . , 135
Travels Through the Interior Parts of North-America. . . , 56, 232
Treaties, xxiii, 31, 41, 60, 64, 76, 85, 144, 257
Treaty of Paris (1763), 144
Treaty of Payne's Landing, 85
Trickster tales, xxvi, 171-172
Triplett, Frank, 136
True History, 209
True Narrative of the Sufferings of Mary Kinnan. . . , A, 51
True Relation (Smith), 12
True Relation of the Gentleman of Elvas. . . , xvi, 3
Tuckerman, Henry T., 260
Tupi Indians, 4
Turkey-snake, 56; description of, 59
Tyler, Moses Coit, 60
Typee, xiv, xxix, xxx, 264-267; selection from, 267-274

Uncertain Glory, 172
Utah, 165, 166
Ute Indians, 166, 170
Utica, N.Y., 260
Utopias, xxvii, 209, 254

Vanderlyn, John, 141
Venus de' Medici, 260, 261
Vermont, 134, 166
Vicksburg, Miss., 60
Virginia, xvi, 12, 14, 53, 213
Virginian, The, 200
Virginia Richly Valued. . . , 3
Visual arts, xiv, 12, 253-254, 260-261; selections from, 255, 262. *See also* Cole, Thomas; Palmer, Erastus Dow
Vrooman, Peter, 172

Wadsworth, Daniel, 254
Wadsworth Atheneum, 254
Walnut Hills. *See* Vicksburg, Miss.
Wampanoag Indians, 219
Warhaftige Historia. . . , 4
War of 1812, 264
"War! War!! War!!! Women and Children Butchered. . . ," 86. *See also* broadsides
Wars (Anglo-Indian), xxii, xxiii, xxiv, xxv, 23, 31, 50-51, 64-65, 76-77, 85, 90, 111, 131-132, 143-144, 157, 165, 166, 218, 231, 254, 267
Washington, D.C., 267
Washington, George, 51, 111
Wayne, Gen. "Mad Anthony," 160
Webb, Thomas, 237
Week on the Concord and Merrimack Rivers, A, 156-167; selection from, 157-159. *See also* Thoreau, Henry David
Welsh, Indian language similar to, 61, 62

Wept of Wish-ton-Wish, The, 219
West Palm Beach, Fla., 40
"White Captive" (statue by Palmer), 260-261; illustration of, 262; story about, from *Atlantic Monthly,* 261-263. *See also* visual arts
"White Captive, The" (ballad), 165-166; reprinted, 166-168. *See also* ballads
White, Henry, xxiv; 132
White, John, 70
White into Red, 125
Whitelock, Kenly W., 168
Whittier, John Greenleaf, 156
Williams, Eunice, 131, 132, 133-134. *See also* Deerfield, Mass.; Williams, Rev. John
Wiliams, Rev. John, xviii, xxiv, xxvi, 131-134. *See also* Deerfield, Mass.
Williams, Roger, xvii
Williamson, Peter, xx
Williamstown, Mass., 47
Wimer, James, xxv, 132
Winnebago Indians, 76, 78, 81, 82
Winthrop, John, xvii, xix
Wister, Owen, 200
Wolf, Edwin II, 70
Women, stereotypes of, 91, 156, 188
Woolman, John, xvi
Worcester, Mass., 156
Wounded Knee, S.D., xxiv
Württemberg, 145
Wyandot Indians, 62, 148, 150
Wyoming, 90, 200
Wyoming Massacre, 111

Yamoyden, xxvii, 218-219, 257; selection from, 219-223
Yazoo River, 65
Yellow Bird. *See* Ridge, John Rollin
Yellowstone Park, 136

About the Editors

A former Newberry Library Research Fellow, James Levernier is now an assistant professor of English at the University of Arkansas, Little Rock. Specializing in American literature, he has written articles for such journals as *Keystone Folklore Quarterly* and *Research Studies.* He is currently working on an edition of Increase Mather's *An Essay for the Recording of Illustrious Providences.*

Hennig Cohen, professor of English at the University of Pennsylvania, Philadelphia, specializes in American literature and has written articles for such journals as *American Speech, Journal of American Folklore,* and *The Explicator.* His previous books include *The South Carolina Gazette, 1932-1975.*

Recent titles in Contributions in American Studies
SERIES EDITOR: ROBERT H. WALKER

The Muse and the Librarian
Roy P. Basler

Henry B. Fuller of Chicago: The Ordeal of a Genteel Realist in Ungenteel America
Bernard R. Bowron, Jr.

Mother Was a Lady: Self and Society in Selected American Children's Periodicals, 1865-1890
R. Gordon Kelly

The *Eagle* and Brooklyn: A Community Newspaper, 1841-1955
Raymond A. Schroth, S.J.

Black Protest: Issues and Tactics
Robert C. Dick

American Values: Continuity and Change
Ralph H. Gabriel

Where I'm Bound: Patterns of Slavery and Freedom in Black American Autobiography
Sidonie Smith

William Allen White: Maverick on Main Street
John D. McKee

American Studies Abroad
Robert H. Walker, Editor

American Studies: Topics and Sources
Robert H. Walker, Editor

In the Driver's Seat: The Automobile in American Literature and Popular Culture
Cynthia Golomb Dettelbach

The United States in Norwegian History
Sigmund Skard

Milestones in American Literary History
Robert E. Spiller

A Divided People
Kenneth S. Lynn

The American Dream in the Great Depression
Charles R. Hearn